Lecture Notes in Computer Science 2735
Edited by G. Goos, J. Hartmanis, and J. van Leeuwen

Springer
*Berlin
Heidelberg
New York
Hong Kong
London
Milan
Paris
Tokyo*

Frans Kaashoek   Ion Stoica (Eds.)

Peer-to-Peer Systems II

Second International Workshop, IPTPS 2003
Berkeley, CA, USA, February 21-22, 2003
Revised Papers

 Springer

Series Editors

Gerhard Goos, Karlsruhe University, Germany
Juris Hartmanis, Cornell University, NY, USA
Jan van Leeuwen, Utrecht University, The Netherlands

Volume Editors

Frans Kaashoek
MIT Laboratory of Computer Science
200 Technology Square, Cambridge, MA, USA
E-mail: kaashoek@lcs.mit.edu

Ion Stoica
University of California
Computer Science Division, EECS Department
645 Soda Hall, Berkeley
CA 94720-1776, USA
E-mail: istoica@cs.berkeley.edu

Cataloging-in-Publication Data applied for

A catalog record for this book is available from the Library of Congress.

Bibliographic information published by Die Deutsche Bibliothek
Die Deutsche Bibliothek lists this publication in the Deutsche Nationalbibliografie;
detailed bibliographic data is available in the Internet at <http://dnb.ddb.de>.

CR Subject Classification (1998): C.2, H.3, H.4, D.4, F.2.2, E.1, D.2

ISSN 0302-9743
ISBN 3-540-40724-3 Springer-Verlag Berlin Heidelberg New York

Springer-Verlag Berlin Heidelberg New York
a member of BertelsmannSpringer Science+Business Media GmbH

http://www.springer.de

© Springer-Verlag Berlin Heidelberg 2003
Printed in Germany

Typesetting: Camera-ready by author, data conversion by DA-TeX Gerd Blumenstein
Printed on acid-free paper   SPIN: 10929131   06/3142   5 4 3 2 1 0

Preface

In a very short time, peer-to-peer computing has evolved into an exciting research field which brings together researchers from systems, networking and theory. This workshop is the second installment in what we hope to be a long series of successful workshops that are focused on examining peer-to-peer technologies, applications and systems, and on identifying key research challenges and solutions.

The program of the 2nd International Workshop on Peer-to-Peer Systems (IPTPS) consisted of 27 position papers and four invited talks. The authors were asked to submit position papers not exceeding five pages. We had a record 166 submissions covering a broad range of topics. This diversity was reflected in the final program, which included sessions covering theory and algorithms, incentives and fairness, naming and searching, file sharing, networking and applications, and experience with existing peer-to-peer systems.

Submissions went through two rounds of reviews. In the first round each submission received two reviews. In the second round we targeted the submissions with first-round reviews that expressed differing opinions, and submissions that were neither clear rejects nor accepts. In addition to the technical merit, the reviewing process emphasized originality, and the potential of the submission to lead to interesting discussions during the workshop.

In addition to the position papers, the workshop included four invited talks that aimed to expose the academic community to some of the problems and issues faced by the developers of peer-to-peer systems in the industry and the public domain. Bernard Traversat from Sun gave a talk on the JXTA platform, Christian Huitema from Microsoft presented a peer-to-peer toolkit for Windows XP, Ian Clarke presented the Freenet project, and Jed McCaleb gave a talk on the Overnet system.

The workshop was crossdisciplinary, well focused, with emphasis on innovation. As a result, a considerable amount of time was devoted to informal discussion. To ensure a productive workshop environment, attendance was limited to 65 participants.

This volume includes a report on the discussions that took place at the workshop during technical sessions. We thank Michal Feldman and Shelley Zhuang for taking notes and putting together this report. Many thanks to a wonderful program committee that coped with an unexpectedly large number of submissions in a very short timeframe. The hard and diligent work of the program committee was a key reason behind the success of this workshop. We would like to thank Bob Miller for the flawless local arrangements, and Keith Sklower for maintaining the IPTPS Web server and providing wireless connectivity during the workshop. We thank our sponsors, NSF, and Microsoft, for their generous support.

Finally, we thank all authors who submitted papers to this year's workshop, and all participants for making the workshop a success!

May 2003   Frans Kaashoek and Ion Stoica

Workshop Co-chairs

Frans Kaasheok   MIT, USA
Ion Stoica   UC Berkeley, USA

IPTPS Steering Committee

Peter Druschel   Rice University, USA
Frans Kaasheok   MIT, USA
Anthony Rowstron   Microsoft Research, UK
Scott Shenker   ICSI, Berkeley, USA
Ion Stoica   UC Berkeley, USA

Program Committee

Miguel Castro   Microsoft Research
Joe Hellerstein   UC Berkeley
Richard Karp   UC Berkeley
Frans Kaashoek   MIT
Nancy Lynch   MIT
David Mazières   New York University
Robert Morris   MIT
Ion Stoica   UC Berkeley
Marvin Theimer   Microsoft Research
Amin Vahdat   Duke University
Geoffrey Voelker   UC San Diego
Ellen Zegura   Georgia Tech
Hui Zhang   CMU

Administrative Assistant

Robert Miller
University of California at Berkeley

Sponsoring Institutions

National Science Foundation   Microsoft Corp.

Table of Contents

IV   Incentive and Fairness

V   New DHT Designs

VI   Naming, Indexing and Searching

VII File Sharing

VIII Networking and Applications

Workshop Report
for 2nd International Workshop
on Peer-to-Peer Systems (IPTPS '03)
21-22 February 2003 – Claremont Hotel, Berkeley, CA, USA

Michal Feldman[1] and Shelley Zhuang[2]

[1] School of Information Management and Systems
University of California Berkeley
[2] Computer Science Division
University of California Berkeley

Attendees were welcomed by Frans Kasshoek and Ion Stoica. The workshop had attracted 166 submissions out of which 27 position papers had been accepted for presentation. In addition, the program included four invited talks.

1 Experience with P2P

Ratul Mahajan, Miguel Castro, Antony Rowstron, **Controlling the Cost of Reliability in Peer-to-Peer Overlays, presented by Ratul Mahajan.** This paper defines two metrics in an overlay: message loss rate, and cost of overlay maintenance in terms of control traffic. The paper then presents techniques to adapt times between liveness probes to changing network conditions to meet a specified target loss rate. Simulation results based on traces of recent p2p measurement studies show that this self-tuning technique works well. Finally, the authors describe mechanisms to deal with massive failures such as network partitions.

Discussion: **Q:** We may expect failure rates in p2p networks to be highly variable, with a long-tail distribution? How does that affect your tuning mechanism? **A:** We can make it more sophisticated by distinguishing between the two types of nodes, otherwise some hops may be more reliable than others.

Q: Why don't you use a passive approach instead of active probing to detect node failures? **A:** We don't send probes if we send messages, but neighbor relationship may not be symmetric in Pastry.

Frank Dabek, Ben Zhao, Peter Druschel, John Kubiatowicz, Ion Stoica, **Towards a Common API for Structured Peer-to-Peer Overlays, presented by Ben Zhao.** Currently there are lots and lots of p2p applications built on top of structured p2p overlays with different APIs. This work attempts to identify the fundamental abstractions provided by structured overlays and to define APIs for the common services they provide. A key-based routing API

F. Kaashoek and I. Stoica (Eds.): IPTPS 2003, LNCS 2735, pp. 1–20, 2003.

(KBR) is defined (tier-0), and a number of higher level abstractions including DHT, CAST, and DOLR are identified as tier-1 services.

Discussion: **Q:** Will scalable overlays used across multiple administrative domains, and security issues affect these API's? **A:** We are trying to find the smallest pieces possible, a lot of layers like replication, caching, and security can be layered on top. Nothing in the current proposal precludes additional layer on the top that includes administrative boundaries or security.

Q: This reminds me of work in the mid 90's on extensible systems, and that's a very hard thing to do. It's very hard to assure other people that your API is general enough. Can you use language techniques? Perhaps you can use reduction to show that the API is general enough. **A:** We tried to stay away from language-dependency simply because protocols are all implemented using different languages. Nothing here precludes additional input from outside components like statistical inference components.

Q: API's make me think of sockets, but I fail to see that here, instead you have levels of abstractions. **A:** We want to go ground-up, identify the minimum core, at each level, we clearly define the functions and semantics, and then we can build additional tier-0 primitives.

Michael Freedman, David Mazières, Sloppy Hashing and Self-Organizing Clusters, presented by Michael Freedman. DHTs are not well-suited to implement file-sharing, or replace proprietary CDNs because of two problems. First, hotspots are created on nodes that store pointers to popular data, and replication helps only with fetches, but not stores. Second, DHTs have poor locality; a node might need to send a query far away to learn that its neighbor is caching a particular web page. Coral provides a new distributed sloppy hash table (DSHT) abstraction. Instead of storing actual data, it stores weakly-consistent lists of pointers to nodes that actually store the data. Coral assigns RTT thresholds to clusters to bound cluster diameter and ensure fast lookups. A decentralized clustering algorithm by which nodes form clusters of varying network diameters is presented.

Discussion: **Q:** You have the same kind of pointer locality in Pastry, Tapestry, why do we need a new mechanism? **A:** It's not quite the same. You can always go to nearby neighbors first, but then you break the $\log N$ hops property.

Q: The rings you're building are isomorphic to the lower-layer routing layer in Tapestry/Pastry. **A:** Coral provides a layer of flexibility on which a variety of clustering criteria can be leveraged. When the lower-system doesn't give us pointer locality, such as in Chord, Coral can optimize it. When the layer provides routing locality, such as in Pastry or Kademlia, Coral can still optimize data placement, which isn't possible in such systems.

Q: How do you have multiple values for one key? **A:** This question asks what key/value naming is on the application layer. For example, one could use Coral to store content URLs or node addresses as "values" under a key.

Sean Rhea, Timothy Roscoe, John Kubiatowicz, Structured Peer-to-Peer Overlays Need Application-Driven Benchmarks, presented by

Sean Rhea. Structured peer-to-peer overlays share the common property of mapping identifiers to a set of nodes in a network. However, they embody a wide variety of design alternatives. Thus, application-driven benchmarks for such overlays are needed for application writers. Two benchmarks, find_owner and locate, are evaluated over two overlays, Chord and Tapestry.

Discussion: **Q:** Did you turn off location caching in Chord, maybe all nodes are cached? **A:** Not sure, but most lookups are short, like two hops. (**Note:** Subsequent investigations showed that the location caching was turned on. The final version of the paper published in this proceedings shows results with the location caching turned off.)

Q: You need to take the overhead of overlay maintenance into consideration, otherwise we compare oranges to apples. **A:** Yes, that's the great thing about Emulab, we can get full bandwidth numbers.

Joint Discussion: **Q:** (for Ratul Mahajan) It seems to me that during extreme times of congestion, you are actually making it worse by increasing the probing rate? Essentially, you can't tell the difference between node failure rates and high congestion! **A:** Yes, there's nothing in the system that distinguishes between the two. **Q:** The general principle in Internet is that if you have losses, you slow down, and not send more packets. **A:** A huge correlated loss in a link would be detected as a partition, and we don't actually count that in the failure rate calculation.

Q: (for Ben Zhao and Sean Rhea)) How does attack resilience and others fit into this? **A:** Performance is due to the core functionality. **A:** Right now, we don't even have benchmarks of simple things.

Q: (for Ben Zhao) Do you have any thoughts to deal with next generation applications, such as databases? **A:** We took care of supporting all the applications we know about.

Q: (for Sean Rhea) From personal experience, these algorithms are very sensitive to little hacks, like caching, how do you know why one is better? The paper does not match the implementation! **A:** The problem now is that we're treating these protocols as blackboxes. In the direction of reliability metrics, we will break apart components. For example, what's the difference between iterative and recursive lookups. **A:** One thing that should be done is to look at exactly what these add-ons add to the system? **A:** There are two types of benchmarks, one is teasing apart mechanisms and utilities, and the other is application-level benchmarks.

Q: (for Ben Zhao) A DOLR is very similar to a DHT, do we really need two APIs? **A:** Yes, with a DOLR, you don't actually put data in the network, only pointers. **Q:** By looking at all the applications and commonalities, worried about benchmarks, tweaking all the different parameters would gain better understanding of what's fundamentally required? **A:** It turned out to be very hard to look at, mainly because the lack of a large network.

2   Theory and Algorithms

Ananth Rao, Karthik Lakshminarayanan, Sonesh Surana, Richard Karp, Ion Stoica, **Load Balancing in Structured P2P Systems, presented by Karthik Lakshminarayanan.** Most P2P systems that provide a DHT abstraction distribute objects among "peer nodes" by choosing random identifiers for the objects. This could result in an $O(\log N)$ imbalance. Our goal is to maintain the system in a state in which every node is less loaded than the maximum load it is willing to hold. The problems we address are: (a) Sizes of objects might not be the same. (b) Object IDs might not be chosen at random. c). Nodes are heterogeneous in their capabilities. We explore the space of designing load balancing algorithms that use the notion of "virtual servers". We present three schemes that differ primarily in the amount of information transferred for the load re-arrangement : (a) One-to-one: light node picks a random ID, contacts the node responsible for it, and accepts load if it is heavy. (b) One-to-many: directories keep data about light nodes. (c) Many-to-many: both light and heavy nodes report information to directories. Our simulation results show that the simplest scheme is able to balance the load within 80% of the optimal value, while 95% is reached with the most complex scheme.

Discussion: **Q:** If nodes of the system have restrictions to choose IDs based on things such as hash of the IP addresses, would the schemes work? **A:** Since virtual servers are used, the restriction should allow use of multiple virtual servers per node. The greater the flexibility the restriction allows in moving virtual servers, the better it would perform.

Q: What happens when there is only one popular object? **A:** Caching can be still used on top of our scheme to achieve different goals.

John Byers, Jeffrey Considine, Michael Mitzenmacher, **Simple Load balancing for DHT, presented by Jeffrey Considine.** We argue that load balancing can be achieved in a simple and cost-effective way. Our goal is to minimize the maximum amount of items assigned to a server. We suggest the direct application of the "power of two choices" paradigm, whereby an item is stored at the less loaded of two or more random alternatives. Given d choices of servers, the max load is $\log \log n / \log d + O(1)$. Insertion and search use d parallel chord lookups instead of just one. Similar results are observed for the choice of two servers or unlimited number of servers, but they differ in the minimum number of items. Recognizing that the main overhead is from d parallel chord lookups, we optimize through redirection. Search cost is one chord lookup as before plus traversal of redirection pointer with probability $(1 - 1/d)$. Storage cost is $d - 1$ redirection pointers per item inserted. Redirection pointers are not load balanced, but are much smaller than items. Redirection pointers can also facilitate active load balancing. Our work doesn't deal with hot spots and caching.

Discussion: **Q:** The problems that are presented in these works on load-balancing all come from the assumption that data is stored in the DHT. So maybe DHT is not the best model? **A:** If we're using the DOLR model, we're basically using redirection pointers.

C: If nodes are performing some computation (e.g. seti@home), pointers won't help you. In these cases, unlike fetching a file, when the data is a result of some processing, you can't use pointers. **A:** this assumption is not made in our work (Karthik).

Q: What's your notion of load? It seems like message processing time has a big overhead. if load is measured in CPU cycles, then redirection may not help. what exactly is it that you are worried about ? **A:** we are assuming that all items are the same. We don't handle popularity, but caching can handle this.

Udi Wieder, Moni Naor, **A Simple Fault Tolerant DHT, presented by Udi Wieder.** The main goal of our work is to enable an efficient location of all items under scenarios of processor failures. We introduce a new distributed hash table with logarithmic degree and logarithmic dilation. We present two lookup algorithms. The first has a message complexity of $\log n$ and is robust under random deletion of nodes. The second has parallel time of $\log n$ and message complexity of $\log 2n$. It is robust under spam induced by a random subset of the nodes. We also show a construction which is fault tolerant against random deletions and has an optimal degreedilation tradeoff. The construction has improved parameters when compared to other DHT's. Its main merits are its simplicity, its flexibility and the fresh ideas introduced in its design. It is very easy to modify and to add more sophisticated protocols, such as dynamic caching and erasure correcting codes.

Discussion: **Q:** How do nodes change their estimation of $n/\log n$ when the network size changes ? **A:** When nodes join and leave other nodes need to re-evaluate their estimation of $\log n/n$.

Frans Kaashoek, David R. Karger, **Koorde: A Simple Degree-Optimal Hash Table, presented by David Karger.** Koorde is a new DHT based on chord and the de Bruijn graphs. It inherits the simplicity of chord, but meets various lower bounds such as such as $O(\log n)$ hops per lookup request with only two neighbors per node , and $O(\log n/\log \log n)$ hops per lookup request with $O(\log n)$ neighbors per node. Most DHT's have $O(\log n)$ degree, hop count, and ratio load balance. If max degree is d, then hop count is at least $\log_d^n$. To tolerate half nodes failing, need degree $\Omega(\log n)$. Koorde differs from chord only in its routing protocol. Routing is done by shifting in destination bits one by one, taking b hops to complete a route. In order to avoid colliding identifiers as nodes join, we need a $b \gg \log n$. That implies a use of $b \gg \log n$ hops to route. Our solution is to use imaginary routing, where present nodes simulate routing actions of absent nodes.

Discussion: **Q:** I believe the Viceroy construction does offer constant degrees with high probability. **A:** It does take another simple mechanism (more coordination) to do it.

Q: Aren't the in-degrees logarithmic? **A:** Indegrees are logarithmic, but they do not have maintenance cost. Large indegrees only mean a larger load of communication.

Q: What about better hop-count? If hop-count is large, there is a delay penalty. **A:** we first worry about a low-level routing layer that guarantees correct routing. Of course, you can then put on top of it a proximity layer, but it's important to separate the proximity from the routing to simplify the correctness of routing. Proximity is not fundamental to the robustness of the system.

Joint Discussion: **Q:** (for David Karger) You say that correctness should be a first concern and efficiency should be built on top of it. Why shouldn't we look at it the other way around (i.e. find an efficient solution and then verify its correctness). **A:** I'm a theoretician ! Efficiency should be put on top of a correct design. Otherwise, every time you tweak the proximity, you have to question your correctness all over again. **Q:** I disagree with you. Once you tweak proximity, it doesn't mean that you have to question correctness. Tweaking proximity is only about efficiency, not about correctness. **A:** We have to start with one of them. I prefer correctness. **C:** There are some systems that perform well, but their problem is their correctness, so David is right that the main point should be correctness. However, I also disagree with David that tweaks with the proximity layer may ruin the correctness. **Q:** What about the context of Denial of Service attacks? **A:** correctness is even more important in the context of denial of service attacks.

Q: (for Jeffrey Considine) It seems like the advantage of your approach over the other paper (first load-balancing paper) is that the performance is independent of n (the number of servers). **A:** Yes.

Q: (for Karthik Lakshminarayanan and Jeffrey Considine) All of these schemes assume uniform access to all of the space. However, in practice there are certain keys being much more popular than others. Do you have an application in mind that shows uniform load against keys **A:** No. **Q:** Would the schemes that you present adopt to a non-uniform distribution of popularity? **A:** I believe it can be done. **C:** One can have multiple hash functions. and use only a smaller number of them at one point in time. With more hash functions, there is a better chance of finding a light node, but it's not necessary to use it, unless needed. A possible approach would be to set d to be high, but not only use it d times. Rather, sometimes use a small number, and for popular keys use d.

Q: (for Udi Wider) What are the differences between your construction and Koorde? **A:** My algorithm is a $2 \log n$ hop algorithm that may follow n different paths. The Koorde algorithm presented a $2 \log n$ algorithm that may follow exactly one path, and therefore is less fault tolerant. My algorithm actually routes to a random location and then back, but I can use a different routing algorithm that would use exactly $\log n$ hops. The $2 \log n$ hops means that there are no bottlenecks for permutation routing. This is a property of the de Bruijn graph.

3   P2P in a Broader Perspective

Fred von Lohmann, **Peer-to-Peer File Sharing and Copyright Law: A Primer for Developers, presented by Fred von Lohmann.** Lawsuits are brought against file-sharing applications such as Napster, Morpheus, Aimster, Audiogalaxy, Scour, Kazaa, Grokster, ReplayTV, and even against ancillary services, such as www.mp3board.com. p2p developers can become indirect (contributory or vicarious) infringers of copyright laws. Lessons and guidelines for developers are to make and store no copies, total control or total anarchy, sell stand-alone products rather than services, ask whether you can plausibly deny what users are up to, what are your substantial non-infringing uses, do not promote infringing users, disaggregate functions, give up EULA, auto-updates, or customer support, and be open source.

Discussion: **Q:** All these lawsuits are against companies, does that mean loose organizations or regular open-source individuals are off-the-hook? **A:** Not entirely, there's nothing to prevent that, so far it's because they don't want to go that far. There were threats against the CEO of Napster.

Q: Record companies are going after end-users, universities, employees, what's going to happen? **A:** It's hard to say, there has not been a single law-suit against an end-user in the US yet.

Q: I heard about ISP being sued over not wanting to disclose information about a particular user? **A:** ISPs have always been a popular place to put pressure in the Internet infrastructure, there's an effort to cut off Internet access for anyone who's doing file sharing, and to force ISPs to handover customer information. Yeah, that's a whole other piece of this fight.

Ian Foster, Adriana Iamnitchi, **On Death, Taxes, and the Convergence of Peer-to-Peer and Grid Computing, presented by Ian Foster.** Both p2p and Grid are concerned with the pooling and coordinated use of resources within distributed communities and are constructed as overlay structures. Currently, Grid addresses infrastructure but not yet failure, whereas p2p addresses failure but not yet infrastructure. Grid has established communities with restricted participation, and implicit incentives. Resources are diverse, powerful, and well connected, and approaches to failure reflect assumptions about centralized components. In contrast, p2p is composed of very large number of entities with no implicit incentives for good behavior. Resources are less powerful, intermittent, and approaches to failures vary from centralized to highly self-configuring. It will be highly beneficial for Grid and p2p communities to recognize key commonalities and accelerate progress in both disciplines.

Discussion: **Q:** Is defense against DoS being looked at in the Grid community? **A:** It hasn't gotten to the top of anyone's priority list now.

Q: What do you think is the main reason that led to the fairly quick standardization of this toolkit? **A:** It's a combination of good technology, open source, and good marketing. A lot of groups were eager to deploy Grid technologies a few years ago.

Jonathan Ledlie, Jeff Shneidman, Margo Seltzer, John Huth, **Scooped, again, presented by Jonathan Ledlie.** The p2p and Grid communities are addressing an overlapping set of problems. The Grid infrastructure is a great customer waiting for future p2p products. p2p research should at least address the needs of Grid users, otherwise it may eventually be sidelined by standard algorithms that are less elegant but were used to solve Grid problems.

Discussion: **Q:** p2p is about making scalable services, it's a technique not infrastructure. **A:** I've noticed pointers to p2p ideas on grid-related websites, what I'm talking about more is that p2p people need to ask how can my ideas be used in Grid applications?

Q: p2p is a very lightweight, organic thing, which is very much the reason behind the success of the web. In contrast, the Grid toolkit is a very thick piece of toolkit. **A:** There's a first-mover's advantage though. **C:** Butler Lampson's quote is wrong, the success of a design is being able to support applications that they didn't even dream of. **C:** Once you remove the human and replace it by a machine, 5 years from now, we'll be able to revert Lampson's quote, and say that the web was invented by us 30 years ago.

Joint Discussion: **Q:** (for Fred von Lohmann) Your talk leaves us depressed. So we should not do caching in the network? **A:** You should push caching to your end-users, and decentralize as much as you can. **Q:** The way you use an infrastructure is to get reliability and services out of it, which means that there's someone offering the service, and that's not the end-user. Is there no future for such a company? **A:** It's complicated, before you do it, just beware of copyright laws. There's a strong incentive towards decentralization and disaggregation of functionalities. **Q:** If you've got Kazaa, which does file-sharing, but also does indexing, would that be a good case? **A:** It certainly helps, the more non-infringing uses the applications have, the better.

Q: (for Ian Foster) It's not clear that this convergence picture is consistent with the incentives. **A:** I disagree strongly with your implications. The international astronomy community have many computational devices that they want to be federated and utilized. It's getting to a point where they have enough diversity and users where work in this community is becoming relevant. **Q:** What are the fault-tolerance and scalability limits needed by the Grid community? **A:** It depends, hopefully we can define architectures where you can instantiate different parts of the design. **Q:** Do you envision having 5 billion hosts running the Grid or more having 100,000 research communities around the world? **A:** The common problem is that they need to do distributed resource management. **Q:** It seems like Grid has at least two things associated with it, one is infrastructure, and the other is sharing computation. p2p is more about moving information, I know how to protect data, encrypt, but computation seems less amenable to less secure elements, how do you prevent viruses? **A:** There are two fundamental limitations, one is homogeneity, and the other is you're not going to get very far with only information sharing, you need transformation as well which involves computing.

4   Incentive and Fairness

Jeff Shneidman, David Parkes, **Rationality and Self-Interest in P2P Networks, presented by Jeff Shneidman** Rational users in peer to peer networks can have deleterious effect on the system. Problems occur when system designers don't anticipate rational behavior. Some examples occur in computation systems (false submissions) and sharing systems (free riding, false files). Therefore, p2p designers need to consider user behavior model when designing a system. Designers responses to rationality in p2p networks can be divided into four groups: ignore it (rely on altruism or obedience), limit it (restrict computation to specialized hardware), punish (although might be computationally expensive), or embrace it, that is, use incentives and design techniques to encourage proper behavior. Our work takes the fourth approach. Mechanism design studies how to achieve a good system by incentivizing rational agents. Some example mechanisms are the vickery auction and reputation system in eBay and reputation and resource allocation in Kazaa. Traditional MD is centralized and usually NP-hard to compute. A recent research area is DAMD (distributed algorithmic mechanism design), where the mechanism computation is distributed across the nodes of the network. Unlike contemporary mechanism design, DAMD looks at how to deal with communication and computational complexity. However, it does impose a lot of open questions.

Discussion: **Q:** It seems like your assumption is that users are rational and act to maximize their utility. However, in reality, users are usually in a binary state (hurt / no hurt), and have to make a binary choice. Furthermore, most of the things are constant cost. **A:** I agree.

Q: It is common thought now that human behavior is often not rational. Therefore, once we assume rational users, it might not help or even worsen performance. **A:** You refer to the notion of bounded rationality. Usually it's because the user cannot compute what is best for him. Regarding computational capabilities, machines are better than humans.

Q: You gave Kazaa as an example to a system that is being manipulated by its users. However, at the same time, Kazaa is extremely popular. **A:** Kazaa, though, is not a good example of a system that embraces rationality. **C:** We should distinguish between the terms selfish and rational.

Tsuen-Wan Ngan, Dan Wallach, Peter Druschel, **Enforcing fair sharing of P2P Resources, presented by Tsuen-Wan Ngan** Users of p2p systems do not have incentives to donate resources to the system if they can get it for free. Our goal is to design an architecture for enforcement of fair sharing of storage resources. we consider "fair" as equal exchange of space. We take two different approaches: quota management and auditing. The drawback of the quota management approach is that it can only work with small percentage of malicious nodes. With auditing, nodes maintain and publish their own quota information and audit each other to ensure correctness. We argue that nodes have incentives to report their usage truthfully, and our simulation results show that auditing incurs a small communication overhead (linear in the avg number of files per node).

Discussion: **Q:** When a node audits a random node it should check every entry in its list. In the worst case a node would have to talk to every node in the system. **A:** It could happen in the worst case, but we don't expect that it would happen.

Q: What happens when two people are lying about each other (e.g. A says she holds B's file and vice versa). **A:** As long as it is balanced it's not violating the system.

Q: What if Bob renames the file, so it seems like he is storing another file? **A:** Storing a file is a form of payment to the system.

Q: In your presentation you mention payment, but in the paper you claim that there is no actual payment, but rather a barter economy. Which one of these is true? **A:** It is a barter economy (i.e. I store for you; you store for me), and no money is involved. In the presentation, I refer to putting an entry in the list as a form of payment. **Q:** It's not necessarily a symmetric payment. **A:** correct. It's not necessarily mutual.

Joint Discussion: **Q:** (for Tsuen-Wan Ngan) The enforcement seems like a zero-sum game. I don't understand how money is produced when new node arrives, and why economy doesn't go to zero once nodes leave. **A:** Each node advertises its capacity. If capacity is greater than what it stores then that node can use the system. **Q:** The graph shows that average bandwidth per node goes up linearly in the number of files in the system. **A:** The x-axis represents the number of files per node in the system.

Q: (for Jeff Shneidman) Mechanism design can fit in different layers of the networks model. How can we decide where to put it? What if two mechanisms that are implemented in different layers compete with each other? **A:** This can happen. In fact, if one of the mechanism design is broken, it can hurt the performance of the other mechanisms. **Q:** Do you have any examples of where rationality was taken into account in the design process? **A:** Economics is used in many systems. The problem is that there are too many assumptions on obedience on the node's part. **Q:** How can you deal with the problem of cheap (zero-cost) pseudonyms? **A:** These are questions of trust and identity. One way to go with that is that you can only get from the system as much as you put on the table. However, I dont have a very good answer to that. **Q:** It is not clear that you can get Nash Equilibrium in p2p systems. **A:** It is not about Nash Equilibrium. MD schemes work to encourage truth telling (truth revelation). **C:** We should consider anti-social nodes who enjoy from hurting others even in the cost of hurting themselves too. **C:** My view is that we should see mechanism design as a tool, not as an answer.

5   New DHT Designs

Indranil Gupta, Kenneth Birman, Prakash Linga, Al Demers, Robbert Van Renesse, Kelips: Building an Efficient and Stable p2p DHT

Through Increased Memory and Background Overhead, presented by Indranil Gupta. Kelips explores a new design point for DHT systems. Increased memory usage (for replication of tuples and membership information), and constant background overhead at a node are tolerated to achieve $O(1)$ file lookup operations and ensure stability despite high failure and churn rates.

Discussion: **Q:** I like the idea of using epidemics to maintain file pointers, but how do you get rid of them? **A:** There's an expiration time associated with membership entries, or file pointers. Or you can epidemically propagate remove file pointer information.

Q: With $\sqrt{N}$ memory, you can have a quorum system with a lot of other properties. How do you build and maintain affinity groups? **A:** Affinity groups are totally virtual, by hashing on node ID, each affinity group consists of a fairly random selection of nodes.

Zheng Zhang, Shuming Shi, Jing Zhu, **SOMO: self-organized metadata overlay for resource management in p2p DHT, presented by Zheng Zhang.** Data overlay is a mechanism to implement arbitrary data structure on top of any structured p2p DHT. SOMO, an example of a data overlay, is designed to perform resource management for p2p DHTs by gathering and disseminating system metadata in $O(\log N)$ time. The authors also demonstrate how to use SOMO to balance routing traffic with node capacities in a prefix-based overlay.

Discussion: **Q:** So you are making use of hierarchy here? **A:** I think hierarchy is a consequence. For each node, we've a constant number of interactions with its children. You can send delta's to compress information. SOMO can also discover high-capacity nodes to act as root.

Q: Are there bounds or guarantees on the maximum height of the tree as this might degenerate badly? **A:** You can choose a bigger branching factor.

Nicholas Harvey, Michael Jones, Marvin Theimer, Alec Wolman, **Efficient Recovery From Organizational Disconnects in SkipNet, presented by Nicholas Harvey.** SkipNet is a peer-to-peer overlay network that provides controlled data placement and routing locality by organizing data primarily by lexicographic ordering of string names. As a result, an organization forms one or a few contiguous overlay segments, which enables efficient recovery from organizational disconnects.

Discussion: **Q:** Doesn't having all nodes in the same part of the address space make it more vulnerable to attacks? **A:** In some sense it does, a malicious user outside of Microsoft could bracket microsoft.com, and then these nodes would receive forwarding traffic outside of Microsoft to microsoft.com. We feel that this is a small disadvantage to the locality and load balancing benefits.

Q: Nodes within Microsoft may well be moving, so the tying of identifier and location may not be a good idea? **A:** You're just 1 employee out of a lot of Microsoft employees. The majority of nodes are still in Microsoft, so they may all fail at the same time if Microsoft is disconnected.

Q: I'm surprised that you chose to lexicographically organize by DNS names, an alternative might be to pick IDs by using IP addresses and then random 128 bits at the end. **A:** The SkipNet ID space is an arbitrary space, so you can populate it by DNS names or IP addresses. One reason we chose DNS names is because of the nature of CIDR routing, nodes within a subnet may not have contiguous IP addresses.

Q: You have considered one particular dependent failure mode, i.e., org disconnect, why wouldn't you generalize this to a variety of failure modes? You can have the IDs encode other semantics, like all windows machines or Linux machines? **A:** You could do this as well because the space is arbitrary, however, SkipNet is one-dimensional right now. It's not clear that you would get the locality properties when you have IDs encode OS types. We feel that people want to put data by organizations, and locality is very interesting, but if we could generalize to multiple-dimensions, it'd be great.

Q: If you really want locality inside an organization, why do you put it in a p2p network at all? **A:** There's the additional flexibility of app-level routing, such as multicast, and cachable name-lookups.

Joint Discussion: **Q:** (for all) Regarding the general API for DHT's talk in the morning, are there any aspects of your architectures that don't work with the proposed API? **A:** With Kelips, that works, I've been talking with people that build applications on top of Chord and Pastry, and the interface they use is pretty generic (Indranil Gupta). **A:** From our experience, the data overlay abstraction is important to build other applications on top, but there may be more to come (Zheng Zhang). **A:** It's reasonable to wrap-around SkipNet, but I'd like to see additional work on this API, things such as availability checking, etc (Nicholas Harvey). **C:** A general comment, there needs to be resource management and discovery in systems, storage, computing, and networking. No one has looked at the computing part yet. **C:** It might be interesting to see how to integrate the SkipNet routing layer into the KBR. **C:** DHT is a specification, don't think of it as a ring!

Q: (for Indranil Gupta) How much traffic is there in the gossip protocol? **A:** Usually the amount of network usage depends on node join and leave rates, but it's not dependent on that in Kelips. It's a constant amount of background traffic. **Q:** There's failure versus churn, and for any fixed rate of churn, you can design a system with a fixed rate of traffic that handles the churn. **Q:** Question for Kelips, why do you stop at $\sqrt{N}$? We need an efficient way to update these routing entries. **A:** That's what the constant background traffic is for.

6   Invited Talks

Ian Clarke, **The Freenet Project** The goal of Freenet is to provide a form of free communication in the Internet. It works in a completely decentralized manner and provides a publication mechanism which keeps the anonymity of both publishers and readers. Even the developers themselves are unable to shut down the system. It should be scalable and robust to accidental failures or malicious attacks. Its design is very different from the DHT approach. Yet, finding information in Freenet is somewhat similar to the way it is done in DHT, where every node is aware of where it should route a request for a particular key. Freenet has a web interface, while protection is done using public key cryptography. For practical reasons, nodes cache connections and cryptographic information. For survivability reasons, Freenet also provides a distribution node, through which connection to the network can be done when the web interface is not accessible. To achieve load balancing, every node collects statistics on the load of other nodes and announces itself only if its load is less than the average. Currently, there are a number of third-party applications that run on top of Freenet, such as usenet and audio broadcast.

Discussion: **Q:** What's your experience with attacks on Freenet? **A:** Freenet provides excellent anonymity to its attackers. People have attempted some denial of service attacks and email spamming, but not in a concerted way.

Q: Freenet caches content along the path. How does it deal with large streaming files? **A:** streaming audio is done in Freenet. The file is cut into 1MB chunks, and to retrieve the file, one should query those chunks in sequence and reassemble them.

Q: Is it possible to control which subset of the clients receive some content? **A:** This is not part of the goal of Freenet, but it can be done using encryption before inserting it into the Freenet network.

Q: What is the convergence between anti-censorship tools and Freenet? **A:** Most such tools seem to do something different than Freenet. Freenet allows people within countries with strong censorship regimes to publish and consume information.

Q: What is your experience with free riding on Freenet (e.g. people not caching along the path) **A:** People generally do whatever the default is. Therefore, one of the best way in practice to combat free riding is to make the default beneficial for the system.

Jed McCaleb, **Overnet: a Real World p2p Application** Overnet uses the same transfer protocol as eDonkey, which allows parallel downloads, and search is done through "Kademlia" (DHT). Overnet is an open-source free code, with approximately 250,000 users. The load on most nodes as well as the bandwidth is very low. People have tried to create clones of the system. However, unlike eDonkey, people have failed to clone overnet because of the complexity of the algorithm. Furthermore, even if they were able to announce themselves, they vanished once they were not able to provide the specified key. We haven't noticed any attacks from overpeers yet. As for network growth: in the beginning it doubled every two months, but it has slowed down since.

Discussion: **Q:** How do the web pages for authentication work? **A:** It is based on three values: file name, hash value and size.

Q: Doesn't the interface create a scalability problem? **A:** The web pages are not part of the network. The motivation behind web pages is the meta data verification.

Q: What happens if I insert a file with the hash of another file? **A:** You'll get collision.

Q: When a node joins the system, it is not successful in retrieving the files. why does that happen? It shouldn't be the case in Kademlia or any other DHT? **A:** A lot of the context was bad, and depending on who you ask, you get different information.

Q: Do you use collision resistant hashing? How do you verify that the hashes are from the real data? **A:** You verify it once you get it (might be too late at this point).

Bernard Traversat, Project JXTA: Open p2p Platform Present and Future The vision of the project is looking into the future of networks (the number of devices that will be attached to the network, new ways to communicate with the network etc). It is essentially an open set of XML protocols. Observing the diversity in ways people want to use their p2p services, our objectives are to provide a ubiquitous interoperable system with security and monitoring capabilities. The system takes advantage of the heterogeneity of its users. It has the notion of a "class society", where nodes can join different groups, but must obey the policies set by these groups (e.g. search mechanism). To reduce the cost of maintaining a DHT structure, the system uses a loosely consistent DHT. There are currently more than 80 projects that are building applications on top of JXTA. File sharing and picture exchange are some typical applications.

Discussion: **Q:** JXTA sounds similar to the idea of Corba, Javabeans, etc. What is the key difference in the infrastructure between JXTA and those? **A:** You could do everything in Javabeans, but JXTA is ubiquitous and doesn't bind you to a certain language.

Q: Wouldn't I be better off with something that already has a language? **A:** We do have a java binding, c binding, python binding etc. We note that in memory constrained devices, one needs to be careful in what protocols are used.

Christian Huitema, Developing a p2p Toolkit for Windows XP The goal of this project is to build a p2p toolkit for windows XP, with a focus on interaction within small groups without the need of an external server. We split the design into the following components: (a) IPv6 overlay - to achieve connectivity, (b) p2p naming system - we use dynamic name resolution with a 2-level hash (128 bits for each level), (c) p2p security - we use the concept of secure groups to organize peers. d) graphing solution - we implement application level multicast by building a graph in real time between the members of the group.

Discussion: **Q:** Do you say that IPv6 will make it easier for p2p applications? **A:** Yes. NAT is one of the major causes of failures. It will fix 90% of the problems.

Q: What about firewalls? **A:** We can write an adequate software that passes firewall, but our customers don't like this idea.

Q: How serious is the problem of getting outside connectivity? **A:** it's quite serious. e.g. people meet in a conference room in a corporation, and have no way to get outside connectivity.

7   Naming, Indexing and Searching

Hari Balakrishnan, Scott Shenker, Michael Walfish, **Semantic-Free Referencing in Linked Distributed Systems, presented by Hari Balakrishnan.** Every linked distributed system requires a reference resolution service (RRS). The nature of reference resolution should be general-purpose (application-independent), and the references themselves should be unstructured and semantic-free. Thus, unstructured keys are ideal references, and DHTs provide a convenient platform for reference resolution. A DHT-based Semantic-Free Referencing (SFR) architecture is proposed, which gives location-independence, human unreadable names, and a shared, lightweight infrastructure.

Discussion: **Q:** There'll be contention, and you're just pushing it one level up? **A:** You want to push it to a level where competition can exist.

Q: AOL keywords? **A:** Competition can co-exist, for example, you have Google and AOL search.

Q: It seems to me that there are hard issues with naming, and you're separating the hard problem with the easy problem, and here's how you are solving the easy problem. Why didn't you use a secure file system-like approach? **A:** Your proposal would rely on DNS. The hard/easy distinction is not exactly accurate as object routing is, in fact, hard.

Jinyang Li, Boon Thau Loo, Joe Hellerstein, Frans Kaashoek, David R. Karger, Robert Morris, **On the Feasibility of Peer-to-Peer Web Indexing and Search, presented by Jinyang Li.** There are two basic P2P search strategies: Gnutella style search via flooding, and inverted index partitioned by keyword. Naive implementations of P2P Web search are not feasible under communication constraints. Optimizations such as caching, precomputation, bloom filters, gap compression, adaptive set, and clustering bring the problem to within an order of magnitude of feasibility. Two possible compromises in the quality of search results, and in the P2P structure will bring us within feasibility range for P2P Web search.

Discussion: **Q:** You are focused on aggregate load on the Internet backbone, but I'm wondering if latency is a better metric? How would one improve the lookup latency? **A:** We just tried to evaluate whether or not it's feasible, so we think bandwidth is the biggest factor.

Q: When searching for conjunction of keywords, how do you know which node holds which keywords? **A:** We can use DHT.

Q: Have you looked at bandwidth-distance product? That's where you might have a significant advantage over Gnutella but disadvantage over centralized server? **A:** No, we've not looked at that yet.

Brian Cooper, Hector Garcia-Molina, **Studying search networks with SIL, presented by Brian Cooper.** The Search/Index Link (SIL) model is a mechanism for describing the topology and properties of p2p search networks. There are four kinds of directed links in the model: forwarding search link (FSL), non-forwarding search link (NSL), forwarding index link (FIL), and non-forwarding index link (NIL). SIL is useful for evaluating networks in terms of metrics such as efficiency or fault tolerance, discovering new network architectures, defining and studying desirable topological properties of networks such as redundancy, and studying new ways of constructing and maintaining dynamic networks.

Discussion: **Q:** When you get a lot of nodes in the network, you'll inevitably have a flooding effect? **A:** How far can you get away from flooding? You can actually tune the system to make the clusters smaller or bigger.

Q: The problem is a tradeoff between flooding within and outside a cluster? **A:** This is why you look at the load in the network, and you can tradeoff searches versus updates to tune your network.

Q: Redundancy is good for failures, do you imagine this overlay that has no redundancy win over others that have redundancy? **A:** We picked one primary thing to optimize, and we picked load. We found that we can build networks that are both efficient and don't need to use super-nodes such as the parallel search clusters. You can eliminate redundancy without creating bottlenecks.

Bobby Bhattacharjee, Sudarshan Chawathe, Vijay Gopalakrishnan, Pete Keleher, Bujor Silaghi, **Efficient Peer-To-Peer Searches Using Result-Caching, presented by Bobby Bhattacharjee.** This paper proposes a new data structure, the view tree, to efficiently store and retrieve prior search results. Use of result-caching can eliminate the vast majority of tuples retrieved across the network for queries with multiple terms, and are effective even with no locality in the query stream but with locality in the distribution of attributes across documents, and update cost should be relatively insignificant.

Discussion: **Q:** You can permute the set of ids and get better balances in the tree, but you get a taller tree. **A:** Here we're missing potential parents.

8   File Sharing

Daniel Bernstein, Zhengzhu Feng, Brian Levine, Shlomo Zilberstein, **Adaptive Peer Selection, presented by Daniel Bernstein** In file sharing systems a node has to choose a good source from a list of potential servers and to switch among peers when it is advantageous to do so. The challenge is enlarged by the fact that many peers have slow and unreliable connections, and some peers may not be encountered more than once. Our approach is to let nodes learn their own selection strategy by techniques from machine learning. ITI decision trees are used for rating peers based on low-cost information (attributes from search response, such as speed or busy-flag), and Markov decision processes are used for deriving a policy for switching among nodes. Preliminary results with some nodes of the Gnutella network demonstrate that these selection strategies perform better than random selection, while we get mixed results when comparing them to ping-time-based strategies.

Discussion: **Q:** Can you think of other applications (besides peer selection) that can benefit from the techniques you described? **A:** The algorithm can take into account more information such as the quality of the data, and can optimize not just download time but some combination of time and quality.

Q: I can imagine much simpler schemes. What drove you to use machine learning schemes? **A:** I'm coming from an AI background and I'm familiar with all these techniques. It's still preliminary work and we hope that as it gets more complicated, it will be able to solve things in a way you can't do in simpler ways.

Petar Maymounkov, David Mazières, **Rateless Codes and Big Downloads, presented by Petar Maymounkov** This paper presents a novel algorithm for downloading big files from multiple sources in peer-to-peer networks. The problem is enlarged by the fact that transfer time of a big file is much longer than the average uptime of a node. Some previous approaches like partial downloads and suboptimal reconciliation protocols tend to have overlapping information and waste bandwidth. Our objective is to achieve a better bandwidth utilization, along with high file availability. The algorithm is simple, but offers several compelling properties. It ensures low hand-shaking overhead between peers that download parts of files from each other. Its computational cost is linear in the amount of data transfered. Most importantly, when nodes leave the network in the middle of uploads, the algorithm minimizes the duplicate information shared by nodes with truncated downloads. Thus, any two peers with partial knowledge of a given file can almost always fully benefit from each other's knowledge. Our algorithm is made possible by the recent introduction of lineartime, rateless erasure codes.

Discussion: **Q:** What is the overhead of the scheme? **A:** One overhead comes from the fact that code is suboptimal. Another overhead comes from the fact that each block has to be accompanied with its ID.

Q: What is the 1% overhead that you mentiones? **A:** Once you push overhead lower and lower, the codes become optimal only for very big sizes. To apply also to small files, a good parameter is 1% overhead. It makes it more practical.

Ranjita Bhagwan, Stefan Savage, Geoffrey Voelker, **Understanding Availability, presented by Ranjita Bhagwan** This paper addresses the question of what is "availability". The availability of a resource can be quantified at many different timescales, and can vary from a packet loss to a crash failure. Once we understand what "availability" means the challenge is to build highly available systems in the dynamic environments of p2p systems. We argue that existing measurements and models do not capture the complex timevarying nature of availability in today's peer-to-peer environments. Our goals are to build a P2P file system that automatically and dynamically guarantees a specified level of availability, to model redundancy requirements for building high-availability systems, and to accurately measure time-varying nature of availability in P2P environments. We empirically characterize the availability of the Overnet network (to overcome aliasing) over a period of 7 days, and analyze and measure availability distributions. Data become unavailable for two reasons: transient host disconnections and long-term host departures. Redundancy mechanisms can be used to keep data available in the short-term, while periodic data refreshes are required to keep data available in the long-run.

Discussion: **Q:** Do you have some statistics regarding how often addresses vary? **A:** We have the data, but we haven't looked at it yet. It might be interesting.

Q: Your crawler runs periodically, every 4 hours. Is it possible that we see a new study with a crawler that runs more frequently than every 4 hours, whose results will override yours? **A:** It's possible.

Joint Discussion: **Q:** (for Ranjita Bhagwan) The availability statistics that are presented here are taken from a world with a lot of piracy. How do you think the world will look like without piracy? **A:** I view it as a chicken and egg problem. We can't get data unless we have a piracy-free system. I still think that some of the effects that we see (e.g. machine switching off in night time) will still be seen, provided that we also care about home machines. **C:** In a corporation, most machines stay up most of the time. For example, it was shown that in Microsoft, the vast majority of machines were up most of the time. **C:** It depends on the corporation's policy. In some cases the policy is to leave everything off, whereas in others, it is to leave it on. **C:** Another factor that affects the behavior is the connection (dialup/DSL). I can imagine the world going in all kind of directions. **C:** I also wonder how valid free riding studies are given that wake up time is so low. **Q:** You claim that other studies underestimated availability. Your results show four times more availability than the Kazaa study. So, if you multiply all of the results of previous studies by 4, do you get similar results? **A:** Not the same results, because we report avg results. **Q:** But all studies report avg results. **A:** The Kazaa people checked availability by Kazaa IDs (rather than IP address), and they found an increase in availability on the factor of 2-3.One way to explain it is that Kazaa IDs are not completely unique. **Q:** Kazaa is much bigger than the network you played with, so why didn't you use Kazaa for your study? **A:** We didn't have the data from Kazaa, and besides, Kazaa IDs are not completely unique.

9   Networking and Applications

Jakob Eriksson, Michalis Faloutsos, Srikanth Krishnamurthy, **Peer-Net: Pushing Peer-to-Peer Down the Stack, presented by Jakob Eriksson.** PeerNet is a peer-to-peer-based network layer. It is not an overlay on top of IP, but an alternative to the IP layer. The key idea in PeerNet is the separation of the identity and address of a node. It provides an address allocation algorithm and a node lookup service using a per-node state of $O(\log N)$. Before sending a packet to some destination, the sender looks up the current address of the destination node using the lookup service. Packet routing is done in a Distance Vector fashion, but with a routing table size of $O(\log N)$.

Discussion: **Q:** How easy is it to add new nodes, and links that disconnect as a result? **A:** Links will break when nodes move, and they'll reconnect. Good thing is that addresses are locally allocated. Nodes change their addresses, but that doesn't really affect the routing table, only the lookup table is affected.

Marcelo Pias, Jon Crowcroft, Steve Wilbur, Tim Harris, Saleem Bhatti, Lighthouses for Scalable Distributed Location, presented by Marcelo Pias. Existing location mechanisms such as GNP uses a fixed set of reference points, which could become communication bottlenecks and single points of failure. Lighthouse overcomes this issue of well-known pivots by using multiple local bases together with a transition matrix in vector spaces. Lighthouse achieves similar levels of accuracy as GNP with a 3-D vector space.

Discussion: **Q:** How is it related to the work at Berkeley about Internet-isobar? **A:** It's actually quite different, Internet-isobar is more like ID-maps.

Miguel Castro, Peter Druschel, Anne-Marie Kermarrec, Animesh Nandi, Antony Rowstron, Atul Singh, SplitStream: High-bandwidth content distribution in a cooperative environment, presented by Antony Rowstron. In conventional tree-based multicast, a small number of interior nodes carry the burden of splitting and forwarding multicast traffic, while a large number of leaf nodes contribute no resources. In SplitStream, the multicast content is split into k stripes, and each stripe is multicasted in a separate multicast tree. The forest of multicast trees is constructed such that an interior node in one tree is a leaf node in all the remaining trees, which spreads the forwarding load across all participating nodes.

Discussion: **Q:** There are 20% nodes with link stress 100? **A:** This is much better than n-way unicast and the median is well below 100.

Q: Is the number of streams in SplitStream tied to the b-parameter in pastry, $16 = 2^b$? **A:** You can actually route using $b = 1$ with a $b = 4$ routing table because it's just a subset of $b = 4$ routing table.

Luc Onana Alima, Sameh El-Ansary, Per Brand and Seif Haridi, $DKS(N, k, f)$: A Family of Low Communication, Scalable and Fault-Tolerant Infrastructure for p2p Applications, presented by Luc Onana Alima. DKS(N,k,f) builds on four design principles. First, "distributed k-ary search", which can serve for understanding most of the existing DHT-based designs. Second, "Correction-on-use", which eliminates unnecessary bandwidth consumption that existing DHTs have, because of the use of active correction for maintaining routing tables. Third, "local atomic action" to handle join and leave operations in a way that avoids lookup failures. Fourth, "f+1 replication" for fault-tolerance. With the correction-on-use, in DKS(N,k,f) out-of-date routing information is corrected on-the-fly while performing lookups and insertions of (key, value) pairs. Each lookup is resolved in at most $\log_k(N)$ overlay hops under normal operations, and each node maintains only $(k - 1) \log_k(N) + 1$ addresses of other nodes for routing purposes. (Note: The presentation was on a different topic than the paper included in the proceedings.)

Discussion: **Q:** Have you compared this to a regular Chord network in terms of overhead? **A:** We have done an analytical evaluation of Chord that shows high communication overhead assuming (1) the worst case scenario (i.e., when the system evolution is synchronous), and (2) that each node updates all its fingers every 30 sec (using the stabilization procedure). However, we have not done a simulation-based comparison due to some problems we had with our simulation environment. We are working on fixing these problems.

Q: When you join, it involves three nodes. You don't update neighbor entries when you don't need to use them, but do you still need to monitor whether these entries are up or down? **A:** We detect failure of a node when the node is contacted for lookup or insertion. If the node does not respond, it may just be a communication problem. In this case, the node is bypassed. The only way to be sure that a node has failed is for the remote site to return an error code.

Acknowledgement

We thank the authors for their useful comments.

Controlling the Cost of Reliability
in Peer-to-Peer Overlays

Ratul Mahajan[1*], Miguel Castro[2], and Antony Rowstron[2]

[1] University of Washington
Seattle, WA
ratul@cs.washington.edu
[2] Microsoft Research
Cambridge, United Kingdom
{mcastro,antr}@microsoft.com

Abstract. Structured peer-to-peer overlay networks provide a useful substrate for building distributed applications but there are general concerns over the cost of maintaining these overlays. The current approach is to configure the overlays statically and conservatively to achieve the desired reliability even under uncommon adverse conditions. This results in high cost in the common case, or poor reliability in worse than expected conditions. We analyze the cost of overlay maintenance in realistic dynamic environments and design novel techniques to reduce this cost by adapting to the operating conditions. With our techniques, the concerns over the overlay maintenance cost are no longer warranted. Simulations using real traces show that they enable high reliability and performance even in very adverse conditions with low maintenance cost.

1 Introduction

Structured peer-to-peer (p2p) overlay networks (e.g., [6, 12, 7, 14]) are a useful substrate for building distributed applications because they are scalable, self-organizing and reliable. They provide a hash table like primitive to route messages using their keys. These messages are routed in a small number of hops using small per-node routing state. The overlays update routing state automatically when nodes join or leave, and can route messages correctly even when a large fraction of the nodes crash or the network partitions.

But scalability, self-organization, and reliability have a cost; nodes must consume network bandwidth to maintain routing state. There is a general concern over this cost [10, 11] but there has been little work studying it. The current approach is to configure the overlays statically and conservatively to achieve the desired reliability and performance even under uncommon adverse conditions. This results in high cost in the common case, or poor reliability in worse than expected conditions.

---

* This work was done while Ratul Mahajan was visiting Microsoft Research.

F. Kaashoek and I. Stoica (Eds.): IPTPS 2003, LNCS 2735, pp. 21–32, 2003.
© Springer-Verlag Berlin Heidelberg 2003

This paper studies the cost of overlay maintenance in realistic environments where nodes join and leave the system continuously. We derive analytic models for routing reliability and maintenance cost in these dynamic conditions.

We also present novel techniques that reduce the maintenance cost by observing and adapting to the environment. First, we describe a self-tuning mechanism that minimizes the overlay maintenance cost given a performance or reliability target. The current mechanism minimizes the probe rate for fault detection given a target message loss rate. It estimates both the failure rate and the size of the overlay, and uses the analytic models to compute the required probe rate. Second, we present mechanisms to effectively and efficiently deal with uncommon conditions such as network partitions and extremely high failure rates. These mechanisms enable the use of less conservative overlay configurations with lower maintenance cost. Though presented in the context of Pastry [7, 2], our results and techniques can be directly applied to other overlays.

Our results show that concerns over the maintenance cost in structured p2p overlays are not warranted anymore. It is possible to achieve high reliability and performance even in adverse conditions with low maintenance cost. In simulations with a corporate network trace [1], over 99% of the messages were routed efficiently while control traffic was under 0.2 messages per second per node. With a much more dynamic Gnutella trace [10], similar performance levels were achieved with a maintenance cost below one message per second per node most of the time.

The remainder of the paper is organized as follows. We provide an overview of Pastry and our environmental model in Section 2, and present analytic reliability and cost models in Section 3. Techniques to reduce maintenance cost appear in Section 4. In Section 5 we discuss how our techniques can be generalized for other structured p2p overlays. Related work is in Section 6, and conclusions in Section 7.

2   Background

This section starts with a brief overview of Pastry with a focus on aspects relevant to this paper. Then, it presents our environment model.

PASTRY   Nodes and objects are assigned random identifiers from a large sparse 128-bit *id space*. These identifiers are called *nodeIds* and *keys*, respectively. Pastry provides a primitive to send a message to a key that routes the message to the live node whose nodeId is numerically closest to the key in the id space.

The routing state maintained by each node consists of the *leaf set* and the *routing table*. Each entry in the routing state contains the nodeId and IP address of a node. The leaf set contains the $l/2$ neighboring nodeIds on either side of the local node's nodeId in the id space. In the routing table, nodeIds and keys are interpreted as unsigned integers in base 2^b (where b is a parameter with typical value 4). The routing table is a matrix with $128/b$ rows and 2^b columns. The entry in row r and column c of the routing table contains a nodeId that shares the first r digits with the local node's nodeId, and has the $(r+1)$th digit equal to c. If there is no such nodeId or the local nodeId satisfies this constraint, the entry is left empty. On average only $log_{2^b} N$ rows have non-empty entries.

Pastry routes a message to a key using no more than $log_{2^b} N$ hops on average. At each hop, the local node normally forwards the message to a node whose nodeId shares with the key a prefix that is at least one digit longer than the prefix that the key shares with the local node's nodeId. If no such node is known, the message is forwarded to a node whose nodeId is numerically closer to the key and shares a prefix with the key at least as long. If there is no such node, the message is delivered to the local node.

Pastry updates routing state when nodes join and leave the overlay. Joins are handled as described in [2] and failures are handled as follows. Pastry uses periodic probing for failure detection. Every node sends a keep-alive to the members of its leaf set every T_{ls} seconds. Since the leaf set membership is symmetric, each node should receive a keep-alive message from each of its leaf set members. If it does not, the node sends an explicit probe and assumes that a member is dead if it does not receive a response within T_{out} seconds. Additionally, every node sends a liveness probe to each entry in its routing table every T_{rt} seconds. Since routing tables are not symmetric, nodes respond to these probes. If no response is received within T_{out}, another probe is sent. The node is assumed faulty if no response is received to the second probe within T_{out}.

Faulty entries are removed from the routing state but it is necessary to replace them with other nodes. It is sufficient to replace leaf set entries to achieve correctness but it is important to replace routing table entries to achieve logarithmic routing cost. Leaf set replacements are obtained by piggybacking information about leaf set membership in keep-alive messages. Routing table maintenance is performed by periodically asking a node in each row of the routing table for the corresponding row in its routing table, and when a routing table slot is found empty during routing, the next hop node is asked to return any entry it may have for that slot. These mechanisms are described in more detail in [2].

ENVIRONMENT MODEL Our analysis and some of our cost reduction techniques assume that nodes join according to a Poisson process with rate λ and leave according to an exponential distribution with rate parameter μ (as in [4]). But we also evaluate our techniques using realistic node arrival and departure patterns and simulated massive correlated failures such as network partitions. We assume a fail-stop model and conservatively assume that all nodes leave ungracefully without informing other nodes and that nodes never return with the same nodeId.

3   Reliability and Cost Models

Pastry forwards messages using UDP with no acknowledgments by default. This is efficient and simple, but messages forwarded to a faulty node are lost. The probability of forwarding a message to a faulty node at each hop is $P_f(T, \mu) = 1 - \frac{1}{T\mu}(1 - e^{-T\mu})$, where T is the maximum time it takes to detect the fault. There are no more than $log_{2^b} N$ overlay hops in a Pastry route on average. Typically,

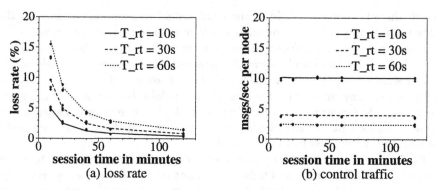

Fig. 1. Verifying loss rate and control traffic models

the last hop uses the leaf set and the others use the routing table. If we ignore messages lost by the underlying network, the message loss rate, L, is:

$$L = 1 - (1 - P_f(T_{ls} + T_{out}, \mu)).(1 - P_f(T_{rt} + 2T_{out}, \mu))^{log_{2^b} N - 1}$$

Reliability can be improved by applications if required [9]. Applications can retransmit messages and set a flag indicating that they should be acknowledged at each hop. This provides very strong reliability guarantees [2] because nodes can choose an alternate next hop if the previously chosen one is detected to be faulty. But waiting for timeouts to detect that the next hop is faulty can lead to very bad routing performance. Therefore, we use the message loss rate, L, in this paper because it models both performance and reliability – the probability of being able to route efficiently without waiting for timeouts.

We can also derive a model to compute the cost of maintaining the overlay. Each node generates control traffic for five operations: leaf set keep-alives, routing table entry probes, node joins, background routing table maintenance, and locality probes. The control traffic in our setting is dominated by the first two operations. So for simplicity, we only consider the control traffic per second per node, C, due to leaf set keep-alives and routing table probes:

$$C = \frac{l}{T_{ls}} + \frac{2 \times \sum_{r=0}^{\frac{128}{b}}((2^b - 1) \times (1 - b(0; N, \frac{1}{(2^b)^{(r+1)}})))}{T_{rt}}$$

The first term is the cost of leaf set keep-alives: l keep-alives every T_{ls} seconds. The second is the cost of routing table probing: two messages (probe and response) for each routing table entry every T_{rt}. The summation computes the expected number of routing table entries, where $b(k; n, p)$ is the binomial distribution.

We verified these equations using simulation. We started by creating a Pastry overlay with 10,000 nodes. Then we let new nodes arrive and depart according to a Poisson processes with the same rate to keep the number of nodes in the system

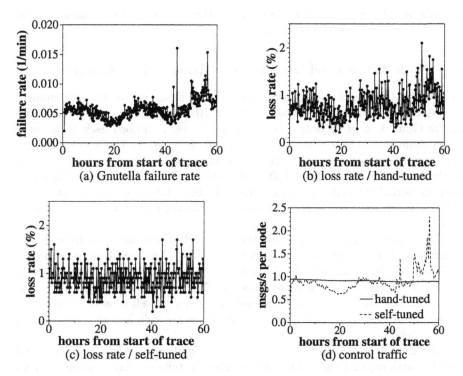

Fig. 2. Self-tuning: (a) shows the measured failure rate in the Gnutella network; (b) and (c) show the loss rate in the hand-tuned and self-tuned versions of Pastry; and (d) shows the control traffic in the two systems

roughly constant. After ten simulated minutes, 500,000 messages were sent over the next ten minutes from randomly selected nodes to randomly selected keys. Figure 1a shows the message loss rate for three different values of T_{rt} (10, 30 and 60 seconds) with T_{ls} fixed at 30 seconds. The x-axis shows the mean session lifetime of a node ($\mu = 1/lifetime$). The lines correspond to the values predicted with the loss rate equation and the dots correspond to the simulation results (three simulation runs for each parameter setting). Figure 1b shows a similar graph for control traffic. The results show that both equations are quite accurate. As expected, the loss rate decreases when T_{rt} (or T_{ls}) decrease but the control traffic increases.

4   Reducing Maintenance Cost

This section describes our techniques to reduce the amount of control traffic required to maintain the overlay. We start by motivating the importance of observing and adapting to the environment by discussing the characteristics of realistic environments. Then, we explain the self-tuning mechanism and the techniques to deal with massive failures.

4.1 Node Arrivals and Departures in Realistic Environments

We obtained traces of node arrivals and failures from two recent measurement studies of p2p environments. The first study [10] monitored 17,000 unique nodes in the Gnutella overlay over a period of 60 hours. It probed each node every seven minutes to check if it was still part of the overlay. The average session time over the trace was approximately 2.3 hours and the number of active nodes in the overlay varied between 1300 and 2700. Figure 2a shows the failure rate over the period of the trace averaged over 10 minute intervals. The arrival rate is similar. There are large daily variations in the failure rate of more than a factor of 3.

The Gnutella trace is representative of conditions in an open Internet environment. The second trace [1] is representative of a more benign corporate environment. It monitored 65,000 nodes in the Microsoft corporate network, probing each node every hour for a month. The average session time over the trace was 37.7 hours. This trace showed large daily as well as weekly variations in the failure rate, presumably because machines are switched off during nights and weekends.

These traces show that failure rates vary significantly with both daily and weekly patterns, and the failure rate in the Gnutella overlay is more than an order of magnitude higher than in the corporate environment. Therefore, the current static configuration approach would require not only different settings for the two environments, but also expensive configurations if good performance is desired at all times. The next sections show how to achieve high reliability with lower cost in all scenarios.

4.2 Self-Tuning

The goal of a self-tuning mechanism is to enable an overlay to operate at the desired trade-off point between cost and reliability. In this paper we show how to operate at one such point – achieve a target routing reliability while minimizing control traffic. The methods we use to do this can be easily generalized to make arbitrary trade-offs.

In the loss rate and control traffic equations, there are four parameters that we can set: T_{rt}, T_{ls}, T_{out}, and l. Currently, we choose fixed values for T_{ls} and l that achieve the desired resilience to massive failures (Section 4.3). T_{out} is fixed at a value higher than the maximum expected round trip delay between two nodes; it is set to 3 seconds in our experiments (same as the TCP SYN timeout). We tune T_{rt} to achieve the specified target loss rate by periodically recomputing it using the loss rate equation with the current estimates of N and μ. Below we describe mechanisms that, without any additional communication, estimate N and μ.

We use the density of nodeIds in the leaf set to estimate N. Since nodeIds are picked randomly with uniform probability from the 128-bit id space, the average distance between nodeIds in the leaf set is $2^{128}/N$. It can be shown that this estimate is within a small factor of N with very high probability, which is sufficient for our purposes since the loss rate depends only on $log_{2^b}N$.

The value of μ is estimated by using node failures in the routing table and leaf set. If nodes fail with rate μ, a node with M unique nodes in its routing state should observe K failures in time $\frac{K}{M\mu}$. Every node remembers the time of the last K failures. A node inserts its current time in the history when it joins the overlay. If there are only $k < K$ failures in the history, we compute the estimate as if there was a failure at the current time. The estimate of μ is $\frac{k}{M \times T_{k_f}}$, where T_{k_f} is the time span between the first and the last failure in the history.

The accuracy of μ's estimate depends on K; increasing K increases accuracy but decreases responsiveness to changes in the failure rate. We improve responsiveness when the failure rate decreases by using the current estimate of μ to discard old entries from the failure history that are unlikely to reflect the current behavior of the overlay. When the probability of observing a failure given the current estimate of μ reaches a threshold (e.g., 0.90) without any new failure being observed, we drop the oldest failure time from the history and compute a new estimate for μ.

We evaluated our self-tuning mechanism using simulations driven by the Gnutella trace. We simulated two versions of Pastry: *self-tuned* uses the self-tuning mechanism to adjust T_{rt} to achieve a loss rate of 1%; and *hand-tuned* sets T_{rt} to a fixed value that was determined by trial and error to achieve the same average loss rate. Hand-tuning is not possible in real settings because it requires perfect knowledge about the future. Therefore, a comparison between these two versions of Pastry provides a conservative evaluation of the benefits of self-tuning.

Figures 2b and 2c show the loss rates achieved by the self-tuned and the best hand-tuned versions, respectively. The loss rate is averaged over 10 minute windows, and is measured by sending 1,000 messages per minute from random nodes to random keys. T_{ls} was fixed at 30 seconds in both versions and T_{rt} at 120 seconds for hand-tuned. The results show that self-tuning works well, achieving the target loss rate independent of the failure rate.

Figure 2d shows the control traffic generated by both the hand-tuned and the self-tuned versions. The control traffic generated by hand-tuned is roughly constant whereas the one generated by self-tuned varies according to the failure rate to meet the loss rate target. It is interesting to note that the loss rate of hand-tuned increases significantly above 1% between 52 and 58 hours due to an increased failure rate. The control traffic generated by the self-tuned version clearly increases during this period to achieve the target loss rate with the increased failure rate. If the hand-tuned version was instead configured to always keep loss rate below 1%, it would have generated over 2 messages per second per node all the time.

We simulated the Microsoft corporate network trace also and obtained similar results. The self-tuned version achieved the desired loss rate with under 0.2 messages per second per node. The hand-tuned version required a different setting for T_{rt} as the old value would have resulted in an unnecessarily high overhead.

4.3   Dealing with Massive Failures

Next we describe mechanisms to deal with massive but rare failures such as network partitions.

BROKEN LEAF SETS   Pastry relies on the invariant that each node has at least one live leaf set member on each side. This is necessary for the current leaf set repair mechanism to work. Chord relies on a similar assumption [12]. Currently, Pastry uses large leaf sets ($l = 32$) to ensure that the invariant holds with high probability even when there are massive failures and the overlay is large [2].

We describe a new leaf set repair algorithm that uses the entries in the routing table. It can repair leaf sets even when the invariant is broken. So it allows the use of smaller leaf sets, which require less maintenance traffic.

The algorithm works as follows. When a node n detects that all members in one side of its leaf set are faulty, it selects the nodeId that is numerically closest to n's nodeId on that side from among all the entries in its routing state. Then it asks this seed node to return the entry in its routing state with the nodeId closest to n's nodeId that lies between the seed's nodeId and n's nodeId in the id space. This process is repeated until no more live nodes with closer nodeIds can be found. The node with the closest nodeId is then inserted in the leaf set and its leaf set is used to complete the repair. To improve the reliability of the repair process, we explore several paths in parallel starting with different seeds.

The expected number of rounds to complete the repair is $log_{2^b} N$. We improve convergence by adding a *shadow leaf set* to the routing state. The shadow leaf set of node n contains the $l/2$ nodes in the right leaf set of its furthest leaf on the right, and the $l/2$ nodes in the left leaf set of its furthest leaf on the left. This state is acquired at no additional cost as leaf set changes are already piggybacked on keep-alive messages, and is inexpensive to maintain since nodes in it are not directly probed. Most leaf set repairs complete in one round using the nodes in the shadow leaf set. We also use the shadow leaf set to increase the accuracy of the estimate of N.

The experiments in this paper use a small leaf set with $l = 8$. This is sufficient to ensure reliable operation with high probability even when half the nodes fail simultaneously. At the same time it ensures that the leaf set repair algorithm does not need to be invoked very often. For example, the probability of all nodes in half of a leaf set failing within $T_{ls} = 30s$ is less than 10^{-10} with the average session time in the Gnutella trace.

MASSIVE FAILURE DETECTION   The failure of a large number of nodes in a small time interval results in a large number of faulty entries in nodes' routing tables,

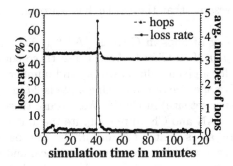

Fig. 3. Impact of half the nodes in the overlay failing together

which increases loss rate. This is resolved when nodes detect that the entries are faulty and repair the routing tables. But it can take very long in environments with low average failure rate because the self-tuning mechanism sets T_{rt} to a large value. We reduce the time to repair routing tables using a mechanism to detect massive failures.

The members of a leaf set are randomly distributed throughout the underlying network. So a massive failure such as a network partition is likely to manifest itself as failure of several nodes in the leaf set within the same probing period. When a node detects a number of faults in the same probing period that exceeds a specified fraction of l, it signals the occurrence of a massive failure and probes all entries in its routing table (failures discovered during this probing are not used for estimating μ as the background failure rate has not changed). This reduces the time to repair the routing tables after the failure to $T_{ls} + T_{out}$ seconds. We set an upper bound on the value of T_{ls} that achieves the desired repair time. In the experiments described in this paper, the threshold on the number of faults for failure detection is 30% and $T_{ls} = 30s$.

We evaluated our mechanisms to deal with massive failures using a simulation with 10,000 nodes where we failed half the nodes 40 minutes into the simulation. In addition to this failure, nodes were arriving and departing the overlay according to a Poisson process with a mean lifetime of 2 hours. 10,000 messages per minute were sent from random sources to random keys. Figure 3 shows the average loss rate and number of overlay hops in each minute. There is a large peak in the loss rate when the massive failure occurs but Pastry is able to recover in about a minute. Recovery involved not only detecting the partition and repairing routing tables but also repairing several broken leaf sets.

5   Applicability beyond Pastry

The work presented in this paper is relevant to other structured p2p overlay networks as well. In this section, we briefly outline how it applies to other networks. Due to space constraints, we only describe how it can be applied to CAN [6] and

Chord [12], and we assume that the reader has a working knowledge of CAN and Chord.

The average number of hops in CAN is $\frac{d}{4}N^{1/d}$ (where d is the number of dimensions) and is $\frac{1}{2}log_2 N$ in Chord. We can use these equations to compute the average loss rate for a given failure rate (μ) and number of nodes (N) as we did for Pastry. The average size of the routing state is $2d$ in CAN and $log_2 N + l$ (where l is the successor set size) in Chord. We can use these equations and the probing rates used in CAN and Chord to compute the amount of control traffic.

Self-tuning requires an estimate of N and μ. Our approach for estimating N using density can be generalized easily – the size of local and neighboring zones, and the density of the successor set can be used respectively for CAN and Chord. We can estimate μ in CAN and Chord using the failures observed in the routing state exactly as we did in Pastry.

The leaf set repair algorithm applies directly to Chord's successor set. A similar iterative search mechanism can be used when a CAN node loses all its neighbors along one dimension (the current version uses flooding). Finally, partition detection can be done using the successor set in Chord and neighbors in CAN.

6   Related Work

Most previous work has studied overlay maintenance under static conditions but the following studied dynamic environments where nodes continuously join and leave the overlay. Saia et al use a butterfly network to build an overlay that routes efficiently even with large adversarial failures provided that the network keeps growing [8]. Pandurangan et al present a centralized algorithm to ensure connectivity in the face of node failures [5]. Liben-Nowell et al provide an asymptotic analysis of the cost of maintaining Chord [12]. Ledlie et al [3] present some simulation results of Chord in an idealized model with Poisson arrivals and departures. We too study the overlay maintenance cost in dynamic environments but we provide an exact analysis in an idealized model together with simulations using real traces. Additionally, we describe new techniques to reduce this cost while providing high reliability and performance.

Weatherspoon and Kubiatowicz have looked at efficient node failure discovery [13]; they propose that nodes further away be probed less frequently to reduce wide area traffic. In contrast, we reduce the cost of failure discovery through adapting to the environment. The two approaches can potentially be combined though their approach makes the later hops in Tapestry (and Pastry) less reliable, with messages more likely to be lost after having been routed for a few initial hops.

7   Conclusions and Future Work

There are general concerns over the cost of maintaining structured p2p overlay networks. We examined this cost in realistic dynamic conditions, and presented novel techniques to reduce this cost by observing and adapting to the environment. These techniques adjust control traffic based on observed failure rate and they detect and recover from massive failures efficiently. We evaluated these techniques using mathematical analysis and simulation with real traces. The results show that concerns over the overlay maintenance cost are no longer warranted. Our techniques enable high reliability and performance even in adverse conditions with low maintenance cost. Though done in the context of Pastry, this work is relevant to other structured p2p networks such as CAN, Chord and Tapestry.

As part of ongoing work, we are exploring different self-tuning goals and methods. These include i) operating at arbitrary points in the reliability vs. cost curve and using different performance or reliability targets; ii) choosing a self-tuning target that takes into account the application's retransmission behavior, such that total traffic is minimized; and iii) varying T_{ls} (has implications for detecting leaf set failures since keep-alives are unidirectional) along with T_{rt} under the constraint that T_{ls} has an upper bound determined by the desired resilience to massive failures. We are also studying the impact of failures on other performance criteria such as locality.

Acknowledgements

We thank Ayalvadi Ganesh for help with mathematical analysis, and John Douceur and Stefan Saroiu for the trace data used in this paper.

References

[1] W. J. Bolosky, J. R. Douceur, D. Ely, and M. Theimer. Feasibility of a serverless distributed file system deployed on an existing set of desktop PCs. In *ACM SIGMETRICS*, June 2000.

[2] Miguel Castro, Peter Druschel, Y. Charlie Hu, and Antony Rowstron. Exploiting network proximity in peer-to-peer overlay networks. Technical Report MSR-TR-2002-82, Microsoft Research, May 2002.

[3] Jonathan Ledlie, Jacob Taylor, Laura Serban, and Margo Seltzer. Self-organization in peer-to-peer systems. In *ACM SIGOPS European Workshop*, September 2002.

[4] David Liben-Nowell, Hari Balakrishnan, and David Karger. Analysis of the evolution of peer-to-peer systems. In *ACM Principles of Distributed Computing (PODC)*, July 2002.

[5] G. Pandurangan, P. Raghavan, and E. Upfal. Building low-diameter peer-to-peer networks. In *IEEE FOCS*, October 2001.

[6] Sylvia Ratnasamy, Paul Francis, Mark Handley, Richard Karp, and Scott Shenker. A scalable content-addressable network. In *SIGCOMM*, August 2001.

[7] Antony Rowstron and Peter Druschel. Pastry: Scalable, distributed object location and routing for large-scale peer-to-peer systems. In *IFIP/ACM Middleware*, November 2001.

[8] Jared Saia, Amos Fiat, Steve Gribble, Anna Karlin, and Stefan Saroiu. Dynamically fault-tolerant content addressable networks. In *IPTPS*, March 2002.

[9] Jerry Saltzer, David Reed, and David Clarke. End-to-end arguments in system design. *ACM TOCS*, 2(4), November 1984.

[10] Stefan Saroiu, Krishna Gummadi, and Steven Gribble. A measurement study of peer-to-peer file sharing systems. In *MMCN*, January 2002.

[11] Shubho Sen and Jia Wang. Analyzing Peer-to-Peer Traffic Across Large Networks. In *Proc. ACM SIGCOMM Internet Measurement Workshop*, Marseille, France, November 2002.

[12] Ion Stoica, Robert Morris, David Karger, M. Frans Kaashoek, and Hari Balakrishnan. Chord: A scalable peer-to-peer lookup service for Internet applications. In *ACM SIGCOMM*, August 2001.

[13] Hakim Weatherspoon and John Kubiatowicz. Efficient heartbeats and repair of softstate in decentralized object location and routing systems. In *ACM SIGOPS European Workshop*, September 2002.

[14] Ben Y. Zhao, John D. Kubiatowicz, and Anthony D. Joseph. Tapestry: An infrastructure for fault-resilient wide-area location and routing. Technical Report UCB-CSD-01-1141, U. C. Berkeley, April 2001.

Towards a Common API
for Structured Peer-to-Peer Overlays[*]

Frank Dabek[1], Ben Zhao[2], Peter Druschel[3],
John Kubiatowicz[2], and Ion Stoica[2]

[1] MIT Laboratory for Computer Science
Cambridge, MA.
[2] University of California
Berkeley, CA.
[3] Rice University
Houston, TX

Abstract. In this paper, we describe an ongoing effort to define common APIs for structured peer-to-peer overlays and the key abstractions that can be built on them. In doing so, we hope to facilitate independent innovation in overlay protocols, services, and applications, to allow direct experimental comparisons, and to encourage application development by third parties. We provide a snapshot of our efforts and discuss open problems in an effort to solicit feedback from the research community.

1 Introduction

Structured peer-to-peer overlay networks have recently gained popularity as a platform for the construction or resilient, large-scale distributed systems [6, 7, 8, 10, 11]. Structured overlays conform to a specific graph structure that allows them to locate objects by exchanging $O(\lg N)$ messages where N is the number of nodes in the overlay.

Structured overlays can be used to construct services such as distributed hash tables [4], scalable group multicast/anycast [3, 12], and decentralized object location [5]. These services in turn promise to support novel classes of highly scalable, resilient, distributed applications, including cooperative archival storage, cooperative content distribution and messaging.

Currently, each structured overlay protocol exports a different API and provides services with subtly different semantics. Thus, application designers must understand the intricacies of each protocol and the services they provide to decide which system best meets their needs. Subsequently, applications are locked into one system and unable to leverage innovations in other protocols. Moreover, the semantic differences make a comparative evaluation of different protocol designs difficult.

---

[*] This research was conducted as part of the IRIS project (http://project-iris.net/), supported by the National Science Foundation under Cooperative Agreement No. ANI-0225660.

F. Kaashoek and I. Stoica (Eds.): IPTPS 2003, LNCS 2735, pp. 33–44, 2003.

This work attempts to identify the fundamental abstractions provided by structured overlays and to define APIs for the common services they provide. As the first step, we have identified and defined a *key-based routing API (KBR)*, which represents basic (tier 0) capabilities that are common to all structured overlays. We show that the KBR can be easily implemented by existing overlay protocols and that it allows the efficient implementation of higher level services and a wide range of applications. Thus, the KBR forms the common denominator of services provided by existing structured overlays.

In addition, we have identified a number of higher level (tier 1) abstractions and sketch how they can be built upon the basic KBR. These abstractions include distributed hash tables (DHT), group anycast and multicast (CAST), and decentralized object location and routing (DOLR). Efforts to define common APIs for these services are currently underway.

We believe that defining common abstractions and APIs will accelerate the adoption of structured overlays, facilitate independent innovation in overlay protocols, services, and applications, and permit direct experimental comparisons between systems.

Our APIs will not be universal. Certain applications will wish to use protocol-specific APIs that allow them to exploit particular characteristics of a protocol. This is necessary and desirable to facilitate innovation. However, we expect that such non-standard APIs, once properly understood and abstracted, can be added to the common APIs over time.

The rest of this paper is organized as follows. Section 2 provides an overview of structured overlays and the key services they provide. Next, Section 3 defines and differentiates current tier 1 services. Section 4 describes our KBR API and Section 5 evaluates our proposed API by demonstrating how it can be used to implement a variety of services and how existing overlay protocols can efficiently implement the API. Section 6 discusses future work: developing commons API for higher level tier 1 services like distributed hash tables. We conclude in Section 6.

2   Background

In this section, we define application-visible concepts common to all structured overlay protocols.

A *node* represents an instance of a participant in the overlay (one or more nodes may be hosted by a single physical IP host). Participating nodes are assigned uniform random *nodeIds* from a large *identifier space*. Application-specific objects are assigned unique identifiers called *keys*, selected from the same id space. Tapestry [11, 5], Pastry [8] and Chord [10] use a circular identifier space of n-bit integers modulo 2^n ($n = 160$ for Chord and Tapestry, $n = 128$ for Pastry). CAN [7] uses a d-dimensional cartesian identifier space, with 128-bit nodeIds that define a point in the space.

Each key is dynamically mapped by the overlay to a unique live node, called the key's *root*. To deliver messages efficiently to the root, each node maintains a *routing table* consisting of the nodeIds and IP addresses of the nodes to which

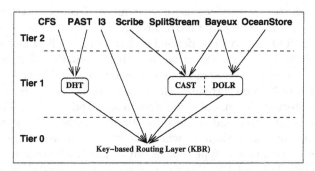

Fig. 1. Basic abstractions and APIs, including Tier 1 interfaces: distributed hash tables (DHT), decentralized object location and routing (DOLR), and group anycast and multicast (CAST)

the local node maintains overlay links. Messages are forwarded across overlay links to nodes whose nodeIds are progressively closer to the key in the identifier space.

Each system defines a function that maps keys to nodes. In Chord, keys are mapped to the live node with the closest nodeId clockwise from the key. In Pastry, keys are mapped to the live node with the closest nodeId. Tapestry maps a key to the live node whose nodeId has the longest prefix match, where the node with the next higher nodeId value is chosen for each digit that cannot be matched exactly. In CAN, neighboring nodes in the identifier space agree on a partitioning of the space surrounding their nodeIds; keys are mapped to the node responsible for the space that contains the key.

3 Abstractions

All existing systems provide higher level abstractions built upon the basic structured overlays. Examples are Distributed Hash Tables (DHT), Decentralized Object Location and Routing (DOLR), and group anycast/multicast (CAST).

Figure 1 illustrates how these abstractions are related. Key-based routing is the common service provided by all systems at tier 0. At tier 1, we have higher level abstractions provided by some of the existing systems. Most applications

Table 1. Tier 1 Interfaces

DHT	DOLR	CAST
put (key, data)	*publish (objectId)*	*join(groupId)*
remove (key)	*unpublish (objectId)*	*leave(groupId)*
value = get (key)	*sendToObj (msg, objectId, [n])*	*multicast(msg, groupId)* *anycast(msg, groupId)*

and higher-level (tier 2) services use one or more of these abstractions. Some tier 2 systems, like *i3* [9], use the KBR directly.

The KBR API at tier 0 will be defined in detail in the following section. Here, we briefly explain the tier 1 abstractions and their semantic differences. The key operations of each of these abstractions are sketched in Table 1.

The DHT abstraction provides the same functionality as a traditional hashtable, by storing the mapping between a key and a value. This interface implements a simple store and retrieve functionality, where the value is always stored at the live overlay node(s) to which the key is mapped by the KBR layer. Values can be objects of any type. For example, the DHT implemented as part of the DHash interface in CFS [4] stores and retrieves single disk blocks by their content-hashed keys.

The DOLR abstraction provides a decentralized directory service. Each object replica (or endpoint) has an *objectID* and may be placed anywhere within the system. Applications announce the presence of endpoints by *publishing* their locations. A client message addressed with a particular *objectID* will be delivered to a *nearby* endpoint with this name. Note that the underlying distributed directory can be implemented by annotating trees associated with each *objectID*; other implementations are possible. One might ask why DOLR is not implemented on top of a DHT, with data pointers stored as values; this is not possible because a DOLR routes messages to the nearest available endpoint—providing a locality property not supported by DHTs. An integral part of this process is the maintenance of the distributed directory during changes to the underlying nodes or links.

The CAST abstraction provides scalable group communication and coordination. Overlay nodes may join and leave a group, multicast messages to the group, or anycast a message to a member of the group. Because the group is represented as a tree, membership management is decentralized. Thus, CAST can support large and highly dynamic groups. Moreover, if the overlay that provides the KBR service is proximity-aware, then multicast is efficient and anycast messages are delivered to a group member near the anycast originator.

The DOLR and CAST abstractions are closely related. Both maintain sets of endpoints in a decentralized manner and by their proximity in the network, using a tree consisting of the routes from the endpoints to a common root associated with the set. However, the DOLR abstraction is more tailored towards object location, while the CAST abstraction targets group communication. Thus, their implementations combine different policies with the same basic mechanism. The DHT abstraction, on the other hand, provides a largely orthogonal service, namely a scalable repository for key, value pairs.

Defining APIs for the DHT, DOLR and CAST interfaces is the subject of ongoing work. By defining an API for key-based routing and identifying the key tier 1 abstractions, we have taken a major first step.

4 Key-Based Routing API

In this section we describe the proposed key-based routing API. We begin by defining notation and data types we will use to describe the API. Section 5.1 will show how we can use these calls to implement the DHT, DOLR and CAST higher level abstractions.

4.1 Data Types

A *key* is a 160-bit string. A *nodehandle* encapsulates the transport address and nodeId of a node in the system. The nodeId is of type *key*; the transport address might be, for example, an IP address and port. Messages (type *msg*) contain application data of arbitrary length.

We adopt a language-neutral notation for describing the API. A parameter p will be denoted as $\rightarrow p$ if it is a read-only parameter and $\leftrightarrow p$ if it is a read-write parameter. We denote an ordered set p of objects of type T as $T[]$ p.

4.2 Routing Messages

void route(key →K, msg →M, nodehandle →hint) This operation forwards a message, M, towards the root of key K. The optional *hint* argument specifies a node that should be used as a first hop in routing the message. A good hint, e.g. one that refers to the key's current root, can result in the message being delivered in one hop; a bad hint adds at most one extra hop to the route. Either K or *hint* may be NULL, but not both. The operation provides a best-effort service: the message may be lost, duplicated, corrupted, or delayed indefinitely.

The **route** operation delivers a message to the key's root. Applications process messages by executing code in upcalls which are invoked by the KBR routing system at nodes along a message's path and at its root. To permit event-driven implementations, upcall handlers must not block and should not perform long-running computations.

void forward(key ↔K, msg ↔M, nodehandle ↔nextHopNode) This upcall is invoked at each node that forwards message M, including the source node, and the key's root node (before deliver is invoked). The upcall informs the application that message M with key K is about to be forwarded to *nextHopNode*. The application may modify the M, K, or *nextHopNode* parameters or terminate the message by setting *nextHopNode* to NULL.

By modifying the *nextHopNode* argument the application can effectively override the default routing behavior. We will demonstrate examples of the use of this flexibility in Section 5.1.

void deliver(key →K, msg →M) This function is invoked on the the node that is the root for key K upon the arrival of message M. The **deliver** upcall is provided as a convenience for applications.

4.3   Routing State Access

The API allows applications to access a node's routing state via the following calls. All of these operations are strictly local and involve no communication with other nodes. Applications may query the routing state to, for instance, obtain nodes that may be used by the forward upcall above as a next hop destination.

Some of the operations return information about a key's r-root. The r-root is a generalization of a key's root. A node is an r-root for a key if that node becomes the root for the key if all of the i-roots fail for $i < r$. The node may be the r-root for keys in one or more contiguous regions of the ID space.

nodehandle[] local_lookup(key →K, int →num, boolean →safe) This call produces a list of nodes that can be used as next hops on a route towards key K, such that the resulting route satisfies the overlay protocol's bounds on the number of hops taken.

If *safe* is true, the expected fraction of faulty nodes in the list is guaranteed to be no higher than the fraction of faulty nodes in the overlay; if false, the set may be chosen to optimize performance at the expense of a potentially higher fraction of faulty nodes. This option allows applications to implement routing in overlays with byzantine node failures. Implementations that assume fail-stop behavior may ignore the *safe* argument. The fraction of faulty nodes in the returned list may be higher if the *safe* parameter is not true because, for instance, malicious nodes have caused the local node to build a routing table that is biased towards malicious nodes [1].

nodehandle [] neighborSet (int →num) This operation produces an unordered list of nodehandles that are neighbors of the local node in the ID space. Up to *num* node handles are returned.

nodehandle [] replicaSet (key →k, int →max_rank) This operation returns an ordered set of nodehandles on which replicas of the object with key k can be stored. The call returns nodes with a rank up to and including *max_rank*. If *max_rank* exceeds the implementation's maximum replica set size, then its maximum replica set is returned. Some protocols ([11], [7]) only support a *max_rank* value of one. With protocols that support a rank value greater than one, the returned nodes may be used for replicating data since they are precisely the nodes which become roots for the key k when the local node fails.

update(nodehandle →n, bool →joined) This upcall is invoked to inform the application that node n has either joined or left the neighbor set of the local node as that set would be returned by the neighborSet call.

boolean range (nodehandle →N, rank →r, key ↔lkey, key ←rkey) This operation provides information about ranges of keys for which the node N is currently a r-root. The operations returns *false* if the range could not be determined, *true* otherwise. It is an error to query the range of a node not present in the neighbor set as returned by the **update** upcall or the **neighborSet** call. Certain implementations may return an error if r is greater than zero. $[lkey, rkey]$ denotes an inclusive range of key values.

Some protocols may have multiple, disjoint ranges of keys for which a given node is responsible. The parameter *lkey* allows the caller to specify which region should be returned. If the node referenced by N is responsible for key *lkey*, then the resulting range includes *lkey*. Otherwise, the result is the nearest range clockwise from *lkey* for which N is responsible.

5   Validating the API

To evaluate our proposed API, we show how it can be used to implement the tier 1 abstractions, and give examples of other common usages. We believe that the API is expressive enough to implement all the applications known to the authors that have to date been built on top of CAN, Chord, Pastry and Tapestry. We also discuss how the API can be supported on top of several representative structured overlay protocols.

5.1   Use of the API

Here we briefly sketch how tier 1 abstractions (DHT, DOLR, CAST) can be implemented on top of the routing API. We also show how to implement a tier 2 application, Internet Indirection Infrastructure [9], and other mechanisms and protocols such as caching and replication.

DHT. A distributed hash table (DHT) provides two operations: (1) *put(key, value)*, and (2) *value = get(key)*. A simple implementation of *put* routes a *PUT* message containing *value* and the local node's nodehandle, S, using **route(key, [PUT,value,S], NULL)**. The key's root, upon receiving the message, stores the (key, value) pair in its local storage. If the value is large in size, the insertion can be optimized by returning only the nodehandle R of the key's root in response to the initial *PUT* message, and then sending the value in a single hop using **route(key, [PUT,value], R))**.

The *get* operation routes a *GET* message using **route(key, [GET,S], NULL)**. The key's root returns the value and its own nodehandle in a single hop using **route(NULL, [value,R], S)**. If the local node remembers R from a previous access to *key*, it can provide R as a hint.

CAST. Group communication is a powerful building block in many distributed applications. We describe one approach to implementing the CAST abstraction described in Section 3. A key is associated with a group, and the key's root becomes the root of the group's multicast tree. Nodes join the group by routing a SUBSCRIBE message containing their nodehandle to the group's key.

When the **forward** upcall is invoked at a node, the node checks if it is a member of the group. If so, it terminates the SUBSCRIBE message; otherwise, it inserts its nodehandle into the message and forwards the message towards the group key's root, thus implicitly subscribing to the group. In either case, it adds the nodehandle of the joining node to its list of children in the group multicast tree.

Any overlay node may multicast a message to the group, by routing a MCAST message using the group key. The group key's root, upon receiving this message, forwards the message to its children in the group's tree, and so on recursively. To send an anycast message, a node routes an ACAST message using the group key. The first node on the path that is a member of the group forwards the message to one of its children and does not forward it towards the root (returns NULL for nexthop). The message is forwarded down the tree until it reaches a leaf, where it is delivered to the application. If the underlying KBR supports proximity, then the anycast receiver is a group member near the anycast originator.

DOLR. A decentralized object location and routing (DOLR) layer allows applications to control the placement of objects in the overlay. The DOLR layer provides three operations: *publish(objectId)*, *unpublish(ObjectID)*, and *sendToObj(msg, objectId, [n])*.

The *publish* operation announces the availability of an object (at the physical node that issues this operation) under the name *objectID*. The simplest form of *publish* calls **route(objectId, [PUBLISH, objectId, S], NULL)**, where S is the name of the originating node. At each hop, an application upcall handler stores a local mapping from *objectId* to S. More sophisticated versions of *publish* may deposit pointers along secondary paths to the root. The *unpublish* operation walks through the same path and removes mappings.

The *sendToObj* operation delivers a message to n nearby replicas of a named object. It begins by routing the message towards the object root using **route(objectId, [n, msg], NULL)**. At each hop, the upcall handler searches for local object references matching objectId and sends a copy of the message directly to the closest n locations. If fewer than n pointers are found, the handler decrements n by the number of pointers found and forwards the original message towards objectID by again calling **route(objectId, [n, msg], NULL)**.

Internet Indirection Infrastructure (*i3*). *i3* is a communication infrastructure that provides indirection, that is, it decouples the act of sending a packet from the act of receiving it [9]. This allows *i3* to provide support for mobility, multicast, anycast and service composition.

There are two basic operations in *i3*: sources send packets to a logical *identifier* and receivers express interest in packets by inserting a *trigger* into the network. In their simplest form, packets are of the form (*id, data*) and triggers are of the form (*id, addr*), where *addr* is either an identifier or an IP address.[1]

---

[1] To support service composition and scalable multicast, *i3* generalizes the packet and trigger formats by replacing the *id* of a packet and the *addr* field of a trigger with a stack of identifiers. However, since these generalizations do not affect our discussion, we ignore them here.

Given a packet $(id, data)$, $i3$ will search for a trigger $(id, addr)$ and forward $data$ to $addr$. $i3$ IDs in packets are matched with those in triggers using longest prefix matching. $i3$ IDs are 256-bit long, and their prefix is at least 128-bit long.

To insert a trigger $(id, addr)$, the receiver calls **route**($H(id_{255:128})$, $[id_{127:0}$, **addr**], **NULL**), where $H()$ is a hash function that converts an 128-bit string into an unique 160-bit string (eventually by padding $id_{255:128}$ with zeros). This message is routed to the node responsible for $H(id_{255:128})$, where the trigger is stored. Note that all triggers whose IDs have the same prefix are stored at the same node; thus the longest prefix matching is done locally. Similarly, a host sending a packet $(id, data)$ invokes **route**($H(id_{255:128})$, $[id_{127:0}$, **data**], **NULL**). When the packet arrives at the node responsible for $H(id_{255:128})$, the packet's id is matched with the trigger's id and forwarded to the corresponding destination. To improve efficiency, a host may cache the address S of the server where a particular id is stored, and use S as a hint when invoking the **route** primitive for that id.

Replication. Applications like DHTs use replication to ensure that stored data survives node failure. To replicate a newly received key (k) r times, the application calls **replicaSet (k,r)** and sends a copy of the key to each returned node. If the implementation is not able to return r suitable neighbors, then the application itself is responsible for determining replica locations.

Data Maintenance. When a node's identifier neighborhood changes, the node will be required to move keys to preserve the mapping of keys to nodes, or to maintain a desired replication level. When the **update** upcall indicates that node (n) has joined the identifier neighborhood, the application calls **range (n, i)** with $i = 0 \ldots r$ and transfers any keys which fall in the returned range to n. This has the effect of both transferring data to a node which has taken over the local node's key space $(i = 0)$ and maintaining replicas $(i > 0)$. This description assumes that a node is using r replicas as returned by **replicaSet**.

Caching. Applications like DHTs use dynamic caching to create transient copies of frequently requested data in order to balance query load. It is desirable to cache data on nodes that appear on the route request messages take towards a key's root because such nodes are likely to receive future request messages. A simple scheme places a cached a copy of a data item on the last node of the route prior to the node that provides the data. Caching can be implemented as follows. A field is added to the request message to store the nodehandle of the previous node on the path. When the **forward** upcall is invoked, each node along the message's path checks whether it stores the requested data. If not, it inserts its nodehandle into the message, and allows the lookup to proceed. If the node does store the data, it sends the data to the requester and sends a copy of the data to the previous node on the request path. The node then terminates the request message by setting *nextHopNode* to NULL.

5.2 Implementation

Here we sketch how existing structured overlay protocols can implement the proposed API. While the chosen example systems (CAN, Chord, Pastry, Tapestry) do not constitute an exhaustive list of structured overlays, they represent a cross-section of existing systems and support our claim the the API can be widely implemented easily.

CAN   The **route** operation is supported by existing operations, and the hint functionality can be easily added. The **range** call returns the range associated with the local node, which in CAN can be represented by a binary prefix. **local_lookup** is a local routing table lookup and currently ignores the value of **safe**. The **update** operation is triggered every time a node splits its namespace range, or joins its range with that of a neighbor.

Chord   Route is implemented in an iterative fashion in Chord. At each hop, the local node invokes an RPC at the next node in the lookup path; this RPC invokes the appropriate upcall (route or deliver) and returns a next hop node. If a hint is given, it is used as the first hop in the search instead of a node taken from the local routing table. The **local_lookup** call returns the closest *num* successors of K in the node's location table. Calls to **neighborSet** and **replicaSet** return the node's successor list; **neighborSet** calls additionally return the node's predecessor. The range call can be implemented by querying the successor list; given the nth node, it returns the range $[succ[n].ID, succ[n+1].ID$. The exception to this rule is the predecessor; the range of the predecessor cannot be determined.

Pastry   The **route** operation can be trivially implemented on top of Pastry's route operation. The hint argument, if present, supersedes the routing table lookup. The **range** operation is implemented based on nodeId comparisons among the members of Pastry's leafset. **local_lookup** translates into a simple lookup of Pastry's routing table; if *safe* is true, the lookup is performed in Pastry's *constrained* routing table [1]. The **update** operation is triggered by a change in Pastry's leafset, and the neighbor set (returned by **neighborSet**) consists of the leafset.

Tapestry   The **route** operation is identical to the Tapestry API call *Tapestry-RouteMsg* forwarded to the hint argument, if present. Tapestry routing tables optimize performance and maintain a small set (generally three) of nodes which are the closest nodes maintaining the next hop prefix matching property. The **local_lookup** call retrieves the optimized next hop nodes. The *safe* routing mode is not used by the current Tapestry implementation, but may be used in future implementations. The **range** operation returns a set of ranges, one each for all combinations of levels where the node can be surrogate routed to. The **update** operation is trigged when a node receives an acknowledged multicast for a new inserting node, or when it receives an object movement request during node deletion [5].

6   Discussion and Future Work

Settling on a particular key-based routing API were complicated by the tight coupling between applications and the lookup systems on which they were developed. Current block replication schemes, especially the neighbor set replication used by Chord and Pastry, are closely tied to the manner in keys are mapped to nodes. Supporting efficient data replication independent of the lookup system necessitates the **range** and **replicaSet** calls which allow a node to determine where to replicate keys. The common practice of caching blocks along probable lookup paths also requires additional flexibility in the API, namely the upcall mechanism which allows application procedures to execute during the lookup.

The KBR API described here is intended to be language neutral to allow the greatest possible flexibility for implementors of lookup systems. Without specifying a precise binding of the API in a language, application developers will not be able to trivially change which system they use. Instead, the API directs developers to structure their applications in such a way that they can be translated from one system to another with a minimum of effort. One possibility for true portability among structured P2P systems would be to implement the API as an RPC program.

In the future, we will better articulate APIs for tier 1 services such as DHT, DOLR and CAST, including clear definitions of functional and performance expectations. We made a stab at this in Section 3, but more work must be done. In particular, the similarities between DOLR and CAST are striking and demand further exploration. It is at level of tier 1 abstractions that structured peer-to-peer overlays take on their greatest power and utility. We hope that the effort detailed in this paper is the beginning of convergence of functionality toward common services available for all peer-to-peer applications writers.

References

[1] CASTRO, M., DRUSCHEL, P., GANESH, A., ROWSTRON, A., AND WALLACH, D. S. Secure routing for structured peer-to-peer overlay networks. In *Proceedings of OSDI* (December 2002).

[2] CASTRO, M., DRUSCHEL, P., KERMARREC, A.-M., NANDI, A., ROWSTRON, A., AND SINGH, A. SplitStream: High-bandwidth content distribution in a cooperative environment. In *Proceedings of (IPTPS'03)* (February 2003).

[3] CASTRO, M., DRUSCHEL, P., KERMARREC, A.-M., AND ROWSTRON, A. SCRIBE: A large-scale and decentralized application-level multicast infrastructure. *IEEE JSAC 20*, 8 (Oct. 2002).

[4] DABEK, F., KAASHOEK, M. F., KARGER, D., MORRIS, R., AND STOICA, I. Wide-area cooperative storage with CFS. In *Proceedings of SOSP* (Oct. 2001).

[5] HILDRUM, K., KUBIATOWICZ, J. D., RAO, S., AND ZHAO, B. Y. Distributed object location in a dynamic network. In *Proceedings of SPAA* (Winnipeg, Canada, August 2002), ACM.

[6] MAYMOUNKOV, P., AND MAZIERES, D. Kademlia: A peer-to-peer information system based on the xor metric. In *Proceedings of (IPTPS)* (2002).

[7] RATNASAMY, S., FRANCIS, P., HANDLEY, M., KARP, R., AND SHENKER, S. A scalable content-addressable network. In *Proc. ACM SIGCOMM* (San Diego, 2001).

[8] ROWSTRON, A., AND DRUSCHEL, P. Pastry: Scalable, distributed object location and routing for large-scale peer-to-peer systems. In *Proceedings of IFIP/ACM Middleware* (Nov. 2001).

[9] STOICA, I., ADKINS, D., ZHUANG, S., SHENKER, S., AND SURANA, S. Internet indirection infrastructure. In *Proceedings of SIGCOMM* (August 2002), ACM.

[10] STOICA, I., MORRIS, R., KARGER, D., KAASHOEK, M. F., AND BALAKRISHNAN, H. Chord: A scalable peer-to-peer lookup service for internet applications. In *Proc. ACM SIGCOMM* (San Diego, 2001).

[11] ZHAO, B., KUBIATOWICZ, J., AND JOSEPH, A. Tapestry: An infrastructure for fault-tolerant wide-area location and routing. Tech. Rep. UCB/CSD-01-1141, Computer Science Division, U. C. Berkeley, Apr. 2001.

[12] ZHUANG, S. Q., ZHAO, B. Y., JOSEPH, A. D., KATZ, R. H., AND KUBIATOWICZ, J. D. Bayeux: An architecture for scalable and fault-tolerant wide-area data dissemination. In *Proceedings of NOSSDAV* (June 2001).

Sloppy Hashing and Self-Organizing Clusters

Michael J. Freedman and David Mazières

New York University
Dept. of Computer Science
715 Broadway, 7th floor
New York, NY 10003, USA
{mfreed,dm}@cs.nyu.edu
http://www.scs.cs.nyu.edu/coral/

Abstract. We are building Coral, a peer-to-peer content distribution system. Coral creates self-organizing clusters of nodes that fetch information from each other to avoid communicating with more distant or heavily-loaded servers. Coral indexes data, but does not store it. The actual content resides where it is used, such as in nodes' local web caches. Thus, replication happens exactly in proportion to demand.

We present two novel mechanisms that let Coral achieve scalability and high performance. First, a new abstraction called a *distributed sloppy hash table* (DSHT) lets nodes locate nearby copies of a file, regardless of its popularity, without causing hot spots in the indexing infrastructure. Second, based on the DSHT interface, we introduce a decentralized clustering algorithm by which nodes can find each other and form clusters of varying network diameters.

1 Introduction

The academic community has implemented a number of distributed hash tables (DHTs) as efficient, scalable, and robust peer-to-peer infrastructures. However, we should ask whether DHTs are well-suited for the desired applications of the wider Internet population. For example, can DHTs be used to implement file-sharing, by far the most popular peer-to-peer application? Or could DHTs replace proprietary content distribution networks (CDNs), such as Akamai, with a more democratic client caching scheme that speeds up any web site and saves it from flash crowds at no cost to the server operator?

Thus far, the answer to these questions is no. DHTs fail to meet the needs of real peer-to-peer applications for two main reasons.

DHTs provide the wrong abstraction. Suppose many thousands of nodes store a popular music file or cache CNN's widely-accessed home page. How might a hash table help others find the data? Using CNN's URL as a key, one might store a list of every node that has the web page. Of course, any single node responsible for such a URL-to-node-list mapping would quickly be overloaded. DHTs typically replicate popular data, but replication helps only with fetches, not stores. Any node seeking a web page will likely also cache it. Therefore,

F. Kaashoek and I. Stoica (Eds.): IPTPS 2003, LNCS 2735, pp. 45–55, 2003.

any URL-to-node-list mapping would be updated almost as frequently as it is fetched.

An alternative approach, taken by CFS [3], OceanStore [5], and PAST [9], is to store actual content in the hash table. This approach wastes both storage and bandwidth, as data must be stored at nodes where it is not needed. Moreover, while users have clearly proven willing to burn bandwidth by sharing files they themselves are interested in, there is less incentive to dedicate bandwidth to sharing unknown data. Worse yet, storing content in a DHT requires large amounts of data to be shifted around when nodes join and leave the system, a common occurrence [10].

DHTs have poor locality. Though some DHTs make an effort to route requests through nodes with low network latency, the last few hops in any lookup request are essentially random. Thus, a node might need to send a query half way around the world to learn that its neighbor is caching a particular web page. This is of particular concern for any peer-to-peer CDN, as the average DHT node may have considerably worse network connectivity than the web server itself.

This paper presents Coral, a peer-to-peer content distribution system we are building. Coral is based on a new abstraction we call a *distributed sloppy hash table* (DSHT). It is currently being built as a layer on the Chord lookup service [13], although it is equally designed to support Kademlia [6] or other existing systems [7, 8, 14]. Coral lets nodes locate and download files from each other by name. Web caches can use it to fetch static data from nearby peers. Users can employ it directly to share directories of files. Coral's two principal goals are to avoid hot spots and to find nearby data without querying distant nodes.

The DSHT abstraction is specifically suited to locating replicated resources. DSHTs sacrifice the consistency of DHTs to support both frequent fetches and frequent stores of the same hash table key. The fundamental observation is that a node doesn't need to know every replicated location of a resource—it only needs a single, valid, nearby copy. Thus, a sloppy insert is akin to an append in which a replica pointer appended to a "full" node spills over to the previous node in the lookup path. A sloppy retrieve only returns some randomized subset of the pointers stored under a given key.

In order to restrict queries to nearby machines, each Coral node is a member of several DSHTs, which we call *clusters*, of increasing network *diameter*. The diameter of a cluster is the maximum desired round-trip time between any two nodes it contains. When data is cached somewhere in a Coral cluster, any member of the cluster can locate a copy without querying machines farther away than the cluster's diameter. Since nodes have the same identifiers in all clusters, even when data is not available in a low-diameter cluster, the routing information returned by the lookup can be used to continue the query in a larger-diameter cluster.

Note that some DHTs replicate data along the last few hops of the lookup path, which increases the availability of popular data and improves performance in the face of many readers. Unfortunately, even with locality-optimized routing, the last few hops of a lookup are precisely the ones that can least be optimized. Thus, without a clustering mechanism, even replication does not avoid the need to query distant nodes. Perhaps more importantly, when storing pointers in a DHT, nothing guarantees that a node storing a pointer is near the node pointed to. In contrast, this property follows naturally from the use of clusters.

Coral's challenge is to organize and manage these clusters in a decentralized manner. As described in the next section, the DSHT interface *itself* is well-suited for locating and evaluating nearby clusters.

2 Design

This section first discusses Coral's DSHT storage layer and its lookup protocols. Second, it describes Coral's technique for forming and managing clusters.

2.1 A Sloppy Storage Layer

A traditional DHT exposes two functions. *put*(*key*, *value*) stores a value at the specified *m*-bit key, and *get*(*key*) returns this stored value, just as in a normal hash table. Only one value can be stored under a key at any given time. DHTs assume that these keys are uniformly distributed in order to balance load among participating nodes. Additionally, DHTs typically replicate popular key/value pairs after multiple *get* requests for the same *key*.

In order to determine where to insert or retrieve a key, an underlying lookup protocol assigns each node an *m*-bit *nodeid* identifier and supplies an RPC *find_closer_node*(*key*). A node receiving such an RPC returns, when possible, contact information for another a node whose *nodeid* is closer to the target key. Some systems [6] return a set of such nodes to improve performance; for simplicity, we hereafter refer only to the single node case. By iterating calls to *find_closer_node*, we can map a key to some closest node, which in most DHTs will require an expected $O(\log n)$ RPCs. This $O(\log n)$ number of RPCs is also reflected in nodes' routing tables, and thus provides a rough estimate of total network size, which Coral exploits as described later.

DHTs are well-suited for keys with a single writer and multiple readers. Unfortunately, file-sharing and web-caching systems have multiple readers *and* writers. As discussed in the introduction, a plain hash table is the wrong abstraction for such applications.

A DSHT provides a similar interface to a DHT, except that a key may have multiple values: *put*(*key*, *value*) stores a value under *key*, and *get*(*key*) need only return some subset of the values stored. Each node stores only some maximum number of values for a particular key. When the number of values exceeds this maximum, they are spread across multiple nodes. Thus multiple stores on the same key will not overload any one node. In contrast, DHTs replicate the exact same data everywhere; many people storing the same key will all contact the same closest node, even while replicas are pushed back out into the network from this overloaded node.

More concretely, Coral manages values as follows. When a node stores data locally, it inserts a pointer to that data into the DSHT by executing *put*(*key*, *addr*). For example, the key in a distributed web cache would be *hash*(*URL*). The inserting node calls *find_closer_node*(*key*) until it locates the first node whose list stored under *key* is full, or it reaches the node closest to *key*. If this located node is full, we backtrack one hop on the lookup path. This target node appends *addr* with a timestamp to the (possibly new) list stored under *key*. We expect records to expire quickly enough to keep the fraction of stale pointers below 50%.

A *get*(*key*) operation traverses the identifier space and, upon hitting a node storing *key*, returns the key's corresponding contact list. Then, the requesting node can contact these nodes, in parallel or in some application-specific way, to download the stored data.

Coral's "sloppy store" method inserts pointers along the lookup path for popular keys. Its practice of "spilling-over" when full helps to balance load while inserting pointers, retrieving pointers, and downloading data. Rapid membership changes remain inexpensive as the system only exchanges pointers.

While sloppy stores eliminate hot spots, we still must address the problem of latency. In particular, *find_closer_node*(*key*) may circle the globe to find some nearby host with the data. To take advantage of data locality, Coral introduces *hierarchical* lookup.

2.2   A Hierarchical Lookup Layer

Instead of one global lookup system as in [3, 5, 9], Coral uses several *levels* of DSHTs called clusters. Coral nodes belong to one DSHT at each level; the current implementation has a three-level DSHT hierarchy. The goal is to establish many fast clusters with regional coverage (we refer to such "low-level" clusters as level-2), multiple clusters with continental coverage (referred to as "higher" level-1 clusters), and one planet-wide cluster (level-0). Reasonable round-trip time thresholds are 30 msec for level-2 clusters, 100 msec for level-1, and ∞ for the global level-0. Section 3 presents some experimental measurements to support these choices. Each cluster is named by an m-bit cluster identifier, cid_i; the global cid_0 is predefined as 0^m.

Coral uses this hierarchy for distance-optimized lookup, visualized in Figure 1 for both the Chord [13] and Kademlia [6] routing structures.

To **insert** a key/value pair, a node performs a *put* on all levels of its clusters. This practice results in a loose hierarchical data cache, whereby a higher-level cluster contains nearly all data stored in the lower-level clusters to which its members also belong.

To **retrieve** a key, a requesting node r first performs a *get* on its level-2 cluster to try to take advantage of network locality. *find_closer_node* on this level may hit some node caching the key and halt (a *hit*). If not, the lookup will reach the node in that cluster closest to the target key, call it t_2. r then continues its search in its level-1 cluster. However, t_2 has already returned routing information in the level-1 cluster. Thus, r begins with the closest level-1 node in t_2's routing table. Even if the search eventually switches to the global cluster, Coral does not

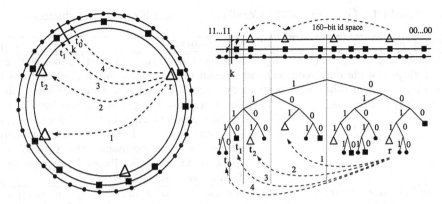

Fig. 1. Coral's hierarchical lookup visualized on the Chord (left) and Kademlia (right) routing structures. Nodes maintain the same id in each of their clusters; smaller-diameter low-level lusters are naturally sparser. For a lookup on key k, a node first searches on its lowest cluster. This lookup fails on that level if the node closest to k, node t_2, does not store the key. If this occurs, Coral continues its lookup on a higher-level cluster, having already traversed the id space up to t_2's prefix. Route RPCs are shown with sequential numbering

require any more RPCs than a single-level lookup service, as a lookup always restarts where it left off in the id space. Moreover, Coral *guarantees* that all lookups at the beginning are fast. This functionality arises naturally from a node having the same *nodeid* in all DSHTs to which it belongs. Note that Coral achieves this property independent of any distance optimization in its underlying lookup protocol.

Two conflicting criteria impact the effectiveness of Coral's hierarchical DSHTs. First, clusters should be large in terms of membership. The more peers in a DSHT, the greater its capacity and the lower the *miss* rate. Second, clusters should have small network diameter to achieve fast lookup. That is, the expected latency between randomly-selected peers within a cluster should be below the cluster's specified threshold.

The remainder of this section describes Coral's mechanisms for managing its multiple DSHT clusters. These mechanisms are summarized in Table 1.

2.3   Joining a Cluster

Coral largely inherits its join and leave protocols from its underlying lookup service, with one difference. Namely, a node will only join an *acceptable* cluster, that is, one in which the latency to 90% of the nodes is below the cluster's diameter. This property is easy for a node to test by collecting round trip times to some subset of nodes in the cluster, perhaps by simply looking up its own identifier as a natural part of joining.

Table 1. Overview of the Coral's design for self-organizing clusters

The Task	Coral's Solution
Discovering and joining a low-level cluster, while only requiring knowledge of *some* other node, not necessarily a close one.	Coral nodes insert their own contact information and Internet topology hints into higher-level clusters. Nodes reply to unexpected requests with their cluster information. Sloppiness in the DSHT infrastructure prevents hotspots from forming when nodes search for new clusters and test random subsets of nodes for acceptable RTT thresholds. Hotspots would otherwise distort RTT measurements and reduce scalability.
Merging close clusters into the same name-space without experiencing oscillatory behavior between the merging clusters.	Coral's use of cluster size and age information ensures a clear, stable direction of flow between merging clusters. Merging may be initiated as the byproduct of a lookup to a node that has switched clusters.
Splitting slow clusters into disjoint subsets, in a manner resulting in an acceptable and stable partitioning without causing hotspots.	Coral's definition of a cluster center provides a stable point about which to separate nodes. DSHT sloppiness prevents hotspots while a node determines its relative distance to this known point.

As in any peer-to-peer system, a node must initially know some other Coral node to join the system. However, Coral adds a RTT requirement for a node's lower-level clusters. A node unable to find an acceptable cluster creates a new one with a random *cid*. A node joins a better cluster whenever it learns of one.

Several mechanisms could have been used to discover clusters, including using IP multicast or merely waiting for nodes to learn about clusters as a side effect of normal lookups. However, Coral exploits the DSHT interface to let nodes find nearby clusters. Upon joining a low-level cluster, a node inserts itself into its higher-level clusters, keyed under the IP addresses of its gateway routers, discovered by `traceroute`. For each of the first five routers returned, it executes $put(hash(router.ip), addr)$. A new node, searching for a low-level acceptable cluster, can perform a *get* on each of its own gateway routers to learn some set of topologically-close nodes.

2.4   Merging Clusters

While a small cluster diameter provides fast lookup, a large cluster capacity increases the hit rate in a lower-level DSHT. Therefore, Coral's join mechanism for individual nodes automatically results in close clusters merging if nodes in both clusters would find either acceptable. This merge happens in a totally decentralized way, without any expensive agreement or leader-election protocol. When a node knows of two acceptable clusters at a given level, it will join the larger one.

When a node switches clusters, it still remains in the routing tables of nodes in its old cluster. Old neighbors will still contact it; the node replies to level-i requests originating outside its current cluster with the tuple $\{cid_i, size_i, ctime_i\}$, where $size_i$ is the estimated number of nodes in the cluster, and $ctime_i$ is the cluster's creation time. Thus, nodes from the old cluster will learn of this new cluster that has more nodes and the same diameter. This produces an avalanche effect as more and more nodes switch to the larger cluster.

Unfortunately, Coral can only count on a rough *approximation* of cluster size. If nearby clusters A and B are of similar sizes, inaccurate estimations could in the worst case cause oscillations as nodes flow back-and-forth. To perturb such oscillations into a stable state, Coral employs a preference function δ that shifts every hour. A node selects the larger cluster only if the following holds:

$$\left| \log(size_A) - \log(size_B) \right| > \delta \left(\min(age_A, age_B) \right)$$

where age is the current time minus $ctime$. Otherwise, a node simply selects the cluster with the lower cid.

We use a square wave function for δ that takes a value 0 on an even number of hours and 2 on an odd number. For clusters of disproportionate size, the selection function immediately favors the larger cluster. However, should clusters of similar size continuously exchange members when δ is zero, as soon as δ transitions, nodes will all flow to the cluster with the lower cid. Should the clusters oscillate when $\delta = 2$, the one 2^2-times larger will get all members when δ returns to zero.

2.5 Splitting Clusters

In order to remain acceptable to its nodes, a cluster may eventually need to split. This event may result from a network partition or from population over-expansion, as new nodes may push the RTT threshold. Coral's split operation again incorporates some preferred direction of flow. If nodes merely atomized and randomly re-merged into larger clusters, the procedure could take too long to stabilize or else form highly sub-optimal clusters.

To provide a direction of flow, Coral specifies some node c within cid as a *cluster center*. When splitting, all nodes near to this center c join one cluster; all nodes far from c join a second cluster. Specifically, define $cid^N = hash(cid)$ and let cid^F be cid^N with the high-order bit flipped. The cluster center c is the node closest to key cid^N in the DSHT. However, nodes cannot merely ping the cluster center directly, as this would overload c, distorting RTT measurements.

To avoid this overload problem, Coral again leverages its sloppy replication. If a node detects that its cluster is no longer acceptable, it performs a get first on cid^N, then on cid^F. For one of the first nodes to split, $get(cid^N)$ resolves directly to the cluster center c. The node joins cid_i based on its RTT with the center, and it performs a $put(cid_i, addr)$ on its old cluster and its higher-level DSHTs.

One concern is that an early-adopter may move into a small successor cluster. However, before it left its previous level-i cluster, the latency within its old cluster was approaching that of its larger level-$(i-1)$ cluster. Thus, the node actually gains little benefit from maintaining membership in its old (larger yet slower) lower-level cluster.

As more nodes transition, their *gets* begin to hit the sloppy replicas of cid^N and cid^F: They learn a random subset of the nodes already split off into the two new clusters. Any node that finds cluster cid^N acceptable will join it, without having needed to ping the old cluster center. Nodes that do not find cid^N acceptable will attempt to join cluster cid^F. However, cluster cid^F could be even worse than the previous cluster, in which case it will split again. Except in the case of pathological network topologies, a small number of splits should suffice to reach a stable state. (Otherwise, after some maximum number of unsuccessful splits, a node could simply form a new cluster with a random ID as before.)

3   Measurements

Coral assigns system-wide RTT thresholds to the different levels of clusters. If nodes otherwise choose their own "acceptability" levels, clusters would experience greater instability as individual thresholds differ. Also, a cluster would not experience a distinct merging or splitting period that helps to return it to an acceptable, stable state. Can we find sensible system-wide parameters?

To measure network distances in a deployed system, we performed latency experiments on the Gnutella network. We collected host addresses while acting as a Gnutella peer, and then measured the RTT between 12 RON nodes [1] and approximately 2000 of these Gnutella peers. Both operations lasted for 24 hours. We determined round-trip times by attempting to open several TCP connections to high ports and measuring the minimum time elapsed between the SYN and RST packets.

Figure 2 shows the cumulative distribution function (CDF) of the measured RTT's between Gnutella hosts and the following RON sites: New York University (NYU); Nortel Networks, Montreal (Nortel); Intel research, Berkeley (Intel); KAIST, Daejon (South Korea); Vrije University (Amsterdam); and National Technical University of Athens (Athens).

If the CDFs had multiple "plateaus" at *different* RTT's, system-wide thresholds would not be ideal. A threshold chosen to fall within the plateau of some set of nodes sets the cluster's most natural size. However, this threshold could bisect the rising edge of other nodes' CDFs and yield greater instability for them.

Instead, our measurements show that the CDF curves are rather smooth. Therefore, we have relative freedom in setting cluster thresholds to ensure that each level of cluster in a particular region can capture some expected percentages of nearby nodes.

Our choice of 30 msec for level-2 covers smaller clusters of nodes, while the level-1 threshold of 100 msec spans continents. For example, the expected RTT between New York and Berkeley is 68 msec, and 72 msec between Amsterdam and Athens. The curves in Figure 2 suggest that most Gnutella peers reside in North America. Thus, low-level clusters are especially useful for sparse regions

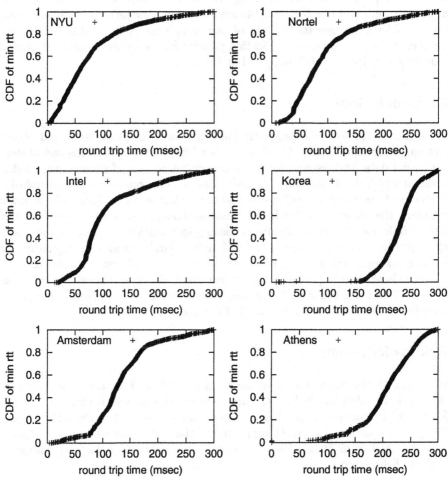

Fig. 2. CDFs of round-trip times between specified RON nodes and Gnutella peers

like Korea, where most queries of a traditional peer-to-peer system would go to North America.

4   Related Work

Several projects have recently considered peer-to-peer systems for web traffic. Stading *et. al.* [11] uses a DHT to cache replicas, and PROOFS [12] uses a randomized overlay to distribute popular content. However, both systems focus on mitigating flash crowds, not on normal web caching. Therefore, they accept higher lookup costs to prevent hot spots. Squirrel [4] proposed web caching on a traditional DHT, although only for LANs. It examines storing pointers in the

DHT, yet reports poor load-balancing. We attribute this result to the fact that a *limited* number of pointers (only 4) are stored on a *single* node. In some sense, both problems are due to the lack of any sloppiness in the system's DHT interface. SCAN [2] examined replication policies for data disseminated through a multicast tree from a DHT deployed at ISPs.

5   Conclusions

Coral introduces the following techniques to enable distance-optimized object lookup and retrieval. First, Coral provides a DSHT abstraction. Instead of storing actual data, the system stores weakly-consistent lists of pointers that index nodes at which the data resides. Second, Coral assigns round-trip-time thresholds to clusters to bound cluster diameter and ensure fast lookups. Third, Coral nodes maintain the same identifier in all clusters. Thus, even when a low-diameter lookup fails, Coral uses the returned routing information to continue the query efficiently in a larger-diameter cluster. Finally, Coral provides an algorithm for self-organizing merging and splitting to ensure acceptable cluster diameters.

Coral is a promising design for performance-driven applications. We are in the process of building Coral and planning network-wide measurements to examine the effectiveness of its hierarchical DSHT design.

Acknowledgments

We thank David Andersen for access to the RON testbed, and Vijay Karamcheti, Eric Freudenthal, Robert Grimm, Sameer Ajmani, and Rodrigo Rodrigues for helpful comments. This research was conducted as part of the IRIS project (http://project-iris.net/), supported by the NSF under Cooperative Agreement No. ANI-0225660. Michael Freedman was supported by the ONR under an NDSEG Fellowship.

References

[1] David Andersen. Resilient overlay networks testbed. http://nms.lcs.mit.edu/projects/ron/
[2] Yan Chen, Randy H. Katz, and John D. Kubiatowicz. SCAN: A dynamic, scalable, and efficient content distribution network. In *Proceedings of the International Conference on Pervasive Computing*, Zurich, Switzerland, August 2002
[3] Frank Dabek, M. Frans Kaashoek, David Karger, Robert Morris, and Ion Stoica. Wide-area cooperative storage with CFS. In *Proceedings of the 18th ACM Symposium on Operating Systems Principles (SOSP '01)*, Banff, Canada, October 2001
[4] Sitaram Iyer, Antony Rowstron, and Peter Druschel. Squirrel: A decentralized, peer-to-peer web cache. In *Principles of Distributed Computing (PODC)*, Monterey, CA, July 2002

[5] John Kubiatowicz, David Bindel, Yan Chen, Steven Czerwinski, Patrick Eaton, Dennis Geels, Ramakrishna Gummadi, Sean Rhea, Hakim Weatherspoon, Westley Weimer, Chris Wells, and Ben Zhao. OceanStore: An architecture for global-scale persistent storage. In *Proc. ASPLOS*, Cambridge, MA, Nov 2000

[6] Petar Maymounkov and David Mazières. Kademlia: A peer-to-peer information system based on the xor metric. In *Proceedings of the 1st International Workshop on Peer-to-Peer Systems (IPTPS02)*, Cambridge, MA, March 2002

[7] Sylvia Ratnasamy, Paul Francis, Mark Handley, Richard Karp, and Scott Shenker. A scalable content-addressable network. In *Proc. ACM SIGCOMM*, San Diego, CA, Aug 2001

[8] Antony Rowstron and Peter Druschel. Pastry: Scalable, distributed object location and routing for large-scale peer-to-peer systems. In *Proc. IFIP/ACM Middleware*, November 2001

[9] Antony Rowstron and Peter Druschel. Storage management and caching in PAST, a large-scale, persistent peer-to-peer storage utility. In *Proc. 18th ACM Symposium on Operating Systems Principles (SOSP '01)*, Banff, Canada, October 2001

[10] Subhabrata Sen and Jia Wang. Analyzing peer-to-peer traffic across large networks. In *Proc. ACM SIGCOMM Internet Measurement Workshop*, Marseille, France, November 2002.

[11] Tyron Stading, Petros Maniatis, and Mary Baker. Peer-to-peer caching schemes to address flash crowds. In *Proceedings of the 1st International Workshop on Peer-to-Peer Systems (IPTPS02)*, Cambridge, MA, March 2002.

[12] Angelos Stavrou, Dan Rubenstein, and Sambit Sahu. A lightweight, robust p2p system to handle flash crowds. In *IEEE International Conference on Network Protocol (ICNP)*, Paris, France, November 2002.

[13] Ion Stoica, Robert Morris, David Liben-Nowell, David R. Karger, M. Frans Kaashoek, Frank Dabek, and Hari Balakrishnan. Chord: A scalable peer-to-peer lookup protocol for internet applications. In *IEEE/ACM Trans. on Networking*, 2002.

[14] Ben Zhao, John Kubiatowicz, and Anthony Joseph. Tapestry: An infrastructure for fault-tolerant wide-area location and routing. Technical Report UCB/CSD-01-1141, Computer Science Division, U.C. Berkeley, April 2000.

Structured Peer-to-Peer Overlays Need Application-Driven Benchmarks

Sean C. Rhea[1], Timothy Roscoe[2], and John Kubiatowicz[1]

[1] Department of Electrical Engineering and Computer Science
University of California, Berkeley
{srhea,kubitron}@cs.berkeley.edu
[2] Intel Research Berkeley
troscoe@intel-research.net

Abstract. Considerable research effort has recently been devoted to the design of *structured peer-to-peer overlays*, a term we use to encompass Content-Addressable Networks (CANs), Distributed Hash Tables (DHTs), and Decentralized Object Location and Routing networks (DOLRs). These systems share the property that they consistently map a large set of identifiers to a set of nodes in a network, and while at first sight they provide very similar services, they nonetheless embody a wide variety of design alternatives. We present the case for developing application-driven benchmarks for such overlays, give a model of the services they provide applications, describe and present the results of two preliminary benchmarks, and discuss the implications of our tests for application writers. We are unaware of other empirical comparative work in this area.

1 Introduction and Motivation

This paper reports on our ongoing work to devise useful benchmarks for implementations of structured peer-to-peer overlays, a term we use to encompass Content-Addressable Networks (CANs), Distributed Hash Tables (DHTs), and Decentralized Object Location and Routing networks (DOLRs). We argue that benchmarks are essential in understanding how overlays will behave in a particular application. Our work is driven partly by our experience implementing the OceanStore [6] and Mnemosyne [4] systems.

We want to benchmark structured peer-to-peer overlays for three reasons. The first is naturally for pure performance comparisons. However, in this paper we are not interested in declaring one overlay "better" or "worse" than another by measuring them on the same scale. The real value of application-driven benchmarks is to demonstrate how the design choices embodied in different overlay designs lead to different performance characteristics in different applications. Our aim is to relate three different areas: the design choices of the various overlays, their measured performance against our benchmarks, and the kind of performance and scaling behavior that users might see for their own applications. Our final motivation in benchmarking is our desire to provide overlay designers with

F. Kaashoek and I. Stoica (Eds.): IPTPS 2003, LNCS 2735, pp. 56–67, 2003.

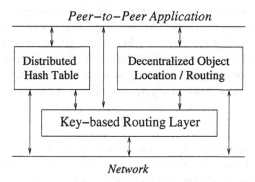

Peer–to–Peer Application

Fig. 1. *Overlay Service Decomposition.* The functionality exposed by structured peer-to-peer overlays can be divided into a mapping of keys onto nodes, mechanisms to store and retrieve data items, and mechanisms to route to or locate data items stored according to a policy outside the overlay's control

a metric of success as expressed by application builders. Even a less-than-perfect benchmark would allow the designers of new algorithms to compare their work against previous designs, raising the barrier to entry for algorithms which hope to lure a large user base.

In the next section, we present a generic service model for structured peer-to-peer overlays which we use as a framework for measurement. Such a model attempts to capture the characteristics of an overlay which are of interest to an application writer. In Section 3, we describe our benchmarking environment, consisting of the Chord [13] and Tapestry [5, 16] implementations running on the PlanetLab testbed. In Section 4 we discuss two benchmarks for overlays, and the results of running them against our Chord and Tapestry deployments. In Section 5 we draw some conclusions and discuss future work.

2   A Common Service Model

Before describing our benchmarking work, we present a generic service model for structured peer-to-peer overlays which we use as a framework for measurement. Such a model attempts to capture the characteristics of overlays which are of interest to an application writer.

The service model is in some ways like an Application Programming Interface (API), but it differs from an API in that it tries to capture the possible behavior of functionality presented to a user of the overlay, rather than explicitly specifying how the functionality is invoked. Furthermore, the model does not attempt to capture the routing mechanisms of the overlay except insofar as they manifest themselves in observed application performance, under "normal" conditions. We are not at this stage concerned with benchmarking overlays under attack in the ways described in [3], though this is clearly a direction for future work.

Figure 1 shows a functional decomposition of the services offered by various structured peer-to-peer overlays.[1] All existing overlays of which we are aware consist of a set of *identifiers,* $\mathcal{I}$ (often the set of 160-bit unsigned integers), and a set of *nodes,* $\mathcal{N}$ (often some subset of the set of IPv4 addresses), which consists of the nodes participating in the overlay at a given moment. The lowest level of an overlay, the *key-based routing layer*, embodies a surjective mapping

$$owner : \mathcal{I} \to \mathcal{N}$$

which maps every identifier $i \in \mathcal{I}$ to a node $n \in \mathcal{N}$. We chose the name *owner* to embody the idea that the *owner* is the node ultimately responsible for some portion of the set of identifiers. To compute *owner*, it is generally necessary to gather state from several successive nodes in the system; these nodes may all be contacted from the querying node itself, as in the MIT Chord implementation, or the query may be routed through the network, with each relevant node contacting the next, as in the Berkeley Tapestry implementation. In the original Chord paper [13], these two styles are respectively termed *iterative* and *recursive*; we will continue the use of that terminology in this work.

The most basic operations application writers are interested in is evaluating this function for some $i \in \mathcal{I}$, and/or sending a message to the node $owner(i)$. In Chord, the *owner* function is directly implemented, and called *find_successor*, while in Tapestry it is provided by the *route_to_root(i, m)* function which sends a message m to $owner(i)$.

Above this basic facility many applications are also interested using overlays to store or retrieve data. To date, there are to our knowledge two different ways in which this functionality is achieved. In the first, a DHT is implemented atop the routing layer by mapping the names of data items into $\mathcal{I}$, and storing each object at the owner of its identifier.[2] In this case, an application may call the function $put(i, x)$ to store the datum x with name i, or $get(i)$ to retrieve the datum named i. For load balancing and fault tolerance, data items are often replicated a nodes other than the owner.

The second common method of implementing a storage layer in an overlay is to place data throughout the system independent of the overlay, but use the overlay to place pointers to where the data is stored. Algorithms using this second technique are called DOLRs to emphasize that they locate or route to data without specifying a storage policy. The functionality exposed by DOLRs consists of a *publish(i)* operation, by which a node advertises that it is storing a datum with name i, and a *route_to_object(i, m)* operation, by which a message m is routed to a node which has previously published i.

While many applications benefit from the higher levels of abstraction provided by some overlays, others are hindered by them. To Mnemosyne, for ex-

---

[1] This figure is a simplified version of that presented in the work to establish a common API for such systems [2].

[2] A common mapping of this sort is exemplified by CFS [1], which associates a data block b with an identifier $i = SHA1(b)$ and stores the block contents at node $n = owner(SHA1(b))$.

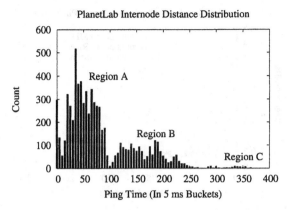

Fig. 2. *Distribution of round-trip times in PlanetLab.* Region A (0–100 ms) contains 72.3% of the times, Region B (100–275 ms) contains 26.6%, and Region C (275–400 ms) contains the the negligible remainder

ample, the additional performance cost of DHT or DOLR-like functionality is a disadvantage; in contrast, the DOLR properties of Tapestry are integral to the OceanStore design. We conclude this section by noting that the decomposition in Figure 1 is not a strict layering. While at a functional level, a DOLR may be implemented by a DHT and vice-versa, we show in the results section of this paper that there are performance consequences of doing so.

3   Experimental Setup

Our experiments are performed on PlanetLab [9], an open, shared testbed for developing and deploying wide-area network services. This testbed consists of sites spread across the United States and Europe with up to three nodes at each site. While the hardware configuration of the machines varies slightly, most of the nodes are 1.2 GHz Pentium III CPUs with 1 GB of memory.

To gain some notion of the shape of the network, we performed two simple experiments using 83 of the machines on November 1, 2002. First, we pinged every host from every other hosts ten times and stored the minimum value seen for each pair; the results are graphed in Figure 2. The median inter-node ping time is 64.9 ms. Next, we had each node use the Unix *scp* command to transfer a 4 MB file from each of the machines planlab1.cs.caltech.edu, planetlab1.lcs.mit.edu, and ricepl-1.cs.rice.edu. This test is crude, but we only wanted a rough idea of the throughput available. The median observed throughput was 487 kB/s. The correlation between observed throughput and ping time is shown in Figure 3; as predicted analytically by Padhye et al. [8], TCP throughput and round-trip time show an inverse correlation. Since well-behaved peer-to-peer applications are likely to use TCP for data transfer in the foreseeable future, this correlation

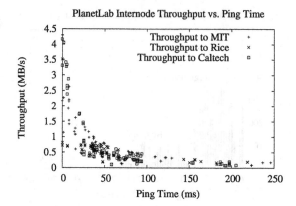

Fig. 3. *PlanetLab Inter-node Throughput.* Throughput is inversely proportional to ping time

is significant; it implies that nearby nodes are likely to observe higher throughput on data transfers than distant nodes.

In the first version of this paper, we used the MIT Chord implementation from September 23, 2002.[3] We later discovered that this implementation caches the IP addresses and Chord identifiers of the last several hundred nodes it has contacted; since our test uses less than a hundred nodes, with this cache each lookup takes at most a single network hop. This behavior will clearly not scale, so we reran some of our experiments with the Chord implementation from March 2, 2003, which allows us to disable this cache. For our Tapestry experiments, we used the Berkeley implementation of Tapestry,[4] also from either September or March. The implementation used in each experiment is noted below.

Chord is implemented in C++ while Tapestry is implemented in Java atop SandStorm [15]. To test them both under the same framework, we extended the Chord implementation to export the *find_successor* functionality to the local machine through an RPC interface over UDP. We then built a stage which used this interface to provide access to Chord's functionality from within SandStorm. To test the overhead of this wrapping, we started a single node network and performed 1000 calls to *find_successor* from within SandStorm; the average call took 2.4 ms.[5] As we show below, this is a small percentage of the overall time taken by each *find_successor* operation.

To run an experiment with Chord, we start a Chord instance running this gateway for each node in the test, allow the network to stabilize, and then bring up the benchmarking code for each machine. To run an experiment with

---

[3] Available at http://www.pdos.lcs.mit.edu/chord/.

[4] Available at http://oceanstore.cs.berkeley.edu/.

[5] This small delay only occurs once for each computation of the successor of a given identifier, not once per hop during that computation.

Tapestry, we bring up the Tapestry network first and allow it to stabilize, then we begin the benchmark.

4   Experimental Results

In this section we describe our experiments and analyze their results.

4.1   Find Owner Test

Our first benchmark measures the *find_owner* function. It tests the *find_successor* function under Chord; under Tapestry it is implemented as a *route_to_root* function with a response from the root to the query source over TCP. This test was run on March 4, 2003, on 79 PlanetLab nodes using the implementations of Chord and Tapestry from March. In the test, each node in the network chooses 400 identifiers uniformly and randomly from the identifier space and evaluates *find_owner* on each, timing the latency of each operation and waiting one second between them. All nodes perform the test concurrently.

Relevance The *find_owner* functionality is used by almost every system built on an overlay. It is used to read and write data in CFS, PAST, and Mnemosyne, and to find candidate archival storage servers in OceanStore. With systems such as CFS and Mnemosyne, where the individual units of storage are small (on the order of disk blocks), the latency of the *find_owner* operation can drastically affect the time to perform a read or write.

Results Figure 4 shows the median latency of the *find_owner* operation implemented using Chord as a function of the ping time between the query source and the discovered owner. In theory, this function can be implemented without contacting the owner; if an identifier lies between a node and its successor, that node knows the successor of the identifier. The MIT Chord implementation always contacts the owner node in the the process of finding it, however, so there is a correlation between the *find_owner* and ping times.

Figure 5 shows the same graph, but using Tapestry to implement *find_owner*. As in the MIT Chord implementation, the owner is always contacted in computing this function in Tapestry, so the *find_owner* latency should never be lower than the ping time. Ping times do vary between when they are measured and the test in question however, so some points fall below the line $y = x$. In general, though, Tapestry behaves as predicted in previous work [11]; the time to find the owner is roughly proportional to the network distance between the owner and the query source.

Discussion A summary of the *find_owner* results is shown in Table 1. The median *find_owner* time in Chord is 2.9 times slower than in Tapestry. Also shown in Table 1 are estimated times to send a message to the owner of an identifier using each algorithm; we call this operation *call_owner*. In both networks, the

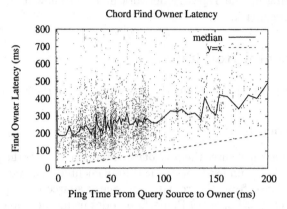

Fig. 4.   *Chord* find_owner *latency*

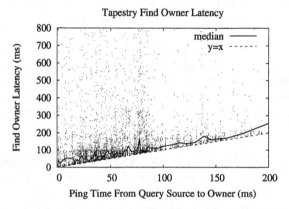

Fig. 5.   *Tapestry* find_owner *latency*

time to compute *call_owner* can be estimated as one half ping time less than the *find_owner* time. In this test, Chord is 3.9 times slower than Tapestry.

There are two main reasons to expect that the Chord implementation would be slower than Tapestry on *find_owner*. First, the Tapestry network is built for locality; although both networks take $O(\log N)$ hops in locating an owner, network hops early in the Tapestry location process are expected to be short. Second, the MIT Chord implementation performs iterative lookup; each node in the lookup process is contacted from the query node, rather than routing the query through the network as in Tapestry. Since the query node is in control of the lookup process from start to finish, iterative lookup is attractive from a robustness standpoint. Our timing results show some cost associated with this increased robustness, although we leave separating this cost from that of locality in neighbor links as a topic for future work.

Table 1. *Summary of* find_owner *results.* Times for the *call_owner* operation are estimated using the ping times shown in Figure 2. All times are in milliseconds

Median latency of. . .	Chord	Tapestry
find_owner (measured)	269	93
call_owner (estimated)	236	61

We can also use the *find_owner* times to make a rough estimate of the median time to retrieve a data block from the owner. We first note that the time to retrieve a block of negligible size is the same as the *find_owner* time in our experiments. Estimating the time to retrieve larger blocks is a matter of adding the time to transfer the additional bytes. Assuming the throughput between the query source and the owner is the median throughput of 487 kB/s, a 4 kB block takes only 8 ms to transfer, resulting in Chord being 2.8 times slower than Tapestry. This difference fades with increasing block size, however; for 1.7 MB blocks, the Chord retrieval time would be within 5% of the Tapestry time.

Our computed times, of course, are only estimates; if such computations were sufficient for judging algorithmic performance, there would be no need for benchmarking. As such, we have already begun further testing to directly measure *call_owner* and block retrieval times.

4.2 Replica Location Test

Our next test is a replica location test; it was run on October 29, 2002, on 83 of the PlanetLab nodes. In Chord, this test is simply the *get* operation implemented in DHASH, the storage layer underlying CFS. In Tapestry, it is implemented as the *locate* operation, followed by a response over TCP with the requested data. In these tests we measure not the latency of the replica location, but the *location stretch*, which we define as the the distance to the replica that was located divided by the distance to the replica closest to the query source. Location stretch is a measure of the *quality* of location; it shows the degree to which an overlay finds close replicas when they are available. In these tests, we use the implementations of both algorithms from September 2002; since location stretch is independent of the time to find a replica, these results are not affected by the presence of Chord's cache.

Relevance An important feature of Tapestry is that it tries to route to the *closest* replica to the query source if more than one replica is available. In contrast, although DHASH generally provides several replicas of each data block in CFS, there is no direct mechanism in Chord to locate the nearest replica. Instead, it always locates the one stored on the *owner* of the block's identifier, and provisions to find closer replicas must be implemented at the application layer.

Locating nearby replicas has several benefits, the most obvious of which is performance; as Figure 3 shows, there is some correlation between ping time and

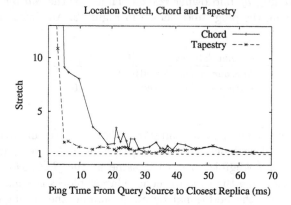

Fig. 6. *Location stretch in Chord and Tapestry*

throughput. Replicas close in ping time to the query source are more likely to have a high throughput path to the latter; they can thus not only deliver the first byte of a data item faster than replicas further from the query source, but they can also provide the last byte faster. Applications with high performance needs and multiple replicas of each data object should thus value locality highly.

In addition to performance, locality can also help provide availability; the closer a discovered replica is, the less likely it will fall on the other side of a network partition than the query source. Finally, by serving each read from the replica closest to the reader, a system may achieve better resource utilization and load balance.

Results To test the locality features of the overlays, we first built a Chord network and stored 4 replicas of 10 different zero-byte objects as in DHASH. Then, we read the objects from each node in the system, one at a time, and recorded the total read latency and the node on which the replica was found. Next, we built a Tapestry network in which we stored the replicas on the same nodes as in the Chord test, and read the data as before.

After performing the tests, we calculated for each operation the distance to the closest replica from the query source, and the ping time to the replica that was actually discovered. The median ping time to the located replica in Chord was 55 ms; in Tapestry it was 39 ms, a 39% improvement. For reference, the median ping time to the closest available replica in each case was 29 ms, so Tapestry underperforms an ideal algorithm by 36%. Figure 6 graphs the location stretch of the two overlays.

Discussion We first observe that neither overlay performs well when the query source is within 5 ms of the closest replica; we believe that other techniques are necessary to achieve high performance in this range [11].

Next, we can see from Figure 6 that Tapestry significantly outperforms Chord when the closest available replica is within 5–15 ms of the query source. Referring back to Figure 3, a replica in this range generally sees high throughput to the query source as well, further increasing the benefits of locality.

Finally, we note that although Chord is not designed to find replicas according to locality, it could be extended to achieve low location stretch by finding all available replicas and then choosing the one with the lowest ping time. The CFS paper seems to imply that their implementation does something of this sort. Finding the latency to each replica would take time, but in some cases it might be justified. For example, if a *service* is being located (as in I^3 [14]), rather than a replica, if the number of replicas is very small, or if the replica is for a very large file, the location time may be dwarfed by the remainder of the operation. Further study is needed to determine the performance of such a scheme relative to Tapestry, and we plan to test the CFS implementation in our future work.

5 Conclusions and Future Work

One can observe structured peer-to-peer overlay designs from several angles: simplicity, robustness, efficiency, and/or performance. In this work we have focused on the latter, primarily because it is the easiest to measure, when the implementations of some of these algorithms are still in the early stages. Moreover, regardless of which of these features one studies, one can take an algorithmic approach, as in [10], or an application-level approach as we have taken. We view these two as complementary: at the same time that it is necessary for overlay builders to be exploring their design space, it is important for application writers to explore the differences between designs and the ways they affect the systems built on them.

In this paper we presented two benchmarks, *find_owner* and *locate*, evaluated over two overlays, Chord and Tapestry. We showed that for systems storing and retrieving blocks only from their *owner* nodes, *find_owner* provides insight into the choice of overlay. For systems that store files larger than 1.7 MB at the *owner*, there is little performance difference between Tapestry and Chord; for systems that store files as 4 kB blocks, each on their own *owner* however, there is a significant performance advantage to Tapestry. Depending on the application, however, this performance advantage may not be sufficient enough to justify the extra mechanism. Moreover, at least some of the latency advantage seen by Tapestry is due to its recursive—as opposed to iterative—routing style. In our future work, we plan to also study a recursive implementation of Chord so as to study each of these differences separately.

Our second benchmark, *locate*, showed that there is still work to be done on improving the ability of overlays to locate nearby replicas when they exist. We hope this result motivates the designers of these algorithms to further improve them; the correlation of throughput and ping times shown in Figure 3 indicate that there are significant performance gains available if they do.

Our ongoing work in the short term is to extend our benchmarks to other overlay implementations, and to track the increasing size of PlanetLab with more measurements. However, we believe we have only scratched the surface of the set of interesting and important benchmarks. We have not yet examined (for example) the cost of a new node joining a network, or the cost of one leaving. Neither have we examined the cost of a high rate of node turnover on a network, as highlighted by others [7, 12]. Finally, we have not analyzed the behavior of these overlays during node failure or maliciousness. The design of good application-driven benchmarks for such cases is a rich topic for future work. Nevertheless, we hope our existing work will help application designers to better understand the tradeoffs in choosing an overlay, and that it will motivate further design and implementation improvements by the networks' designers.

References

[1] F. Dabek, M. F. Kaashoek, D. Karger, R. Morris, and I. Stoica. Wide-area cooperative storage with CFS. In *Proc. of ACM SOSP*, 2001.

[2] F. Dabek, B. Zhao, P. Druschel, J. Kubiatowicz, and I. Stoica. Towards a common API for structured peer-to-peer overlays. In *Proc. of IPTPS*, 2003.

[3] M. Freedman, E. Sit, J. Cates, and R. Morris. Tarzan: A peer-to-peer anonymizing network layer. In *Proc. of IPTPS*, 2002.

[4] S. Hand and T. Roscoe. Mnemosyne: Peer-to-peer steganographic storage. In *Proc. of IPTPS*, 2002.

[5] K. Hildrum, J. Kubiatowicz, S. Rao, and B. Zhao. Distributed data location in a dynamic network. In *Proc. of ACM SPAA*, 2002.

[6] J. Kubiatowicz et al. Oceanstore: An architecture for global-scale persistent storage. In *Proc. of ASPLOS*, 2000.

[7] D. Liben-Nowell, H. Balakrishnan, and D. Karger. Observations on the dynamic evolution of peer-to-peer networks. In *Proc. of IPTPS*, 2002.

[8] J. Padhye, V. Firoiu, D. Towsley, and J. Kurose. Modeling TCP throughput: A simple model and its empirical validation. In *Proc. of ACM SIGCOMM*, 1998.

[9] Larry Peterson, David Culler, Tom Anderson, and Timothy Roscoe. A blueprint for introducing disruptive technology into the Internet. In *Proc. of HOTNETS*, 2002.

[10] S. Ratnasamy, S. Shenker, and I. Stoica. Routing algorithms for DHTs: Some open questions. In *Proc. of IPTPS*, 2002.

[11] S. Rhea and J. Kubiatowicz. Probabilistic location and routing. In *Proc. of INFOCOM*, 2002.

[12] S. Saroiu, P. K. Gummadi, and S. Gribble. A measurement study of peer-to-peer file sharing systems. In *Multimedia Computing and Networking*, 2002.

[13] I. Stoica, R. Morris, D. Karger, M. F. Kaashoek, and H. Balakrishnan. Chord: A scalable peer-to-peer lookup service for Internet applications. In *Proceedings of SIGCOMM*, 2001.

[14] Ion Stoica, Dan Adkins, Sylvia Ratnasamy, Scott Shenker, Sonesh Surana, and Shelley Zhuang. Internet indirection infrastructure. In *Proc. of IPTPS*, 2002.

[15] M. Welsh, D. Culler, and E. Brewer. SEDA: An architecture for well-conditioned, scalable internet services. In *Proc. of ACM SOSP*, 2001.

[16] B. Zhao, A. Joseph, and J. Kubiatowicz. Tapestry: An infrastructure for fault-tolerant wide-area location and routing. Technical Report UCB//CSD-01-1141, U. C. Berkeley, 2001.

Load Balancing in Structured P2P Systems*

Ananth Rao, Karthik Lakshminarayanan, Sonesh Surana, Richard Karp, and
Ion Stoica

Computer Science Division
University of California at Berkeley
Berkeley, CA 94720, USA
{ananthar,karthik,sonesh,karp,istoica}@cs.berkeley.edu

Abstract. Most P2P systems that provide a DHT abstraction distribute objects among "peer nodes" by choosing random identifiers for
the objects. This could result in an O(log N) imbalance. Besides, P2P
systems can be highly heterogeneous, i.e. they may consist of peers that
range from old desktops behind modem lines to powerful servers connected to the Internet through high-bandwidth lines. In this paper, we
address the problem of load balancing in such P2P systems. We explore
the space of designing load-balancing algorithms that uses the notion of
"virtual servers". We present three schemes that differ primarily in the
amount of information used to decide how to re-arrange load. Our simulation results show that even the simplest scheme is able to balance the
load within 80% of the optimal value, while the most complex scheme is
able to balance the load within 95% of the optimal value.

1 Introduction

In this work, we address the problem of load balancing in peer-to-peer (P2P)
systems that provide a distributed hash table (DHT) abstraction ([1, 2, 4, 5]).
In such structured systems, each data item that is stored is mapped to a unique
identifier ID. The identifier space is partitioned among the nodes and each node
is responsible for storing all the items that are mapped to an identifier in its
portion of the space. Thus, the system provides an interface comprising two
functions: *put(ID, item)*, which stores the item associating an identifier ID with
it, and *get(ID)* which retrieves the item corresponding to the identifier ID.

While peer-to-peer algorithms are symmetric, that is, all peers play the same
role in the protocol, P2P systems can be highly heterogeneous. A P2P system like
Gnutella or Kazaa may consist of peers that range from old desktops behind modem lines to powerful servers connected to the Internet through high-bandwidth
lines.

If node identifiers are chosen at random (as in [1, 2, 4, 5]), a random choice of
item IDs results in an $O(\log N)$ imbalance factor in the number of items stored
at a node. Furthermore, applications may associate semantics with IDs, which

---

* This research was supported by the NSF under Cooperative Agreement No. ANI-
0225660 (http://project-iris.net), and Career Award ANI-0133811.

F. Kaashoek and I. Stoica (Eds.): IPTPS 2003, LNCS 2735, pp. 68–79, 2003.
© Springer-Verlag Berlin Heidelberg 2003

means that IDs are no longer uniformly distributed. For example, in a database application, each item can be a tuple whose ID represents the value of its primary key [6].

A popular technique to deal with hot-spots is *caching*. However, caching will not work for certain types of resources such as storage. Furthermore, if the load is caused by the popularity of a large number of small items (as can be expected in database applications), then caching has to push out a significant fraction of the items before it is effective. On the other hand, the techniques we propose are not very effective in dealing with hot-spots. Therefore, we believe that caching is both orthogonal and complementary to the load-balancing techniques we describe in this paper.

This paper presents three simple load-balancing schemes that differ primarily in the amount of information used to decide how to rearrange load. Our simulation results show that even the simplest scheme is able to balance the load within 80% of the optimal value, while the most complex scheme is able to balance the load within 95% of the optimal value.

2   Preliminaries

In this work, we use the concept of *virtual servers* [3] for load balancing. A virtual server looks like a single peer to the underlying DHT, but each physical node can be responsible for more than one virtual server. For example, in Chord, each virtual server is responsible for a contiguous region of the identifier space but a node can own non-contiguous portions of the ring by having multiple virtual servers. The key advantage of splitting load into virtual servers is that we can move a virtual server from any node to any other node in the system. This operation looks like a *leave* followed by a *join* to the underlying DHT, and hence is supported by all DHTs. In contrast, if each node has only one virtual server, it can only transfer load to nodes that are its neighbors in the ID space (for example, its successor and predecessor in Chord). Even though splitting load into virtual servers will increase the path length on the overlay, we believe that the flexibility to move load from any node to any other node is crucial to any load-balancing scheme over DHTs.

Even though a large number of applications have been suggested in the literature for DHT-based P2P systems, little can be predicted about which applications will eventually turn out to be popular or about the typical workloads that might be experienced. Since it is very hard to address the load balancing problem in its full generality, we make some simplifying assumptions, which we believe are reasonable in practice. First, while we do not restrict ourselves to a particular type of resource (storage, bandwidth or CPU), we assume that there is only one bottleneck resource we are trying to optimize for. Second, we consider only schemes that achieve load balancing by moving virtual servers from heavily loaded nodes to lightly loaded nodes. Such schemes are appropriate for balancing storage in distributed file systems, bandwidth in systems with a web-server like load, and processing time when serving dynamic HTML content or performing distributed join operations [6]. Third, we assume that the load on a virtual server is stable (or can otherwise be predicted, as in a distributed join operation) over the timescale it takes for the load balancing algorithm to operate.

3   Load-Balancing Schemes

In this section, we present three simple load-balancing schemes. All these schemes try to balance the load by transferring virtual servers from heavily loaded nodes to lightly loaded nodes. The key difference between these three schemes is the amount of information required to make the transfer decision. In the simplest scheme, the transfer decision involves only two nodes, while in the most complex scheme, the transfer decision involves a set consisting of both heavy and light nodes. Before delving into the details of the schemes, we first define the notion of light and heavy nodes more precisely.

3.1   Heavy and Light Nodes

Let L_i denote the load of node i, where L_i represents the sum of the loads of all virtual servers of node i. We assume that every node also has a *target load* (T_i) chosen beforehand. A node is considered to be *heavy* if $L_i > T_i$, and is *light* otherwise. The goal of all our load balancing algorithms is to decrease the total number of heavy nodes in the system by moving load from heavy nodes to light nodes.

While this binary modeling of the state of a node may seem very restrictive at first glance, we believe that it is both simple and sufficient for a number of applications. For systems with a well-defined cliff in the load-response curve, the load at which the cliff occurs is a natural choice for the target load. On the other hand, if the goal is to equalize the load on all the nodes in the system, we can choose the target close to average load in the system (a rough estimate by random sampling might be good enough). Assume that C_i denotes the capacity of a node[1], and that the goal is to divide the load in proportion to the capacity. Ideally, we want the load on node i to be $(\bar{L}/\bar{C})C_i$, where N is the total number of nodes in the system, the average load $\bar{L} = (\sum_{i=1}^{N} L_i)/N$, and the average capacity $\bar{C} = (\sum_{i=1}^{N} C_i)/N$. However, since in practice this target may be hard to achieve, we approximate it with $T_i = (\bar{L}/\bar{C} + \delta)C_i$, where δ is a slack variable and represents a trade-off between the amount of load moved and the quality of balance achieved.

3.2   Virtual Server Transfer

The fundamental operation performed for balancing the loads is transferring a virtual server from a heavy node to a light node. Given a heavy node h and a light node l, we define the *best virtual server* to be transferred from h to l as the virtual server v the transfer of which satisfies the following constraints:

---

[1] For example, the up-link bandwidth in the case of a web server.

1. Transferring v from h to l will not make l heavy.
2. v is the lightest virtual server that makes h light.
3. If there is no virtual server whose transfer can make h light, transfer the heaviest virtual server v from h to l.

Intuitively, the above scheme tries to transfer the minimum amount of load to make h light while still maintaining l light. If this is not possible, the scheme will transfer the largest virtual server that will not change l's status. The idea is to increase the chance of h finding another light node that eventually will allow h to shed all its excess load.

Note that this scheme guarantees that a transfer can only decrease the number of heavy nodes. In addition, we do not consider transfers between nodes of the same type (i.e., when both nodes are either heavy or light). This way, we guarantee that when the load in the system is high ($\bar{L} > \bar{T}$), no thrashing will occur. Also, we *can stop at any time* if the desired performance is reached.

3.3 Splitting of Virtual Servers

If no virtual server in a heavy node can be transferred in its entirety to another node, then a possibility is to split it into smaller virtual servers and transfer a smaller virtual server to a light node. While this would improve the time taken to achieve balance and possibly reduce the total load transferred, there is a risk of excessively fragmenting the identifier space. An increase in the number of virtual servers would imply an increase in the overlay hop length and size of routing tables. Hence, a scheme to periodically merge virtual servers would be needed to counteract the increase in the number of virtual servers caused by splitting.

Since this would complicate our algorithms considerably, we consider only load-balancing schemes that do not need to split virtual servers. Instead, we assume that the load of all virtual servers is bounded by a predefined threshold. Each node is responsible for enforcing this threshold by splitting the virtual servers when needed. In our simulations, we set the threshold for splitting to $\bar{T}$. This choice has the property that if the target is achievable ($\bar{L} < \bar{T}$), no more than N virtual servers need to be split. Recall that N is the number of nodes in the system.

3.4 One-to-One Scheme

The first scheme is based on a one-to-one rendezvous mechanism, where two nodes are picked at random. A virtual server transfer is initiated if one of the nodes is heavy and the other is light.

This scheme is easy to implement in a distributed fashion. Each light node can periodically pick a random ID and then perform a lookup operation to find the node that is responsible for that ID. If that node is a heavy node, then a transfer may take place between the two nodes.

In this scheme only light nodes perform probing; heavy nodes do not perform any probing. There are three advantages of this design choice. First, heavy nodes are relieved of the burden of doing the probing as well. Second, when the system load is very high and most of the nodes are heavy, there is no danger of either overloading the network or thrashing. Third, if the load of a node is correlated with the length of the ID space owned by that node, a random probe performed by a light node is more likely to find a heavy node.

3.5   One-to-Many Scheme

Unlike the first scheme, this scheme allows a heavy node to consider more than one light node at a time. Let h denote the heavy node and let $l_1, l_2, \ldots, l_k$ be the set of light nodes considered by h. For each pair (h, l_i) we pick a virtual server v_i using the same procedure described in Section 3.2. Among the virtual servers that this procedure gives, we choose the lightest one that makes heavy node h light. If there is no such a virtual server, we pick the heaviest virtual server among the virtual server v_i $(1 \le i \le k)$ to transfer.

We implement this scheme by maintaining *directories* that store load information about a set of light nodes in the system. We use the same DHT system to store these directories. Assume that there are d directories in the system, where d is significantly smaller than the number of physical nodes N. A light node l is hashed into a directory by using a well-known hash function h' that takes values in the interval $[0, d)$. A directory i is stored at the node which is responsible for the identifier $h(i)$, where h is another well-known hash function.

A light node l will periodically advertise its target load and current load to node $i = h(h'(l))$, which is responsible for directory $h'(l)$. In turn, the heavy nodes will periodically sample the existing directories. A heavy node n picks a random number $k \in [0, d]$ and sends the information about its target load and the loads of all its virtual servers to node $j = h(h'(k))$. Upon receiving such a message, node j looks at the light nodes in its directory (i.e., directory $h'(k)$) to find the best virtual server that can be transferred from n to a light node in its directory. This process repeats until all the heavy nodes become light.

3.6   Many-to-Many Scheme

This scheme is a logical extension of the first two schemes. While in the first scheme we match one heavy node to a light node and in the second scheme we match one heavy node to many light nodes, in this scheme we match many heavy nodes to many light nodes.

We first start with the description of a centralized scheme that has full information about all nodes in the system. Our goal is to bring the loads on each node to a value less than the corresponding target. To allow many heavy nodes and many light nodes to interact together, we use the concept of a *global pool* of virtual servers, an intermediate step in moving a virtual server from a heavy node to a light node. The *pool* is only a local data structure used to compute the final allocation; no load is actually moved until the algorithm terminates.

The scheme consists of three phases:

- **Unload:** In this phase, each heavy node i transfers its virtual servers greedily into a global *pool* till it becomes light. At the end of this phase, all the nodes are light, but the virtual servers that are in the pool must be transferred to nodes that can accommodate them.
- **Insert:** This phase aims to transfer all virtual servers from the pool to light nodes without creating any new heavy nodes. This phase is executed in stages. In each stage, we choose the heaviest virtual server v from the pool, and then transfer it to the light node k determined using a best-fit heuristic, i.e., we pick the node that minimizes $T_k - L_k$ subject to the condition that $(T_k - L_k) \geq load(v)$. This phase continues until the pool becomes empty, or until no more virtual servers can be transferred. In the former case, the algorithm terminates, as all the nodes are light and there are no virtual servers in the pool. In the latter case, the algorithm continues with the dislodge phase.
- **Dislodge:** This phase swaps the largest virtual server v from the pool with another virtual server v' of a light node i such that $L_i + load(v) - load(v') \leq T_i$. Among all light nodes, we pick the one from which we can remove the lightest virtual server. If we cannot identify a light node i such that $load(v') < load(v)$, the algorithm terminates. Otherwise the algorithm returns to the insert phase. Since we are considering nodes from the pool in descending order of their load, insert might work for the next node in the pool.

To implement this scheme in a distributed fashion we can use similar techniques as in the One-to-Many scheme. The main difference in this case is that we hash heavy nodes into directories as well. In particular, each node i chooses a random number k between 1 and d (where d is the number of directories) and then sends its complete load information to node $j = h(h'(k))$. After it receives information from enough nodes, node j performs the algorithm presented above and then sends the solution back to these nodes. The solution specifies to each node the virtual servers it has to transfer. The algorithm continues with nodes rehashing periodically to other directories. In the distributed version, at any stage if an insert fails, we have the choice of either going into the dislodge phase or just moving the virtual server v being considered back to the node from which it came into the pool. After re-hashing, we may be able to find a better light node to move v to in the next round. Thus, we avoid the overhead of moving load out of a light node at the cost of having to go through more rounds.

4   Simulations

We simulated all three algorithms under a variety of conditions to understand their performance and their limitations. The goal of our simulations is to understand the fundamental trade-offs in the different approaches; we do not claim that we have a bullet-proof algorithm that can be used efficiently in all DHT based systems. Given the lack of information about applications and their work-loads, we only make conservative assumptions that stress our algorithms. We consider two types of distributions to generate the load on a virtual server.

- **Gaussian Distribution** Let f be the fraction of the identifier space owned by a given virtual server. This fraction is assumed to be exponentially distributed (this is true in both Chord and CAN). The load on the virtual server is then chosen from a Gaussian distribution with mean μf and standard deviation $\sigma \sqrt{f}$. Here, μ and σ are the mean and the standard deviation of the total load on the system (we set $\sigma/\mu = 10^{-3}$). This distribution would result if the total load on a virtual server is due to a large number of small items it stores, and the individual loads on the items are independent.
- **Pareto Distribution** The load on a virtual server is chosen from a power-law distribution with exponent 3 and mean μf. The standard deviation for this distribution is ∞. The heavy-tailed nature of this distribution makes it a particularly bad case for load balancing.

We consider two key metrics in our simulations: the **total load** moved between the nodes to achieve a state where all nodes are light, and the **number of probes** (or the *number of rounds*). The second metric gives us an idea of the total time taken to converge and the control traffic overhead caused by the load balancing algorithm.

Scalability: First, we look at the scalability of the different algorithms. In the one-to-many and the many-to-many schemes, the fraction of load moved and the number of probes per node depend only on N/d, where N is the number of nodes in the system and d is the number of directories. This is because each directory contains a random sample of size N/d, and the characteristics of this sample do not depend on N for a large enough N. A similar argument holds for the one-to-one scheme also. Thus, *all three schemes do very well in terms of scalability*. In the remainder of this section we consider only simulations with 4096 nodes. However, from the above reasoning, the results should hold for larger systems as well.

Efficiency: Next, we look at the efficiency of the different schemes in terms of the amount of load transferred. Fig. 1 plots the the total load moved (as a fraction of the total load of the system) as a function of $\bar{L}/\bar{T}$ for different schemes when the load is Pareto-distributed. Due to space limitations we do not present the results for Gaussian distribution. However, we note that, not surprisingly, all schemes perform better under Gaussian distribution. The plot in Fig. 1 shows the trade-off between the slack δ (defined in Section 3) and the load moved in the system. There are two points worth noting. First, the load moved depends only on the distribution of the load and not on the particular load balancing scheme. This is because all three schemes do only "useful" moves and hence *move only the minimum required to make nodes light*.

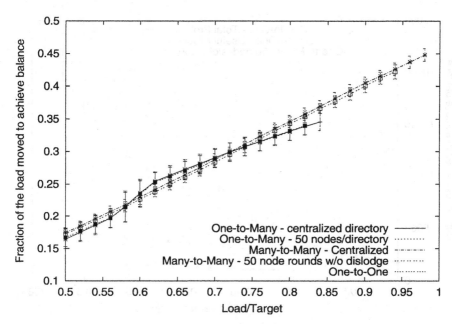

Fig. 1. The fraction of the total load moved for different schemes. In the beginning, each node is assigned 5 virtual servers at random

Second, we plot a point in this graph only if all 10 runs of the simulation result in a scenario where *all nodes are light*. This means that the range on the x-axis of a line is the range of loads over which the algorithm converged. Thus, the many-to-many scheme is capable of balancing the load within a factor of 0.94 from the ideal case (i.e., the case when $\delta = 0$), whereas the other two algorithms are able to balance the load only within a factor of 0.8 from the ideal case. The reason why the many-to-many scheme performs better than the other two schemes is that it uses a best-fit heuristic to match a set of heavy nodes to a set of light nodes. In contrast, with the first two schemes, there is a higher chance that a very light node i may not be able to accept a large virtual server v, despite the fact that $load(v) < T_i - L_i$. This can happen when other heavy nodes with smaller virtual servers contact node i first. To conclude, *the many-to-many scheme is capable of achieving balance even at very small δ* within a reasonable number of rounds [2], whereas the other two schemes cannot.

Total Number of Probes: The above results show that the one-to-one scheme achieves similar results with respect to load moved and the quality of balance achieved as the one-to-many scheme. But the main problem for the one-to-one scheme is the number of probes, which negatively impacts both the convergence

---

[2] Approximately 50 rounds with the Pareto distribution with $\bar{L}/\bar{T} = 0.94$.

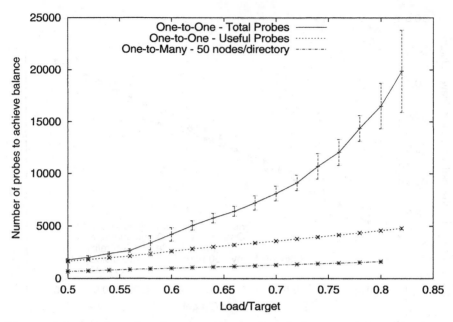

Fig. 2. The number of probes (total over all nodes) required for all nodes to become light

time and the control traffic overhead. To quantify this overhead, in Fig. 2 we plot the total number of probes performed by heavy nodes before they completely shed their excess load. A probe is considered *useful* if it results in the transfer of a virtual node. This graph shows that the *one-to-one scheme may be sufficient if loads remain stable over long time scales*, and if the control traffic overhead does not affect the system adversely.

Effect of Size of Directory: Given that we need to look at more than two nodes at a time to reduce the number of probes, the question arises as to how many nodes we must look at to perform efficiently in terms of control traffic. To answer this question, we look at the effect of the size of the directory on the number of probes in the one-to-many scheme. In Fig. 3, the x-axis shows the average size of a directory N/d, and the y-axis shows the total and the useful number of probes performed. Note that the initial number of heavy nodes is a lower bound on the number of probes. The graph shows that *even when $N/d = 16$, most heavy nodes are successful in shedding their load by probing only one directory*. We have observed the same trend in the number of rounds taken by the many-to-many scheme.

Trade-Off Involved in Doing Dislodge: In the the many-to-many scheme with dislodge, it is no longer true that only useful moves are done. We found

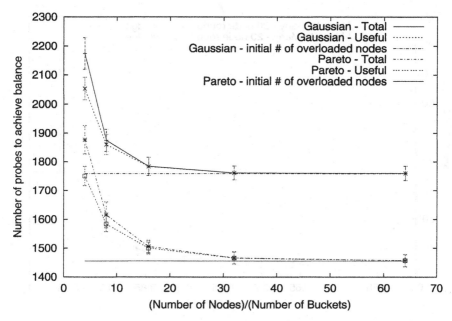

Fig. 3. The number of probes needed as a function of the expected number of nodes that will get hashed into a single directory ($\bar{L}/\bar{T} = 0.75$)

that with dislodge enabled, around 10% to 20% more of the total load was being moved than with dislodge disabled. The natural question is whether the extra load moved is justified by the reduction in the number of rounds. Fig. 4 shows that dislodging is useful only when $\bar{T}$ is very close to $\bar{L}$ even if we are trying to optimize only for the number of rounds. Also, note that even when the number of rounds required to make *all* nodes light is as high as 40, almost 95% of the heavy nodes became light after the first round. So, we conclude that *dislodge may not be a useful operation in practice.*

5   Related Work

Most structured P2P systems ([1, 2, 4, 5]) assume that object IDs are uniformly distributed. Under this assumption, the number of objects per node varies within a factor of $O(\log N)$, where n is the number of nodes in the system. CAN [1] improves this factor by considering a subset of existing nodes (i.e., a node along with neighbors) instead of a single node when deciding what portion of the ID space to allocate to a new node. Chord [2] was the first to propose the notion of virtual servers as a means of improving load balance. By allocating $\log N$ virtual servers per real node, Chord ensures that with high probability the number of objects per node is within a constant factor from optimal. However, to achieve

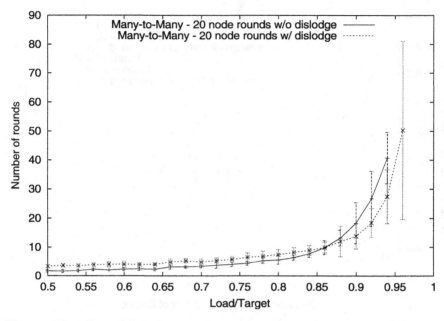

Fig. 4. The effect of dislodges on the number of rounds. The load distribution is Gaussian

load balancing, these schemes assume that nodes are homogeneous, objects have the same size, and object IDs are uniformly distributed.

CFS [3] accounts for node heterogeneity by allocating to each node, some number of virtual servers proportional to the node capacity. In addition, CFS proposes a simple solution to shed the load from an overloaded node by having the overloaded node remove some of its virtual servers. However, this scheme may result in thrashing as removing some virtual nodes from an overloaded node may result in another node becoming overloaded, and so on.

Douceur and Wattenhofer [7] have proposed algorithms for replica placement in a distributed filesystem which are similar in spirit with our algorithms. However, their primary goal is to place object replicas to maximize the availability in an untrusted P2P system, while we consider the load-balancing problem in a cooperative system.

Triantafillou *et al.* [9] have recently studied the problem of load-balancing in the context of content and resource management in P2P systems. However, their work considers an unstructured P2P system, in which meta-data is aggregated over a two-level hierarchy. A re-assignment of objects is then computed using the aggregated global information.

6   Conclusions and Future Work

We have presented three simple techniques to achieve load-balancing in structured peer-to-peer systems. The simulation results demonstrate the effectiveness of these schemes by showing that it is possible to balance the load within 95% of the optimal value with minimal load movement.

We plan to extend this work along three directions. First, we plan to study the effectiveness of our schemes in a dynamic system where items are continuously inserted and deleted, or/and where the access patterns of the items changes continuously. Second, we plan to develop the theoretical underpinnings of the proposed schemes. This would allow us to study the trade-offs between the transfer overhead and the effectiveness of each scheme better. Third, we plan to build a prototype of the load-balancing schemes on top of the Chord lookup system.

References

[1] S. Ratnasamy and P. Francis and M. Handley and R. Karp and S. Shenker. "A Scalable Content-Addressable Network", *Proc. ACM SIGCOMM 2001.*

[2] I. Stoica and R. Morris and D. Karger and M. F. Kaashoek and H. Balakrishnan. "Chord: A scalable Peer-to-Peer Lookup Service for Internet Applications", *Proc. ACM SIGCOMM 2001.*

[3] F. Dabek and M. F. Kaashoek and D. Karger and R. Morris and I. Stoica. "Wide-area Cooperative Storage with CFS", *Proc. ACM SOSP 2001.*

[4] K. Hildrum and J. Kubiatowicz and S. Rao and B. Y. Zhao. "Distributed Object Location in a Dynamic Network", *Proc. ACM SPAA, 2002.*

[5] A. Rowstron and P. Druschel. "Pastry: Scalable, Distributed Object Location and Routing for Large-Scale Peer-to-Peer Systems", Proc. IFIP/ACM International Conference on Distributed Systems Platforms (Middleware), Heidelberg, Germany, pages 329-350, November, 2001.

[6] M. Harren and J. M. Hellerstein and R. Huebsch and B. T. Loo, S. Shenker and I. Stoica. "Complex Queries in DHT-based Peer-to-Peer Networks", *Proc. IPTPS 2002.*

[7] J. R. Douceur and R. P. Wattenhofer. "Competitive Hill-Climbing Strategies for Replica Placement in a Distributed File System", *Lecture Notes in Computer Science, Vol. 2180, 2001.*

[8] J. R. Douceur and R. P. Wattenhofer. "Optimizing File Availability in a Secure Serverless Distributed File System", *Proc. of 20th IEEE SRDS, 2001.*

[9] P. Triantafillou and C. Xiruhaki and M. Koubarakis and N. Ntarmos. "Towards High Performance Peer-to-Peer Content and Resource Sharing Systems", *Proc. of CIDR, 2003.*

Simple Load Balancing
for Distributed Hash Tables

John Byers[1]*, Jeffrey Considine[1]*, and Michael Mitzenmacher[2]**

[1] Department of Computer Science
Boston University
Boston, MA, USA
{byers,jconsidi}@cs.bu.edu
[2] EECS
Harvard University
Cambridge, MA, USA
michaelm@eecs.harvard.edu

Abstract. Distributed hash tables have recently become a useful building block for a variety of distributed applications. However, current schemes based upon consistent hashing require both considerable implementation complexity and substantial storage overhead to achieve desired load balancing goals. We argue in this paper that these goals can be achieved more simply and more cost-effectively. First, we suggest the direct application of the "power of two choices" paradigm, whereby an item is stored at the less loaded of two (or more) random alternatives. We then consider how associating a small constant number of hash values with a key can naturally be extended to support other load balancing strategies, including load-stealing or load-shedding, as well as providing natural fault-tolerance mechanisms.

1 Introduction

Distributed hash tables have been proposed as a fundamental building block for peer-to-peer systems [6, 9, 8, 10, 12]. In the current design of distributed hash tables (DHTs), it is conventionally assumed that keys are mapped to a single peer — that peer is then responsible for storing a value associated with the key, such as the contents of a file with a given name. A widely used design to support such a DHT [10] consists of two components: consistent hashing over a one-dimensional space [6] and an indexing topology to quickly navigate this space.

In a basic consistent hashing approach, both peers and keys are hashed onto a one dimensional ring. Keys are then assigned to the nearest peer in the clockwise direction. Servers are connected to their neighbors in the ring (i.e. the ring

---

* Supported in part by NSF grants ANI-0093296 and ANI-9986397.
** Supported in part by NSF grants CCR-9983832, CCR-0118701, CCR-0121154, and an Alfred P. Sloan Research Fellowship.

F. Kaashoek and I. Stoica (Eds.): IPTPS 2003, LNCS 2735, pp. 80–87, 2003.

structure is embedded in the overlay) and searching for a key reduces to traversing the ring. Fast searches are enabled through additional overlay edges spanning larger arcs around the ring; for example, in Chord [10], a carefully constructed "finger table" of logarithmic size enables searches in a logarithmic number of steps.

However, with the naive implementation of consistent hashing described so far, considerable load imbalance can result. In particular, a peer that happens to be responsible for a larger arc of the ring will tend to be assigned a greater number of items.[1] If there are n peers, the maximum arc length for a peer will be $\Theta(\log n/n)$ with high probability, even though the average arc length is $1/n$.

A solution proposed in [10] is for each peer to simulate a logarithmic number of "virtual peers", thus assigning each peer several smaller segments whose total size is more tightly bounded around the expectation $1/n$. While theoretically elegant, virtual peers do not completely solve the load balancing issue. First, even with perfectly uniform assignments of segments to peers, the load need not be well balanced. In the extreme case where there are n items and n peers, this is the standard balls and bins problem, and with high probability one peer will be responsible for $\Theta(\log n/\log\log n)$ items. Second, the proposal to use $O(\log n)$ virtual peers with $O(\log n)$ edges in each finger table leads to $O(\log^2 n)$ edges per peer. Using the numbers of [10], a network of 100,000 peers will need to maintain 400 edges per peer. Although this number is small in terms of memory consumption, maintaining 400 edges per peer incurs a rather hefty messaging cost since each edge will need to be probed at regular intervals to detect failures and to perform general maintenance.

As a practical alternative to virtual peers, we propose the application of the "power of two choices" paradigm [1, 7] to balance load. These methods are used in standard hashing scenarios using bins (chaining) to reduce the maximum bin load with high probability. Using these methods, two or more hash functions are used to pick candidate bins for each item to be inserted. Prior to insertion, the load of each bin is compared and the item is inserted into the bin with the lowest load. Similarly, to search for an item, one applies the hash functions and examines each bin to locate the item. If there are n items, n bins, and $d \geq 2$ hash functions, the maximum load of any bin is only $\log\log n/\log d + O(1)$ with high probability. Moreover, the maximum load is more tightly concentrated around the mean for any number of balls.

Returning to DHTs, suppose that we have each peer represented by just one point in the circle. Each item chooses $d \geq 2$ possible points in the circle, and is associated with the corresponding peer with the least load from these choices. Previous results for the power of two choices cannot be immediately applied, since in this case the probability of a ball landing in a bin is not uniform. Our first

---

[1] For now, we will make the unrealistic assumption that all items are of equal size and popularity. Very popular items, or "hot spots", can be specially handled by appropriate replication, as in [6, 10]. Here, we are concerned with balancing load associated with the bulk of less popular items.

contribution is to examine this interesting case, both theoretically and through simulation.

Our second contribution is to apply these methods in the context of the Chord architecture. We present low-overhead searching methods which are compatible with the two choice storage model and then provide a comparative performance evaluation against the virtual peers approach.

Our final contribution is a consideration of the broader impact of having a key map to a small constant number of peers rather than to a single peer. We argue that the power of two choices paradigm facilitates other load balancing methods, such as load-stealing and load-shedding in highly dynamic DHTs, and enables new methods for addressing fault-tolerance.

2   Two Choices

We first consider the following problem, which is interesting theoretically in its own right. Suppose that we have each of n peers represented by just one point in the circle, to avoid the need for multiple finger tables. Then n items are placed sequentially. Each item uses $d \geq 2$ hash functions to choose locations on the circle; each point is associated with the closest peer (in the clockwise direction). The item is then associated with the peer from this set of at most d peers storing the fewest other items; ties are broken arbitrarily. A natural question to help assess the utility of two choices in this setting is whether in this case, we maintain a $\log \log n / \log d + O(1)$ maximum load with high probability.

Theorem 1. *In the setting above, the maximum load is at most* $\log \log n / \log d + O(1)$ *with high probability.*

Our proof (not included for reasons of space) uses the layered induction technique from the seminal work of [1] (see also [7]). Because of the variance in the arc length associated with each peer, we must modify the proof to take this into account. The standard layered induction uses the fact that if there are β_k bins that have load at least k, then the probability each ball causes a bin to reach load $k + 1$ is most $(\beta_k/n)^2$. This is used to derive bounds on β_k that hold with high probability for each k. The key insight that is required for our modification is that the largest β_k arcs have total length "not too much longer" than β_k/n. This result therefore applies to other settings in which the bin sizes are non-uniform, or equivalently, when the probabilities associated with selecting bins are non-uniform.

Our results hold regardless of how ties are broken when more than one choice has the same smallest load. Vöcking uses an improved tie-breaking scheme to improve the d-choice balls and bins result [11]; his extension can also be applied here. However, in this setting we have a natural criterion that can be used to break ties: the length of the arcs. Intuitively, choosing the least loaded arc with the smallest length appears best, since that arc is the least likely to obtain further load in the future. Simulations bear out that this tie-breaking approach is better than breaking ties at random, and in fact in simulations, the resulting load balance is better than that achieved using Vöcking's scheme; however, we cannot yet demonstrate this analytically. We employ this "shorter arc" tie-breaking scheme in our subsequent experiments.

Although this theoretical result is for the simplest setting (items have equal weight, and are inserted sequentially), the paradigm of using two choices is generally successful in more complex situations, including weighted items and cases where items enter and leave the system dynamically [7]. We therefore expect good behavior in the more complex peer-to-peer settings; we plan to continue to derive related theoretical results.

3   DHT Implementation

Now we describe the application of this idea to DHTs. Let h_0 be a universally agreed hash function that maps peers onto the ring. Similarly, let $h_1, h_2, \ldots h_d$ be a series of universally agreed hash functions mapping items onto the ring. To insert an item x using d hash functions, a peer first calculates $h_1(x), h_2(x), \ldots, h_d(x)$. Then, d lookups are executed in parallel to find the peers $p_1, p_2, \ldots, p_d$ responsible for these hash values, according to the mapping given by h_0. After querying the load of each peer, the peer p_i with lowest load is chosen to store x. A straightforward, but naive, implementation of a search requires the peer performing the search to again calculate $h_1(x), h_2(x), \ldots, h_d(x)$. The peer then initiates lookups to find the peers associated with each of these d values, of which at least one will successfully locate the key-value pair. While these searches are inherently parallelizable, and thus enable searching in little more time than their classic counterparts, this approach uses a factor of d more network traffic to perform each search, which may be unacceptable.

To reduce the overhead searching for additional peers, we introduce *redirection pointers*. Insertion proceeds exactly as before. But in addition to storing the item at the least loaded peer p_i, all other peers p_j where $j \neq i$ store a redirection pointer $x \rightarrow p_i$. To search for x, a peer now performs a single query, by choosing a hash function h_j at random in an effort to locate p_i. If p_j does not have x, then p_j forwards the query using a redirection pointer $x \rightarrow p_i$. Lookups now take at most one more step; if h_j is chosen uniformly at random from the d choices, the extra step is necessary with probability $(d-1)/d$. Although this incurs the overhead of keeping these additional pointers, unless the items stored are very small or inexpensive to calculate, storing actual items and any associated computation will tend to dominate any stored pointers.

One hazard with this approach is that the use of explicit redirection pointers introduces a dependence on a particular peer staying up. We assume that a soft state approach [4] is used and the provider of the key periodically re-inserts it, both to ensure freshness and to recover from failures. Replication to nearby peers as in DHash [5] will allow recovery, but a new search will need to be performed to find the replicating peers. This is easily remedied by keeping pointers to some or all of the replicating peers, and similarly, replicating those pointers.

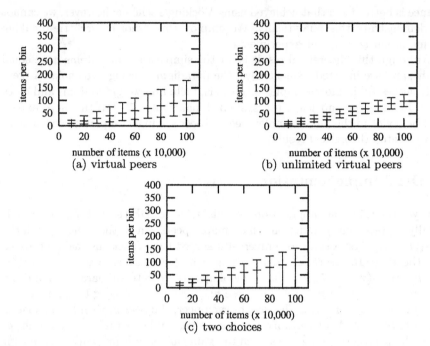

Fig. 1. 1st percentile, mean and 99th percentile loads using various load balancing strategies

4   Other Virtues of Redirection

While using two or more choices for placement improves load balancing, it still forces a static placement of the items, which may lead to poor performance when the popularity of items changes over time. As mentioned earlier, one means of coping with this issue is to use soft state and allow items to change location when they are re-inserted if their previous choice has become more heavily loaded.[2] However, since redirection pointers give the peers responsible for a key explicit knowledge of each other, they can be used to facilitate a wide range of load balancing methods that react more quickly than periodic re-insertion allows. We briefly explore some of these possibilities here.

Load-stealing and load-shedding become simple in this context. For example, consider load-stealing, whereby an underutilized peer p_1 seeks out load to take from more heavily utilized peers. In the case where items are placed using multiple choices, a natural idea is to have p_1 attempt to steal items for which p_1 currently has a redirection pointer. This maintains the invariant that an item is associated with one of its d hash locations. Alternatively, the stealing peer could break this invariant, but at the risk of additional implementation complexity. In general, a load-stealing peer could identify an arbitrary peer p_2 and take respon-

---

[2] This is essentially a dynamic balls and bins problem [7].

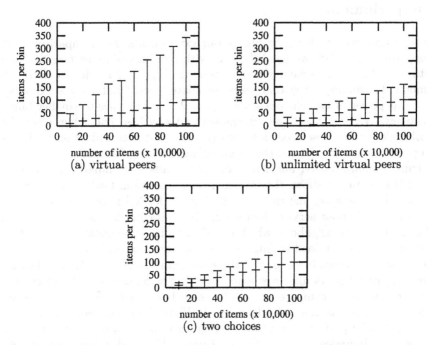

Fig. 2. Minimum, mean and maximum loads using various load balancing strategies

sibility for an item x by making a replica of x and having p_2 create a redirection pointer to p_1 for item x.

Load-shedding, whereby an overloaded peer attempts to offload work to a less loaded peer, is also well suited to peer-to-peer networks. An overloaded peer p_1 must pass on an item x and create a redirection pointer to a peer p_2. Alternatively, the item x could be *replicated* at p_2, both adding redundancy and allowing p_1 to control how much of the load to shed, although this then introduces issues of consistency. Again, in the case where items are placed using multiple choices, load shedding can attempt to maintain the invariants of the hashing paradigm, although this is not strictly necessary.

An interesting alternative combining replication and the multiple-choice schemes above is to replicate an item x at the k least loaded out of d possible locations given by hash functions. Such replication can maintain balanced load while also allowing additional functionality, such as parallel downloading from multiple sources [2, 3]. Indeed, parallel downloading may further improve load balancing in the system. This remains an interesting possibility for future study.

5   Experiments

In this section, we detail the results of our experiments. For comparison with the experiments of [10], we use 10^4 peers with numbers of items ranging from 10^5 to 10^6. The three schemes we consider use 1) $\lfloor \log_2 n \rfloor$ virtual peers, 2) an unbounded number of virtual peers (simulated using uniformly sized arcs), and 3) our power of two choices scheme ($d = 2$, breaking ties to smaller bins), respectively. We omit the basic scheme without any load balancing, since the virtual node scheme described in Chord [10] and in the introduction is clearly far superior.[3] All statistics are the results of aggregating 10^4 trials.

Figure 1 shows the 1st and 99th percentile loads for comparison to the results of [10]. Figure 2 shows the minimum and maximum loads – we view the maximum load as a key metric since the highest loaded peers are most likely to fail or provide poor service. Moreover, when a highly loaded node fails, its load cascades to its neighbors, which can then cause subsequent failures. Both figures show the mean load to illustrate how far or close each scheme is to the ideal. Figure 1(a) reproduces some of those experiments of [10].[4] As noted there, the use of virtual peers improves load balancing significantly and reduces the fraction of idle peers compared to a scheme without load balancing. However, the corresponding maximum loads shown in Figure 2(a) are much higher and reveal a potential performance problem. Figures 1(b) and 2(b) show the results of using an unbounded number of virtual peers. The load balancing is significantly better in this case, but the maximum load is very similar to that shown in Figures 1(c) and 2(c), which show the benefits of employing two choices.

Overall, this means that even given unlimited resources to allocate to virtual peers in this scenario, the end result is a maximum load like that of using two choices. The distribution of load is slightly different – there is less variation in load than when using two choices – but we emphasize that we are comparing an unlimited resource scenario with a limited one. In particular, approximating the unlimited scenario is expensive, and the use of $\lfloor \log_2 n \rfloor$ virtual peers as proposed in [10] introduces a large amount of topology maintenance traffic but does not provide a very close approximation. Finally, we observe that while we are illustrating the most powerful instantiation of virtual peers, we are comparing it to the weakest choice model – further improvements are available to us just by increasing d to 3.

6   Conclusion

We advocate generalizing DHT's to enable a key to map to a set of d possible peers, rather than to a single peer. Use of this "power of two choices" paradigm

---

[3] The high loads that result when no load balancing is used (with 10^6 items and 10^4 peers, the 99th percentile load was 463 items per bin and the maximum load was 1820 items per bin) dwarf those of the three schemes we compare and make them difficult to distinguish when plotted on the same axes.

[4] The maximum load of a peer was not considered in [10].

facilitates demonstrably better load-balancing behavior than the virtual peers scheme originally proposed in Chord; moreover, it does so with considerably less shared routing information stored at each peer. We also make a preliminary case for other benefits of multiple storage options for each key ranging from fault-tolerance to better performance in highly dynamic environments.

At first glance, the prospect of having keys map to a small set of possible peers in a DHT runs the risk of incurring a substantial performance penalty. In practice, the cost is only a modest amount of extra static storage at each peer as well as a small additive constant in search lengths.

References

[1] AZAR, Y., BRODER, A., KARLIN, A., AND UPFAL, E. Balanced allocations. *SIAM Journal on Computing 29*, 1 (1999), 180–200.

[2] BYERS, J., CONSIDINE, J., MITZENMACHER, M., AND ROST, S. Informed content delivery across adaptive overlay networks. In *SIGCOMM* (2002), pp. 47–60.

[3] BYERS, J. W., LUBY, M., AND MITZENMACHER, M. Accessing multiple mirror sites in parallel: Using tornado codes to speed up downloads. In *INFOCOM (1)* (1999), pp. 275–283.

[4] CLARK, D. The design philosophy of the DARPA internet protocols. In *ACM SIGCOMM* (1988), ACM Press, pp. 106–114.

[5] DABEK, F., KAASHOEK, M. F., KARGER, D., MORRIS, R., AND STOICA, I. Wide-area cooperative storage with CFS. In *Proceedings of the 18th ACM Symposium on Operating Systems Principles (SOSP '01)* (Chateau Lake Louise, Banff, Canada, Oct. 2001).

[6] KARGER, D. R., LEHMAN, E., LEIGHTON, F. T., PANIGRAHY, R., LEVINE, M. S., AND LEWIN, D. Consistent hashing and random trees: Distributed caching protocols for relieving hot spots on the world wide web. In *ACM Symposium on Theory of Computing* (May 1997), pp. 654–663.

[7] MITZENMACHER, M., RICHA, A., AND SITARAMAN, R. *The Power of Two Choices: A Survey of Techniques and Results*. Kluwer Academic Publishers, Norwell, MA, 2001, pp. 255–312. edited by P. Pardalos, S. Rajasekaran, J. Reif, and J. Rolim.

[8] RATNASAMY, S., FRANCIS, P., HANDLEY, M., KARP, R., AND SHENKER, S. A scalable content addressable network. In *ACM SIGCOMM* (2001), pp. 161–172.

[9] ROWSTRON, A., AND DRUSCHEL, P. Pastry: Scalable, distributed object location and routing for large-scale peer-to-peer systems. In *Proceedings of Middleware 2001* (2001).

[10] STOICA, I., MORRIS, R., KARGER, D., KAASHOEK, M. F., AND BALAKRISHNAN, H. Chord: A scalable peer-to-peer lookup service for internet applications. In *ACM SIGCOMM* (2001), pp. 149–160.

[11] VÖCKING, B. How asymmetry helps load balancing. In *Proceedings of the 40th IEEE-FOCS* (1999), pp. 131–140.

[12] ZHAO, B. Y., KUBIATOWICZ, J. D., AND JOSEPH, A. D. Tapestry: An infrastructure for fault-tolerant wide-area location and routing. Tech. Rep. UCB/CSD-01-1141, UC Berkeley, Apr. 2001.

A Simple Fault Tolerant Distributed Hash Table*

Moni Naor** and Udi Wieder

The Weizmann Institute of Science
Rehovot 76100 Israel
{naor,uwieder}@wisdom.weizmann.ac.il

Abstract. We introduce a distributed hash table (DHT) with logarithmic degree and logarithmic dilation. We show two lookup algorithms. The first has a message complexity of $\log n$ and is robust under random deletion of nodes. The second has parallel time of $\log n$ and message complexity of $\log^2 n$. It is robust under spam induced by a random subset of the nodes. We then show a construction which is fault tolerant against random deletions and has an optimal degree-dilation tradeoff. The construction has improved parameters when compared to other DHT's. Its main merits are its simplicity, its flexibility and the fresh ideas introduced in its design. It is very easy to modify and to add more sophisticated protocols, such as dynamic caching and erasure correcting codes.

1 Introduction

We propose a very simple and easy to implement distributed hash table. Our construction offers logarithmic linkage, load and dilation. It can operate in a highly dynamic environment and is robust against random deletions and random spam generating nodes, in the sense that with high probability *all* nodes can locate *all* data items.

There are two commonly used methods for modelling the *occurrence* of faults. The first is the random fault model, in which every node becomes faulty with some probability and independently from other nodes. The other is the worst case model in which an adversary which knows the state of the system chooses the faulty subset of nodes. There are several models that describe the *behavior* of faulty nodes. One of them is the fail-stop model in which a faulty node is deleted from the system. Another is a spam generating model in which a faulty node may produce arbitrary false versions of the data item requested. A third model is the Byzantine model in which there are no restrictions over the behavior of faulty nodes.

In the random fault model, if we want that all nodes can access all data items, then it is necessary that the degree be at least $\log n$ and that every data item is stored by at least $\log n$ nodes[1]. Otherwise with non-negligible probability there would be nodes disconnected from the system.

---

* Research supported in part by the RAND/APX grant from the EU Program IST.
** Incumbent of the Judith Kleeman Professorial Chair.

[1] It is not necessary that the item be *replicated* $\log n$ times but rather that $\log n$ processors be *involved* in the storage of it.

F. Kaashoek and I. Stoica (Eds.): IPTPS 2003, LNCS 2735, pp. 88–97, 2003.

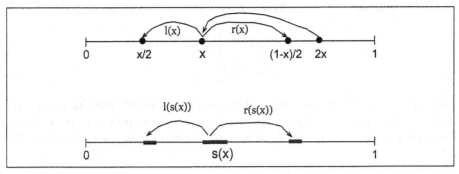

Fig. 1. The upper figure shows the edges of a point in G_c. The lower shows a mapping of a segment into two smaller ones

1.1 Related Work

Several peer-to-peer systems are known to be robust under random deletions ([10], [8], [6]). Stoica *et al* prove that the Chord system [8] is resilient against random faults in the fail-stop model. It does not seem likely that Chord can be made spam resistant without a significant change in its design. Fiat and Saia [7] proposed a content addressable network that is robust against deletion and spam in the *worst case* scenario, when an adversary can choose which nodes fail. Clearly in this model some small fraction of the non-failed nodes would be denied from accessing some of the data items. While their solution handles a more difficult model then ours, it has several disadvantages; *(I)* it is not clear whether the system can preserve its qualities when nodes join and leave dynamically. *(II)* the message complexity is large ($\log^3 n$) and so is the linkage needed ($\log^2 n$). Most importantly their construction is very complicated. Complex constructions and algorithms increase the likelihood of errors in implementation and offer easier opportunities for an adversary to diverge from the designated protocol. In a later paper Fiat *et al* [2] solve the first problem yet they do not describe a spam resistant lookup.

The construction presented here is designed using design rules which we call *continuous - discrete*. These design rules are defined and analyzed in [5], where their power is demonstrated by the suggestion of several distributed dynamic data structures. Among them is a *constant degree* DHT. The only previously known constant degree DHT is Viceroy [4] which is rather involved. The DHT described in [5] enjoys an optimal tradeoff between the degree and the dilation. A degree of $\log n$ results with a dilation of $O(\frac{\log n}{\log\log n})$ which is an improvement over previous constructions.

2 The Overlapping DHT

We describe the construction as a discretization of a continuous graph denoted by G_c. The vertex set of G_c is denoted by I and defined to be the real interval

$[0, 1)$. The edge set of G_c is defined by the following functions:

$$\ell(a) \stackrel{def}{=} \frac{a}{2} \tag{1}$$

$$r(a) \stackrel{def}{=} \frac{a}{2} + \frac{1}{2} \tag{2}$$

where $a \in I$, ℓ abbreviates 'left' and r abbreviates 'right'. Note that the out-degree of each point is 2 while the in-degree is 1. Sometimes we may enhance the notation and write $r, \ell([a, b])$ meaning the image of the interval $[a, b]$ under r, ℓ.

Properties of G_c: We set some useful notations. For any two points $a, b \in I$ define $d(a, b)$ to be $|a - b|$. Let σ denote a sequence of binary digits, and σ_t denote its prefix of length t. For every point $a \in I$ define $\sigma_t(a)$ in the following manner:

$$\sigma_0(a) = a$$
$$(\sigma_t.0)(a) = \ell(\sigma_t(a))$$
$$(\sigma_t.1)(a) = r(\sigma_t(a))$$

In other words $\sigma_t(a)$ is the point reached by a walk that starts at a and proceeds according to σ_t when 0 represents ℓ and 1 represents r. The following lemma justifies the name 'Distance Halving':

Lemma 1 (Distance Halving Property). *For all $a, b \in I$ and for all binary strings σ it holds that:*

$$d(r(a), r(b)) = d(\ell(a), \ell(b)) = \tfrac{1}{2}d(a, b) \tag{3}$$

$$d(\sigma_t(a), \sigma_t(b)) = 2^{-t} \cdot d(a, b) \tag{4}$$

For every point $a \in [0, 1)$ and t there is a string σ_t and a point a' such that $\sigma_t(a') = a$. The string σ_t could be easily calculated from a and in fact it consists of the first t bits from the binary representation of a.

Lemma 2. *Let $a, b \in [0, 1)$ and let σ be the binary representation of a. For all t it holds that*

$$d(a, \sigma_t(b)) \leq 2^{-t}$$

Proof. Let a' be such that $\sigma_t(a') = a$; i.e. a walk that starts at a' and follows the binary representation of the prefix of length t of a, reaches a. We have $d(a, \sigma_t(b)) = d(\sigma_t(a'), \sigma_t(b))$. By Lemma 1 it holds that $d(\sigma_t(a'), \sigma_t(b)) = 2^{-t}d(a', b) \leq 2^{-t}$.

The Discrete graph G: We show how to construct the discrete graph G. Each node i $(1 \leq i \leq n)$ in the graph is associated with a *segment* $s(i) \stackrel{def}{=} [x_i, y_i]$. These segments should have the following properties:

Property I - The set of points $x = x_1, x_2, \ldots, x_n$ is evenly distributed along I. Specifically we desire that every interval of length $\frac{\log n}{n}$ contains $\Theta(\log n)$ points from x. The point x_i is fixed and would not change as long as i is in the network.

Property II - The point y_i is chosen such that the length of each segment is $\Theta(\frac{\log n}{n})$. It is important to notice that for $i \neq j$, $s(i)$ and $s(j)$ may *overlap*. The point y_i would be updated as nodes join and leave the system. The precise manner in which y_i is chosen and updated would be described in the next section.

The edge set of G is defined as follows. A pair of vertices i, j is an edge in G if $s(i)$ and $s(j)$ are connected in G_c or if $s(i)$ and $s(j)$ overlap. The edges of G are anti-parallel. It is convenient to think of G as an undirected graph. A point $a \in I$ is said to be *covered* by i if $a \in s(i)$. We observe the following:

1. Each point in I is covered by $\Theta(\log n)$ nodes of G. This means that each data item is stored at $\Theta(\log n)$ processors.
2. Each node in G has degree $\Theta(\log n)$.

Join and Leave: Our goal in designing the Join and Leave operations is to make sure that properties I,II remain valid. When node i wishes to join the system it does the following:

1. It chooses at random $x_i \in [0, 1)$ [2].
2. It calculates q_i which is an estimation of $\frac{\log n}{n}$.
3. It sets $y_i = x_i + q_i \mod 1$.
4. It updates all the appropriate neighbors according to the definition of the construction.
5. The neighbors may decide to update their estimation of $\frac{\log n}{n}$ and therefore change their y value.

When node i wishes to leave the system (or is detected as down) all its neighbors should update their routing tables and check whether their estimation of $\frac{\log n}{n}$ should change. If so they should change their y value accordingly. The following lemma is straight forward:

Lemma 3. *If n points are chosen randomly, uniformly and independently from the interval $[0, 1]$ then with probability $1 - \frac{1}{n}$ each interval of length $\Theta(\frac{\log n}{n})$ would contain $\Theta(\log n)$ points.*

---

[2] It may be that x_i is chosen by hashing some i.d. of i. In this case it is important that the hash function distribute the x values evenly.

If each node chooses its x-value uniformly at random from I then property-I holds. Observe that if each node's estimation of $\frac{\log n}{n}$ is accurate within a multiplicative factor then property II holds as well. The procedure for calculating q_i is very simple. Assume x_j is the predecessor of x_i along I. It is proven in [4] that with high probability[3]

$$\log n - \log \log n - 1 \leq \log \left(\frac{1}{d(x_i, x_j)} \right) \leq 3 \log n$$

Conclude that node i can easily estimate $\log n$ within a multiplicative factor. Call this estimation $(\log n)_i$. A multiplicative estimation of $\log n$ implies a *polynomial* estimation of n, therefore an additional idea should be used. Let q_i be such that in the interval $[x_i, x_i + q_i]$ there are *exactly* $(\log n)_i$ different x-values.

Lemma 4. *With high probability the number q_i estimates $\frac{\log n}{n}$ within a multiplicative factor.*

The proof follows directly from lemma 3. Each node in the system updates its q value and holds an accurate estimation of $\frac{\log n}{n}$ at all times. Therefore property II holds at all times.

Mapping the Data Items to Nodes: The mapping of data items to nodes is done in the same manner as other constructions of distributed hash tables (such as Chord [8], Viceroy [4] and CAN [6]). First data items are mapped into the interval I using a hash function. Node i should hold all data items mapped to points in $s(i)$. The use of consistent hashing [3] is suggested in Chord [8]. Note that all nodes holding the same data item are connected to one another so they form a clique. If a node storing a data item is located, then other nodes storing the same data item are quickly located as well. This means that accessing different copies of the same data item in parallel can be simple and efficient. It suggests storing the data using an erasure correcting code, (for instance the digital fountains suggested by Byers *et al* [1]) and thus avoid the need for replication. The data stored by any small subset of the nodes would suffice to reconstruct the date item. Weatherspoon and Kubiatowicz [9] suggest that an erasure correcting code may improve significantly the bandwidth and storage used by the system.

3   The Lookup Operation

The lookup procedure emulates a walk in the continuous graph G_c. Assume that processor i wishes to locate data item V and let $v = h(V)$ where h is a hash function, i.e. data item V is stored by every processor which covers the point v. Let $z_i = \frac{x_i + y_i}{2}$ and let σ be the binary representation of z_i. Lemma 2 states that $\sigma_t(v)$ is within the interval $[z_i - 2^{-t}, z_i + 2^{-t}]$. Conclude that when $t = \log n - \log \log n + O(1)$ it holds that $\sigma_t(v) \in s(i)$. Let t to be the minimum

---

[3] The term 'with high probability' (w.h.p) means with probability $1 - n^{-\epsilon}$

integer for which $\sigma_t(v) \in s(i)$. Call the path between $\sigma_t(v)$ and v the *canonical path* between v and $s(i)$. This gives rise to a natural lookup algorithm. The canonical path exists is G_c, yet by the definition of G, if (a, b) is an edge in G_c, a is covered by i and b is covered by j then the edge (i, j) exists in G. This means that the canonical path can be *emulated* by G.

Simple Lookup: Every point in I is covered by $\Theta(\log n)$ nodes. This means that when node i wishes to pass a message to a node covering point $z \in I$ it has $\Theta(\log n)$ *different* neighbors that cover z. In the Simple Lookup it chooses *one* of these nodes at random and sends the message to it.

Theorem 1. *Simple Lookup has the following properties:*

1. *The length of each lookup path is at most $\log n + O(1)$. The message complexity is $\log n + O(1)$.*
2. *If i is chosen at random from the set of nodes and v is chosen at random from I, then the probability a given processor participates in the lookup is $\Theta\left(\frac{\log n}{n}\right)$.*

Proof (Proof Sketch:). The proof of statement (1) is immediate. To show the correctness of statement (2) we prove the following: Fix a processor i. The probability processor i participates in the kth step of the routing $1 \leq k \leq \log n$ is $\Theta(\frac{1}{n})$. Summing up over k yields the result. This statement is proved by induction on k.

Theorem 2. *If each node is faulty independently with fixed probability p, then for sufficiently low p (which depends entirely on the parameters chosen when constructing G), with high probability each surviving node can locate every data-item.*

Proof. We prove the following lemma:

Lemma 5. *If p is small enough, then w.h.p every point in I is covered by at least one node.*

Proof. Assume for simplicity that $x_1 < x_2 < \cdots < x_n$. Each point in an interval $[x_i, x_{i+1}]$ is covered by the *same* set of $\Theta(\log n)$ nodes. Call this set S_i. We have

$$\Pr[\text{ All nodes in } S_i \text{ were deleted }] = p^{\Theta(\log n)}$$

Therefore for sufficiently small p this probability is smaller than n^{-2}. Applying the union bound over all i yields that with probability greater than $1 - \frac{1}{n}$ every point in I is covered by at least one node. It is important to notice that for an arbitrary value of p it is possible to adjust the q values, so that each point in I is covered by sufficiently many nodes, and the lemma follows.

For every edge (a, b) in G_c there exists at least one edge in G whose nodes cover a and b, therefore the canonical path could be emulated in G and the simple lookup succeeds. We stress that after the deletions the lookup still takes $\log n$ time and $\log n$ messages. Furthermore the average load induced on each node does not increase significantly.

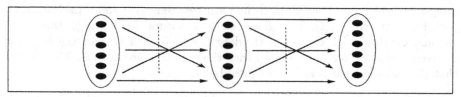

Fig. 2. The message is sent through *all* the nodes covering the canonical path

Spam Resistant Lookup: Assume that a faulty node may generate arbitrarily false data items. We wish to show that every node can find all *correct* data items w.h.p. Just as in the simple lookup, the spam resistant lookup between i and v emulates the canonical path between $s(i)$ and v. The main difference is that now when node i wishes to pass a message to a node covering point a it will pass the message to all $\Theta(\log n)$ nodes covering a. At each time step each node receives $\Theta(\log n)$ messages, one from each node covering the previous point of the path. The node sends on a message only if it were sent to it by a *majority* of nodes in the previous step.

Theorem 3. *The spam resistant lookup has the following properties:*

1. *With high probability all surviving nodes can obtain all correct data items.*
2. *The lookup takes (parallel) time of $\log n$.*
3. *The lookup requires $O(\log^2 n)$ messages in total.*

Proof. Statements $(2,3)$ follow directly from the definitions of the spam resistant lookup. Statement (1) follows from the following:

Lemma 6. *If each node fails with probability p, then for sufficiently small p (which depends entirely on the parameters chosen when constructing G) it holds that with high probability every point in I is covered by a majority of non-failed processors.*

The proof of lemma 6 is similar to that of lemma 5. Now the proof of theorem 3 is straight forward. It follows by induction on the length of the length of the path. Every point of the canonical is covered by a majority of good nodes, therefore every node along the path would receive a majority of the authentic message. It follows that with high probability *all* nodes can find *all* true data items.

The easy proofs of theorems 2 and 3 demonstrate the advantage of designing the algorithms in G_c and then migrating them to G.

4   Reducing the Dilation

We now show how to decrease the lookup length and the congestion by increasing the degree. For any integer $c \geq 2$ construct a continuous graph G_c with edges defined by the following functions:

$$f_i(y) = \frac{y}{c} + \frac{i}{c} \ (i = 0, 1, \ldots, c-1)$$

The equivalent of Lemma 1 is

$$d(f_i(y), f_i(z)) = \tfrac{1}{c}d(y, z)$$

and the equivalent of Lemma 2 is $d(y, \sigma_t(z)) \le c^{-t}$. Therefore:

Theorem 4. *A discretization of G_c would result with a graph of degree $\Theta(c \log n)$ and with dilation $\log_c n$.*

Two interesting options are setting $c = \log n$ or $c = n^\epsilon$ (for some constant ϵ), as the first results with a lookup length of $\frac{\log n}{\log \log n}$, and the second with a lookup length of $O(1)$. It is worth noting that the same analysis of Theorem 1 shows that for each choice of c, the probability a processor participates in a lookup is $\Theta(\frac{\log_c n}{n})$.

Optimizing the Degree-Dilation Tradeoff: We show how to achieve a dilation of $\Theta(\frac{\log n}{\log \log n})$ while maintaining a degree of $\Theta(\log n)$, thus improving the lookup and congestion while maintaining the same degrees as Chord. First set $c = \log n$. The previous construction yields a graph with the desired dilation yet with a degree of $\Theta(\log^2 n)$. The reduction of the degree is achieved by connecting each processor to only *one* other processor for each projection of its segment. More formally, for each $0 \le j \le \log n$ the length of $f_j([x_i, y_i])$ is $\Theta(\frac{1}{n})$, therefore it is *covered* by $\Theta(\log n)$ different processors. processor i is connected to *exactly one* randomly chosen processor whose segment covers $f_j([x_i, y_i])$. As before there exists a link between processor i and all processors with segments that overlap $s(i)$. Lookup is done in the same manner as Simple Lookup; i.e. the route a message takes emulates the canonical path of the continuous graph. Clearly the maximum degree of the construction is $\Theta(c + \log n) = \Theta(\log n)$ and when there are no faults the dilation is only $\Theta(\frac{\log n}{\log \log n})$. It is left to show that this construction remains fault tolerant under random deletions of processors and connections.

As before we assume that each processor fails with some fixed probability p. Assume that processor i tries to move the message from point $a \in s(i)$ to point $f(a)$. Processor i should do the following

1. If the processor which is connected to i and covers $f(a)$ is alive then i moves the message to it.
2. If i fails moving the message to $f(a)$ then it picks at random a processor covering a and moves the message to it.

We need to bound the number of times Step (2) occurs, i.e. the number of hops in which the message remains in the same spot on the continuous graph.

Lemma 7. *W.h.p the number of hops a message stays in point a in G_c, (before moving to $f(a)$), is dominated by a geometric random variable with a constant success probability.*

Proof (Proof Sketch:). For sake of simplicity assume that first each processor fails with probability p and then processors randomly choose their links. Let i

be a processor which covers $a \in s(i)$. There are $\Theta(\log n)$ processors which covers $f(s(i))$ (and therefore cover $f(a)$) out of which i chooses at random one. W.h.p out of the $\Theta(\log n)$ processors which cover $f(s(i))$ a constant fraction survived. Therefore the probability i is connected to a live processor that covers $f(a)$ is at least a constant and is independent from the choices of other processors. Conclude that the number of hops a message remains in a is dominated by a geometric random variable

Theorem 5. *The expected dilation of a message after faults is* $\Theta(\frac{\log n}{\log \log n})$. *The actual dilation is at most* $\Theta(\frac{\log n}{\log \log n})$ *with probability* $1 - n^{-\frac{1}{\epsilon \log \log n}}$.

Proof (Proof Sketch:). The expectation of a geometric random variable is constant. Lemma 7 and the linearity of expectation implies that even after random faults the expected dilation of a message is $\Theta(\frac{\log n}{\log \log n})$.

The total number of hops a message remains in the same spot is at most the sum of $\Theta(\frac{\log n}{\log \log n})$ independent geometric variables. Standard use of tail bounds for hypergeometric distributions yields the second assertion.

5 Extensions

Dynamic Caching: The simplicity of the construction implies that it is easy to modify and add protocols. In [5] we show a simple protocol that performs dynamic caching of a popular data items, thus relieving hot spots in the system. The protocol can provably prevent the existence of hot spots in the network. The protocol was designed for a constant degree non overlapping DHT. It is rather straightforward to modify it for the overlapping DHT.

Expander Graphs: It is shown in [5] that similar techniques could be used to build a graph that is guaranteed to be and expander. The idea is to use the Gabber Galil continuous expander over $[0, 1) \times [0, 1)$ and then compose it into cells using a Voronoi diagram.

6 Future Work

The main challenge ahead is to prove robustness against a worst case scenario, where an adversary chooses which nodes fail. We believe that a slight variation of the construction might be able to route messages successfully in the worst case model as well.

None of the known constructions (including [2],[7]) can handle the case in which an adversary controls the nodes *prior to their insertion*. This means that an adversary may control the actual construction of the network, and thus cause faults that otherwise would have been beyond its capability. It seems likely that robustness against such an adversary would require the use of cryptographic means.

References

[1] J. W. Byers, M. Luby, M. Mitzenmacher, and A. Rege. A digital fountain approach to reliable distribution of bulk data. In *SIGCOMM*, pages 56–67, 1998.

[2] A. Fiat and J. Saia. Censorship resistant peer-to-peer content addressable networks. In *Symposium on Discrete Algorithms (SODA)*, 2002.

[3] D. R. Karger, E. Lehman, F. T. Leighton, R. Panigrahy, M. S. Levine, and D. Lewin. Consistent hashing and random trees: Distributed caching protocols for relieving hot spots on the world wide web. In *ACM Symposium on Theory of Computing*, pages 654–663, May 1997.

[4] D. Malkhi, M. Naor, and D. Ratajczak. Viceroy: A scalable and dynamic emulation of the butterfly. In *PODC*, 2002.

[5] M. Naor and U. Wieder. Novel architectures for p2p applications: the continuous-discrete approach. *www.wisdom.weizmann.ac.il/ ~uwieder*, 2002.

[6] S. Ratnasamy, P. Francis, M. Handley, R. Karp, and S. Shenker. A scalable content addressable network. In *Proc ACM SIGCOMM*, pages 161–172, San Diego CA, Augost 2001.

[7] J. Saia, A. Fiat, S. Gribble, A. R. Karlin, and S. Saroiu. Dynamically fault-tolerant content addressable networks. In *First International Workshop on Peer-to-Peer Systems*, MIT Faculty Club, Cambridge, MA, USA, 2002.

[8] I. Stoica, R. Morris, D. Karger, F. Kaashoek, and H. Balakrishnan. Chord: A scalable Peer-To-Peer lookup service for internet applications. In *Proceedings of the 2001 ACM SIGCOMM Conference*, pages 149–160, 2001.

[9] H. Weatherspoon and J. D. Kubiatowicz. Erasure coding vs. replication: A quantitative comparison. In *First International Workshop on Peer-to-Peer Systems*, MIT Faculty Club, Cambridge, MA, USA, 2002.

[10] B.Y. Zhao and J. Kubiatowicz. Tapestry: An infrastructure for fault-tolerant wide-area location and routing. Technical Report UCB CSD 01-1141, University of California at Berkeley, Computer Science Department, 2001.

Koorde: A Simple Degree-Optimal Distributed Hash Table

M. Frans Kaashoek and David R. Karger*

MIT Laboratory for Computer Science
{kaashoek,karger}@lcs.mit.edu

Abstract. *Koorde*[1] is a new distributed hash table (DHT) based on Chord [15] and the de Bruijn graphs [2]. While inheriting the simplicity of Chord, Koorde meets various lower bounds, such as $O(\log n)$ hops per lookup request with only 2 neighbors per node (where n is the number of nodes in the DHT), and $O(\log n/ \log \log n)$ hops per lookup request with $O(\log n)$ neighbors per node.

1 Introduction

A number of different performance measures exist for DHTs; optimizing one tends to put pressure on the others. These measures include:

1. **Degree**: the number of *neighbors* with which a node must maintain continuous contact;
2. **Hop Count**: the number of hops needed to get a message from any source to any destination;
3. The degree of **Fault Tolerance**: what fraction of the nodes can fail without eliminating data or preventing successful routing;
4. The **Maintenance Overhead**: how often messages are passed between nodes and neighbors to maintain coherence as nodes join and depart;
5. The degree of **Load Balance**: how evenly keys are distributed among the nodes, and how much load each node experiences as an intermediate node for other routes.

There are other measures for DHTs, such as delay (i.e., proximity routing) and resilience against malicious nodes, but because of the page limit we mostly ignore them in this paper.

A quick survey of existing systems shows some common trends. Degree tends to be logarithmic, or at worst polylogarithmic. Hop count is generally logarithmic as well. These bounds turn out to be close to optimal, but not optimal.

We point out that for any constant degree k, $\Theta(\log n)$ hops is optimal. We also show that to provide a high degree of fault tolerance, a node must maintain

---

* This research was conducted as part of the IRIS project (http://project-iris.net/), supported by the National Science Foundation under Cooperative Agreement No. ANI-0225660.

[1] A mathematical chord is a koorde in the Dutch language.

F. Kaashoek and I. Stoica (Eds.): IPTPS 2003, LNCS 2735, pp. 98–107, 2003.

$O(\log n)$ neighbors; in that case, however, an $O(\log n / \log \log n)$ hop count may be achieved.

Koorde is a simple DHT that exploits de Bruijn graphs to achieve these lower bounds. Koorde may be important in practice, because it has low maintenance overhead.

2   Bounds and Tradeoffs

In this section, we discuss lower-bounds and tradeoffs between some of the DHT measures.

2.1   Degree and Hop Count

Our first observation relates the degree and routing hops in any system:

Lemma 1. *An n-node system with maximum degree d requires at least $\log_d n - 1$ routing hops in the worst case and $\log_d n - O(1)$ on average.*

Proof. Since the maximum degree is d, the number of nodes within distance h is, by induction, at most $d^{h+1}/(d-1)$. Since $d^{\log_d n} = n$, it follows that some node is at distance at least $\log_d n - 1$. The average-case claim follows from the corollary that in fact almost all nodes are at distance $\log_d n - O(1)$. □

Many protocols (Chord, Kademlia [9], Pastry [11], Tapestry [5]) offer $O(\log n)$ degree and hop count. CAN [10] uses degree d to achieve $O(dn^{1/d})$ hops. These are near-optimal bounds but the lower bound allows for (i) $O(\log n)$ hops using only constant degree and (ii) a degree of $O(\log n)$ achieving $O((\log n)/\log \log n)$ hops.

The Viceroy DHT [8] provides constant *expected* degree. However, its *high probability* bound is $O(\log n)$—in fact, it is likely that a few unlucky nodes will have $\Omega(\log n)$ degree. Viceroy is also relatively complex. For example, it involves estimating the size of the network to select various "levels" for nodes in the system. Furthermore, fault tolerance is not discussed in the Viceroy paper.

2.2   Fault Tolerance and Maintenance

A strong notion of fault tolerance is one that requires all live nodes to remain connected in the presence of node failures. Connectivity is a necessary (but not sufficient) condition for efficient routing.

Lemma 2. *In order for a network to stay connected with constant probability when all nodes fail with probability $1/2$, some nodes must have degree $\Omega(\log n)$.*

Proof. Suppose that the maximum degree $d < \log n - 2 \log \log n - 1$. Then the probability that a particular node is *isolated*, staying up but losing all of its neighbors, is at least $(1/2)^{d+1} \geq 2^{2 \log \log n}/2^{\log n} = (\log^2 n)/n$. Since there are n nodes, we expect at least $\log^2 n$ nodes to become isolated. This almost gives what we want, but we must deal technically with the fact that node isolations are not independent: if one node is not isolated then it has a living neighbor, which decreases the odds of other nodes being isolated.

However, since the maximum degree is d, each node has at most d^2 neighbors at distance 2. It follows that there is a set S of n/d^2 nodes such that no two share any neighbors (the set can be found by a greedy algorithm: take a node, include it in S, delete its distance-2 neighbors, repeat). Since none of the nodes in S share any neighbors, their "isolation events" are independent; thus the probability that no node in S gets isolated is at most $(1 - (\log^2 n)/n)^{n/d^2} < 1/e$ (using the inequality $(1 - x)^{1/x} < 1/e$ for any x). In other words, such an event happens with constant probability.   □

A star graph has only one node with degree exceeding 1 and still manages to stay connected with constant probability in the above model. However. in a P2P system we want no node to be of substantially above-average degree. Under such a restriction the lemma can be strengthened: the *average* degree must be $\Omega(\log n)$. Space precludes a proof.

As a particular case, a network partition can also be thought of as a collection of failures of the nodes on the "other side" of the partition; tolerating a failure rate of $1/2$ means that the larger half of the system will stay connected after the partition. This argument generalizes to failure probabilities $p \neq 1/2$; roughly speaking, d must be such that the expected number of *surviving* neighbors $pd = \Omega(\log n)$.

A similar argument can be applied to the maintenance traffic. Liben-Nowell, Balakrishnan, and Karger [7] introduce the notion of "half-life" as the time it takes for a peer-to-peer network to replace half its nodes through departures and new arrivals, and prove that every node must be notified about $\Omega(\log n)$ other nodes per half-life if the network is to remain connected.

Most DHTs support some mechanism for handling nonbyzantine failures, but few provide analytical results. The Chord DHT uses "successor lists" of $O(\log n)$ neighbors of each node and proves that with these successor lists, the network remains connected (and continues to route efficiently) with high probability even if half the nodes fail simultaneously. Building on the successor lists, Liben-Nowell, Balakrishnan and Karger show how to limit maintenance traffic to $O(\log^2 n)$ per node per half-life (compared to the lower bound of $\Omega(\log n)$).

Saia, Fiat, Gribble, Karlin, and Saroiu [12] provide a DHT with analytical results in the presence of malicious nodes. Their DHT is "adversarially fault tolerant" in that an adversary killing *any* half of the nodes (not necessarily at random) is only able to disconnect an ϵ fraction of the surviving nodes. To achieve this high level of fault tolerance, however, some performance is sacrificed. Each node maintains $O(\log^3 n)$ state. Lookups take $O(\log n)$ time but require $O(\log^3 n)$ messages. Every data item must be replicated $\log N$ times. Metadata about various items must be distributed to $O(\log^3 N)$ nodes.

2.3   Load Balance

All the DHTs discussed above offer some load balance, in both the amount of data stored and the amount of routing traffic carried. In general, any one node-load is within an $O(\log n)$ factor of the average load over the system with high probability. The Chord DHT shows how, by replicating each node into $O(\log n)$ "virtual nodes," it is possible to improve the maximum-to-average load ratio to a constant (arbitrarily close to 1). A similar technique can be applied to many of the DHTs mentioned above, including Koorde. However, such replication does increase the state needed at a node, and the maintenance overhead, by a logarithmic factor. Thus, the schemes with optimal degree and hop count (Koorde and Viceroy) must give up their optimality if constant-factor load balance is to be achieved. It is an open question to find a system that is both degree optimal and load balanced.

3   Koorde: A Constant-Degree DHT

Koorde combines Chord with de Bruijn graphs. It looks up a key by contacting $O(\log n)$ nodes with $O(1)$ state per node.

Like Chord, Koorde uses consistent hashing [6] to map keys to nodes. A node and a key have identifiers that are uniformly distributed in a 2^b identifier space. A key k is stored at its *successor*, the first node n that follows k on the identifier circle, where node $2^b - 1$ is followed by node 0. The successor of key k is identified as *successor*(k).

3.1   De Bruijn Graphs and Routing

Koorde embeds a de Bruijn graph on the identifier circle for forwarding lookup requests. A de Bruijn graph has a node for each binary number of b bits. A node has two outgoing edges: node m has an edge to node $2m$ mod 2^b and an edge to node $2m + 1$ mod 2^b (see Figure 1). In other words, a node m points at the nodes identified by shifting a new low order bit into m and dropping the high order bit. We represent these nodes using *concatenation* mod 2^b, writing $m \circ 0 = 2m$ mod 2^b and $m \circ 1 = 2m + 1$ mod 2^b.

If we assume a P2P system in which every number corresponds to a node (i.e., $2^b = n$), de Bruijn routing works as follows. With 2^b nodes in the system, consistent hashing will map key k to node k, since *successor*(k) is k.

Routing a message from node m to node k is accomplished by taking the number m and shifting in the bits of k one at a time until the number has been replaced by k (see Figure 1). Each shift corresponds to a routing hop to the next intermediate address; the hop is valid because each node's neighbors are the two possible outcomes of shifting a 0 or 1 onto its own address. Because of the structure of de Bruijn graphs, when the last bit of k has been shifted, the query will be at node k. Node k responds whether key k exists.

This lookup algorithm will contact $b = O(\log n)$ nodes, since after b left shifts the query is at the destination node. To support the forwarding step, each node maintains information only about its two de Bruijn neighbors.

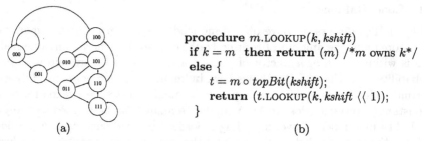

(a)   (b)

Fig. 1. (a) A de Bruijn graph for $b = 3$. (b) Lookup of key k at node m in a de Bruijn graph. Variable *kshift* holds the key k as shifted by previous iterations. On the first call *kshift* $= k$

3.2   Koorde Routing

Most P2P systems contain only a few of the possible 2^b nodes, because only a subset of the nodes will have joined at any given point in time and b is large for other reasons (e.g., to avoid collisions its size is determined by the output of a cryptographic hash function). Thus, some points on the identifier circle correspond to nodes that have have joined the system, while many points on the ring correspond to "imaginary" nodes.

To embed a de Bruijn graph on a sparsely populated identifier ring, each joined node m maintains knowledge about two other nodes: the address of the node that succeeds it on the ring (its successor) and the first node, d, that precedes $2m$ (m's first de Bruijn node). Since the de Bruijn nodes follow each other directly on the ring, there is no reason to keep a variable for the second de Bruijn node ($2m + 1$); it is likely that d is also the predecessor for $2m + 1$.

To look up a key k, the lookup algorithm must find *successor*(k) by walking down the de Bruijn graph. Since the de Bruijn graph is "incomplete," Koorde *simulates* the path taken through the complete de Bruijn graph, passing through the immediate real predecessor, *predecessor*(i), of each imaginary node i on the de Bruijn path.

Figure 2 shows Koorde routing as an extension of the de Bruijn routing of Figure 1. Koorde passes the current imaginary node i as an argument to the routing function. In a single routing step Koorde simulates the hop from imaginary node i to imaginary node $i \circ topBit(k)$, shifting in k. Koorde does so by hopping to $m.d$, which will have value near $2m$ and hopefully be equal to *predecessor*$(i \circ topBit(k))$. If so, Koorde iterates the next routing step.

If at every hop, d is indeed the predecessor of $i \circ topBit(k)$, then Koorde contacts b nodes, where b is the number of bits in identifiers, because the algorithm shifts i left 1 bit at each hop.

Unfortunately, although $m.d$ is by definition the closest predecessor of $2m$, it may not be the closest predecessor of $i \circ topBit(k)$—because the nodes' random distribution around the ring is not perfectly even, some other node might interpose land in between $m.d$ and $2i$. Koorde checks for this case, and corrects.

procedure $m.\text{LOOKUP}(k, kshift, i)$
  if $k \in (m, successor]$ **then return** $(successor)$
  else if $i \in (m, successor]$ **then return** $(d.\text{LOOKUP}(k, kshift \langle\langle 1, i \circ topBit(kshift)))$
  else return $(successor.\text{LOOKUP}(k, kshift, i))$

Fig. 2. The Koorde lookup algorithm at node m. k is the key. i is the imaginary de Bruijn node. d contains the predecessor of $2m$, and *successor* contains the successor of m

When the node d receives the query, it checks whether it is indeed the predecessor of $i \circ topBit(k)$ by examining its own successor pointer. If it is, Koorde takes its next de Bruijn hop. If not, it forwards the query forward along the ring, following *successor* pointers, until the predecessor of $i \circ topBit(k)$ is encountered.

As in Section 3.1, the algorithm makes b calls to $d.\text{LOOKUP}()$. To bound the overall work, we must bound the number of *successor* lookups.

Lemma 3. *In the course of doing a lookup, with high probability the number of routing hops is at most* $3b$.

Proof. To conserve space we analyze the expected number of hops; a high probability extension is standard. In a single step simulating the advance from imaginary node i to imaginary node $i \circ topBit(k)$, we first move from node $m = predecessor(i)$ to node $d = m.d$ and then advance from d to $predecessor(i \circ topBit(k))$ using successor pointers. The nodes we traverse this way are precisely the ones located in identifier space between $2m$ and $2i + 1$. Conditioned on the values m and i, the fact that nodes are randomly distributed around the ring means that the the odds of each node landing in between these two values is $(2i - 2m + 1)/2^b$, so the expected number of nodes in this region of identifier space is $u = n(2i - 2m + 1)/2^b$. To remove the conditioning on m and i, notice that regardless of i, again because n nodes are inserted randomly, the expected value of $i - m$ (distance between i and m in identifier space) is $2^b/n$, so the expected value of u is $n(2 * 2^b/n)/2^b = 2$.

In other words, each imaginary hop involves, in expectation, following two successor pointers. Thus, in total, we expect to follow b de Bruijn pointers and $2b$ successor pointers. $\square$

By maintaining $predecessor(2m)$ *and* its successor (for a total of 3 pointers per node), we reduce the expected number of successor hops per shift to 1, reducing the expected routing cost to $2b$.

3.3 Lookup in $\log n$ Hops

The lookup algorithm described so far contacts $O(b)$ nodes, where b is the (large) number of bits in identifiers. However, we can reduce the number of hops to $O(\log n)$ with high probability by carefully selecting an appropriate imaginary starting node.

In Section 3.2, we started *lookup* with the node m on which the query originated. But since m is responsible for all imaginary nodes between itself and its successor, we can choose (without cost) to simulate starting at any imaginary de Bruijn node i that is between m and its successor. If the ring contains few real nodes, then only i's top bits are significant; we can set i's bottom bits to any value we chose without leaving m's region. If we choose i's bottom bits to be the top bits of the key k, then as soon as the lookup algorithm has shifted out the top bits of i, it will have reached the node responsible for k. With high probability, the distance in identifier space from m to its successor exceeds $2^b/n^2$, which means that m's region contains imaginary nodes with all possible values of the lowest $\lg(2^b/n^2) = b - 2\lg n$ significant bits; this means we can set this many bits to equal the high order bits of k and be left to shift out only the $2\lg n$ most significant bits of the current address, which requires $O(\log n)$ hops.

3.4 Maintenance and Concurrency

Just like finger pointers in Chord, Koorde's de Bruijn pointer is merely an important performance optimization; a query can always reach its destination slowly by following successors. Because of this property, Koorde can use Chord's join algorithm. Similarly, to keep the ring connected in the presence of nodes that leave, Koorde can use Chord's successor list and stabilization algorithm.

Chord has a nice "self stabilizing" property in which a ring consisting only of successor pointers can quickly construct all its fingers by pointer jumping; it is unclear whether the Koorde can similarly self-stabilize.

4 Extensions

To allow users to trade-off degree for hop count, we extend Koorde to degree-k de Bruijn graphs. When choosing $k = \log n$, Koorde can also be made fault tolerant.

4.1 Degree-k de Bruijn Graphs

Koorde can be generalized to provide a simple optimal trade-off between routing table size and routing hop count. In a traditional de Bruijn graph, a node m has edges to nodes $2m$ and $2m + 1$. This graph allows us to shift in one new address bit with a single edge traversal. The same idea can be generalized to a different, non-binary base. For any k, a *base-k de Bruijn graph* connects node m to the k nodes labeled km, $km + 1$, $\ldots$, $km + (k - 1)$. The resulting graph has out degree k but, since we are shifting by a factor of k each time, has diameter $\log_k n$.

This idea can be carried over to Koorde. Instead of letting node m point at *predecessor*$(2m)$, each Koorde node points at *predecessor*(km) and the k nodes immediately following. It can be shown that under this scheme, we expect to use only a constant number of hops through real nodes to simulate a single imaginary-node hop (correcting a single base-k digit). We thus expect to complete the routing in $O(\log_k n)$ hops, matching the optimum lower bound for degree k networks.

4.2   Fault Tolerance

Base Koorde has constant degree and thus, by the Lemma 2 earlier, cannot be fault tolerant against nodes failing with constant probability. To achieve such fault tolerance, we need to increase to minimum degree $\log n$. The approach is straightforward. To provide fault tolerance for immediate successors, we use the "successor list" maintenance protocol developed for Chord: rather than m maintaining only its immediate successor, it maintains the $O(\log n)$ nodes immediately following it. Even if nodes fail with probability $1/2$, at least one of the nodes in each successor list will stay alive with high probability. In such case, routing is always possible, at worst by following live successor pointers to the correct node.

Koorde must provide a similar "backup" in case the "distant" node that m points at, $predecessor(2m)$, fails. If that node fails, its immediate predecessor on the ring becomes the new "correct" node for m to point at. Therefore, Koorde proactively points, not at $predecessor(2m)$, but at $O(\log n)$ nodes on the ring immediately preceding $2m$. One might think that the easiest way to provide such a set is to use a "predecessor list" construction similar to the successor list. However, this construction would violate several of the key invariants used to prove correctness of the Chord protocol. In particular, unlike successor pointers, predecessor pointers may point "off the ring" at nodes that have initiated the Chord join protocol but have not yet completed it; pointing at such new nodes could make lookup operations incorrect.

Fortunately, a slightly different approach does work. To set up its pointers, node m uses a lookup to find not the immediate predecessor of $2m$, but the immediate predecessor p of $2m - x$, where $x = O(\log n/n)$ is chosen so that, with high probability, $\Theta(\log n)$ nodes occupy the interval between $2m - x$ and $2m$. Node m can retrieve the successor list of p, which gives it a set of $O(\log n)$ nodes reaching to point $2m$ on the interval. These nodes provide the necessary redundancy: even if half the nodes fail, with high probability m will have a pointer to the immediate predecessor of address $2m$. This scheme requires an estimate of n, which is easy to achieve in practice by considering the distribution of a nodes' successors.

This attempt to gain fault tolerance has eliminated the constant degree attraction of Koorde. But Koorde can make good use of the extra degree: instead of working with a base-2 de Bruijn graph, Koorde can work with a base-$O(\log n)$ de Bruijn graph. With such a graph, Koorde has fault tolerance *and* the number of routing hops is $O((\log n)/\log\log n)$, which is optimal.

5   Related Work

We are not the first to use de Bruijn graphs in routing [1, 3, 13, 14], and concurrent with our work others have noted their application to DHTs [4]. Compared to the related work, our primary contribution is how to simulate a lookup using a de Bruijn graph in a sparsely-populated identifier space.

Koorde's approach of using de Bruijn graphs is different than D2B's [4]. The D2B DHT attempts to organize its nodes such that the nodes form a de Bruijn graph, but cannot guarantee that the graph constructed is a de Bruijn graph. As a result, D2B can guarantee only with high probability that the out degree is $O(1)$. D2B also modifies node identifiers to create a de Bruijn graph. Koorde puts no restrictions on applications in how they choose node identifiers. Finally, Koorde inherits Chord's algorithms for handling concurrent joins; the D2B technical report doesn't discuss this topic.

6   Summary

Koorde allows its users to tune the out-degree from 2 to $O(\log n)$ to achieve hop counts ranging from $O(\log n)$ to $O(\log n/\log\log n)$. This lets users trade maintenance overhead against hop count, which may be important in practice for systems in flux. An implementation of Koorde is available as part of the Chord software distribution (http://www.pdos.lcs.mit.edu/chord).

References

[1] BERMOND, J.-C., AND FRAIGNIAUD, P. Broadcasting and gossiping in de Bruijn networks. *SIAM Journal on Computing 23*, 1 (1994), 212–225.

[2] DE BRUIJN, N. A combinatorial problem. In *Proc. Koninklijke Nederlandse Akademie van Wetenschappen* (1946), vol. 49, pp. 758–764.

[3] ESFAHANIAN, A., AND HAKIMI, S. Fault-tolerant routing in de bruijn communication networks. *IEEE Trans. on Computers 34*, 9 (1985), 777–788.

[4] FRAIGNIAUD, P., AND GAURON, P. The content-addressable network D2B. Tech. Rep. 1349, CNRS Universié de Paris Sud, January 2003.

[5] HILDRUM, K., KUBATOWICZ, J. D., RAO, S., AND ZHAO, B. Y. Distributed Object Location in a Dynamic Network. In *Proc. 14th ACM Symp. on Parallel Algorithms and Architectures* (Aug. 2002).

[6] KARGER, D., LEHMAN, E., LEIGHTON, F., LEVINE, M., LEWIN, D., AND PANIGRAHY, R. Consistent hashing and random trees: Distributed caching protocols for relieving hot spots on the World Wide Web. In *Proc. 29th Annual ACM Symposium on Theory of Computing* (El Paso, TX, May 1997), pp. 654–663.

[7] LIBEN-NOWELL, D., BALAKRISHNAN, H., AND KARGER, D. R. Analysis of the evolution of peer-to-peer systems. In *Proc. PODC 2002* (Aug. 2002).

[8] MALKHI, D., NAOR, M., AND RATAJCZAK, D. Viceroy: A scalable and dynamic emulation of the butterfly. In *Proceedings of Principles of Distributed Computing (PODC 2002)* (July 2002).

[9] MAYMOUNKOV, P., AND MAZIERES, D. Kademlia: A peer-to-peer information system based on the XOR metric. In *Proc. 1st International Workshop on Peer-to-Peer Systems* (Mar. 2002).

[10] RATNASAMY, S., FRANCIS, P., HANDLEY, M., KARP, R., AND SHENKER, S. A scalable content-addressable network. In *Proc. ACM SIGCOMM* (San Diego, CA, August 2001), pp. 161–172.

[11] ROWSTRON, A., AND DRUSCHEL, P. Pastry: Scalable, distributed object location and routing for large-s cale peer-to-peer systems. In *Proceedings of the 18th IFIP/ACM International Conference on Distributed Systems Platforms (Middleware 2001)* (Nov. 2001).

[12] SAIA, J., FIAT, A., GRIBBLE, S., KARLIN, A., AND SAROIU, S. Dynamically fault-tolerant content addressable networks. In *Proc. 1st International Workshop on Peer-to-Peer systems* (Mar. 2002).

[13] SAMATHAM, M., AND PRADHAM, D. The de bruijn multiprocessor network: A versatile parallel processing and sorting network for VLSI. *IEEE Trans. on Computers 38*, 4 (1989), 567–581.

[14] SIVARAJAN, K., AND RAMASWAMI, R. Multihop lightwave networks based on de bruijn graphs. In *INFOCOM'92*, pp. 1001–1011.

[15] STOICA, I., MORRIS, R., KARGER, D., KAASHOEK, M. F., AND BALAKRISHNAN, H. Chord: A scalable peer-to-peer lookup service for Internet applications. In *Proc. ACM SIGCOMM* (San Diego, Aug. 2001).

Peer-to-Peer File Sharing and Copyright Law:
A Primer for Developers

Fred von Lohmann

Senior Intellectual Property Attorney
Electronic Frontier Foundation
454 Shotwell Street, San Francisco, CA 94110
fred@eff.org

Abstract. The future of peer-to-peer file-sharing and related technologies is entwined, for better or worse, with copyright law. This paper aims to present a layperson's introduction to the copyright law principles most pertinent to peer-to-peer developers, including contributory and vicarious liability principles and potential legal defenses. After describing the current shape of the law, the paper concludes with twelve specific strategies that peer-to-peer developers can undertake to reduce their copyright vulnerabilities.

1 What This Is, and Who Should Read It

The future of peer-to-peer file-sharing and related technologies is entwined, for better or worse, with copyright law. If the early legal skirmishes yield any lesson for P2P developers, it is that an appreciation of the legal environment should be part of any development effort from the beginning, rather than bolted on at the end.

This piece is meant as a general explanation of the U.S. copyright law principles most relevant to P2P file-sharing technologies. It is aimed primarily at:

- Developers of core P2P file-sharing technology, such as the underlying protocols, platform tools, and specific client implementations; and
- Developers of ancillary services that depend upon or add value to P2P file-sharing networks, such as providers of search, security, metadata aggregation, and other services.

This paper is aimed not at giving you all the answers, but rather at allowing you to recognize the right questions to ask.[1]

What This Is Not: The following discussion focuses only on U.S. copyright law. While non-copyright principles may also be mentioned, this discussion does not attempt to examine other legal principles that might apply to P2P file-sharing, including patent, trademark, trade secret, or unfair competition. Nothing contained

---

[1] A longer version of this paper, updated from time to time, is available at www.eff.org.

F. Kaashoek and I. Stoica (Eds.): IPTPS 2003, LNCS 2735, pp. 108-117, 2003.

herein constitutes legal advice—please discuss your individual situation with your own attorney.

2   Copyright Basics and the Intersection with P2P File-Sharing

The nature of digital file-sharing technology inevitably implicates copyright law. First, since every digital file is "fixed" for purposes of copyright law (whether on a hard drive, CD, or merely in RAM), the files being shared generally qualify as copyrighted works. Second, the transmission of a file from one person to another results in a reproduction, a distribution, and possibly a public performance (in the world of copyright law, "public performance" includes the act of transmitting a copyrighted work to the public). To a copyright lawyer, every unauthorized reproduction, distribution, and public performance requires an explanation, and thus file-sharing systems seem suspicious from the outset.

2.1   The End-Users: "Direct" Infringement

For the end-users who are sharing files, the question becomes whether the reproductions, distributions, and public performances are authorized by the copyright owner or otherwise permitted under copyright law (as "fair use" for example). If not, the end-users are what copyright lawyers call "direct infringers"—they have directly violated one or more of the copyright owner's exclusive rights.

In a widely-used public peer-to-peer file-sharing environment, it is a virtual certainty that at least some end-users are engaged in infringing activity (unless specific technical measures are taken to prevent this, like permitting only the sharing of files that have been cryptographically marked as "authorized").

2.2   The P2P Tool Maker: "Contributory" and "Vicarious" Infringement

But what does this have to do with those who develop and distribute peer-to-peer file-sharing tools? After all, in a pure peer-to-peer file-sharing network, the developer of the file-sharing tool has no direct involvement in the discovery, copying or transmission of the files being shared.

Copyright law, however, sometimes reaches beyond the direct infringer to those who were only indirectly involved. As in many other areas of the law (think of the "wheel man" in a stick up, or supplying a gun to someone you know is going to commit a crime), copyright law will sometimes hold one individual accountable for the actions of another. So, for example, if a swapmeet owner rents space to a vendor with the knowledge that the vendor sells counterfeit CDs, the swapmeet owner can be held liable for infringement alongside the vendor.

This indirect, or "secondary," liability can take two distinct forms: contributory and vicarious.

2.2.1 Contributory Infringement

Contributory infringement is similar to "aiding and abetting" liability: "one who, with knowledge of the infringing activity, induces, causes, or materially contributes to the infringing conduct of another, may be held liable as a contributory infringer." In order to prevail on a contributory infringement theory, a copyright owner must prove:

Direct Infringement: There has been a direct infringement by someone.

Knowledge: The accused contributory infringer knew of the underlying direct infringement. This element can be satisfied by showing either that the contributory infringer *actually* knew about the infringing activity, or that he reasonably *should have known* given all the facts and circumstances. At a minimum, however, the contributory infringer must have some specific information about infringing activity—the mere fact that the system is capable of being used for infringement, by itself, is not enough.

Material Contribution: The accused contributory infringer induced, caused, or materially contributed to the underlying direct infringement. Merely providing the "site and facilities" that make the direct infringement possible can be enough.

2.2.2 Vicarious Infringement

Vicarious infringement is derived from the same legal principle that holds an employer responsible for the actions of its employees. A person will be liable for vicarious infringement if he has the right and ability to supervise the direct infringer and also has a direct financial interest in his activities. Thus, in order to prevail on a vicarious infringement theory, a copyright owner must prove each of the following:

Direct Infringement: There has been a direct infringement by someone.

Right and Ability to Control: The accused vicarious infringer had the right and ability to control or supervise the underlying direct infringement. This element does not set a high hurdle. For example, the Napster court found that the ability to terminate user accounts or block user access to the system was enough to constitute "control."

Direct Financial Benefit: The accused vicarious infringer derived a "direct financial benefit" from the underlying direct infringement. In applying this rule, however, the courts have not insisted that the benefit be especially "direct" or "financial"—almost any benefit seems to be enough. For example, the Napster court found that "financial benefit exists where the availability of infringing material acts as a draw for customers" and the growing user base, in turn, makes the company more attractive to investors.

The nature of vicarious infringement liability creates a strong incentive to monitor the conduct of users. This stems from the fact that knowledge is not required for vicarious infringement liability—a person can be a vicarious infringer even if they are completely unaware of infringing activity.

In other words, if you exercise control over your users and derive a benefit from their activities, you remain ignorant of their conduct at your own risk.

3   Potential Defenses to Contributory and Vicarious Liability

3.1   No Direct Infringer: "All of My Users Are Innocent"

If there is no direct infringement, there can be no indirect liability. Consequently, if a peer-to-peer developer can plausibly claim that no users in the network are sharing copyrighted works without authorization, this would be a complete defense to any contributory or vicarious infringement claims.

Unfortunately, this may be extremely difficult to demonstrate, given the decentralized nature of most P2P networks and the wide variety of uses to which they may be put. It will likely be difficult to show that *every* user is innocent. Nevertheless, in certain specialized networks that permit the sharing of only secure, authorized file types, this may be a viable defense.

3.2   The *Betamax* Defense: "Capable of Substantial Noninfringing Uses"

Holding   technology developers responsible for the unlawful acts of end-users obviously can impose a crushing legal burden on those who make general-purpose tools. Fortunately, the Supreme Court has defined an outer limit to copyright's indirect liability theories.

In a case involving the Sony Betamax VCR, the Supreme Court found that contributory infringement liability could not reach the manufacturer of a device that is "capable of substantial noninfringing use." In that case, the Court found that the VCR was capable of several noninfringing uses, including the time-shifting of television broadcasts by home viewers. In the Court's view, it does not matter what proportion of the uses are noninfringing, only whether the technology is "capable" of substantial noninfringing uses.

Unfortunately, the "*Betamax* defense" has been under sustained legal attack in the cases involving P2P technology. In the *Napster* case, the court found that this defense does not apply at all to vicarious liability. Accordingly, if you have control over, and derive a financial benefit from, direct infringement, the existence of "substantial noninfringing uses" for your service is irrelevant.

Moreover, the *Napster* court concluded that the *Betamax* defense may only apply until the copyright owner notifies you regarding specific infringing activity by end-users. At that point, a failure to act to prevent further infringing activity will give rise to liability, and the existence of "substantial noninfringing uses" becomes irrelevant.

The "*Betamax* defense" has also come under attack in the *Aimster* case, where a court stated that the defense was not available where the technology is primarily used for infringement. (This notwithstanding the fact that the "proportion of uses" test was explicitly rejected in the Supreme Court's *Betamax* ruling.) The scope of the "*Betamax* defense" is also at the heart of the case against Kazaa, Morpheus and Grokster, currently pending in Los Angeles.

The recent court interpretations of the "*Betamax* defense" have at least two important implications for P2P developers. First, it underscores the threat of vicarious liability—at least in the Ninth Circuit, a court will not be interested in hearing about your "substantial noninfringing uses" if you are accused of vicarious infringement.

Accordingly, "control" and "direct financial benefit," as described above, should be given a wide berth.

This will likely reduce the attractiveness of business models built on an on-going "service" or "community-building" model, to the extent that these models allow the provider to control user activity (i.e., terminate or block users) and create value by attracting a large user base.

Second, with respect to contributory infringement, the recent interpretations of the *Betamax* defense suggest that, once you receive specific notices from copyright owners about infringing activities, your "substantial noninfringing uses" may no longer serve as a complete shield to contributory liability. The risk then arises that a developer may have a legal duty to "do something" about the infringing activities.

But what "something" must be done? The *Napster* decision recognizes that the ability to respond to these notices may be limited by the technology behind the challenged service or product. In cases involving decentralized P2P networks, there may be nothing a software developer can do to stop future infringements (just as Xerox cannot control what a photocopier is used for after it is sold).

Nevertheless, copyright owners are arguing that technologists should have a duty to redesign technologies once they are put on notice regarding infringing end-users. What this might entail is difficult to predict, but may include, in some cases, modification of the architecture and capabilities of the tool, service or system.

The exact contours of the *Betamax* defense are still being developed in the courts, some of which seem to have embraced conflicting interpretations. Breaking developments on this front may have important ramifications for P2P developers and should be closely monitored.

3.3   DMCA Section 512 "Safe Harbors"

In 1998, Congress enacted a number of narrow "safe harbors" for copyright liability. These safe harbors appear in section 512 of the Copyright Act (*see* 17 U.S.C. § 512). These safe harbors apply only to "online service providers," and only to the extent that the infringement involves four functions: (1) transitory network transmissions; (2) certain kinds of caching; (3) storage of materials on behalf of users (e.g., web hosting, remote file storage); and (4) the provision of information location tools (e.g., providing links, directories, search engines).

Because Congress did not anticipate P2P when it enacted the safe harbors, many P2P products may not fit within the four enumerated functions. For example, according to an early ruling by the district court in the *Napster* case, an OSP cannot use the "transitory network transmission" safe harbor unless the traffic in question passes through its own private network. Many P2P products will, by their very nature, flunk this requirement, just as Napster did.

In addition to being limited to certain narrowly-circumscribed functions, the safe harbors are only available to entities that comply with a number of complex, interlocking statutory requirements.

In the final analysis, qualifying for any of the DMCA safe harbors requires careful attention to the legal and technical requirements and obligations that the statute imposes. Any P2P developer who intends to rely on them should seek qualified legal counsel at an early stage of the development process—an after-the-fact effort to comply is likely to fail (as it did for Napster).

4   Lessons and Guidelines for P2P Developers

Because the relevant legal principles are in flux, these guidelines represent merely one, general analysis of the legal landscape—please consult with an attorney regarding your particular situation.

4.1   Make and Store No Copies

This one may be obvious, but remember that if you make or distribute any copies (even if only in RAM) of copyrighted works, you may be held liable as a direct infringer. The court will not be interested in "control" or "knowledge" or "financial benefit" or "material contribution." If you made or transmitted copies, you're probably liable for infringement.

Of course, this shouldn't be a problem for most P2P developers, since the great insight of peer-to-peer architectures is that the actual resources being shared need not pass through any central server. Nevertheless, be careful where caching or similar activities are concerned.

4.2   Your Two Options: Total Control or Total Anarchy

In the wake of recent decisions on indirect copyright liability, it appears that copyright law has foisted a binary choice on P2P developers: either build a system that allows for thorough monitoring and control over user activities, or build one that makes such monitoring and control completely impossible.

Contributory infringement requires that you have "knowledge" of, and "materially contribute" to, someone else's infringing activity. In most cases, it will be difficult to avoid "material contribution"—after all, if your system adds any value to the user experience, a court may conclude that you have "materially contributed" to any infringing user activities.

So the chief battleground for contributory infringement will likely be the "knowledge" issue. The applicable legal standards on this question are still very much in dispute —especially as relates to the *Betamax* defense." The *Napster* court's analysis suggests that once you receive notice that your system is being used for infringing activity (e.g., a "cease and desist" letter from a copyright owner), you have a duty to "do something" to stop it.

What might that "something" be? Well, it should be limited by the architecture of your system, but may ultimately be decided by a court. So, in order to avoid the unpleasant surprise of a court telling you to re-engineer your technology to stop your infringing users, you can either include mechanisms that enable monitoring and control of user activities (and use them to stop allegedly infringing activity when you receive complaints), or choose an architecture that will convince a judge that such monitoring and control is impossible. (Copyright owners have begun arguing that you must at least redesign future versions of your software to prevent infringement. This remarkable argument has not yet been accepted by any court.)

The *Napster* court's vicarious liability analysis also counsels for either a total control or total anarchy approach. Vicarious liability requires that you "control," and receive "benefit" from, someone else's infringing activity. The "benefit" element will be difficult to resist in many P2P cases (at least for commercial products)—so long as the software permits or enables the sharing of infringing materials, this will serve as a "draw" for users, which can be enough "benefit" to result in liability.

So the fight will likely center on the "control" element. The *Napster* court found that the right to block a user's access to the service was enough to constitute "control." The court also found that Napster had a duty to monitor the activities of its users "to the fullest extent" possible. Accordingly, in order to avoid vicarious liability, a P2P developer would be wise to either incorporate mechanisms that make it easy to monitor and block infringing users, or choose an architecture that will convince a judge that monitoring and blocking is impossible.

4.3   Better to Sell Stand-Alone Software Products than On-Going Services

Vicarious liability is perhaps the most serious risk facing P2P developers. Having the power to terminate or block users constitutes enough "control" to justify imposing vicarious liability. Add "financial benefit" in the form of a business model that depends on a large user base, and you're well on your way to joining Napster as a vicarious infringer. This is true even if you are completely unaware of what your users are up to—the pairing of "control" and "financial benefit" are enough.

Of course, most "service" business models fit this "control" and "benefit" paradigm. What this means is that, after the Napster decision, if you offer a "service," you may have to monitor your users if you want to escape liability. If you want to avoid monitoring obligations, you'll have to give up on "control."

Vendors of stand-alone software products may be in a better position to resist monitoring obligations and vicarious infringement liability. After Sony sells a VCR, it has no control over what the end-user does with it. Neither do the makers of photocopiers, optical scanners, or audio cassette recorders. Having built a device with many uses, only some of which may infringe copyrights, the typical electronics manufacturer has no way to "terminate" end-users or "block" their ability to use the device. The key here is to let go of any control you may have over your users—no remote kill switch, automatic updates feature, contractual termination rights, or other similar mechanisms.

4.4   Can You Plausibly Deny Knowing What Your End-Users Are up to?

Assuming that you have escaped vicarious infringement by eliminating "control" or "financial benefit," there is still the danger of contributory infringement. To avoid liability here, you will need to address whether you knew, or should have known, of the infringing activity of your users.

Have you built a level of "plausible deniability" into your product architecture and business model? If you promote, endorse, or facilitate the use of your product for infringing activity, you're asking for trouble. Similarly, software that sends back usage reports may lead to more knowledge than you want. Customer support channels can also create bad "knowledge" facts. Instead, talk up all the great legitimate capabilities, sell it (or give it away), and then leave the users alone. Again, your choices are total control, or total anarchy.

4.5   What Are Your Substantial Noninfringing Uses?

If your product is intended to work solely (or best) as a mechanism for copyright piracy, you're asking for legal trouble. More importantly, you're thinking too small. Almost all peer-to-peer systems can be used for many different purposes, some of which the creators themselves fail to appreciate.

So create a platform that lends itself to many uses. Actively, sincerely, and enthusiastically promote the noninfringing uses of your product. Gather testimonials from noninfringing users. The existence of real, substantial noninfringing uses will increase the chances that you can invoke the *"Betamax* defense" if challenged in court.

4.6   Do Not Promote Infringing Uses

Do not promote any infringing uses. Be particularly careful with marketing materials and screenshot illustrations—entertainment company attorneys are very good at making hay out of the fact that Beatles songs were included in sample screenshots included in marketing materials or documentation. Have an attorney review these materials closely.

4.7   Disaggregate Functions

Separate different functions and concentrate your efforts on a discrete area. In order to be successful, peer-to-peer networks will require products to address numerous functional needs—search, namespace management, security, dynamic file redistribution—to take a few examples. There's no reason why one entity should try to do all of these things. In fact, the creation of an open set of protocols, combined with a competitive mix of interoperable, but distinct, applications is probably a good idea from a product-engineering point of view.

This approach may also have legal advantages. If Sony had not only manufactured VCRs, but also sold all the blank video tape, distributed all the TV Guides, and sponsored clubs and swap meets for VCR users, the Betamax case might have turned out differently. Part of Napster's downfall was its combination of indexing, searching, and file sharing in a single piece of software. If each activity is handled by a different product and vendor, on the other hand, each entity may have a better legal defense to a charge of infringement.

A disaggregated model, moreover, may limit what a court can order you to do to stop infringing activity by your users. As the Napster court recognized, you can only be ordered to police your own "premises"—the smaller it is, the less you can be required to do.

Finally, certain functions may be entitled to special protections under the "safe harbor" provisions of the Digital Millennium Copyright Act ("DMCA"). Search engines, for example, enjoy special DMCA protections. Thus, the combination of a P2P file sharing application with a third party search engine might be easier to defend in court than Napster's integrated solution.

4.8   Don't Make Your Money from the Infringing Activities of Your Users

Avoid business models that rely on revenue streams that can be directly traced to infringing activities. For example, a P2P file-sharing system that includes a payment mechanism might pose problems, if the system vendor takes a percentage cut of all payments, including payments generated from sales of bootleg Divx movie files.

4.9   Give up the EULA

Although end-user license agreements ("EULAs") are ubiquitous in the software world, copyright owners have used them in P2P cases to establish "control" for vicarious liability purposes. On this view, EULAs represent "contracts" between vendors and their users, and thus give software vendors legal control over end-user activities. EULAs that permit a vendor to terminate at any time for any reason may raise particular concerns, insofar as they leave the impression that a vendor has the legal right to stop users from using the software.

P2P software vendors should consider distributing their code without a EULA. Even without a EULA, a software developer retains all of the protections of copyright law to prevent unauthorized duplication and modifications.

4.10   No "Auto-Updates"

Stay away from any "auto-update" features that permit you to automatically patch, update, or otherwise modify software on the end-user's machine. Copyright owners have argued that these features establish "control" for vicarious liability purposes (on the theory that you can always "update" software to prevent its use for infringement, by retrofitting acoustic filtering, for example).

At a minimum, users should always retain the ability to decline any update. Control should rest in the end-user's hands, not the software vendor's (this as much for security reasons as legal reasons).

4.11   No Customer Support

Any evidence that you have knowingly assisted an end-user in committing copyright infringement will be used against you. In the P2P cases so far, one source for this kind of evidence is from customer support channels, whether message board traffic or email. A user writes in, explaining that the software acted strangely when he tried to download *The Matrix*. If you answer him, copyright owners will make it seem that you directly assisted the user in infringement, potentially complicating your contributory infringement defense.

Even if you read the message but don't answer, or answer in a general FAQ, copyright owners may argue that support requests were enough to create "knowledge" of infringing activities.

So let the user community support themselves in whatever forums they like. Keep your staff out of it. (This will be easier if you are open source, of course.)

4.12   Be Open Source

In addition to the usual litany of arguments favoring the open-source model, the open source approach may offer special advantages in the peer-to-peer realm. It may be more difficult for a copyright owner to demonstrate "control" or "financial benefit" with respect to an open source product. After all, anyone can download and compile open source code, and no one has the ability to "terminate" or "block access" or otherwise control the use of the resulting applications.

"Financial benefit" may also be a problematic concept where the developers do not directly realize any financial gains from the code (as noted above, however, the Napster court has embraced a very broad notion of "financial benefit," so this may not be enough to save you). Finally, by making the most legally dangerous elements of the P2P network open source (or relying on the open source projects of others), you can build your business out of more legally defensible ancillary services (such as search services, bandwidth enhancement, file storage, file meta-data services, etc.).

References

[1]   A&M Records, Inc. v. Napster, Inc., 239 F.3d 1004 (9th Cir. 2001).

[2]   *A&M Records, Inc. v. Napster, Inc.*, 2000 WL 573136 (N.D. Cal. May 12, 2000) (ruling on DMCA 512 safe harbor).

[3]   *In re Aimster Copyright Litigation*, 2002 WL 31006142 (N.D. Ill. Sept. 4, 2002) (granting preliminary injunction against Aimster).

[4]   *MGM v. Grokster* (Kazaa/Morpheus/Grokster) summary judgment briefs: http://www.eff.org/IP/P2P/MGM_v_Grokster/

On Death, Taxes, and the Convergence of Peer-to-Peer and Grid Computing

Ian Foster[1, 2] and Adriana Iamnitchi[1]

[1] Department of Computer Science, University of Chicago, Chicago, IL 60637
{foster,anda}@cs.uchicago.edu
[2] Mathematics and Computer Science, Argonne National Laboratory
Argonne, IL 60439

1   Introduction

It has been reported [25] that life holds but two certainties, death and taxes. And indeed, it does appear that any society—and in the context of this article, any large-scale distributed system—must address both death (failure) and the establishment and maintenance of infrastructure (which we assert is a major motivation for taxes, so as to justify our title!).

Two supposedly new approaches to distributed computing have emerged in the past few years, both claiming to address the problem of organizing large-scale computational societies: peer-to-peer (P2P) [15, 36, 49] and Grid computing [21]. Both approaches have seen rapid evolution, widespread deployment, successful application, considerable hype, and a certain amount of (sometimes warranted) criticism. The two technologies appear to have the same final objective—the pooling and coordinated use of large sets of distributed resources—but are based in different communities and, at least in their current designs, focus on different requirements.

In this article, we take some first steps toward comparing and contrasting P2P and Grid computing. Basing our discussion whenever possible on the characteristics of deployed systems, rather than the unverified claims abundant in the literature, we review their target communities, resources, scale, applications, and technologies. On the basis of this review, we draw some initial conclusions concerning their interrelationship and future evolution. In brief, we argue that (1) both are concerned with the same general problem, namely, the organization of resource sharing within virtual communities; (2) both take the same general approach to solving this problem, namely the creation of overlay structures that coexist with, but need not correspond in structure to, underlying organizational structures; (3) each has made genuine technical advances, but each also has—in current instantiations—crucial limitations, which we characterize (simplistically, but, we believe, usefully) as "Grid computing addresses infrastructure but not yet failure, whereas P2P addresses failure but not yet infrastructure"; and (4) the complementary nature of the strengths and weaknesses of the two approaches suggests that the interests of the two communities are likely to grow closer over time.

F. Kaashoek and I. Stoica (Eds.): IPTPS 2003, LNCS 2735, pp. 118-128, 2003.

2   Defining Terms

The popularity of both Grid and P2P has led to a number of (often contradictory) definitions. We assume here that Grids are sharing environments implemented via the deployment of a persistent, standards-based service infrastructure that supports the creation of, and resource sharing within, distributed communities. Resources can be computers, storage space, sensors, software applications, and data, all connected through the Internet and a middleware software layer that provides basic services for security, monitoring, resource management, and so forth. Resources owned by various administrative organizations are shared under locally defined policies that specify what is shared, who is allowed to share, and under what conditions. We call a set of individuals and/or institutions defined by such sharing rules a virtual organization (VO) [24].

We define *P2P* as a class of applications that takes advantage of resources— storage, cycles, content, human presence—available at the edges of the Internet [49]. Because accessing these decentralized resources means operating in an environment of unstable connectivity and unpredictable IP addresses, P2P design requirements commonly include independence from DNS and significant or total autonomy from central servers. Their implementations frequently involve the creation of overlay networks [53] with a structure independent of that of the underlying Internet. We prefer this definition to the alternative "decentralized, self-organizing distributed systems, in which all or most communication is symmetric," because it encompasses large-scale deployed (albeit centralized) "P2P" systems (such as Napster and SETI@home) where much experience has been gained.

3   Comparing Grids and P2P

Current Grids provide many services to moderate-sized communities [19] and emphasize the integration of substantial resources to deliver nontrivial qualities of service within an environment of at least limited trust. For example, NASA's Information Power Grid links supercomputers at four NASA laboratories [26]. In contrast, current P2P systems deal with many more participants (e.g., Limewire [31] reports hundreds of thousands in Gnutella) but offer limited and specialized services, have been less concerned with qualities of service, and have made few if any assumptions about trust.

These characterizations and examples might not suggest commonality of interest. Nevertheless, we shall argue that in fact the two environments are concerned with the same general problem, namely, resource sharing within VOs that may not overlap with any existing organization. Clearly, the two types of system have both conceptual and concrete distinctions, which we shall identify and illuminate, focusing as noted above on characteristics of deployed systems. We shall show that the distinctions seem to be the result of different target communities and thus different evolutionary paths. Grids have incrementally scaled the deployment of relatively sophisticated services and application, connecting small numbers of sites into collaborations engaged in complex scientific applications. As system scale increases, Grid developers are now facing and addressing problems relating to autonomic configuration and management. P2P communities developed rapidly around unsophisticated, but popular, services such as file sharing and are now seeking to expand to more sophisticated applications as well as continuing to innovate in the area of large-scale autonomic system management. We expect the definition of persistent and multipurpose infrastructure to emerge as an important theme.

3.1   Target Communities and Incentives

The development and deployments of **Grid** technologies were motivated initially by the requirements of professional communities needing to access remote resources, federate datasets, and/or pool computers for large-scale simulations and data analyses. Although Grid technologies were initially developed to address the needs of scientific collaborations, commercial interest is growing. Participants in contemporary Grids thus form part of established communities that are prepared to devote effort to the creation and operation of required infrastructure and within which exist some degree of trust, accountability, and opportunities for sanctions in response to inappropriate behavior. At the same time, the dynamic nature of VO existence and membership and the often-limited engagement of VO participants circumscribe the ability to impose solutions at individual sites (where local VO participants may have only limited authority) and VO-specific administration.

In contrast, **P2P** has been popularized by grass-roots, mass-culture (music) file-sharing and highly parallel computing applications [4, 5] that scale in some instances to hundreds of thousands of nodes. The "communities" that underlie these applications comprise diverse and anonymous individuals with little incentive to act cooperatively. Thus, for example, we find that in file sharing applications, there are few providers and many consumers [2]; the operators of SETI@home [4] devote significant effort to detecting deliberately submitted incorrect results; and people tend to intentionally misreport their resources [46]. Thus, rule enforcing mechanisms as well as incentives for good behavior must be provided by the system (more in Section 3.5).

The need for other participation models based, for example, on payment, contracts, markets, and licensing is recognized in both systems [28, 30, 54] but is not yet standard practice.

3.2   Resources

In general, **Grid** systems integrate resources that are more powerful, more diverse, and better connected than the typical **P2P** resource. A Grid resource might be a cluster, storage system, database, or scientific instrument of considerable value that is administered in an organized fashion according to some well-defined policy. This explicit administration enhances the resource's ability to deliver desired qualities of service and can facilitate, for example, software upgrades, but it can also increase the cost of integrating the resource into a Grid. Diversity in architecture and policy makes the publication of resource properties important [16]. Explicit administration, higher cost of membership, and the stronger community links within scientific VOs mean that resource availability tends to be higher and more uniform. In contrast, P2P systems often deal with intermittent participation and highly variable behavior: for example, in the case of Mojo Nation it is reported [54] that average connection time was only 28% and highly skewed (one sixth of the nodes always connected).

Grids integrate not only "high-end" resources: desktop systems with variable availability [34] form a major component of many contemporary Grids [12]. However, the ensemble of all such resources within a Grid are not treated as an undifferentiated swarm of global scope. Rather, they are aggregated within administrative domains via technologies such as Condor [32, 33] to create local resource pools that are integrated into larger Grids via the same Grid protocols as other computational resources.

Resources in Grids, traditionally from research and educational organizations, tend to be more powerful than home computers that arguably represent the majority of P2P resources (e.g., 71% of SETI@home systems are home computers [4]). The difference in capabilities between home and work computers is illustrated by the average CPU time per work unit in SETI@home: home computers are 30% slower than work computers (13:45 vs. 10:16 hours per work unit).

3.3   Applications

We see considerable variation in the range and scope of scientific **Grid** applications, depending on the interest and scale of the community in question. As three (real, not demonstration) examples, we mention the HotPage portal, providing remote access to supercomputer hardware and software [51]; numerical solution of the long-open "nug30" quadratic optimization problem using hundreds of computers at many sites [7]; and the NEESgrid system that integrate earthquake engineering facilities into a national laboratory [38].

In contrast, **P2P** systems tend to be vertically integrated solutions to specialized resource-sharing problems: currently deployed systems share either compute cycles or files. Diversification comes from differing design goals, such as scalability [41, 44, 50, 55], anonymity [13], or availability [13, 29].

One significant point of differentiation between applications on deployed Grid and P2P systems is that the former tend to be far more data intensive. For example, a recent analysis of Sloan Digital Sky Survey data [6] involved, on average, 660 MB input data per CPU hour; the Compact Muon Solenoid [35] data analysis pipeline involves from 60 MB to 72 GB input data per CPU hour. In contrast, SETI@home moves at least four orders of magnitude less data: a mere 21.25 KB data per CPU hour. The reason is presumably, in part at least, better network connectivity, which also allows for more flexibility in Grid application design: in addition to loosely coupled applications [1, 10, 12], Grids have been used for numerical simulation [3, 43] and branch-and-bound-based optimization problems [7].

3.4   Scale and Failure

We can measure "scale" in terms of at least two different dimensions: number of participating entities and amount of activity. We discussed above the necessity of dealing with failure—seen as intermittent participation in collaboration—as imposed by resource and community characteristics. Dealing effectively and automatically with failure is both a consequence of and a prerequisite for scaling up in both dimensions.

The community orientation of scientific **Grid** communities means that they often involve only modest numbers of participants, whether institutions (tens), pooled computers (thousands), or simultaneous users (hundreds). For example, the high energy physics collaboration that shares and analyzes data from the D0 Experiment [17] spans 73 institutions in 18 countries, with thousands of scientists involved, of which hundreds access its resources (data and computers) simultaneously. The amount of activity, on the other hand, can be large. For example, during the first half of 2002, about 300 D0 users submitted 2.7 million requests and retrieved 824 TB of data. A consequence of these community characteristics is that early Grid implementations did not address scalability and self-management as priorities. Thus, while the design of core Grid protocols (as instantiated within the Globus Toolkit [20]) does not preclude scalability, actual deployments often employ centralized components. For example, we find central repositories for shared data, centralized resource management components (such as the Condor Matchmaker [39]), and centralized (and/or hierarchical) information directories. This situation is changing, with much work proceeding on such topics as reliable and scalable management of large job pools, distributed scheduling [40], replica location [11], and discovery [16]. Overall, though, scalable autonomic management remains a goal, not an accomplishment, for Grid computing.

Far larger **P2P** communities exist: millions of simultaneous nodes in the case of file-sharing systems [31, 47] and several million total nodes in SETI@home. The amount of activity is also significant, albeit, surprisingly, not always larger than in the relatively smaller-scale Grids: 1-2 TB per day in file sharing systems as of end of 2001 [47], amounting to less than half the data transferred in D0. This large scale has emerged from (and later motivated work on) robust self-management of large numbers of nodes. Over time, P2P systems have evolved from first-generation centralized structures (e.g., Napster index, SETI@home) to second-generation flooding-based (e.g., Gnutella file retrieval) and then third-generation systems based on distributed hash tables. First- and second-generation P2P collaborations have been characterized at the level of both individual nodes (behavior, resources [2, 46]) and network properties (topological properties [42], scale [31], traffic [47]), revealing not only general resilience but also unexpected emergent properties. Third-generation systems have been characterized primarily via simulation studies [41, 50] rather than large-scale deployments. Scalable autonomic management clearly has been achieved to a significant extent in P2P, albeit within specific narrow domains.

3.5   Services and Infrastructure

The technologies used to develop Grid and P2P applications differ both in the specific services provided and in the emphasis placed on persistent, multipurpose infrastructure.

Much work has been expended within the **Grid** community on both technical and organizational issues associated with creating and operating persistent, multipurpose infrastructure services for authentication [23], authorization [37, 52], discovery [16], resource access, data movement, and so forth. (Perhaps because of the relatively self-contained nature of early Grid communities, less effort has been devoted to managing participation in the absence of trust, via accounting, reputation management, and so forth, although these issues are increasingly discussed.) We use the term *persistent* to indicate that services are operated by participants over extended periods as critical and often highly available infrastructure elements, like DNS servers; and *multipurpose* to indicate that the same services are used for multiple purposes (e.g., the same monitoring and discovery service [16] is used by a wide range of higher-level functions, such as computation scheduling, data replication, and fault detection). These services operate as overlays on resources and services maintained by participating institutions. Gatewaying from these overlay structures to local mechanisms and policies is a significant concern.

Many Grid communities use the open source Globus Toolkit [20] as a technology base. Significant effort has been channeled toward the standardization of protocols and interfaces to enable interoperability between different Grid deployments. The Open Grid Services Architecture (OGSA) [22] is such an effort: it integrates Grid and Web services technologies to define a service-oriented architecture within which all services adhere to a set of standard interfaces and behaviors (some required, others optional) for such purposes as service creation, registry, discovery, lifecycle, service data query, notification, and reliable invocation.

P2P systems have tended to focus on the integration of simple resources (individual computers) via protocols designed to provide specific vertically integrated functionality. Thus, for example, Gnutella defines its own protocols for search and network maintenance. Such protocols do, of course, define an infrastructure, but in general (at least for second- and third-generation systems) the persistence properties of such infrastructures are not specifically engineered but are rather emergent properties. Over time, experience with these emergent properties has revealed the need for new services, such as anonymity and censorship resistance [48], incentives for fair sharing and reputation management [14], and result checking [45]—important issues that have not tended to arise to date in Grid computing, because of different underlying trust assumptions.

JXTA [27], XtremWeb [18], and BOINC [9] have been proposed as standard service infrastructure for P2P systems but, to date, have seen little adoption and no interoperability. Thus, for example, a user participating in Gnutella, KaZaA, SETI@home, and FightAIDSatHome must run four independent applications, each coded from scratch and running its own protocols over its own overlay networks. This lack of interest in standard infrastructure may perhaps derive from the simple nature of current P2P applications and the fact that a typical user does not encounter a substantial administrative burden even when running multiple applications. As functionality requirements increase, so presumably will the benefits of standard tooling and infrastructure.

While P2P and Grid service requirements overlap in many regards, there are also important distinctions. First, some services are specific to particular regimes: for example, mechanisms that make up for the inherent lack of incentives for cooperation in P2P. Second, functionality requirements can conflict; for example, Grids might require accountability and P2P systems anonymity. Third, common services may start from different hypotheses, as in the case of trust.

4   Future Directions

Grid and P2P are both concerned with the pooling and coordinated use of resources within distributed communities and are constructed as overlay structures that operate largely independently of institutional relationships. Yet despite these commonalities, there are also major differences in communities, incentives, applications, technologies, resources, and achieved scale.

Nevertheless, we argue that the vision that motivates both Grid and P2P computing—that of a worldwide computer within which access to resources and services can be negotiated as and when needed—will come to pass only if we are successful in developing a technology that combines elements of what we today call both P2P and Grid computing. This technology will address *failure* (death) at a fundamental level, using scalable self-configuring protocols such as those emerging from P2P research. It will also provide persistent and multipurpose *infrastructure* (at some cost, justified because amortized over many uses and users), which like DNS and routing tables will be supported in an organized and distributed fashion and will exploit heterogeneity (whether naturally occurring or artificially imposed) in its environment to achieve goals of robustness, performance, and trust. Diverse discovery, negotiation, and maintenance protocols constructed on some common base will be used to deliver a wide spectrum of services and qualities of service.

The Grid and P2P communities are approaching this nirvana from different directions. Over time, the scale of Grid systems is increasing as barriers to participation are lowered and as commercial deployments enable communities based on purely monetary transactions. For example, the International Virtual Data Grid Laboratory [8] is deploying to scores of sites and many thousands of resources both nationally and internationally, and interest is growing in utility computing models [28] that establish sharing relationships based on commercial transactions rather than common interest. Both trends lead to a greater need for scalability, trust negotiation, self-configuration, automatic problem determination, and fault tolerance [11, 16]—areas where P2P has much to offer. OGSA definition work, proceeding within the Global Grid Forum, and an OGSA-based Globus Toolkit 3 are stimulating much work on service definition and implementation.

Meanwhile, developers of P2P systems are becoming increasingly ambitious in their applications and services, as a result of both natural evolution and more powerful and connected resources. We expect that the developers of such systems are going to become increasingly interested in standard infrastructure and tools for service description, discovery, and access, as well in standardized service definitions and implementations able to support different mixes of logical and physical organizations.

This analysis suggests to us that the Grid and P2P communities have more in common than is perhaps generally recognized and that a broader recognition of key commonalities will tend to accelerate progress in both disciplines—which is why we wrote this article.

Acknowledgments

We are grateful to H. Casanova, K. Ranganathan, and M. Ripeanu for comments. This work was supported in part by the National Science Foundation under contract ITR-0086044.

References

[1]   Berkeley Open Infrastructure for Network Computing. http://boinc.berkeley.edu, 2002.

[2]   DZero Experiment. www-d0.fnal.gov.

[3]   JXTA. www.jxta.org.

[4]   Limewire. www.limewire.com.

[5]   Abramson, D., Sosic, R., Giddy, J. and Hall, B., Nimrod: A Tool for Performing Parameterised Simulations Using Distributed   Workstations. *Proc. 4th IEEE Symp. on High Performance Distributed Computing*, 1995.

[6]   Adar, E. and Huberman, B.A. Free Riding on Gnutella. *First Monday*, *5* (10). 2000.

[7]   Allen, G., Dramlitsch, T., Foster, I., Goodale, T., Karonis, N., Ripeanu, M., Seidel, E. and Toonen, B., Supporting Efficient Execution in Heterogeneous Distributed Computing Environments with Cactus and Globus. *SC'2001*, 2001, ACM Press.

[8]   Anderson, D.P., Cobb, J., Korpella, E., Lebofsky, M. and Werthimer, D. SETI@home: An Experiment in Public-Resource Computing. *Communications of the ACM*, *45* (11). 56-61. 2002.

[9]   Anderson, D.P. and Kubiatowicz, J. The Worldwide Computer. *Scientific American* (3). 2002.

[10] 10.Annis, J., Zhao, Y., Voeckler, J., Wilde, M., Kent, S. and Foster, I., Applying Chimera Virtual Data Concepts to Cluster Finding in the Sloan Sky Survey. *SC'2002*, 2002.

[11] Anstreicher, K., Brixius, N., Goux, J.-P. and Linderoth, J.T. Solving Large Quadratic Assignment Problems on Computational Grids. *Mathematical Programming*, *91* (3). 563-588. 2002.

[12] Avery, P., Foster, I., Gardner, R., Newman, H. and Szalay, A. An International Virtual-Data Grid Laboratory for Data Intensive Science, 2001. www.griphyn.org.

[13] Casanova, H., Obertelli, G., Berman, F. and Wolski, R., The AppLeS Parameter Sweep Template: User-Level Middleware for the Grid. *Proc. SC'2000*, 2000.

[14] Chervenak, A., Deelman, E., Foster, I., Guy, L., Hoschek, W., Iamnitchi, A., Kesselman, C., Kunszt, P., Ripeanu, M., Schwartzkopf, B., Stockinger, H., Stockinger, K. and Tierney, B., Giggle: A Framework for Constructing Scalable Replica Location Services. *SC'02*, 2002.

[15] Chien, A., Calder, B., Elbert, S. and Bhatia, K. Entropia: Architecture and Performance of an Enterprise Desktop Grid System. *Journal of Parallel and Distributed Computing, To appear.*

[16] Clarke, I., Sandberg, O., Wiley, B. and Hong, T.W., Freenet: A Distributed Anonymous Information Storage and Retrieval System. *International Workshop on Designing Privacy Enhancing Technologies*, Berkeley, CA, USA, 2000, Springer-Verlag.

[17] Cornelli, F., Damiani, E., Capitani, S.D., Paraboschi, S. and Samarati, P., Choosing reputable servents in a P2P network. *International World Wide Web Conference*, Honolulu, Hawaii, USA, 2002, ACM Press, 376 - 386.

[18] Crowcroft, J. and Pratt, I., Peer to Peer: peering into the future. *IFIP-TC6 Networks 2002 Conference*, Pisa, Italy, 2002, Springer Verlag.

[19] Czajkowski, K., Fitzgerald, S., Foster, I. and Kesselman, C., Grid Information Services for Distributed Resource Sharing. *10th IEEE International Symposium on High Performance Distributed Computing*, 2001, IEEE Press, 181-184.

[20] Fedak, G., Germain, C., Néri, V. and Cappello, F., XtremWeb : A Generic Global Computing System. *Workshop on Global Computing on Personal Devices (CCGRID2001)*, Berlin, Germany, 2001, IEEE Press.

[21] Foster, I. The Grid: A New Infrastructure for 21st Century Science. *Physics Today, 55* (2). 42-47. 2002.

[22] Foster, I. and Kesselman, C. Globus: A Toolkit-Based Grid Architecture. Foster, I. and Kesselman, C. eds. *The Grid: Blueprint for a New Computing Infrastructure*, Morgan Kaufmann, 1999, 259-278.

[23] Foster, I. and Kesselman, C. (eds.). *The Grid: Blueprint for a New Computing Infrastructure*. Morgan Kaufmann, 1999.

[24] Foster, I., Kesselman, C., Nick, J. and Tuecke, S. The Physiology of the Grid: An Open Grid Services Architecture for Distributed Systems Integration, Globus Project, 2002. www.globus.org/research/papers/ogsa.pdf.

[25] Foster, I., Kesselman, C., Tsudik, G. and Tuecke, S. A Security Architecture for Computational Grids. *ACM Conference on Computers and Security*, 1998, 83-91.

[26] Foster, I., Kesselman, C. and Tuecke, S. The Anatomy of the Grid: Enabling Scalable Virtual Organizations. *International Journal of High Performance Computing Applications, 15* (3). 200-222. 2001.

[27] Franklin, B., Letter to Jean-Baptiste Leroy, 1789.

[28] Johnston, W.E., Gannon, D. and Nitzberg, B., Grids as Production Computing Environments: The Engineering Aspects of NASA's Information Power Grid. *8th IEEE Symposium on High Performance Distributed Computing*, 1999, IEEE Press.

[29] Kenyon, C. and Cheliotis, G., Architecture Requirements for Commercializing Grid Resources. *11th IEEE International Symposium on High Performance Distributed Computing*, 2002.

[30] Kubiatowicz, J., Bindel, D., Chen, Y., Czerwinski, S., Eaton, P., Geels, D., Gummadi, R., Rhea, S., Weatherspoon, H., Weimer, W., Wells, C. and Zhao, B., OceanStore: An Architecture for Global-Scale Persistent Storage. *9th Intl. Conf. on Architectural Support for Programming Languages and Operating Systems*, 2000.

[31] Lai, C., Medvinsky, G. and Neuman, B.C. Endorsements, Licensing, and Insurance for Distributed System Services. *Proc. 2nd ACM Conference on Computer and Communication Security*, 1994.

[32] Litzkow, M., Livny, M. and Mutka, M. Condor - A Hunter of Idle Workstations. *Proc. 8th Intl Conf. on Distributed Computing Systems*, 1988, 104-111.

[33] Livny, M. High-Throughput Resource Management. Foster, I. and Kesselman, C. eds. *The Grid: Blueprint for a New Computing Infrastructure*, Morgan Kaufmann, 1999, 311-337.

[34] Mutka, M. and Livny, M. The Available Capacity of a Privately Owned Workstation Environment. *Performance Evaluation, 12* (4). 269--284. 1991.

[35] Negra, M.D. CMS Collaboration, CERN, 1994. http://cmsinfo. cern.ch/Welcome.html.

[36] Oram, A. (ed.), Peer-to-Peer: Harnessing the Power of Disruptive Technologies. O'Reilly, 2001.

[37] Pearlman, L., Welch, V., Foster, I., Kesselman, C. and Tuecke, S., A Community Authorization Service for Group Collaboration. *IEEE 3rd International Workshop on Policies for Distributed Systems and Networks*, 2002.

[38] Prudhomme, T., Kesselman, C., Finholt, T., Foster, I., Parsons, D., Abrams, D., Bardet, J.-P., Pennington, R., Towns, J., Butler, R., Futrelle, J., Zaluzec, N. and Hardin, J. NEESgrid: A Distributed Virtual Laboratory for Advanced Earthquake Experimentation and Simulation: Scoping Study, NEESgrid, 2001. www.neesgrid.org.

[39] Raman, R., Livny, M. and Solomon, M., Matchmaking: Distributed Resource Management for High Throughput Computing. *IEEE International Symposium on High Performance   Distributed Computing*, 1998, IEEE Press.

[40] Ranganathan, K. and Foster, I., Decoupling Computation and Data Scheduling in Distributed Data Intensive Applications. *International Symposium for High Performance Distributed Computing*, Edinburgh, UK, 2002.

[41] Ratnasamy, S., Francis, P., Handley, M., Karp, R. and Shenker, S., A Scalable Content-Addressable Network. *SIGCOMM Conference*, 2001, ACM.

[42] Ripeanu, M., Foster, I. and Iamnitchi, A. Mapping the Gnutella Network: Properties of Large-Scale Peer-to-Peer Systems and Implications for System Design. *Internet Computing, 6* (1). 50-57. 2002.

[43] Ripeanu, M., Iamnitchi, A. and Foster, I. Performance Predictions for a Numerical Relativity Package in Grid Environments. *International Journal of High Performance Computing Applications, 15* (4). 2001.

[44] Rowstron, A.I.T. and Druschel, P., Pastry: Scalable, Decentralized Object Location, and Routing for Large-Scale   Peer-to-Peer Systems. *Middleware,* 2001, 329-350.

[45] Sarmenta, L.F.G. Sabotage-tolerance mechanisms for volunteer computing systems. *Future Generation Computer Systems, 18* (4). 561-572. 2002.

[46] Saroiu, S., Gummadi, P.K. and Gribble, S.D., A Measurement Study of Peer-to-Peer File Sharing Systems. *Proceedings of Multimedia Computing and Networking (MMCN)*, San Jose, CA, USA, 2002.

[47] Sen, S. and Wang, J., Analyzing Peer-to-Peer Traffic Across Large Networks. *Internet Measurement Workshop*, Marseille, France, 2002.

[48] Serjantov, A., Anonymizing Censorship Resistant Systems. *1st International Workshop on Peer-to-Peer Systems (IPTPS'02)*. Cambridge, MA, 2002, Springer Verlag.

[49] Shirky, C. What Is P2P... and What Isn't? www.openp2p.com/pub/a/p2p/2000/11/24/shirky1-whatisp2p.html, 2000.

[50] Stoica, I., Morris, R., Karger, D., Kaashoek, F. and Balakrishnan, H., Chord: A Scalable Peer-to-Peer Lookup Service for Internet Applications. *SIGCOMM Conference*, San Diego, CA, USA, 2001, ACM Press.

[51] Thomas, M.P., Mock, S. and J., B., Development of Web Toolkits for Computational Science Portals: The NPACI HotPage. *Ninth IEEE International Symposium on High Performance Distributed Computing*, 2000.

[52] Thompson, M., Johnston, W., Mudumbai, S., Hoo, G., Jackson, K. and Essiari, A., Certificate-based Access Control for Widely Distributed Resources. *8th Usenix Security Symposium*, 1999.

[53] Touch, J. Overlay networks. *Computer Networks, 3* (2-3). 115-116. 2001.

[54] Wilcox-O'Hearn, B., Experiences Deploying A Large-Scale Emergent Network. *1st International Workshop on Peer-to-Peer Systems   (IPTPS'02)*, Cambridge, MA, 2002, Springer-Verlag.

[55] Zhao, B.Y., Kubiatowicz, J.D. and Joseph, A.D. Tapestry: An infrastructure for fault-tolerant wide-area location and routing, UC Berkeley, 2001.

Scooped, Again

Jonathan Ledlie[1], Jeff Shneidman[1], Margo Seltzer[1], and John Huth[2]

[1] Division of Engineering and Applied Sciences
{jonathan,jeffsh,margo}@eecs.harvard.edu
[2] Department of Physics, Harvard University, Cambridge, MA 02138, USA
huth@physics.harvard.edu

Abstract. The Peer-to-Peer (p2p) and Grid infrastructure communities
are tackling an overlapping set of problems. In addressing these problems,
p2p solutions are usually motivated by elegance or research interest. Grid
researchers, under pressure from thousands of scientists with real file
sharing and computational needs, are pooling their solutions from a wide
range of sources in an attempt to meet user demand. Driven by this need
to solve large scientific problems quickly, the Grid is being constructed
with the tools at hand: FTP or RPC for data transfer, centralization for
scheduling and authentication, and an assumption of correct, obediant
nodes. If history is any guide, the World Wide Web depicts viscerally
that systems that address user needs can have enormous staying power
and affect future research. The Grid infrastructure is a great customer
waiting for future p2p products. By no means should we make them
our *only* customers, but we should at least put them on the list. If p2p
research does not at least address the Grid, it may eventually be sidelined
by defacto distributed algorithms that are less elegant but were used to
solve Grid problems. In essense, we'll have been scooped, again.

1 Introduction

Butler Lampson, in his SOSP '99 Invited Talk, stated that the greatest failure
of the systems research community over the past ten years was that "we did not
invent the Web" [39]. The systems research community laid the groundwork,
but did not follow through. The same situation exists today with the overlapping efforts of the Grid and p2p communities. The former is building and using
a global resource sharing system, while the latter is repeating their mistake of
the past by focusing on elegant solutions without regard to a vast potential user
community.

In 1989, Tim Berner-Lee's need to communicate his own work and the work
of other physicists at CERN led him to develop HTML, HTTP, and a simple
browser [4].

While HTTP and HTML are simple, they have exhibited serious network
and language-based deficiencies as the Web has grown examined and patched to
some extent, but this simple inelegant solution remains at the core of the Web.

A parallel situation exists today with the p2p and Grid communities. A large
group of users (scientists) are pushing for immediately useable tools to pool large

F. Kaashoek and I. Stoica (Eds.): IPTPS 2003, LNCS 2735, pp. 129–138, 2003.

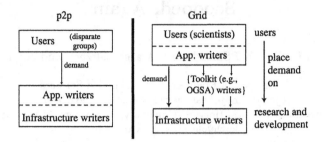

Fig. 1. In serving their well-defined user base, the Grid community has needed to draw from both its ancestry of supercomputing and from Systems research (including p2p and distributed computing). P2p has essentially invented its user base through its technology

sets of resources. The Grid is currently building these tools. The Systems community is in danger of falling victim to the contemporary version of Lampson's admonishment if we do not participate in this process.

The Grid is an active area of research and development. The number of academic grids has jumped six-fold in the last year [43]. As Figure 1 depicts, the "customer base" of scientists, who are often also application writers, drive Grid developers to produce tangible solutions, even when the solutions are not ideal, from a computer systems perspective. Most current p2p users are people sharing files; sometimes these people are pursuing noble causes like anonymous document distribution, but more often they are simply trying to circumvent copyright, and rarely are they interacting with the systems' developers. P2p does not have the driving force that interactive users provide and therefore has focused on solutions that are interesting primarily from a research perspective.

The difficulty with this parallel development is not that it is wasteful, but that, without the p2p community's input, the Grid will most likely be built in a way incompatible and non-inclusive of many of p2p's strong points: search and storage scalability, decentralization, anonymity and pseudonymity, and denial of service prevention.

In the rest of this paper, we first discuss the charters of the two different communities. We introduce three fallacies that may have kept the communities separate. We then describe common problems being attacked by the two communities and compare solutions from each camp, and discuss problems that seem to be truly disjoint. We conclude with a call to action for the p2p community to examine the Grid needs and consider future research problems in that context.

2   Grids

2.1   What Is the Grid?

Buyya defines the Grid as "a type of parallel and distributed system that enables the sharing, selection, and aggregation of resources distributed across multiple administrative domains based on their (resources) availability, capability, performance, cost, and users' quality-of-service requirements" [8]. The Grid is "distinguished from conventional distributed computing by its focus on large-scale resource sharing, innovative applications, and in some cases, high performance orientation" [27].

2.2   Goals of the Grid

The Grid aims to be self-configuing, self-tuning, and self-healing, similar to the goals in autonomic computing [2]. It aims to fulfill the vision of Corbato's Multics [13]: like a utility company, a massive resource to which a user gives his or her computational or storage needs. The Grid's goal is to utilize the shared storage and cycles from the middle *and* edges of the Internet.

2.3   Manifestations

Grids historically arose out of a need to perform massive computation. A manifestation of shared computation, Condor accepts compiled jobs, schedules and runs them on remote idle machines [42]. Exemplifying its focus on computation, it issues RPCs back to the job originator's machine for data. An example of computational middleware is Globus [23]; it "meta-schedules" jobs among Grids like Condor and ships host data between them using GridFTP, an FTP wrapper. Manifestations of Data Grids include the European Data Grid project [20].

The Grid community is currently authoring a Web Services-oriented API called Open Grid Services Architecture (OGSA) [24, 25]. The next generation of Globus is intended to be a reference implentation of this API.

3   P2P

3.1   What Is P2P?

Unintentionally, Shirky describes p2p much like a Grid: "Peer-to-peer is a class of applications that take advantage of resources — storage, cycles, content, human presence — available at the edges of the Internet" [19]. Stoica *et al.* offer a more restrictive definition focusing on decentralized and non-hierarchical node organization [54].

P2p's focus on decentralization, instability, and fault tolerance exemplify areas that essentially have been omitted from emerging Grid standards, but will become more significant as the system grows.

3.2   Goals of P2P

The goal of p2p is to take advantage of the idle cycles and storage of the edge of the Internet, effectively utilizing its "dark matter" [19]. This overarching goal introduces issues including decentralization, anonymity and pseudonymity, redundant storage, search, locality, and authentication.

3.3 Manifestations

O'Reilly's p2p site [46] divides p2p systems into nineteen categories, primarily offering file sharing (*e.g.*, Gnutella [28], KaZaA [36]), distributed computation (*e.g.*, distributed.net [17]), and anonymity (*e.g.*, Freenet [12], Publius [44]). Seti@home is another p2p application, although the Grid community considers it one of theirs as well [51].

Prominant research instances of p2p include Chord, Pastry, and Tapestry [48, 53, 56]. File systems built on these include CFS, PAST, and Oceanstore [14, 18, 37]. File systems, however, are not applications and, while a variety of forms of storage have been built, there exists no driving application in this space.

4   Three Falacies that Have Kept the Communities Separate

This paper argues that the p2p and Grid communities are "natural" partners in research. The following are some objections and responses to this claim.

4.1 "The Technical Problems in Grid Systems Are Different from those in P2P Systems."

Conventional wisdom posits "the Grid is for computational problems" and "p2p is about file sharing." Historically, Grids have grown out of the computationally-bound supercomputers and local batch computation systems like Condor. As these localized systems have become linked to one another in the Grid, handling data has become a much larger problem. Some Grid-connected instruments (*e.g.*, specialized telescopes) focus purely on data production for others to use. Similarly, p2p is moving in the computation direction with efforts in desktop collaboration [31] and network computation [5].

Formally stated "open problems" papers from each camp exhibit a striking similarity in their focus on formation, utilization, security, and maintenance [16, 45, 49]. Conference proceedings echo this trend. Section 5 summarizes areas of active overlap.

4.2 "While the Technical Problems Are Similar, the Architectures (Physical Topology, Bandwidth Availibility and Use, Trust Model, etc.) Demand that the Specific Solutions Be Fundamentally Different."

Researchers familiar with both areas claim that the two will blend as they mature, even perhaps to the point of a merging of the two research communities[6, 22, 50]. Regardless of the veracity of this forecast, it indicates that researchers see good ideas in each community that can solve common problems.

This fallacy is application dependent. Some applications (*e.g.*, military missile calculation or totally anonymous file sharing) impose special requirements for assorted (not always technical) reasons. But even in these situations, a general awareness of technical approaches taken by the other community may help solve "physically private" problems.

4.3 "Grid Projects Do Not Have the Flexibility to Try New Algorithms/Ideas because They Have to Get Real Work Done. P2P Research Is All about this Flexibility."

P2p research is very flexible: one version can obsolete the previous and new algorithms can be developed without conforming to any standard. Within the emerging Grid standards, however, there is room for flexible research too.

Grid researchers recognize the need for test-beds as staging grounds for new applications and protocols [52]. Traditional Grid settings have been in university settings where support staff is on hand to test and deploy new software updates [34]. Moreover, as evidenced by the many toolkits and custom Grid implementations [23, 30], Grid users are willing to adopt different technologies to get their work done.

It seems natural for p2p researchers to develop algorithms either independently or within Grid test-beds, and then "publish" their prototypes within a Grid setting. For example, Systems researchers could build to a particular aspect of the OGSA, benchmark their solution to this API, and then release it as a fresh, improved implementation.

5   Shared Technical Problems

We list and compare the two communities' approaches to problems in four categories and conclude this section with problems that are not shared.

5.1   Formation

Topology formation and peer discovery deals with the problem of how nodes join a system and learn about their neighbors, often in an overlay network [38]. Membership protocols have been explored in both settings [34, 40]. While espousing the autonomous ideal, much Grid infrastructure is hardcoded and could benefit from the active formation found in p2p research prototypes.

5.2   Utilization

Resource discovery determines how we find "interesting items," which can include sets of files, computers, services (compute/storage services), or devices (such as printers or telescopes). Data is also searched within files [16] and across relational tuples [32]. Search requirements exhibit tradeoffs in expressiveness, robustness, efficiency, and autonomy. For some, but not all applications, the ubiquitous hash-based lookup schemes of the p2p world are appropriate.

Resource management and optimization problems deal with how "best" to utilize resources in a network. This category includes data placement, computation, fairness, and communication usage decisions such as, "Where/How do we distribute data/metadata?", "Who performs a certain computation?", "Which links do we use to transmit/receive information?", and "How can I speed up access to popular files?" Both communities have examined data replication and caching algorithms to increase performance [3, 12].

Scheduling and handling of contention has been examined in both communities. P2p has focused on bandwidth usage (*e.g.*, Gnutella's maximum connections) with solutions that are often resolved with dynamic programming at the node level. Grids are often centered around scheduling and use traditional scheduling techniques involving cost functions implemented by a central scheduler and often lack QoS or fairness guarentees [7]. Agoric solutions in Grids have been centralized thus far; distributed economic scheduling mechanisms may be more appropriate for fault tolerance reasons [55].

Load balancing/splitting schemes in both communities attempt to reduce the load of a particular file, link, or computation by breaking larger blobs into many smaller distributed atoms.

Popular p2p file sharing programs are trivial to join, use, and leave, with get, put, and delete as their primative operations. Grid users (scientists) cannot use some simple p2p solutions, mainly because what they are trying to do (*e.g.*, distributed code instrumentation) is complex. The lack of tools for application developers (and the complexity of the existing tools) is also a major stumbling block [49].

5.3   Coping with Failure

Partial and arbitrary failure must be addressed in any realistic distributed network. Most p2p systems punt on guarenteeing accessibility by accepting lossy storage in their model [12, 28]. If the ideas from p2p storage are going to be successfully applied to the Grid, p2p researchers need to consider revising the common loss model. They also should consider the order-of-magnitude of storage some Grid experiments will produce: some are expected to produce on the order of half a petabyte per month [47], about the current capacity of KaZaA. This data, however, cannot be lossy.

Traditional distributed systems techniques for dealing with failure often make assumptions on connectivity and complexity that may not be appropriate for traditional p2p systems or Grid systems, as both Daswani *et al.* [16] and Schopf *et al.* [49] note in their respective open problems papers. The same replication algorithms used to increase availability can also serve to ensure correctness in the face of data, computation, or communication failures.

Security-related research in the two communities includes authenticity issues (such as verification of data or computation, or handling man-in-the-middle style attacks), availibility issues (surviving denial of service attacks), and authorization issues (such as access control), but research from p2p would help address some DoS problems introduced by the Grid's frequent reliance on centralized structures [1, 9]. Chang *et al.* examine enforcing safety with certifying compilers in a Grid environment [10].

These aspects have been identified and explored in the context of data sharing p2p systems [16]. Computational p2p systems have similar problems: more than fifty percent of the Seti@Home's project resources were at one time spent dealing with security problems, including the problem of "cheating" on the distributed computation [35].

The Grid community faces the same security problems [49]. The work on the Grid Security Infrastructure [26] addresses the problem of authentication, but inter-testbed authentication remains to be resolved [33]. Focus on decentralized authentication schemes like SPKI may be a step in the right direction [11].

5.4   Maintenance

In the areas of deployment and managability, p2p has essentially no standards or APIs; with the possible exception of Gnutella, each version obsoletes the previous one. Many Grid papers profess the need for a standardized programming interface [49], and by necessary, the Grid is being forced to standardize and the OGSA is beginning to help. Similar efforts in p2p standardization are the Berkeley BOINC [5], Google Compute [29], and overly standardization [15].

5.5   Disjoint Problems

Not every problem in "pure" p2p research has an analog in the Grid community. Anononymity (often grouped with security issues) for instance, may not be so useful, but a middleground of pseudonymity may exist. Anonymizing systems are important and offer a prime example of a consideration left out of the emerging Grid standards: for example, they are currently being used to promote free speech in China [41].

6   Call to Action

How do we avoid being scooped again? Given the large degree of commonality between the two worlds, "coming up to speed" on the Grid is not a difficult undertaking. As a community and individuals, we must familiarize ourselves with the set of problems the Grid is addressing, so we can identify the areas where we have solutions or are actively working on solutions. We must also work to understand Grid users' day to day needs; how robust must a solution be in order to be appropriate for deployment on a Grid? We should understand the standards they are developing and to which they expect all systems to comply (OSGA). We can make a significant contribution helping them create a standard that allows the evolution and experimentation that "outside" researchers can provide. Perhaps the answer lies in a directive as simple as: "Find a user and figure out what that user needs."

References

[1] A. Adya, W. Bolosky, M. Castro, G. Cermak, R. Chaiken, J. Douceur, J. Howell, J. Lorch, M. Theimer, and R. Wattenhofer. FARSITE: Federated, available, and reliable storage for an incompletely trusted environment. In *OSDI '02*, Boston, MA, 2002.

[2] Autonomic computing. http://www.research.ibm.com/autonomic/.

[3] William H. Bell, David G. Cameron, Luigi Capozza, A. Paul Millar, Kurt Stocklinger, and Floriano Zini. Simulation of dynamic grid replication strategies in optorsim. In *Grid 2002*, November 2002.

[4] Tim Berners-Lee and R. Cailliau. WorldWideWeb: Proposal for a HyperText project, 1990.

[5] Berkeley BOINC. http://boinc.berkeley.edu.

[6] Scott Bradner. The rest of peer-to-peer. *Network World Fusion*, October 2002.

[7] R. Buyya, H. Stockinger, J. Giddy, and D. Abramson. Economic models for management of resources in peer-to-peer and grid computing. In *ITCom 2001*, August 2001.

[8] Rajkumar Buyya. Grid computing info centre. http://www.gridcomputing.com, 2002.

[9] M. Castro, P. Drushel, A. Ganesh, A. Rowstron, and D. Wallach. Secure routing for structured peer-to-peer overlay networks. In *OSDI '02*, Boston, MA, 2002.

[10] Bor-Yuh Evan Chang, Karl Crary, Margaret DeLap, Robert Harper, Jason Liszka, Tom Murphy VII, and Frank Pfenning. Trustless Grid Computing in ConCert. In *Grid Computing - GRID 2002, Third International Workshop*, November 2002.

[11] Dwaine Clarke, Jean-Emile Elien, Carl Ellison, Matt Fredette, Alexander Morcos, and Ronald L. Rivest. Certificate chain discovery in SPKI/SDSI. *Journal of Computer Security*, January 2001.

[12] Ian Clarke, Oskar Sandberg, Brandon Wiley, and Theodore Hong. Freenet: A distributed anonymous information storage and retrieval system. http://freenetproject.org/cgi-bin/twiki/view/Main/ICSI, 2001.

[13] F. J. Corbato and V. A. Vyssotsky. Introduction and overview of the multics system. In *Proceedings of AFIPS FJCC*, 1965.

[14] Frank Dabek, M. Frans Kaashoek, David Karger, Robert Morris, and Ion Stoica. Wide-area cooperative storage with CFS. In *SOSP '01*, October 2001.

[15] Frank Dabek, Ben Zhao, Peter Druschel, and Ion Stoica. Towards a common API for structured peer-to-peer overlays. In *IPTPS '03*, Berkeley, CA, February 2003.

[16] Neil Daswani, Hector Garcia-Molina, and Berverly Yang. Open problems in data-sharing peer-to-peer systems. In *9th International Conference on Database Theory*, January 2003.

[17] Distributed.net. http://distributed.net.

[18] Peter Druschel and Antony Rowstron. PAST: A large-scale, persistent peer-to-peer storage utility. In *SOSP '01*, October 2001.

[19] Andy Oram (ed.). Gnutella. In *Peer-to-Peer: Harnessing the power of disruptive technologies*. O'Reilly & Associates, 2001.

[20] European union data grid project. http://eu-datagrid.web.cern.ch/eu-datagrid/, 2001.

[21] Roy Fielding. Representational state transfer: An architectural style for distributted hypermedia interactive (research talk), 1998.

[22] John Fontana. P2p getting down to some serious work. *Network World Fusion*, August 2002.

[23] I. Foster and C. Kesselman. Globus: A metacomputing infrastructure toolkit. *International Journal of Supercomputer Applications and High Performance Computing*, Summer 1997.

[24] I. Foster, C. Kesselman, J. Nick, and S. Tuecke. The physiology of the grid: An open grid services architecture for distributed systems integration. http://www.globus.org/research/papers/ogsa.pdf, 2002.

[25] I. Foster, C. Kesselman, J.M. Nick, and S. Tuecke. Grid services for distributed systems integration. *IEEE Computer*, 35(6), 2002.

[26] I. Foster, C. Kesselman, G. Tsudik, and S. Tuecke. A security architecture for computational grids. In *ACM Conference on Computers and Security*, November 1998.

[27] I. Foster, C. Kesselman, and S. Tuecke. The anatomy of the grid. *The International Journal of Supercomputer Applications*, 15(3), Fall 2001.

[28] Gnutella. Gnutella protocol specification v0.4. http://www.clip2.com/GnutellaProtocol04.pdf, 2001.

[29] Google compute. http://toolbar.google.com/dc/.

[30] Andrew S. Grimshaw and William A. Wulf. The legion vision of a worldwide virtual computer. *Communications of the ACM*, January 1997.

[31] Groove networks desktop collaboration software. http://www.groove.net/, 2002.

[32] M. Harren, J. Hellerstein, R. Huebsch, B. Loo, S. Shenker, and I. Stoica. Complex queries in DHT-based peer-to-peer networks. In *IPTPS '02*, March 2002.

[33] M. Humphrey and M. Thompson. Security implications of typical grid computing usage scenarios. In *HPDC 10*, August 2001.

[34] Adriana Iamnitchi and Ian Foster. On fully decentralized resource discovery in grid environments. In *International Workshop on Grid Computing*. IEEE, November 2001.

[35] Leander Kahney. Cheaters bow to peer pressure. http://www.wired.com/news/technology/0,1282,41838,00.html, 2001.

[36] KaZaA. http://www.kazaa.com.

[37] John Kubiatowicz, David Bindel, Yan Chen, Patrick Eaton, Dennis Geels, Ramakrishna Gummadi, Sean Rhea, Hakim Weatherspoon, Westly Weimer, Christopher Wells, and Ben Zhao. Oceanstore: An architecture for global-scale persistent storage. In *ASPLOS-IX*, November 2000.

[38] Shay Kutten and David Peleg. Deterministic distributed resource discovery. In *PODC 2002*, July 2000.

[39] Butler Lampson. Computer systems research: Past and future (invited talk). In *SOSP '99*, December 1999.

[40] Jonathan Ledlie, Jacob Taylor, Laura Serban, and Margo Seltzer. Self-organization in peer-to-peer systems. In *10th EW SIGOPS*, September 2002.

[41] Jennifer 8. Lee. Guerrilla warfare, waged with code. *New York Times*, October 2002.

[42] Michael Litzkow, Miron Livny, and Matt Mutka. Condor - a hunter of idle workstations. In *Proceedings of the 8th International Conference of Distributed Computing Systems*, June 1988.

[43] Om Malik. Ian foster = grid computing. *Grid Today*, October 2002.

[44] Aviel D. Rubin Marc Waldman and Lorrie Faith Cranor. Publius: A robust, tamper-evident, censorship-resistant, web publishing system. In *9th USENIX Security Symposium*, August 2000.

[45] Andy Oram. Research possibilities in peer-to-peer networking. http://www.openp2p.com/lpt/a/1312, 2001.

[46] O'Reilly p2p directory. http://www.openp2p.com/pub/q/p2p_category, 2002.

[47] Petascale virtual-data grids. http://www.griphyn.org/projinfo/intro/petascale.php.

[48] Antony Rowstron and Peter Druschel. Pastry: Scalable, decentralized object location, and routing for large-scale peer-to-peer systems. In *Middleware*, November 2001.

[49] Jennifer Schopf. Grids: The top ten questions. *Scientific Programming*, 10(2), 2002.

[50] Second IEEE international conference on peer-to-peer computing: Use of computers at the edge of networks (p2p, grid, clusters). www.ida.liu.su/conferences/p2p/p2p2002, September 2002.

[51] Seti@home. http://setiathome.ssl.berkeley.edu.

[52] H. J. Song, X. Liu, D. Jakobsen, R. Bhagwan, X. Zhang, Kenjiro Taura, and Andrew A. Chien. The microgrid: a scientific tool for modeling computational grids. In *Supercomputing*, 2000.

[53] Ion Stoica, Robert Morris, David Karger, M. Frans Kaashoek, and Hari Balakrishnan. Chord: A scalable peer-to-peer lookup service for internet applications. In *Proceedings of the ACM SIGCOMM '01 Conference*, August 2001.

[54] Ion Stoica, Robert Morris, David Liben-Nowell, David Karger, M. Frans Kaashoek, Frank Dabek, and Hari Balakrishnan. Chord: A scalable peer-to-peer lookup service for internet applications. Research report, MIT, January 2002.

[55] Michael Stonebraker, Paul M. Aoki, Robert Devine, Witold Litwin, and Michael A. Olson. Mariposa: A new architecture for distributed data. In *ICDE*, February 1994.

[56] B. Zhao, J. Kubiatowicz, and A. Joseph. Tapestry: An infrastructure for fault-tolerant wide-area location and routing. Research Report UCB/CSD-01-1141, U. C. Berkeley, April 2001.

Rationality and Self-Interest
in Peer to Peer Networks

Jeffrey Shneidman and David C. Parkes

Harvard University, Division of Engineering and Applied Sciences
{jeffsh,parkes}@eecs.harvard.edu

Abstract. Much of the existing work in peer to peer networking assumes that users will follow prescribed protocols without deviation. This assumption ignores the user's ability to modify the behavior of an algorithm for self-interested reasons. We advocate a different model in which peer to peer users are expected to be rational and self-interested. This model is found in the emergent fields of Algorithmic Mechanism Design (AMD) and Distributed Algorithmic Mechanism Design (DAMD), both of which introduce game-theoretic ideas into a computational system. We, as designers, must create systems (peer to peer search, routing, distributed auctions, resource allocation, etc.) that allow nodes to behave rationally while still achieving good overall system outcomes. This paper has three goals. The first is to convince the reader that rationality is a real issue in peer to peer networks. The second is to introduce mechanism design as a tool that can be used when designing networks with rational nodes. The third is to describe three open problems that are relevant in the peer to peer setting but are unsolved in existing AMD/DAMD work. In particular, we consider problems that arise when a networking infrastructure contains *rational* agents.

1   Introduction

Imagine running an auction over a large peer to peer network. You are the auctioneer and have three directly connected neighbors. You send out an announcement advertising the auction and ask that it be globally propagated. You then sit back, expecting many bids, and are surprised when you only receive three bids – one from each neighbor. What happened? Your three neighbors understood that it was in their best interest not to forward the initial announcement. Assuming each of your neighbors wanted to win the auction, it made sense for them to limit the possible competition.

This trivial example (which shall be used for the remainder of the paper) captures the problem of rationality in peer to peer networks. Perhaps the key defining characteristic of a peer to peer network is that one cannot distinguish between strategic nodes and the network infrastructure. Nodes, representing rational users, sometimes will deviate from a suggested protocol in order to better their own outcome. This paper considers notions of rationality and self-interest in the context of peer to peer networks. Section 2 explores evidence

F. Kaashoek and I. Stoica (Eds.): IPTPS 2003, LNCS 2735, pp. 139–148, 2003.

for the existence of rationality in peer to peer networks and discusses common approaches for dealing with this strategic node behavior. Section 3 reviews some of the requisite mechanism design tools and terminology. Section 4 introduces different node types (the strategic agents) to motivate why mechanism design is applicable to the peer to peer setting. Section 5 describes open problems in DAMD that are particularly relevant to peer to peer settings. Section 6 reviews related work and finally in Section 7, we conclude with our future work in this area.

2   Rationality in Peer to Peer Systems

In the auction example given above, we can speculate that all three bidders had positive utility for winning the auction. *Utility* is a numeric value that agents assign to a particular outcome based on their preference for that outcome. The game-theoretic approach of mechanism design assumes that a *rational* node plays a *strategy* to maximize its own expected utility. A node's equilibrium strategy depends on the information that it has about the preferences and behavior of other nodes, and in some cases may require some effort to calculate.

It is not hard to find evidence of rational behavior in existing peer to peer networks. There is interesting work documenting the "free rider" problem [1] and the "tragedy of the commons" [9] in a data centric peer to peer setting. In this situation, rational users free ride and consume a resource but do not produce at the same level of their consumption.

An additional example can be found in the context of peer to peer search: consider the rational users in simple file sharing networks who refuse to relay other node queries to conserve their own bandwidth. The Kazaa peer to peer file sharing network client supports a similar behavior, allowing powerful nodes to opt-out of network support roles that consume CPU and bandwidth [16]. Our auction example is another case where self-interested message passing and computation presents a challenge.

Although it has not been labeled as such, rational behavior has occurred in computational peer to peer settings as well. One perverse example occurred when users of Seti@Home (a peer to peer computation project) modified their client software to make it appear as if they were doing more work than was actually occurring. These users placed a high utility on their ranking in a leader board that recorded the "computation units contributed" for the Seti@Home project. The scoring system did not prevent these rational players from increasing their utility by modifying the behavior of their software [12].

What should be the response to the problems created by user rationality in peer to peer systems? One common approach has been to ignore rationality problems and hope for the best. Rational users can free ride on systems, create software designed to subvert mechanisms, and generally place themselves into selfishly advantageous situations. This sounds bad, and this paper argues that it is bad, but one should not ignore the fact that this is how many peer to peer systems work. One reason why these systems may work is that there can be enough obedient users following a given protocol, even when it might be rational not to do so. For instance, they might download an obedient client program instead of writing or acquiring a more expressive client. Alternatively, existing systems may work because there are enough "rational" users that maximize their expected utility by the enjoyment of providing a common good. This altruistic behavior is outside of typical game-theoretic models.

Another approach is to limit the effect that a rational user can have on the execution of a system. In peer to peer networks, a node can be required to run some part of a distributed mechanism. If one assumes that users cannot modify the execution of the mechanism (but can only strategize about their inputs), then the rationality problem is much easier. With this assumption, for instance, one would not need to worry about nodes refusing to pass messages in this paper's initial auction example. This is what Perrig et al. [20] can achieve with the help of specially trusted auction hardware.

Another approach comes from failure handling in distributed algorithms, where running nodes are classified into two basic types: correct and faulty. One goal of a distributed algorithm is to identify and ignore faulty behavior. In this model, a rational node that deviates from a protocol is considered faulty. However, ignoring rational nodes is not practical in systems like Gnutella, where in one study 70% of nodes seemed to free ride, thereby acting rationally [1]. It seems suboptimal to use traditional distributed systems techniques that detect and ignore faulty nodes. Doing so creates other problems as well such as network vulnerability, an idea explored in Adar & Huberman [1].

None of these approaches seems optimal, and this leads one naturally to consider designing networks with self-interest in mind. Mechanism design can help here by incentivizing rational nodes to perform as a network designer might intend.

3   A Brief Introduction to Mechanism Design

This section gives a brief introduction to economic mechanism design. Classical mechanism design concepts are covered in more detail in introductory and more advanced game theory textbooks [5, 8].

The idea in mechanism design (MD) is to define the strategic situation, or "rules of the game", so that the system as a whole exhibits good behavior in equilibrium when self-interested nodes pursue self-interested strategies. Formally, a *mechanism* is a specification of possible player strategies and a mapping from the set of played strategies to outcomes. This paper's initial auction example is a mechanism implementation in action: players choose their bids and the auctioneer computes the outcome according to the rules of the mechanism. Mechanism design can be thought of as *inverse* game theory – where game theory reasons about how agents will play a game, MD reasons about how to design games that produce desired outcomes. For instance, in the auction problem, we seek a mechanism that will provide incentives that result in neighbors forwarding the bids and bid announcements, and in nodes implementing the appropriate auction rules.

MD assumes that the players feed their calculated strategies to a special obedient *center* that performs the mechanism calculation and declares the outcome. However, one problem with traditional MD is that many mechanisms are computationally infeasible. For instance, it can be hard for a player to calculate a best strategy. It can be even more difficult for a mechanism implementation to calculate the outcome.

An emerging field, borne out of the theoretical computer science and artificial intelligence communities, deals with *tractable* mechanism design. Algorithmic Mechanism Design (AMD) addresses the computational complexity of the mechanism infrastructure and attempts to construct mechanisms that produce desired outcomes while retaining computational feasibility [17]. Research in mechanism design has also focused on the design of mechanisms that reduce the computational complexity of agent participation (e.g. [19]).

Distributed Algorithmic Mechanism Design (DAMD) is an even newer construction [7]. Whereas AMD is concerned with a centralized implementation, DAMD assumes that a mechanism is carried out via a distributed computation. This more accurately models situations like the Internet and peer to peer networks, where agents and resources are distributed.

In these settings, using obedient centers might not be feasible for a number of reasons, including issues of trust, privacy, and complexity:

- For instance, a node offering to perform a mechanism computation might have a vested interest in the outcome and silently change the result. Distributing a mechanism over many nodes with vested interest is more realistic in real-world networks when the presence of obedient nodes cannot be guaranteed. If the presence of *some* obedient nodes can be assumed, or when tools outside of mechanism design like cryptography or redundancy [2, 22] are available, distributing a mechanism may allow a robustness to cheating that is not possible in a centralized mechanism.
- Furthermore, because of network topology, a node running in a network with a centralized mechanism may have to reveal its strategy to the center via other competing nodes. For instance, a point to point transmission between a node and the center may actually occur via many hops over strategizing nodes. In distributed mechanisms, this problem is made explicit. One way of addressing this problem is to make truthful revelation be an equilibrium strategy (e.g. [6]).
- Finally, a centralized mechanism implementation might be NP-hard. Distributed mechanisms can sometimes achieve better complexity results than centralized mechanisms, and may even be piggybacked on existing network protocols [6].

In all forms of mechanism design, the mechanism designer is aiming to create a *good mechanism*. Mechanisms can be good in different ways: they can be efficient, strategy proof, incentive compatible, budget balanced, etc. (For space considerations, we hope to pique your interest but defer to other good sources [19] for a complete discussion of these properties.) A famous example of a good mechanism (with a center) that you may have used is the second-price sealed-bid auction.[1]

A well designed mechanism will incentivize rational nodes into behaving according to a designer's wishes. A poorly designed mechanism will fail to exact the expected behavior; this paper's auction scenario is a trivial example.

A more subtle problem can occur if the mechanism designer does not build mechanisms with strategies that are simple to compute. For instance, it is reasonable to suppose that different nodes have different computational capabilities in a peer to peer network. If a node is constrained by computational or communication limits, it may fail to pick a strategy that maximizes its expected utility. In game theory, this node is known as a *bounded-rational* player.

Finally, mechanisms can be modeled as one-shot or repeated, and behavior that may not seem rational in the short term (a starving graduate student slaving over a paper submission, when sleep would yield a higher utility) is (hopefully) rational in the long term.

4   Node Types in Peer to Peer Systems

Mechanism design should be viewed as a tool in the network designer's repertoire to help deal with rational nodes. When additional node types are present, additional tools are needed. Distributing the mechanism implementation creates additional challenges [7] that need to be addressed with outside techniques like redundancy or cryptography.

Feigenbaum & Shenker give an enumeration of node types in a network based on node intention [7]. Our listing differs slightly in order to stress how the actual mechanism affects the behavior of strategizing nodes, and to explore techniques for dealing with these strategizing node types.

First, we should mention two classes of non-strategizing node types described in the distributed systems literature:

Correct/Obedient nodes correctly follow a given protocol.

---

[1] If you have used Yahoo! Auctions or Ebay, you have seen this flavor of mechanism at work. For instance, if the current bid for an Enron Ethics Manual [11] is 10, and you tell the auctioneer you are willing to pay 15, your bid will be recorded as 11 (assuming a minimum bid increment of 1). If only one other bid for 13 is received before the auction closes, you win the auction and pay 14 (the second highest price + the minimum bid increment.) The second price sealed-bid auction (for which William Vickrey won the 1996 Economics Nobel Prize) has the nice property that the best (dominant) strategy a bidder can choose is to declare truthfully his/her value for owning the item. This mechanism also happens to be efficient, individual rational, and weakly budget balanced, further nice properties that make Vickrey auctions at least theoretically popular. See Sandholm [21] for a concise overview of various auction types and a discussion of why the interesting Vickrey auction is not used very often in real life.

Faulty nodes have been classified according to their side effects and severity. Elements in this classification set include failstop (a node stops working), send/receive omission (a node drops messages), and Byzantine failure (a node can act arbitrarily) [13].

Economic mechanisms do not affect either correct or faulty nodes, since these node types do not strategize. Correct nodes need no special handling. Typical techniques for dealing with faulty nodes include using redundancy and cryptographic signing to detect and ignore broken nodes [13]. Second, we define two classes of nodes that can strategize about their behavior:

Rational nodes aim to maximize their expected utility from participation, given their beliefs about their environment, including the types of other nodes and the network topology. Rational nodes can exhibit behaviors normally attributed to the *adversarial nodes* found in cryptographic-protocol theory. Namely, rational nodes may use information learned from participation in a protocol to refine their own strategy. Rational nodes also can change or drop messages from other players, and can change or replace local algorithms as part of a utility maximizing strategy.

Irrational nodes behave strategically but do not follow a behavior modeled by the mechanism designer. They behave irrationally with respect to the mechanism. For example, these nodes might have utility functions that depend on more than just their own preferences. Anti-social nodes [3], for instance, prefer strategies that hurt other nodes even when it means reducing their own economic utility.[2] Alternatively, the bounded-rational nodes introduced in Section 3 might be unable to act rationally if the strategy calculation is too onerous.

Both of these node types are affected by the mechanism. The grand goal of the mechanism designer is to build a mechanism that enables strategizing nodes to act rationally, and incentivizes rational nodes to behave well. Irrational nodes can sometimes be brought into the rational node class by changing a poorly-designed mechanism. For instance, simplifying a mechanism might allow nodes that were bounded-rational to compute rational strategies in the new mechanism. Other types of irrational nodes might be made rational by designing repeated mechanisms instead of one-shot mechanisms.

5   Mechanism Design for Peer to Peer Networks

In this section, we highlight some open problems in DAMD that are especially apparent in peer to peer settings. In doing so, we also explore other techniques that can be used with MD to create systems that are proactive in dealing with the problems created by rational nodes.

---

[2] In the real world, companies accept lower profits in attempts to drive out competition. While their behavior may seem irrational in the short term, in the grand scheme of things, their behavior makes sense.

Open Problem #1: What Effect Does Network Topology Have on Message Passing in a Centralized Mechanism Running on a Peer to Peer Network? What about in a Decentralized Mechanism? It seems that network topology can have both positive and negative effects on the ability to implement mechanisms with strategic nodes.

Monderer and Tennenholtz [15] examine the effects of topology on a centralized mechanism when nodes are not connected directly to a center, but instead must pass messages through other rational nodes. In this environment, it might be rational for infrastructure nodes to drop or change messages from their neighbors, as in this paper's initial auction example. They show that redundant message passing, weak cryptography, and a biconnected topology can be used to provide incentives for nodes to forward messages and implement a suggested protocol.

Yet, attempting to apply the same ideas to non-biconnected network leads to a negative result. These graphs can contain rational nodes at articulation points. The rational behavior of these nodes is enough to break the mechanism.

One way to circumvent this negative result when the network topology is known is to use a digital signing scheme. The node implementing the centralized mechanism can send signed messages to all participants and request signed return receipts. Because of the strong cryptography, if an articulation point drops or changes one of these messages, the bad behavior can be caught and the deviating node can be punished.

In the distributed setting, rational infrastructure nodes must pass messages *and* perform computation to determine the outcome of a mechanism. The problem is identified in Feigenbaum et al. [6] as "the need to reconcile the strategic model with the computational model." As an example, the authors give a strategyproof incentive compatible distributed mechanism for computing lowest-cost paths in an interdomain routing setting. But, the model assumes that nodes obediently compute their part of the distributed mechanism. This issue of implementing mechanisms is critical in peer to peer networks when infrastructure nodes might be required to participate in the mechanism even when they are not disinterested in the outcome.

Open Problem #2: What Are the Bounds on the Guarantees that Mechanism Design Can Provide in a Distributed Setting, and What Is the Minimum Set of Helper Technologies that Must Be Employed in Concert with DAMD Ideas in Distributed Networks? When a mechanism is to be computed by strategic agents, DAMD techniques may need to be augmented to ensure that agents perform computations correctly. One approach is to use cryptographic signing techniques [7] to detect cheating. However, a heavy-handed cryptographic approach may not be desirable. Are there other techniques that a designer can use? Another approach may be to use network redundancy with catch-and-punish techniques to ensure compliance [15, 22]. A third approach, mentioned earlier, is to assume some obediency in the network either in the form of specialized hardware [20] or dedicated designer-trusted nodes. (See Open Problem #3.) Reputation systems is an economic area that might be useful in heuristically strengthening mechanisms. Paralleling Monderer and Tennenholtz [15], we are interested in understanding when clever partitioning of a mechanism across nodes can be useful.

Are these alternate techniques valid on all topologies? If one imagines these alternate techniques as the foundation upon which MD should be built, how few helper technologies can one employ?

Open Problem #3: How Can Assumptions about the Distribution (but not the Identity) of Various Node Strategy Types Help to Create Mechanisms with Good Properties? Researchers might take advantage of the fact that some nodes in a peer to peer system do appear to be obedient [1]. Designers can use this idea when creating mechanisms that might need to rely on obedient nodes. For example, a minimum number of obedient nodes are sometimes required in auction protocols (e.g. [10]). Alternatively, one could use these obedient agents to check the behavior of other nodes if the system implements catch-and-punish schemes to enforce good behavior. The system designer can also consider injecting a limited number of obedient nodes into the system to make the mechanism design problem easier.

6   Related Work

The last section of Feigenbaum & Shenker [7] considers applications of DAMD, two of which are peer to peer systems and overlay networks. They pose several open questions, including how rational agents might affect network topology formation. In this paper, we are additionally concerned about how network topology affects mechanism implementation.

There have been some heuristic approaches to addressing these problems, including the introduction of a "barter economy" currency [14] to induce proper node behavior. Mechanism design ideas may provide a useful toolkit to analyze these barter economies.

There has been considerable work in auction protocols. A protocol by Brandt [2] uses costly cryptography to remove the need for either an auctioneer or any obedient nodes. This is actually a side effect of work that concentrates on privacy-preservation in auctions. The work assumes a totally connected physical graph, which probably is not realistic in most peer to peer settings.

Finally, there are several topical papers on "peer to peer auctions" that basically ignore notions of rationality [18]. Similarly, recent papers on economic models for resource scheduling in scientific Grid computing have not explored issues of rationality [4].

7   Conclusions

Rationality is a concern in peer to peer networks, where, in a very real sense, the users are the network. The central challenge in turning to ideas from economics is to provide incentives for nodes to follow protocols that provide the network as a whole with good system-wide performance. Mechanism design, while not a silver bullet to address all network implementation problems, is a good tool to use when designing robust systems.

Our future work in this area will explore the open problems presented in this paper in an attempt to minimize the amount of external support used to successfully implement distributed mechanisms. To this end, our current focus is on how redundancy helps the mechanism designer [22]. We are exploring how to build a real peer to peer resource allocation system using mechanism design as inspiration for dealing with rational nodes.

Acknowledgements

We thank Joan Feigenbaum for her continuing conversations on DAMD and related topics. We also thank Danni Tang for her assistance while putting together this paper.

References

[1] Eytan Adar and Bernardo Huberman. Free Riding on Gnutella. *First Monday*, 5(10), October 2000.

[2] Felix Brandt. A Verifiable, Bidder-Resolved Auction Protocol. In *Proceedings of the 5th International Workshop on Deception, Fraud and Trust in Agent Societies*, pages 18–25, 2002.

[3] Felix Brandt and Gerhard Weiß. Antisocial Agents and Vickrey Auctions. In *Pre-proceedings of the Eighth International Workshop on Agent Theories, Architectures, and Languages (ATAL-2001)*, pages 120–132, 2001.

[4] R. Buyya, H. Stockinger, J. Giddy, and D. Abramson. Economic Models for Management of Resources in Peer-to-Peer and Grid Computing. In *Proceedings of the SPIE International Symposium on The Convergence of Information Technologies and Communications (ITCOM)*, August 2001.

[5] Prajit K. Dutta. *Strategies and Games*. The MIT Press, 1999.

[6] Joan Feigenbaum, Christos Papadimitriou, Rahul Sami, and Scott Shenker. A BGP-based Mechanism for Lowest-Cost Routing. In *Proceedings of the 21st Symposium on Principles of Distributed Computing*, pages 173–182, New York, 2002. ACM Press.

[7] Joan Feigenbaum and Scott Shenker. Distributed Algorithmic Mechanism Design: Recent Results and Future Directions. In *Proceedings of the 6th International Workshop on Discrete Algorithms and Methods for Mobile Computing and Communications*, pages 1–13, New York, 2002. ACM Press.

[8] Drew Fudenberg and Jean Tirole. *Game Theory*. The MIT Press, 1991.

[9] Garrett Hardin. The Tragedy of the Commons. *Science*, 162:1243–1248, 1968. Alternate Location: http://dieoff.com/page95.htm.

[10] Michael Harkavy, J. D. Tygar, and Hiroaki Kikuchi. Electronic Auctions with Private Bids. In *3rd USENIX Workshop on Electronic Commerce*, pages 61–74, September 1998.

[11] C. Bryson Hull. Smithsonian to Enshrine Enron Ethics Manual. http://ca.news.yahoo.com/020227/5/k6vd.html, 2002.

[12] Leander Kahney. Cheaters Bow to Peer Pressure, 2001. http://www.wired.com/news/technology/0,1282,41838,00.html.

[13] Nancy Lynch. *Distributed Algorithms*. Morgan Kaufmann Publishers, 1996.

[14] Jim McCoy. Mojo Nation Responds. http://www.openp2p.com/pub/a/p2p/2001/01/11/mojo.html, 2001.

[15] Dov Monderer and Moshe Tennenholtz. Distributed Games: From Mechanisms to Protocols. In *Proceedings of the 16th National Conference on Artificial Intelligence (AAAI)*, pages 32–37, 1999.

[16] Sharman Networks. Kazaa Guide: Supernode FAQ, 2003. http://www.kazaa.com/us/help/faq/supernodes.htm.

[17] Noam Nisan and Amir Ronen. Algorithmic Mechanism Design. In *Proceedings of the 31st ACM Symposium on Theory of Computing*, pages 129–140, 1999.

[18] E. Ogston and S. Vassiliadis. A Peer-to-Peer Agent Auction. In *Proceedings of the First International Joint Conference on Autonomous Agents and Multi-Agent Systems (AAMAS)*, 2002.

[19] David C. Parkes. *Iterative Combinatorial Auctions: Achieving Economic and Computational Efficiency (Chapter 2)*. PhD thesis, Univesity of Pennsylvania, May 2001. http://www.eecs.harvard.edu/ parkes/pubs/ch2.ps.

[20] Adrian Perrig, Sean Smith, Dawn Song, and J. Doug Tygar. SAM: A Flexible and Secure Auction Architecture Using Trusted Hardware, 1991. Submitted Manuscript.

[21] Tuomas Sandholm. Limitations of the Vickrey Auction in Computational Multiagent Systems. In *Proceedings of the 2nd International Conference on Multi-Agent Systems (ICMAS)*. AAAI Press, 1996. Menlo Park, CA.

[22] Jeffrey Shneidman and David C. Parkes. Using Redundancy to Improve Robustness of Distributed Mechanism Implementations, 2003. Working Paper. Poster version to appear at ACM Conference on Electronic Commerce EC'03.

Enforcing Fair Sharing of Peer-to-Peer Resources

Tsuen-Wan "Johnny" Ngan, Dan S. Wallach, and Peter Druschel

Department of Computer Science, Rice University
{twngan,dwallach,druschel}cs.rice.edu

Abstract. Cooperative peer-to-peer applications are designed to share the resources of each computer in an overlay network for the common good of everyone. However, users do not necessarily have an incentive to donate resources to the system if they can get the system's resources for free. This paper presents architectures for fair sharing of storage resources that are robust against collusions among nodes. We show how requiring nodes to publish auditable records of their usage can give nodes economic incentives to report their usage truthfully, and we present simulation results that show the communication overhead of auditing is small and scales well to large networks.

1 Introduction

A large number of peer-to-peer (p2p) systems have been developed recently, providing a general-purpose network substrate [10, 11, 13, 14, 16] suitable for sharing files [6, 7], among other applications. In practice, particularly with widespread p2p systems such as Napster, Gnutella, or Kazaa, many users may choose to consume the p2p system's resources without providing any of their own resources for the use of others [1]. Users have no natural *incentive* to provide services to their peers if it is not somehow required of them.

This paper considers methods to design such requirements directly into the p2p system. While we could take a traditional quota enforcement approach, requiring some kind of trusted authority to give a user "permission" to store files, such notions are hard to create in a network of peers. Why should some peers be placed in a position of authority over others? If all nodes were to publish their resource usage records, directly, where other nodes are auditing those records as a part of the normal functioning of the system, we might be able to create a system where nodes have natural incentives to publish their records accurately. Ideally, we would like to design a system where nodes, acting selfishly, behave collectively to maximize the common welfare. When such a system has no centralized authority with total knowledge of the system making decisions, this becomes a distributed algorithmic mechanism design (DAMD) problem [9], a current area of study which combines computational tractability in theoretical computer science with incentive-compatible mechanism design in the economics literature.

To illustrate the power of such economic systems, we focus on the specific problem of fair sharing in p2p storage systems, although our techniques can potentially be extended to discuss fairness in bandwidth consumption and other

F. Kaashoek and I. Stoica (Eds.): IPTPS 2003, LNCS 2735, pp. 149–159, 2003.
© Springer-Verlag Berlin Heidelberg 2003

resources. Section 2 discusses adversarial models that a storage system must be designed to address. Section 3 discusses different approaches to implementing fairness policies in p2p storage systems. Section 4 presents some simulation results. Finally, Sect. 5 discusses related work and Sect. 6 concludes.

2 Models

Our goal is to support a notion of fair sharing such as limiting any given node to only consuming as much of the network's storage as it provides space for others on its local disk. A centralized broker that monitored all transactions could accomplish such a feat, but it would not easily scale to large numbers of nodes, and it would form a single point of failure; if the broker was offline, all file storage operations would be unable to proceed.

We will discuss several possible decentralized designs in Sect. 3, where nodes in the p2p network keep track of each others' usage, but first we need to understand the threats such a design must address. It is possible that some nodes may wish to collude to corrupt the system, perhaps gaining more storage for each other than they collectively provide to the network. We consider three adversarial models:

No Collusion Nodes, acting on their own, wish to gain an unfair advantage over the network, but they have no peers with which to collude.

Minority Collusion A subset of the p2p network is willing to form a conspiracy to lie about their resource usage. However, it is assumed that most nodes in the p2p network are uninterested in joining the conspiracy.

Minority Bribery The adversary may choose specific nodes to join the conspiracy, perhaps offering them a bribe in the form of unfairly increased resource usage.

This paper focuses primarily on minority collusions. While bribery is perfectly feasible, and we may well even be able to build mechanisms that are robust against bribery, it is entirely unclear that the lower-level p2p routing and messaging systems can be equally robust. In studying routing security for p2p systems, Castro et al. [3] focused only on minority collusions. Minority bribery would allow very small conspiracies of nodes to defeat the secure routing primitives. For the remainder of this paper, we assume the correctness of the underlying p2p system.

We note that the ability to consume resources, such as remote disk storage, is a form of currency, where remote resources have more value to a node than its local storage. When nodes exchange their local storage for others' remote storage, the trade benefits both parties, giving an incentive for them to cooperate. As such, there is no need for cash or other forms of money to exchange hands; the storage economy can be expressed strictly as a barter economy.

3 Designs

In this section, we describe three possible designs for storage accounting systems. For all of these designs, we assume the existence of a public key infrastructure, allowing any node to digitally sign a document such that any other node can verify it, yet it is computationally infeasible for others to forge.

Likewise, for any of these designs, it is imperative to ensure that nodes are actually storing the files they claim to store. This is guaranteed by the following *challenge* mechanism. For each file a node is storing, it periodically picks a node that stores a replica of the same file as a target, and notifies all other replicas holders of the file that it is challenging that target. Then it randomly selects a few blocks of the file and queries the target for the hash of those blocks. The target can answer correctly only if it has the file. The target may ask another replica holder for a copy of the file, but any such request during a challenge would cause the challenger to be notified, and thus able to restart the challenge for another file.

3.1 Smart Cards

The original PAST paper [7] suggested the use of smart cards to enforce storage quotas. The smart card produces signed endorsements of a node's requests to consume remote storage, while charging that space to an internal counter. When storage is reclaimed, the remote node returns a signed message that the smart card can verify before crediting its internal counter.

Smart cards avoid the bandwidth overheads of the decentralized designs discussed in this paper. However, smart cards must be issued by a trusted organization, and periodically re-issued to invalidate compromised cards. This requires a business model that generates revenues to cover the cost of running the organization. Thus, smart cards appear to be unsuitable for grassroots p2p systems.

3.2 Quota Managers

If each smart card was replaced by a collection of nodes in the p2p network, the same design would still be applicable. We can define the *manager set* for a node to be a set of nodes adjacent to that node in the overlays node identifier (nodeId) space, making them easy for other parties in the overlay to discover and verify. Each manager must remember the amount of storage consumed by the nodes it manages and must endorse all requests from the managed nodes to store new files. To be robust against minority collusion, a remote node would insist that a majority of the manager nodes agree that a given request is authorized, requiring the manager set to perform a Byzantine agreement protocol [4].

The drawback of this design is that request approval has a relatively high latency and the number of malicious nodes in any manager set must be less than one third of the set size. Furthermore, managers suffer no direct penalty if they grant requests that would be correctly denied, and thus could be vulnerable to bribery attacks.

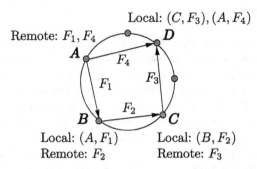

Fig. 1. A p2p network with local/remote lists

3.3 Auditing

While the smart card and quota manager designs are focused on enforcing quotas, an alternative approach is to require nodes to maintain their own records and publish them, such that other nodes can audit those records. Of course, nodes have no inherent reason to publish their records accurately. This subsection describes how we can create natural economic disincentives to nodes lying in their records.

Usage Files. Every node maintains a *usage file*, digitally signed, which is available for any other node to read. The usage file has three sections:

- the *advertised capacity* this node is providing to the system;
- a *local list* of (nodeId, fileId) pairs, containing the identifiers and sizes of all files that the node is storing locally on behalf of other nodes; and
- a *remote list* of fileIds of all the files published by this node (stored remotely), with their sizes.

Together, the local and remote lists describe all the credits and debits to a node's account. Note that the nodeIds for the peers storing the files are not stored in the remote list, since this information can be found using mechanisms in the storage system (e.g., PAST). We say a node is "under quota," and thus allowed to write new files into the network, when its advertised capacity minus the sum of its remote list, charging for each replica, is positive.

When a node A wishes to store a file F_1 on another node B, first B must fetch A's usage file to verify that A is under quota. Then, two records are created: A adds F_1 to its remote list and B adds (A, F_1) to its local list. This is illustrated in Fig. 1. Of course, A might fabricate the contents of its usage file to convince B to improperly accept its files.

We must provide incentives for A to tell the truth. To game the system, A might normally attempt to either *inflate* its advertised capacity or *deflate* the sum of its remote list. If A were to increase its advertised capacity beyond the amount of disk it actually has, this might attract storage requests that A cannot

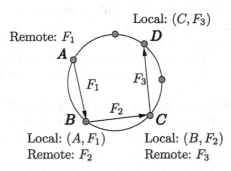

Fig. 2. A cheating chain, where node A is the cheating anchor

honor, assuming the p2p storage system is operating at or near capacity, which is probably a safe assumption. A might compensate by creating fraudulent entries in its local list, to claim the storage is being used. To prevent fraudulent entries in either list, we define an auditing procedure that B, or any other node, may perform on A.

If B detects that F_1 is missing from A's remote list, then B can feel free to delete the file. After all, A is no longer "paying" for it. Because an audit could be gamed if A knew the identity of its auditor, anonymous communication is required, and can be accomplished using a technique similar to Crowds [12]. So long as every node that has a relationship with A is auditing it at randomly chosen intervals, A cannot distinguish whether it is being audited by B or any other node with files in its remote list. We refer to this process as a *normal audit*.

Normal auditing, alone, does not provide a disincentive to inflation of the local list. For every entry in A's local list, there should exist an entry for that file in another node's remote list. An auditor could fetch the usage file from A and then connect to every node mentioned in A's local list to test for matching entries. This would detect inconsistencies in A's usage file, but A could collude with other nodes to push its debts off its own books. To fully audit A, the auditor would need to audit the nodes reachable from A's local list, and recursively audit the nodes reachable from those local lists. Eventually, the audit would discover a *cheating anchor* where the books did not balance (see Fig. 2). Implementing such a recursive audit would be prohibitively expensive. Instead, we require all nodes in the p2p overlay to perform *random auditing*. With a lower frequency than their normal audits, each node should choose a node at random from the p2p overlay. The auditor fetches the usage file, and verifies it against the nodes mentioned in that file's local list. Assuming all nodes perform these random audits on a regular schedule, every node will be audited, on a regular basis, with high probability.

How high? Consider a network with n nodes, where $c < n$ nodes are conspiring. The probability that the cheating anchor is not random audited by any node in one period is $\left(\frac{n-2}{n-1}\right)^{n-c} > 1/e \approx 0.368$, and the cheating anchor would be discovered in three periods with probability higher than 95%.

Recall that usage files are digitally signed by their node. Once a cheating anchor has been discovered, its usage file is effectively a *signed confession* of its misbehavior! This confession can be presented as evidence toward ejecting the cheater from the p2p network. With the cheating anchor ejected, other cheaters who depended on the cheating anchor will now be exposed and subject to ejection, themselves.

We note that this design is robust even against bribery attacks, because the collusion will still be discovered and the cheaters ejected. We also note that since everybody, including auditors, benefits when cheaters are discovered and ejected from the p2p network, nodes do have an incentive to perform these random audits [8].

Extensions

Selling Overcapacity. As described above, a node cannot consume more resources from the network than it provides itself. However, it is easy to imagine nodes who want to consume more resources than they provide, and, likewise, nodes who provide more resources than they wish to consume. Naturally, this overcapacity could be sold, perhaps through an online bidding system [5], for real-world money. These trades could be directly indicated in the local and remote lists. For example, if D sells 1GB to E, D can write (E, 1GB trade) in its remote list, and E writes (D, 1GB trade) in its local list. All the auditing mechanisms continue to function.

Reducing Communication. Another issue is that fetching usage logs repeatedly could result in serious communication overhead, particularly for nodes with slow net connections. To address this, we implemented three optimizations. First, rather than sending the usage logs through the overlay route used to reach it, they can be sent directly over the Internet: one hop from the target node to the anonymizing relay, and one hop to the auditing node. Second, since an entry in a remote list would be audited by all nodes replicating the logs, those replicas can alternately audit that node to share the cost of auditing. Third, we can reduce communication by only transmitting diffs of usage logs, since the logs change slowly. We must be careful that the anonymity of auditors isn't compromised, perhaps using version numbers to act as cookies to track auditors. To address this, the auditor needs to, with some probability, request the complete usage logs.

4   Experiments

In this section, we present some simulation results of the communication costs of the quota managers and the auditing system. For our simulations, we assume all nodes are following the rules and no nodes are cheating. Both storage space and file sizes are chosen from truncated normal distributions[1]. The storage space of each node is chosen from 2 to 200GB, with an average of 48GB. We varied the average file size across experiments. In each day of simulated time, 1% of the files are reclaimed and republished. Two challenges are made to random replicas per file a node is storing per day.

For quota managers, we implemented Castro et al.'s BFT algorithm [4]. With a manager set size of ten, the protocol can tolerate three nodes with Byzantine faults in any manager set. For auditing, normal audits are performed on average four times daily on each entry in a node's remote list and random audits are done once per day. We simulated both with and without the append-only log optimization.

Our simulations include per-node overhead for Pastry-style routing lookups as well as choosing one node, at random, to create one level of indirection on audit requests. The latter provides weak anonymity sufficient for our purposes. Note that we only measure the communication overhead due to storage accounting. In particular, we exclude the cost of p2p overlay maintenance and storing/fetching of files, since it is not relevant to our comparison. Unless otherwise specified, all simulations are done with 10,000 nodes, 285 files stored per nodes, and an average node lifetime of 14 days.

4.1   Results

Figure 3 shows the average upstream bandwidth required per node, as a function of the number of nodes (the average required downstream bandwidth is identical). The per-node bandwidth requirement is almost constant, thus all systems scale well with the size of the overlay network.

Figure 4 shows the bandwidth requirement as a function of the number of files stored per node. The overheads grow linearly with the number of files, but for auditing without caching, it grows nearly twice as fast as the other two designs. Since p2p storage systems are typically used to store large files, this overhead is not a concern. Also, the system could charge for an appropriate minimum file size to give users an incentive to combine small files into larger archives prior to storing them.

Figure 5 shown the overhead versus average node lifetime. The overhead for quota managers grows rapidly when the node lifetime gets shorter, mostly from the cost in joining and leaving manager sets and from voting for file insertions for new nodes.

Our simulations have also shown that quota managers are more affected by the file turnover rate, due to the higher cost for voting. Also, the size of manager sets determines the vulnerability of the quota manager design. To tolerate more malicious nodes, we need to increase the size of manager sets, which would result in a higher cost.

---

[1] The bandwidth consumed for auditing is dependent on the number, rather than the size, of files being stored. We also performed simulations using heavy-tailed file size distributions and obtained similar results.

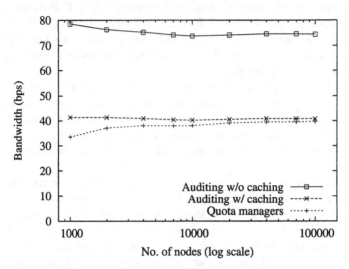

Fig. 3. Overhead with different number of nodes

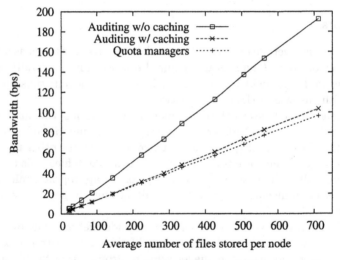

Fig. 4. Overhead with different number of files stored per node

In summary, auditing with caching has performance comparable to quota managers, but is not subject to bribery attacks and is less sensitive to the fraction of malicious nodes. Furthermore, in a variety of conditions, the auditing overhead is quite low — only a fraction of a typical p2p node's bandwidth.

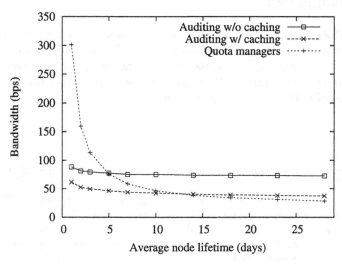

Fig. 5. Overhead with different average node lifetime

5   Related Work

Tangler [15] is designed to provide censorship-resistant publication over a small number of servers (i.e., < 30), exchanging data frequently with one another. To maintain fairness, Tangler requires servers to obtain "certificates" from other servers which can be redeemed to publish files for a limited time. A new server can only obtain these certificates by providing storage for the use of other servers and is not allowed to publish anything for its first month online. As such, new servers must have demonstrated good service to the p2p network before being allowed to consume any network services.

The Eternity Service [2] includes an explicit notion of electronic cash, with which users can purchase storage space. Once published, a document cannot be deleted, even if requested by the publisher.

Fehr and Gachter's study considered an economic game where selfishness was feasible but could easily be detected [8]. When their human test subjects were given the opportunity to spend their money to punish selfish peers, they did so, resulting in a system with less selfish behaviors. This result helps justify that users will be willing to pay the costs of random audits.

6   Conclusions

This paper has presented two architectures for achieving fair sharing of resources in p2p networks. Experimental results indicate small overheads and scalability to large numbers of files and nodes. In practice, auditing provides incentives, allowing us to benefit from its increased resistance to collusion and bribery attacks.

Acknowledgments

We thank Moez A. Abdel-Gawad, Shu Du, and Khaled Elmeleegy for their work on an earlier version of the quota managers design. We also thank Andrew Fuqua and Hervé Moulin for helpful discussions on economic incentives. This research was supported by NSF grant CCR-9985332, Texas ATP grants 003604-0053-2001 and 003604-0079-2001, and a gift from Microsoft Research.

References

[1] E. Adar and B. Huberman. Free riding on Gnutella. *First Monday*, 5(10), October 2000.

[2] R. Anderson. The Eternity service. In *Proc. 1st Int'l Conf. on the Theory and Applications of Cryptology*, pages 242–252, Prague, Czech Republic, October 1996.

[3] Miguel Castro, Peter Druschel, Ayalvadi Ganesh, Antony Rowstron, and Dan S. Wallach. Security for structured peer-to-peer overlay networks. In *Proc. OSDI'02*, Boston, MA, December 2002.

[4] Miguel Castro and Barbara Liskov. Practical Byzantine fault tolerance. In *Proc. OSDI'99*, New Orleans, LA, February 1999.

[5] Brian F. Cooper and Hector Garcia-Molina. Bidding for storage space in a peer-to-peer data preservation system. In *Proc. 22nd Int'l Conf. on Distributed Computing Systems*, Vienna, Austria, July 2002.

[6] F. Dabek, M. F. Kaashoek, D. Karger, R. Morris, and I. Stoica. Wide-area cooperative storage with CFS. In *Proc. SOSP'01*, Chateau Lake Louise, Banff, Canada, October 2001.

[7] Peter Druschel and Antony Rowstron. PAST: A large-scale, persistent peer-to-peer storage utility. In *Proc. 8th Workshop on Hot Topics in Operating Systems*, Schoss Elmau, Germany, May 2001.

[8] Ernst Fehr and Simon Gachter. Altruistic punishment in humans. *Nature*, (415):137–140, January 2002.

[9] Joan Feigenbaum and Scott Shenker. Distributed algorithmic mechanism design: Recent results and future directions. In *Proc. 6th Int'l Workshop on Discrete Algorithms and Methods for Mobile Computing and Communications*, pages 1–13, Atlanta, GA, September 2002.

[10] P. Maymounkov and D. Mazières. Kademlia: A peer-to-peer information system based on the XOR metric. In *Proc. IPTPS'02*, Cambridge, MA, March 2002.

[11] S. Ratnasamy, P. Francis, M. Handley, R. Karp, and S. Shenker. A scalable content-addressable network. In *Proc. SIGCOMM'01*, pages 161–172, San Diego, CA, August 2001.

[12] M. K. Reiter and A. D. Rubin. Crowds: Anonymity for web transactions. *ACM Transactions on Information and System Security*, 1(1):66–92, 1998.

[13] Antony Rowstron and Peter Druschel. Pastry: Scalable, distributed object address and routing for large-scale peer-to-peer systems. In *Proc. IFIP/ACM Int'l Conf. on Distributed Systems Platforms*, pages 329–350, Heidelberg, Germany, November 2001.

[14] I. Stoica, R. Morris, D. Karger, M. F. Kaashoek, and H. Balakrishnan. Chord: A scalable peer-to-peer lookup service for Internet applications. In *Proc. SIGCOMM'01*, San Diego, CA, August 2001.

[15] M. Waldman and D. Mazières. Tangler: A censorship-resistant publishing system based on document entanglements. In *Proc. 8th ACM Conf. on Computer and Communications Security*, November 2001.

[16] B. Y. Zhao, J. D. Kubiatowicz, and A. D. Joseph. Tapestry: An infrastructure for fault-resilient wide-area address and routing. Technical Report UCB//CSD-01-1141, U. C. Berkeley, April 2001.

Kelips: Building an Efficient and Stable P2P DHT through Increased Memory and Background Overhead

Indranil Gupta, Ken Birman, Prakash Linga, Al Demers, and
Robbert van Renesse *

Cornell University, Ithaca, NY, USA
{gupta,ken,linga,ademers,rvr}cs.cornell.edu

Abstract. A peer-to-peer (p2p) distributed hash table (DHT) system allows hosts to join and fail silently (or leave), as well as to insert and retrieve files (objects). This paper explores a new point in design space in which increased memory usage and constant background communication overheads are tolerated to reduce file lookup times and increase stability to failures and churn. Our system, called *Kelips* [1], uses peer-to-peer gossip to partially replicate file index information. In Kelips, (a) under normal conditions, file lookups are resolved within 1 RPC, independent of system size, and (b) membership changes (e.g., even when a large number of nodes fail) are detected and disseminated to the system quickly. Per-node memory requirements are small in medium-sized systems. When there are failures, lookup success is ensured through query rerouting. Kelips achieves load balancing comparable to existing systems. Locality is supported by using topologically aware gossip mechanisms. Initial results of an ongoing experimental study are also discussed.

1 Introduction

A peer-to-peer (p2p) distributed hash table (DHT) implements operations allowing hosts or processes (nodes) to join the system, and fail silently (or leave the system), as well as to insert and retrieve files with known names. Many DHTs have been deployed (e.g. Fasttrack-based systems such as Kazaa) while several others are a focus of academic research, e.g., Chord [3], Pastry [6], Tapestry, etc. [8].

All p2p systems make tradeoffs between the amount of storage overhead at each node, the communication costs incurred while running, and the costs of

---

* The authors were supported in part by DARPA/AFRL-IFGA grant F30602-99-1-0532 and in part by a MURI grant AFOSR F49620-02-1-0233, with additional support from the AFRL-IFGA Information Assurance Institute, from Microsoft Research and from the Intel Corporation.

[1] System name derived from *kelip-kelip*, Malay name for the self-synchronizing fireflies that accumulate after dusk on branches of mangrove trees in Selangor, Malaysia [11]. Our system organizes similarly into affinity groups, and nodes in a group "synchronize" loosely to store information for a common set of file indices.

F. Kaashoek and I. Stoica (Eds.): IPTPS 2003, LNCS 2735, pp. 160–169, 2003.

file retrieval. With the exception of Gnutella, the work just cited has focused on a design point in which storage costs are logarithmic in system size and hence small, and lookup costs are also logarithmic (unless cache hits shortcut the search). However, a study [9] on file sharing systems such as Gnutella and Napster has shown that a significant fraction of nodes could be connected over high latency / low bandwidth links. The presence of even one such slow logical hop on a logarithmically long path is thus likely. This increases the overall cost of the lookup.

We argue that this can be avoided by exploring other potentially interesting points in the design of p2p DHTs. One could vary the soft state memory usage and background network communication overhead at a node in order to realize $O(1)$ lookup costs. For example, complete replication of soft state achieves this, but this approach has prohibitive memory and bandwidth requirements.

The Kelips system uses $O(\sqrt{n})$ space per node, where n is the number of nodes in the system. This soft state suffices to resolve lookups within 1 RPC and with $O(1)$ message complexity. Continuous background communication with a constant overhead is used to maintain the index structure with high quality, as well as guarantee quick convergence after membership changes.

The $\sqrt{n}$ design point is of interest because, within Kelips, both the storage overhead associated with the membership data structure and that associated with replication of file-index (henceforth called *filetuple*) data impose the same $O(\sqrt{n})$ asymptotic cost. Kelips uses query rerouting to ensure lookup success in spite of failures. The mechanism also allows us to use round trip time estimates to select nearby peers for each node.

Memory usage is small for systems with moderate sizes - if 10 million files are inserted into a 100,000-node system, Kelips uses only 1.93 MB of memory at each node. The system exhibits stability in the face of node failures and packet losses, and hence would be expected to ride out "churn" arising in wide-area settings from rapid arrival and failure of nodes. This resilience is achieved through the use of a lightweight Epidemic multicast protocol for replication of system membership data and file indexing data [1, 4]. We note that whereas many DHT systems treat file replication as well as lookup, our work focuses only on the lookup problem, leaving replication to the application. For reasons of brevity, this paper also omits any discussion of privacy and security considerations.

2   Core Design

Kelips consists of k virtual *affinity groups*, numbered 0 through $(k-1)$. Each node lies in an affinity group determined by using a consistent hashing function to map the node's identifier (IP address and port number) into the integer interval $[0, k-1]$. Let n be the number of nodes currently in the system. The use of a cryptographic hash function such as SHA-1 ensures that with high probability, the number of nodes in each affinity group is around $\frac{n}{k}$.
Node soft state consists of the following entries:

• Affinity Group View: A (partial) set of other nodes lying in the same affinity group. Each entry carries additional fields such as round-trip time estimate, heartbeat count, etc. for the other node.

• Contacts: For each of the other affinity groups in the system, a small (constant-sized) set of nodes lying in the foreign affinity group. Entries contain the same additional fields as in the affinity group view.

• Filetuples: A (partial) set of tuples, each detailing a file name and host IP address of the node storing the file (called the file's *homenode*). A node stores a filetuple only if the file's homenode lies in this node's affinity group. Filetuples are also associated with heartbeat counts.

Figure 1 illustrates an example. Entries are stored in AVL trees to support efficient operations.

Memory Usage at a Node: The total storage requirements for a Kelips node are $S(k, n) = \frac{n}{k} + c \times (k - 1) + \frac{F}{k}$ entries (c is the number of contacts per foreign affinity group and F the total number of files present in the system). For fixed n, $S(k, n)$ is minimized at $k = \sqrt{\frac{n+F}{c}}$. Assuming the total number of files is proportional to n, and that c is fixed, the optimal k then varies as $O(\sqrt{n})$. The minimum $S(k, n)$ varies as $O(\sqrt{n})$. This is asymptotically larger than Chord or Pastry, but turns out to be reasonably small for most medium-sized p2p systems.

Consider a system with $n = 100,000$ nodes over $k = \lceil \sqrt{n} \rceil = 317$ affinity groups. Our current implementation uses 60 B filetuple entries and 40 B mem-

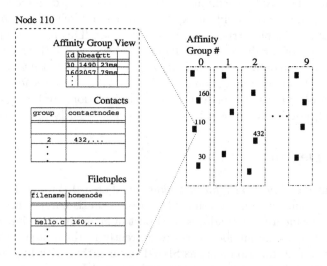

Fig. 1. Soft State at a Node: A Kelips system with nodes distributed across 10 affinity groups, and soft state at a hypothetical node

bership entries, and maintains 2 contacts per foreign affinity group. Inserting a total of 10 million files into the system thus entails 1.93 MB of node soft state. With such memory requirements, file lookup queries return the location of the file within 1 RPC and with $O(1)$ message complexity, i.e., these costs are invariant with system size n.

2.1 Background Overhead

Existing view, contact and filetuple entries are refreshed periodically within and across groups. This occurs through a heartbeating mechanism. Each view, contact or filetuple entry stored at a node is associated with an integer heartbeat count. If the heartbeat count for an entry is not updated over a pre-specified time-out period, the entry is deleted. Heartbeat updates originate at the responsible node (for filetuples, this is the homenode) and are disseminated through a peer-to-peer epidemic-style (or gossip-style) protocol [7]. This gossip communication constitutes the background communication within a group. This continuous *gossip stream* is also used to disseminate new view, contact and filetuple entries to the system.

We first outline gossip-style dissemination within one affinity group. A piece of information (e.g., a heartbeat update for a filetuple) is multicasted to the group by using a constant background bandwidth, incurring latency that increases polylogarithmically with group size. Once a node receives the piece of information to be multicast (either from some other node or from the application), the node gossips about this information for a number of *rounds*, where a round is a fixed local time interval at the node. During each round, the node selects a small constant-sized set of target nodes from the group membership, and sends each of these nodes a copy of the information. Gossiping thus uses constant bandwidth. With high probability, the protocol transmits the multicast to all nodes. The latency can be shown to vary with the logarithm of affinity group size. Gossip messages are transmitted via a lightweight unreliable protocol such as UDP. Gossip target nodes are selected through a weighted scheme based on round-trip time estimates, preferring nodes that are topologically closer in the network. Kelips uses the spatially weighted gossip proposed in [5] towards this. A node with round-trip time estimate rtt is selected as gossip target with probability proportional to $\frac{1}{rtt^r}$. As suggested in [5], we use a value of $r = 2$, where the latency is polylogarithmic ($O(log^2(n))$).

Analysis and experimental studies have revealed that epidemic style dissemination protocols are robust to network packet losses, as well as to transient and permanent node failures. They maintain stable multicast throughput to the affinity group even in the presence of such failures. See references [1, 2, 4].

Information such as heartbeats also need to propagate across affinity groups (e.g., to keep contact entries for this affinity group from expiring). This is achieved by selecting a few of the contacts as gossip targets in each gossip round. Such cross-group dissemination implies a two-level gossiping scheme similar to [7]. With uniform cross-group target selection, latency is more than that of single group gossip by a multiplicative factor of $O(log(k))$ (with $k = \sqrt{n}$ affinity groups, this is the same as $O(log(n))$).

Gossip messages in Kelips carry not just a single entry, but several filetuple and membership entries. This includes entries that are new, were recently deleted, or have an updated heartbeat. Since Kelips limits bandwidth use at each node, not all the soft state can be packed into a gossip message. Maximum rations are imposed on the numbers of view entries, contact entries and filetuple entries that a gossip message may contain. For each entry type, the ration subdivides equally for fresh entries (ones that have so far been included in fewer than a threshold number of gossip messages sent out from this node) and for older entries. Entries are chosen uniformly at random, and unused rations (e.g., due to fewer fresh entries) are filled with older entries.

Ration sizes do not vary with n. With $k = \sqrt{n}$, this increases dissemination latencies a factor of $O(\sqrt{n})$ above that of the Epidemic protocol (since soft state is $O(\sqrt{n})$). Heartbeat timeouts thus need to vary as $O(\sqrt{n} \times log^2(n))$ for view and filetuple entries, and $O(\sqrt{n} \times log^3(n))$ for contact entries.

These numbers are thus the convergence times for the system after membership changes. Such low convergence times are achieved through only the gossip messages sent and received at a node. This gossip stream imposes a constant per-node background overhead. The gossip stream is able to disseminate heartbeats and new entries despite node and packet delivery failures.

2.2   File Lookup and Insertion

Lookup: Consider a node (querying node) that desires to fetch a given file. The querying node maps the file name to the appropriate affinity group by using the same consistent hashing used to decide node affinity groups. It then sends a lookup request to the topologically closest contact among those it knows for that affinity group. A received lookup request is resolved by searching among the filetuples maintained at the node, and returning to the querying node the address of the homenode storing the file. This scheme returns the homenode address to a querying node in 1 RPC and with $O(1)$ message complexity. Finally, the querying node fetches the file directly from the homenode.

Insertion: A node (*origin node*) that wants to insert a given file f, maps the file name to the appropriate affinity group, and sends an insert request to the topologically closest known contact for that affinity group. This contact picks a node h from its affinity group, uniformly at random, and forwards the insert request to it. The node h is now the *homenode* of the file. The file is transferred from the origin node to the homenode. A new filetuple is created to map the file f to homenode h, and is inserted into the gossip stream. Thus, filetuple insertion also occurs within 1 RPC time and with $O(1)$ message complexity. The origin node periodically refreshes the filetuple entry at homenode h in order to keep it from expiring.

Clearly, factors such as empty contact sets or incomplete filetuple replication might cause such one-hop lookup or insertion to fail. Biased partial membership

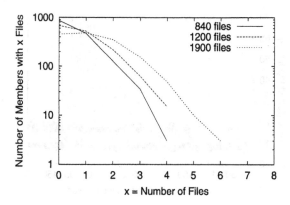

Fig. 2. Load Balancing I: Number of nodes (y-axis) storing given number of files (x-axis), in a Kelips system with 1500 nodes (38 affinity groups)

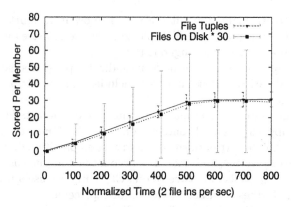

Fig. 3. Load Balancing II: Files are inserted into a 1000 node system (30 affinity groups), 2 insertions per sec between t=0 and t=500. Plot shows variation, over time, of number of files and filetuples at a node (average and one standard deviation)

information might cause uneven load balancing. This is addressed by the general multi-hop multi-try query routing scheme of Section 3.

3   Auxiliary Protocols and Algorithms

We outline Kelips' protocols for node arrival, membership and contact maintenance, topological considerations and multi-hop query routing.

Joining Protocol: Like in several existing p2p systems, a node joins the Kelips system by contacting a well-known introducer node (or group), e.g., a well-known http URL could be used. The joiner view returned by the introducer is used by

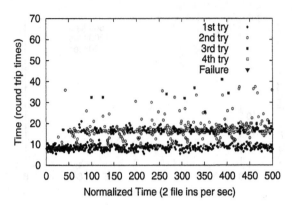

Fig. 4. File Insertion: Turnaround times (in round-trip time units) for file insertion in a 1000-node Kelips system (30 affinity groups)

the new node to warm up its soft state and allow it to start gossiping and populating its view, contact and filetuple set. The gossip stream spreads news about the new node quickly throughout the system.

Spatial Considerations: Each node periodically pings a small set of other nodes it knows about. Response times are included in round-trip time estimates used in spatial gossip.

Contact Maintenance: The maximum number of contacts is fixed, yet the gossip stream supplies potential contacts continuously. *Contact replacement* policy can affect lookup/insert performance and system partitionability. It could be either proactive or reactive, and takes into account factors such as node distance, accessibility (e.g., firewalls in between), etc. Currently, we use a proactive policy that chooses the farthest contact as victim for replacement.

Multi-hop Query Routing: When a file lookup or insert query fails, the querying node retries the query. Query (re-) tries may occur along several axes: a) the querying node could ask multiple contacts, b) contacts could be asked to forward the query within their affinity group (up to a specified TTL), c) the querying node could request the query to be executed at another node in its own affinity group (if this is different from the file's affinity group). Query routing occurs as a random walk within the file affinity group in (b), and within the querying node's affinity group in (c). TTL values on multi-hop routed queries and the maximum numbers of tries trade off between lookup query success rate and maximum processing time. The normal case lookup processing time and message complexity stay $O(1)$.

File insertion occurs through a similar multi-hop multi-try scheme, except the file is inserted exactly at the node where the TTL expires. This helps achieve good load balancing, although it increases the normal case insertion time to grow as $O(log(\sqrt{n}))$. However, this is competitive with existing systems.

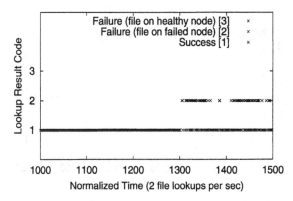

Fig. 5. Fault-Tolerance of Lookups I: In a 1000 node (30 affinity groups) system, lookups are generated 2 per sec. At time $t = 1300$, 500 nodes are selected at random and caused to fail. This plot shows for each lookup if it was successful $[y - axis = 1]$, or if it failed because the homenode failed $[y - axis = 2]$, or if it failed in spite of the homenode being alive $[y - axis = 3]$

4 Experimental Results

We are evaluating a C WinAPI prototype implementation of Kelips. This section reveals preliminary numbers from trace-based experiments, most done along similar lines as previous work [3, 6]. Multiple nodes were run on a single host (1 GHz CPU, 1GB RAM, Win2K) with an emulated network topology layer. Unfortunately, limitations on resources and memory requirements restrict currently simulated system sizes to a few thousand.

Background overhead in the current configuration consists of each node gossiping once every 2 (normalized) seconds. Rations limit gossip message size to 272 B. 6 gossip targets are chosen, 3 of them among contacts.

Load Balancing: Files are inserted into a stable Kelips system. The file name distribution used is a set of anonymized web URLs obtained from the Berkeley Home IP traces at [10]. The load balancing characteristics are better than exponential (Figure 2). File and filetuple distribution as files are inserted (2 insertions per normalized second of time) is shown in Figure 3; the plot shows that filetuple distribution has small deviation around the mean.

File Insertion: This occurs through a multi-try (4 tries) and multi-hop scheme (TTL set to $3 * logN$ logical hops). Figure 4 shows the turnaround times for insertion of 1000 different files. 66.2% complete in 1 try, 33% take 2 tries, and 0.8% take 3 tries. None fail or require more than 3 tries. Views were found to be well replicated in this instance. In a different experiment with 1500 nodes and views only 55.8% of the maximum size, 47.2% inserts required 1 try, 47.04% required 2 tries, 3.76% required 3 tries, 0.96% needed 4 tries, and 1.04% failed. Multi-hop routing thus provides resilience to incomplete replication of soft state.

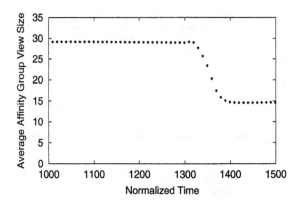

Fig. 6. Fault-Tolerance of Lookups II: At time t=1300, 500 out of 1000 nodes in a 30 affinity group system fail. This plot shows that failure detection and view (and hence filetuple) stabilization occurs by time t=1380

Fault-Tolerance: P2P DHTs are required to be tolerant to dynamic conditions and high churn rates. We measure the resilience of Kelips to a scenario where half of the nodes in the system are caused to fail simultaneously. Figures 5 and 6 show the effectiveness of using background gossip communication. Lookups were initiated at a constant rate and were found to fail only if the homenode had also failed (Figure 5). In other words, multi-hop rerouting and redundant membership information ensures successful lookups despite failures. Responsiveness to failures is good, and membership and filetuple entry information stabilize quickly after a membership change (Figure 6).

5   Conclusion

We are investigating a new design point for DHT systems, based on increased memory usage (for replication of filetuple and membership information), as well as a constant and low background overhead at a node, in order to enable constant cost file lookup operations and ensure stability despite high failure and churn rates. Per-node memory requirements are small in medium-sized systems (less than 2 MB with 10 million files in a 100,000 node system). Multi-hop (and multi-try) query routing enables file lookup and insertion to succeed even when bandwidth limitations or network disconnectivity lead to only partial replication of soft state. We observe satisfactory load balancing.

Kelips and Other DHTs: Memory usage can be traded off for faster lookup times in systems like Chord, Pastry, Tapestry, e.g., by varying the value of the base (the parameter d in Pastry, base value of 2 in Chord) that determines the branching factor of the overlay structure. This would however make routing table entries large and lead to high network traffic to keep them updated as nodes join, leave and fail. Kelips is loosely structured, and it does not need to maintain a structure and invariants (e.g., the ring, routing table entries, etc.) – the soft state allows object lookups and insertions to succeed in spite of stale membership or contact entries.

References

[1] N. T. J. Bailey, "Epidemic Theory of Infectious Diseases and its Applications", Hafner Press, Second Edition, 1975.

[2] K. P. Birman, M. Hayden, O. Ozkasap, Z. Xiao, M. Budiu, Y. Minsky, "Bimodal Multicast", *ACM Trans. Comp. Syst.*, 17:2, pp. 41-88, May 1999.

[3] F. Dabek, E. Brunskill, M. F. Kaashoek, D. Karger, "Building peer-to-peer systems with Chord, a distributed lookup service", *Proc. 8th Wshop. Hot Topics in Operating Syst., (HOTOS-VIII)*, May 2001.

[4] A. Demers, D. H. Greene, J. Hauser, W. Irish, J. Larson, "Epidemic algorithms for replicated database maintenance", *Proc. 6th ACM Symp. Principles of Distributed Computing (PODC)*, pp. 1-12, 1987.

[5] D. Kempe, J. Kleinberg, A. Demers. "Spatial gossip and resource location protocols", *Proc. 33rd ACM Symp. Theory of Computing (STOC)*, pp. 163-172, 2001.

[6] A. Rowstron, P. Druschel, "Pastry: scalable, distributed object location and routing for large-scale peer-to-peer systems", *Proc. IFIP/ACM Middleware*, 2001.

[7] R. van Renesse, Y. Minsky, M. Hayden, "A gossip-style failure detection service", *Proc. IFIP Middleware*, 1998.

[8] *Proc. 1st Intnl. Wshop. Peer-to-Peer Systems (IPTPS), LNCS 2429, Springer-Verlag*, 2002.

[9] S. Saroiu, P. K. Gummadi, S. D. Gribble, "A measurement study of peer-to-peer file sharing systems", *Proc. Multimedia Computing and Networking (MMCN)*, 2002.

[10] Internet Traffic Archive, `http://ita.ee.lbl.gov`

[11] Fireflies of Selangor River, Malaysia, `http://www.firefly-selangor-msia.com/fabout.htm`

SOMO: Self-Organized Metadata Overlay
for Resource Management in P2P DHT

Zheng Zhang[1], Shu-Ming Shi[2][*], and Jing Zhu[2][*]

[1] Microsoft Research Asia
zzhang@microsoft.com
[2] CS Dept. Tsinghua University
{ssm01,zhujing00}@mails.tsinghua.edu.cn

Abstract. In this paper, we first describe the concept of data overlay, which is a mechanism to implement arbitrary data structure on top of any structured P2P DHT. With this abstraction, we developed a highly scalable, efficient and robust infrastructure, called SOMO, to perform resource management for P2P DHT. It does so by gathering and disseminating system metadata in O(log$N$) time with a self-organizing and self-healing data overlay. Our preliminary results of using SOMO to balance routing traffic with node capacities in a prefix-based overlay have demonstrated the utility of data overlay as well as the potential of SOMO.

1 Introduction

For a large P2P overlay to adapt and evolve, there must be a parallel infrastructure to monitor the health of the system (e.g. "top"-like utility in UNIX). The responsibility of such infrastructure is to gather from and distribute to entities comprising the system whatever system metadata of concern, and possibly serve as the channel to communicate various scheduling instructions. The challenge here is that this infrastructure must be embedded in the hosting DHT but is otherwise agonistic to its specific protocols and performance; it must grow along with the hosting DHT system; it must also be fault resilient and, finally, the information gathered and/or disseminated should be as accurate as possible.

In this paper, we describe the *Self-Organized Metadata Overlay*, or SOMO in short, which accomplishes the above goal. By using hierarchy as well as soft-state, SOMO is self-organizing and self-healing, and can gather and disseminate information in O(log$N$) time. SOMO is simple and flexible, and is agnostic to both the hosting P2P DHT and the data being gathered and disseminated. The latter attribute allows it to be programmable, invoking appropriate actions such as merge-sort and aggregation as data flows through.

---

[*] Work done as intern in MSR-Asia.

F. Kaashoek and I. Stoica (Eds.): IPTPS 2003, LNCS 2735, pp. 170-182, 2003.

Through the development of SOMO, we have discovered that there is a consistent and simple mechanism to implement arbitrary data structure on top of a P2P DHT. We refer to a data structure that is distributed onto a DHT a data overlay. Data overlay is discussed in Section-2. Following that, we describe the construction and operations of SOMO in Section-3, and also its application in Section-4. A case study of using SOMO to balance routing traffic to node capacity in a prefix-based overlay is offered in Section-5, along with preliminary results. Related works are discussed in Section-6, and we conclude in Section-7.

2   Data Overlay:
Implement Arbitrary Data Structures on Top of P2P DHT

We observe that hash-table is only one of the fundamental data structures. Sorted list, binary trees and queues etc. all have their significant utilities. One way would be to investigate how to make each of them self-organized (i.e., P2P sorted list). Another is to build on top of a hash table that already has the self-organizing property (i.e. P2P DHT). This second approach, which we call *data overlay*, is what we take in this paper.

Any object of a data structure can be considered as a document. Therefore, as long as it has a key, that object can be deposited into and retrieved from a P2P DHT. Objects relate to each other via pointers, so to traverse to the object *b* pointed by *a.foo*, *a.foo* must now store *b*'s key instead. More formally, the following two are the necessary and sufficient conditions:

- Each object must have a key, obtained at its birth.
- If an attribute of an object, *a.foo*, is a pointer, it is expanded into a structure of two fields: *a.foo.key* and *a.foo.host*. The first substitutes the hard-wired address of a conventional pointer; and the second field is a soft state containing the last known hosting DHT node of the object *a.foo* points to and serves as a routing shortcut.

It is possible to control the generation of object's key to explore data locality in a DHT. For instance, if the keys of *a* and *b* are close enough, it's likely that they will be hosted on the same machine in DHT.

We call a data structure distributed in a hosting DHT a *data overlay*. It differs from traditional sense of overlay in that traversing (or routing) from one entity to another uses the free service of the underlying P2P DHT.

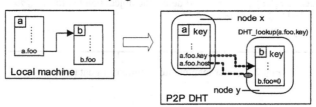

Fig. 1. Implement arbitrary data structure in DHT

Figure 1 contrasts a data structure in local machine versus that on a P2P DHT. Important primitives that manipulate a pointer in a data structure, including *setref, deref* (dereferencing) and *delete*, are outlined in Fig.2. Here, we assume that both DHT_lookup and DHT_insert will, as a side effect, always return the node in DHT that currently hosts the target object. DHT_direct bypasses normal DHT_lookup routing and directly seeks to the node that hosting an object given its key.

The interesting aspect is that it is now possible to host any arbitrary data structure on a P2P DHT, and in a transparent way. What need to be modified are the library routine that creates an object to insert a key as its member, and the few primitives that manipulate pointers as outlined. Therefore, legacy applications can be ported to run on top of a P2P DHT, giving them the illusion of an infinite storage space (here storage can broadly include memory heaps of machines comprising the DHT). The *host* routing shortcut makes the performance independent of the underlying DHT when the overall system dynamism is small.

A data overlay on top of a bare-bone P2P DHT with no internal reliability support can be used to implement distributed data structure that is soft-state in nature (i.e,, data is periodically refreshed and consumed thereafter without ill side-effect). If advanced fault-tolerant techniques are employed, then data overlay can spawn even more interesting research threads. For instance, it may be possible to turn DHT into a parallel computing utility by building a globally accessible and fully-associative memory heap as a repository of shared-variables [14].

```
setref(a.foo, b) {          // initially a.foo==null; b is the object
                            // to which a.foo will points to
   a.foo.key=b.key
   a.foo.host= DHT_insert(b.key, b)
}
deref(a.foo) {              // return the object pointed to by a.foo
   if (a.foo≠null) {
      obj=DHT_direct(a.foo.host, a.foo.key)
      if obj==null {        // object has moved
         obj=DHT_lookup(a.foo.key)
         a.foo.host = node returned
      }
      return obj
   }
   else return "non-existed"
}
delete(a.foo) {             // delete the object pointed to by a.foo
   DHT_delete(a.foo.key)
   a.foo=null
}
```

Fig. 2. Pointer manipulate primitives in data-overlay

3   Self-Organized Metadata Overlay

We now describe the data overlay SOMO (*Self-Organized Metadata Overlay*), an information gathering and disseminating infrastructure on top of any P2P DHT. Such an infrastructure must satisfy a few key properties: *self-organizing* at the same scale as the hosting DHT, fully *distributed* and *self-healing*, and be as *accurate* as possible of the metadata gathered.

Such metadata overlay can take a number of topologies. Given that one of the most important functionalities is aggregation, our implemented SOMO is a tree of k degree whose leaves are planted in each DHT node. Information is gathered from the bottom and propagates towards the root, and disseminated by trickling downwards. Thus, one can think of SOMO as doing *converge cast* from the leaves to the root, and then *multicast* back down to the leaves again. Both the gathering and dissemination phases are $O(\log_k N)$ bounded, where N is total number of entities. Each operation in SOMO involves no more than $k+1$ interactions, making it fully distributed. We deal with robustness using the principle of soft-state, so that data can be regenerated in $O(\log_k N)$ time. The SOMO tree self-organizes and self-heals in the same time bound. We now explain the details of SOMO.

3.1   Building SOMO

Since SOMO is a tree, we call its node the *SOMO node*. To avoid confusion, we denote the DHT nodes as simply the *DHT node*. A DHT node that hosts a SOMO node s, is referred to as *DHT_host(s)*.

The basic structure of the type *SOMO_node* is described in Fig.3. The member Z indicates the region of which this node's *report* member covers. Here, the region is simply a portion of the total logical space of the DHT. The root SOMO node covers the entire logical space. The *key* is produced by a deterministic function of a SOMO node's region Z. Examples of such functions include the center of the region, or a hash of the region coordinates (see Fig.4). Therefore, a SOMO node s will be hosted by a DHT node that covers $s.key$ (e.g. the center of $s.Z$). This allows a SOMO node to be retrieved deterministically as long as we know its region and is particularly useful when we want to query system status in a given key-space range. A SOMO node's responsible region is further divided by a factor of k, each taken by one of its k children, which are pointers in the SOMO data structure. A SOMO node s's i-th child will cover the i-th fraction of region $s.Z$. This recursion continues until termination condition is met (discussed shortly), and since a DHT node will own a piece of the logical space, it is therefore guaranteed a leaf SOMO node will be planted in it.

```
struct SOMO_node {
  string key
  struct SOMO_node *child[1..k]
  DHT_zone_type Z
  SOMO_op op
  Report_type report
}
```

Fig. 3. SOMO node data structure

Initially, when the system contains only one DHT node, there is only the SOMO root. As the DHT system grows, SOMO builds its hierarchy along. This is done by letting each SOMO node periodically execute the routine *SOMO_grow* (Fig.4).

We test first if the SOMO node's responsible zone is smaller or equal to that of the hosting DHT node, if the test comes out to be true, then this SOMO node is already a leaf planted in the right DHT node and there is no point to grow any more children. Otherwise, we attempt to grow. Note that we initialize a SOMO node object and its appropriate fields, and then call the *setref* primitive (See Fig.2) to install the pointer; this last step is where DHT operation is involved.

As this procedure is executed by all SOMO nodes, the SOMO tree will grow as the hosting DHT grows, and the SOMO tree is taller in logical space regions where DHT nodes are denser. This is illustrated in Fig.5.

The procedure is done in a top down fashion, and is executed periodically. A bottom-up version can be similarly derived. When the system shrinks, SOMO tree will prune itself accordingly by deleting redundant children. For an N-node system where nodes populate the total logical space evenly, there will be $2N$ SOMO-nodes when the SOMO fan-out k is 2.

```
SOMO_grow(SOMO_node s) {      // check if any children is necessary
  if (s.Z⊆DHT_host(s).Z) return
  for i=1 to k
    if (s.child[i]==NULL && the i-th sub-space of s.Z ⊄ host(s).Z) {
      t = new(type SOMO_node)
      t.Z = the i-th sub-space of s.Z
      t.key = SOMO_loc(t.Z)
      setref(s.child[i], t)          // inject into DHT
    }
}
SOMO_loc(DHT_zone_type Z) {
  return center of Z
  // optionally
  // return hash_of (Z)
}
```

Fig. 4. SOMO_grow procedure and the SOMO_loc procedure which deterministically calculates a SOMO node's key given the region it covers

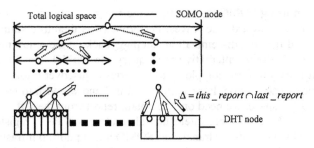

Fig. 5. SOMO tree on top of P2P DHT

The crash of a DHT node will take away the SOMO nodes it is hosting. However, the crashing node's zone will be taken over by another DHT node after repair. Consequently, the periodical checking of all children SOMO nodes ensures that the tree can be completely reconstructed in $O(\log_k N)$ time. Because the SOMO root is always hosted by the DHT node that owns one deterministic point of the total space, that node ensures the existence of the SOMO root and invokes the *SOMO_grow* routine on the SOMO root.

3.2   Gathering and Disseminate Information with SOMO

To gather system metadata, for instance loads and capacities, a SOMO node periodically requests report from its children. The leaf SOMO nodes simply get the required info from their hosting DHT nodes. As a side-effect, it will also re-start a child SOMO node if it has disappeared because the hosting DHT node's crash. Fig.6 illustrates the procedure.

The routine is periodically executed at an interval of T. Thus, information is gathered from the SOMO leaves and flows to its root with a maximum delay of $\log_k N \cdot T$. This bound is derived when flows between hierarchies are completely unsynchronized. If upper SOMO nodes' call immediately triggers the similar actions of their children, then the latency can be reduced to $T + t_{hop} \cdot \log_k N$, where t_{hop} is average latency of a trip in the hosting DHT. The unsynchronized flow has latency bound of $\log_k N \cdot T$, whereas the synchronized version will be bounded by T in practice (e.g., 5 minutes). Note that $O(t_{hop} \cdot \log_k N)$ is the absolute lower bound. For 2M nodes and with $k=8$ and a typical latency of 200ms per DHT hop, the SOMO root will have a global view with a lag of 1.6s.

```
get_report (SOMO_node s) {
  Report_type rep[1..k]
  for i∈ [1..k]
    if (s.child[i] ≠ NULL)           // retrieving via DHT
      rep[i] = deref(s.child[i]).report
  s.report = s.op(rep[])
}
```

Fig. 6. SOMO gathering procedure

Dissemination using SOMO is essentially the reverse: data trickles down through the SOMO hierarchy towards the leaves. Performance is therefore similar to gathering. By some modification, dissemination can piggyback on the return message in the gathering phase. The other alternative is to query the SOMO tree. Since SOMO is hierarchical, it is easy to form complex range queries to discover information relevant to a given logical space region. For example, if k is 2 and we wish to get status report of the first ¼ of the space, we need only to obtain report from the left child of the 2nd level SOMO tree. An even more interesting alternative will be to register queries at SOMO nodes, which essentially transforms SOMO into a pub/sub infrastructure.

Operations in either gathering or disseminating phases involve one interaction with the parent, and then with k children. Thus, the overhead in a SOMO operation is a constant. The entities involved are the DHT nodes that host the SOMO tree. SOMO nodes are scattered among DHT nodes and therefore SOMO processing is distributed and scales with the system.

It seems that towards the SOMO root the hosting DHT nodes need to have increasingly higher bandwidth and stability. As discussed earlier, stability is not a concern because the whole SOMO hierarchy can be recovered in $O(\log_k N)$ time. As for bandwidth, most of the time one needs only to submit delta between reports (Fig. 5.). Compression will further bring down message size. Finally, it is always possible to locate appropriate nodes through SOMO and then let them occupy specific points of the space and thereby take desirable positions in the SOMO topology (e.g. the root). That is to say, SOMO can be self-optimizing as well.

3.3   Discussion

The power of SOMO lies in its simplicity and flexibility: it specifies neither the type of information it should gather and/or disseminate, nor the operation invoked to process them.   That is to say, SOMO operations are programmable and *active*. For this reason, in the pseudo-code we have used *op* as a generic notation for operation used. Using the abstraction of data overlay (especially the *host* routing shortcut), its performance is also insensitive to the hosting DHT.

We have described SOMO in a collaborative environment to start with. If there are malicious nodes, then the trustworthiness of SOMO itself is under doubt. We offer some of our preliminary thoughts here:

- Denial-of-service attacks can be mounted by relentlessly requesting SOMO root. We believe an efficient way to defend against this is by propagating copies throughout the network, thereby stopping the attacks on the system edge. This borrows the idea from Freenet [2].
- SOMO reports can be compromised in multiple ways on the paths of aggregation and dissemination. To guard against this, reports must be signed and redundant SOMO reports need to be generated through multiple SOMO internal nodes, and use voting for consensus and intruder detection.
- Finally, the most difficult attack to solve is that individual node can simply cheat about its own status. Feedback processes among peers external to SOMO should be used to establish trustworthiness of each node.

4   Application of SOMO

As a scalable, fault-tolerant metadata gathering and dissemination infrastructure, the utilities of SOMO are many. In a large scale system, the need to monitor the health of the system itself can not be understated. We have implemented a SOMO-based global performance monitor with which we monitor the servers in our lab on a daily basis. This tool employs SOMO built over a P2P DHT and gathers data from various performance counter on each machine and presents a unified user interface to clients. We tested the SOMO stability by unplugging cables of servers being monitored, and each time the global view is regenerated after a short jitter. Using the data overlay abstraction, the SOMO layer is implemented much like any local procedures, with only a few hundred lines of code.

More advanced usages are chiefly decided by algorithms that built upon the metadata that gathered. It is possible to build a SOMO on top of a basic, mesh-based P2P DHT, and then build a $O(\log N)$ soft-state prefix-based overlay by installing long-range entries because SOMO provides the knowledge of what nodes exist in what portion of the total logic space. Even more useful is the fact that SOMO can create an image of a single resource pool comprised of nodes forming the DHT.

Another instance would be to find powerful nodes, commonly known as *supernodes*. To do this, we will make a SOMO tree where the report type is sorted list, and the *op* is merge-sort. Thus, SOMO can mine out multiple classes of supernodes, as reports available at various internal SOMO nodes, with the SOMO root having the complete list. These supernodes can thus act as indexing [6] or routing hobs [17]. There are also proposals where routing performance is the best but storage uniformity is sacrificed [8], SOMO can discover the density map of node capacities. Such information can guide document placement, or migrate nodes from dense regions to weak ones. In this way, uniformity will improve over time. We have also mentioned the possibility of turning SOMO into a pub/sub infrastructure.

5   Case Study: Balancing Routing Power
with Routing Traffic in Prefix-Based Overlay

Prefix-based overlay includes Tapestry [16], Pastry [9], Chord [11], Kademlia [5] and eCAN [13] (CAN [7] with simple extension). Though some aspects of these proposals differ, they share a few key attributes: 1) the total logical (or key) space is recursively divided and 2) routing greedily seeks out the biggest span into a sub-space and then zoom in towards target quickly. Routing table of prefix-based overlay is an array, recording spaces of exponentially decreasing size and one or several nodes that serve as this node's gateway, or "router" into these spaces. The flexibility of the prefix-based overlays is that, any node in the target sub-space can be a router. This gives rise to many optimization opportunities. Pastry and eCAN explore the possibilities of using the geographically closest node as router candidates to improve routing performance. In this paper, we report our investigation on another complementary axis: choosing the more powerful nodes to serve as routing entrances for larger sub-spaces where traffics are exponentially more than sub-spaces further enclosed. The ultimate solution (and challenge) of selecting these "routers" is to consider all the following three factors: geographic vicinity, routing capacity and load distribution. This remains to be one of our future works.

Our goal is to promote the most capable nodes to handle traffics into larger space, relieving weaker nodes off these responsibilities. Intuitively, the most powerful nodes will take the bulk of the loads in the largest enclosing space, and the weaker ones will serve no more than those designated to its immediate neighbor. Due to space limitation, we refer readers to [15] for the full protocol. Our basic idea is to classify routing loads that a node takes according to the sub-space in which the routing is designated and divide a node's routing capacity accordingly. The end-goal is that each sub-space's load/capacity ratio approaches that of the whole system.

Our optimization consists of four algorithms:

- **Statistic Collection Algorithm.** Aggregate loads and capacity statistics in a bottom-up sweep through SOMO. The goal is to have a "view" of the demographic distribution of both loads and capacities. At this point, the load/capacity ratios of the whole system as well as all enclosing spaces are available.

- **Load Balance Algorithm.** Top-down sweep to determine the amount of routing capacities to be dedicated in each space, so that its load/capacity ratio approaches to that of the whole system where possible.

- **Capacity Selection Algorithm.** Select the right portion of capacities, as recommended by the previous step, from candidate nodes. Also bottom-up sweep. At the end of this algorithm, we have selected the right capacity divide responsible for traffic loads of different space.

- **Entries Dissemination Algorithm.** Notify other nodes to use these new "routers" so that load distribution can take effect.

The core of our algorithm is in the 2nd and the 3rd step. It can be simplified if not for a subtle but important issue. The load and capacity distribution can be so skewed that nodes in a sub-space are already overwhelmed by the traffic designated to them, leaving them virtually no surplus power to share routing duties in enclosing spaces. Our scheduling algorithm has taken this into full account by pardoning heavily loaded sub-spaces (or the ones with meager power).

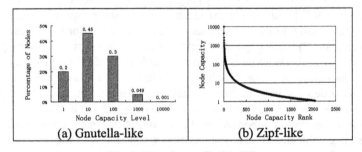

Fig. 7. Capacity profile (N=2K)

We modify an earlier e/CAN simulator by incorporating all the four algorithms described earlier. eCAN [13] is a prefix-based overlay capable of O(lnN) routing performance, and this is achieved with simple extension to CAN [7]. In eCAN, the recursion in resolving routing is by zooming into topology sub-zones rather than shifting bits. However, our algorithm is immediately applicable to other prefix-based overlays such as Pastry [9], Tapestry [16] and Kademlia [5].

Two capacity profiles are used to model heterogeneity:

- **Zipf-Like:** when sorted, the i-th node has capacity $10000 \cdot i^{-\beta}$, we choose β be 1.2 by default.
- **Gnutella-Like:** there are 5 levels of node, and the i-th level has capacity 10^{i-1}, popularity in these levels are 20%, 45%, 30%, 4.9% and 0.1%, going from level 1 to level 5 (see [10]).

The comparison of the two distributions for a 2K node system is shown in Fig.7.

The eCAN configuration we use is equivalent to Pastry/Tapestry of b=1. We tested other configurations [15] and results are similar to those presented here. For each configuration (capacity profile, N and other parameters), an experiment of 5 cycles is run. Each cycle starts with a complete reshuffling of the node capacities, then route $100N$ times, during which load and capacity information are gathered. We then run the four algorithms to perform load balance. Finally another $100N$ routings are performed and various statistics are collected again. This somewhat primitive setup allows us to gain sufficient insight of the algorithms; a more sophisticated one would include node join and leave events and mix SOMO traffics with normal routing, which we plan to conduct in the future.

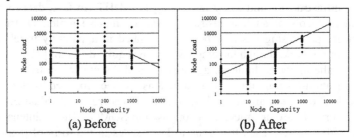

Fig. 8. Results of N=2K, Gnutella-like (the line corresponds to average load of a capacity level)

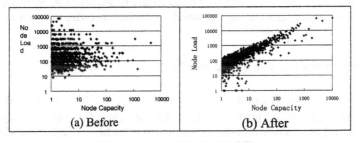

Fig. 9. Results of N=2K, Zipf-like

We found that, in all configurations, load balance converges quickly in $O(\log N)$ time, and that after the full set of the algorithms are run, higher capacity nodes are taking more loads. Fig.8 and Fig.9 show a typical pair of results of the Gnutella-like and Zipf-like capacity distributions, respectively. Note the sharp difference before and after the load redistribution.

6   Related Work

Data overlay relies on the key property of the P2P DHT ([9, 16, 11, 7, 5, 13]) that an item with unique key can be reliably created and retrieved. To our knowledge, extending the principle of self-organizing to arbitrary data structure other than hash table and do it in a way that is agnostic to both semantics and performance of the hosting P2P DHT is new.

A pure "peer-to-peer" mindset will view hierarchy as forbidden word. We believe this is misleading as important functionalities such as aggregation and indexing [6, 1] inherently imply a hierarchical structure. On this, SOMO bears the most similarity to Astrolabe [12], a peer-to-peer management and data mining system, for instance the use of hierarchies and aggregation. SOMO operates at the rudimentary data structure level while Astrolabe is on a virtual, hierarchical database. SOMO's extensibility is much like that of active network, whereas Astrolabe uses SQL queries. The marked difference is that SOMO is designed specifically on top of P2P DHT, for two reasons: 1) we believe P2P DHTs have established a foundation over which many other systems can be built and thus there is a need for a scalable resource management and monitoring infrastructure and 2) by leveraging P2P DHT (in fact, data overlay) the design and protocols of such infrastructure can be much simpler. Distributed, in-network query processing has also been investigated in apparently unrelated fields such as sensor network, though the emphasis there is quite different [2].

The other alternative to build an aggregation and dissemination tree would be to use the application-level multicasting tree such as the one proposed by Scribe [2] and Bayeux [18]. These trees are formed by joining routes from individual nodes to the root and, as a result, are unstructured as opposed to SOMO. The maintenance of the tree would either require each tree node to keep states in the form of pointers to its children, or let DHT nodes route to the root periodically to refresh the tree structure. In SOMO, every node is uniquely identified by the region that its report covers and therefore requires zero states. The structured nature of SOMO also allows queries to arbitrary sub-region of the total space, which would be otherwise impossible.

7   Conclusion and Future Work

This paper makes several novel contributions: we describe how arbitrary data structures can be implemented on P2P DHT using the concept of data overlay; we designed and evaluated a self-organizing and robust metadata gathering and dissemination infrastructure SOMO. We have demonstrated how to balance routing traffic with node capacity in prefix-based overlay using both of these two techniques. Our future work includes more extensive study of these concepts.

Acknowledgement

The authors would like to thank Yu Chen and Qiao Lian for their insightful discussion. Dan Zhao helped to prepare this report as well. We also thank the anonymous reviewers for their useful comments.

References

[1]   Adamic, L., Huberman, B., Lukose, R., and Puniyani, *A. Search in Power Law Networks, Physical Review. E64*(2001), 46135-46143

[2]   Castro M., Druschel P., Kermarrec A., and Rowstron A. SCRIBE: A Large-scale and Decentralized Application-level Multicast Infrastructure. IEEE Journal on Selected Areas in Communications, Vol. 20. No 8. Oct. 2002

[3]   Clarke, I., et al. *Freenet: A distributed anonymous information storage and retrieval system.* In Workshop on Design Issues in Anonymity and Unobservability. 2000. Berkeley, CA, USA.

[4]   Madden, S and et al. TAG: A Tiny AGregation Service for Ad-Hoc Sensor Networks. OSDI'02

[5]   Maymounkov, P. and Mazieres D. Kademlia: a Peer-to-Peer Information System Based on the XOR Metric. In *1st International Workshop on Peer-to-Peer Systems (IPTPS'02)*, (Cambridge, MA March 2002)

[6]   Qin Lv and Sylvia Ratnasamy, *Can Heterogeneity Make Gnutella Scalable?* Proceedings of IPTPS 2002

[7]   Ratnasamy, S., et al. A Scalable Content-Addressable Network. In *ACM SIGCOMM*. 2001. San Diego, CA, USA.

[8]   Ratnasamy, S., et al. Location-Aware Overlay Construction and Server Selection. In *Infocom*. 2002.

[9]   Rowstron, A. and P. Druschel. Pastry: Scalable, distributed object location and routing for largescale peer-to-peer systems. in *IFIP/ACM Middleware*. 2001. Heidelberg, Germany.

[10] Saroiu, S., Gummadi, K., and Gribble, S. A measurement study of peer-to-peer file sharing systems. In *Proceedings of Multimedia Conferencing and Networking* (San Jose, Jan. 2002)

[11] Stoica, I., et al. *Chord:* A scalable peer-to-peer lookup service for Internet applications. In *ACM SIGCOMM*. 2001. San Diego, CA, USA.

[12] Van Renesse, Robert and Birman Kenneth. *Scalable Management and Data Mining using Astrolabe*. Proceedings of IPTPS 2002.

[13] Xu, Zhichen and Zhang, Zheng, *Building Low-maintenance Expressways for P2P Systems*, available at http://www.hpl.hp.com/techreports/2002/HPL-2002-41.html, March 2002

[14] Zhang, Z., Turning P2P DHT into a Parallel Computing Utility. Submitted for publication.

[15] Zhang, Z., Shi, S-M. and Zhu, J.. Self-balanced P2P expressway: when Marxism meets Confucian. MSR-TR-2002-72

[16] Zhao, B., Kubiatowicz, J.D., and Josep, A.D. *Tapestry: An infrastructure for fault-tolerant wide-area location and routing*. Tech. Rep. UCB/CSD-01-1141, UC Berkeley, EECS, 2001.

[17] Zhao, B., and et al. Brocade, Landmark Routing on Overlay Networks. In IPTPS'02

[18] Zhuang S.Q., Zhao B.Y., and Joseph A.D. Bayeux: An Architecture for Scalable and Fault-tolerant Wide-Area Data Dissemination, NOSSDAV'01, New York, USA

Efficient Recovery from Organizational Disconnects in SkipNet

Nicholas J. A. Harvey, Michael B. Jones, Marvin Theimer, and Alec Wolman

Microsoft Research, Redmond, WA, USA
{nickhar,mbj,theimer,alecw}@microsoft.com

Abstract. SkipNet is a scalable overlay network that provides controlled data placement and routing locality guarantees by organizing data primarily by lexicographic ordering of string names. A key side-effect of the SkipNet design is that all nodes from an organization form one or a few contiguous overlay segments. When an entire organization disconnects from the rest of the system, repair of only a few pointers quickly enables efficient routing throughout the disconnected organization; full repair is done as a subsequent background task. These same operations can be later used to efficiently reconnect an organization's SkipNet back into the global one.

1 Introduction

SkipNet is a scalable, peer-to-peer overlay network that organizes nodes into a circular distributed data structure that concurrently supports two separate, but related address spaces. In one space, nodes belong to multiple rings where ring members are lexicographically ordered according to nodes' string names. In the other space, nodes are labeled with uniformly distributed numeric IDs. These numeric IDs define which rings a node belongs to in the first space. The combination of the two spaces enables SkipNet to provide efficient message routing as well as support several important locality properties.

Most notable of these properties is the ability to control the placement of data. SkipNet supports simultaneous use of multiple distributed hash tables (DHTs) that span varying subsets of the overlay nodes. In particular, DHTs can be defined over any set of nodes that share the same string name prefix. For example, if nodes belonging to the same organization all share an organization-specific name prefix then clients of the overlay can define DHTs whose data is load balanced across the nodes of a particular organization while still being accessible from any node in the overlay network.

SkipNet's design also allows it to guarantee that message routes traverse only intermediate nodes sharing the same name prefix as do the source and destination nodes. Thus local access to data stored within an organization can be obtained without having to worry about the associated message traffic having to traverse external nodes that might be either hostile or unavailable.

One of the more common forms of Internet failure is disconnection of an organization due to router misconfigurations and link and router faults [6, 7].

F. Kaashoek and I. Stoica (Eds.): IPTPS 2003, LNCS 2735, pp. 183–196, 2003.

When such a disconnection occurs, SkipNet's locality properties enable a graceful degradation of functionality wherein local overlay traffic and hence access to data stored in locally defined DHTs still remains possible. Assuming that organizations assign node names with one or a few organizational prefixes, an organization's nodes are naturally arranged into one or a few contiguous overlay segments. Should an organization become disconnected, its segments remain internally well-connected and intra-segment traffic can be routed with the same $O(\log N)$ hop efficiency as before.

By forming only a few key routing pointers between the "edge" nodes of each segment, the entire organization can be connected into a separate SkipNet that can route traffic with similar efficiency: cross-segment traffic incurs an additional penalty that is proportional to the number of segments traversed. A background process repairs the additional routing pointers, thereby eliminating the cross-segment penalty. SkipNet's structure enables this repair process to be done in a manner that avoids unnecessary duplication of work. When the organization reconnects to the Internet, these same repair operations can be used to merge the organization's segments back into the global SkipNet.

In contrast, most previous scalable, peer-to-peer overlay designs [9, 10, 11, 13] place nodes in the overlay topology according to a unique random numeric ID only. Disconnection of an organization in most of these systems will result in its nodes fragmenting into many disjoint overlay pieces. During the time that these fragments are reforming into a single overlay, network routing efficiency may be poor or unbalanced, or may even fail.

SkipNet's basic design and performance are described in Section 2; a complete description can be found in in Harvey et al. [3, 4]. Section 3 describes the repair algorithms for disconnection and reconnection, and presents some performance evaluation results. Section 4 concludes the paper.

2   SkipNet Overview

SkipNet is a scalable peer-to-peer overlay network designed to support two key locality properties: *content locality* and *path locality*. These locality properties address two notable disadvantages of many existing overlay designs: it is difficult to control where data is stored and it is difficult to guarantee that routing paths remain within an administrative domain. Content locality is the ability to place data either on specific overlay nodes or to load balance it across the nodes within a specific organization. Path locality is the ability to guarantee that when two overlay nodes within the same organization communicate, any intermediate routing hops also remain within that same organization.

Content and path locality provide a number of key benefits with respect to availability, performance, manageability, and security. As we and others [4, 5, 12] have noted, much of the data stored within peer-to-peer systems can still be expected to exhibit significant locality in clients' access patterns. Thus, for example, organizations may wish to make data globally available while still storing it locally in order to obtain better intra-organizational availability and perfor-

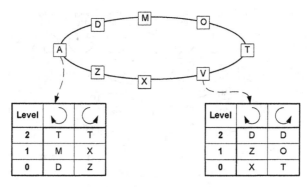

Fig. 1. SkipNet nodes ordered by name ID. Routing tables of nodes A and V are shown

mance. Content and path locality support this style of non-uniform peer-to-peer system. In particular, they also enable an organization to become disconnected from the Internet while still allowing overlay members of the organization to communicate with each other and access data stored within the organization. Explicit content placement onto a single node or across a well-defined set of nodes also enhances overall system manageability because the relevant nodes can be provisioned to support the anticipated access frequency for the set of data items being stored. Finally, path locality provides significant security benefits since potentially malicious routers in other administrative domains cannot affect intra-domain traffic.

2.1   The Basic SkipNet Structure

SkipNet's basic design is derived from ideas underlying the in-memory Skip List data structure [8]. The key idea we take from Skip Lists is the notion of maintaining a sorted list of all data records as well as pointers that "skip" over varying numbers of records. We transform the concept of a Skip List to a distributed system setting by replacing data records with computer nodes, using the string *name IDs* of the nodes as the data record keys, and forming a ring instead of a list. The ring must be doubly-linked to enable path locality, as is explained in Section 2.2.

In the basic SkipNet design each node stores $2 \log N$ pointers, where N is the number of nodes in the overlay system. Each node's set of pointers is called its *routing table*, or R-Table, since the pointers are used to route message traffic between nodes. The pointers at level h of a given node's routing table point to nodes that are roughly 2^h nodes to the left and right of the given node.

Figure 1 depicts a SkipNet containing eight nodes and shows the routing table pointers that nodes A and V maintain. The SkipNet in Figure 1 is a "perfect" SkipNet: each level h pointer traverses exactly 2^h nodes. Figure 2 depicts the same SkipNet of Figure 1, arranged to show all node interconnections at every

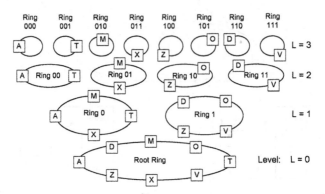

Fig. 2. The full SkipNet routing infrastructure for an 8 node system, including the ring labels

level simultaneously. All nodes are connected by the *root ring* formed by each node's pointers at level 0. The pointers at level 1 point to nodes that are 2 nodes away and hence the overlay nodes are implicitly divided into two disjoint rings. Similarly, pointers at level 2 form four disjoint rings of nodes, and so forth. Note that rings at level $h+1$ are obtained by splitting a ring at level h into two disjoint sets, each ring containing every second member of the level h ring.

Maintaining a perfect SkipNet in the presence of insertions and deletions is very expensive. To facilitate efficient insertions and deletions, we derive a probabilistic SkipNet design. Each ring at level h is split into two rings at level $h + 1$ by having each node randomly and uniformly choose to which of the two rings it belongs. With this probabilistic scheme, insertion/deletion of a node only affects two other nodes in each ring to which the node has randomly chosen to belong. Furthermore, a pointer at level h still skips over 2^h nodes in expectation, and routing is possible in $O(\log N)$ forwarding hops with high probability.

Each node's random choice of ring memberships can be encoded as a unique binary number, which we refer to as the node's *numeric ID*. As illustrated in Figure 2, the first h bits of the number determine ring membership at level h. For example, node X's numeric ID is 011 and its membership at level 2 is determined by taking the first 2 bits of 011, which designate Ring 01. One way to obtain a unique, random numeric ID is by using a collision-resistant hash (such as SHA-1) of the node's DNS name.

Because the numeric IDs of nodes are unique they can be thought of as a second address space that is maintained by the same SkipNet data structure. Whereas SkipNet's string address space is populated by node name IDs that are *not* uniformly distributed throughout the space, SkipNet's numeric address space is populated by node numeric IDs that *are* uniformly distributed. The uniform distribution of numeric IDs in the numeric space is what ensures that our routing table construction yields routing table entries that skip over the appropriate number of nodes.

2.2   Routing by Name ID

Routing/searching by name ID in SkipNet is based on the same basic principle as searching in Skip Lists: Follow pointers that route closest to the intended destination. At each node, a message will be routed along the highest-level pointer that does not point past the destination value. Routing terminates when the message arrives at a node whose name ID is closest to the destination.

Since nodes are ordered by name ID along each ring and a message is never forwarded past its destination, all nodes encountered during routing have name IDs between the source and the destination. Thus, when a message originates at a node whose name ID shares a common prefix with the destination, all nodes traversed by the message have name IDs that share that same prefix. Rings are doubly-linked so that routing can use either right or left pointers depending upon whether the source's name ID is smaller or greater than the destination's.

The number of message hops when routing by name ID is $O(\log N)$ with high probability. For a proof, see [3].

2.3   Routing by Numeric ID

It is also possible to route messages efficiently to a given numeric ID. In brief, the routing operation begins by examining nodes in the level 0 ring until a node is found whose numeric ID matches the destination numeric ID in the first digit. At this point the routing operation jumps up to this node's level 1 ring, which must also contain the destination node. The routing operation then examines nodes in this level 1 ring until a node is found whose numeric ID matches the destination numeric ID in the second digit. As before, we know that this node's level 2 ring must also contain the destination node, and thus the routing operation proceeds in this level 2 ring.

This procedure repeats until we cannot make any more progress — we have reached a ring at some level h such that none of the nodes in that ring share $h+1$ digits with the destination numeric ID. We must now deterministically choose one of the nodes in this ring to be the destination node. Our algorithm defines the destination node to be the node whose numeric ID is numerically closest to destination numeric ID amongst all nodes in this highest ring.

As an example, imagine that the numeric IDs in Figure 2 are 4 bits long and that node Z's ID is 1000 and node O's ID is 1001. If we want to route a message from node A to destination 1011 then A will first forward the message to node D because D is in ring 1. D will then forward the message to node O because O is in ring 10. O will forward the message to Z because it is not in ring 101. Z will forward the message onward around the ring (and hence back) to O for the same reason. Since none of the members of ring 10 belong to ring 101, node O will be picked as the final message destination because its numeric ID is closest to 1011 of all ring 10 members.

The number of message hops when routing by numeric ID is $O(\log N)$ with high probability. For a proof, see [3].

2.4   Constrained Load Balancing

One of the most interesting capabilities that SkipNet supports is *constrained load balancing* (CLB). This is the ability to concurrently support multiple DHTs, each of which may span a client-specified set of nodes that all share the same name prefix. CLB is possible because SkipNet maintains two separate, but related address spaces, one of which supports efficient range queries over node name IDs. To implement CLB, we divide a data object's name into two parts: a part that specifies the set of nodes over which DHT load balancing should be performed (the *CLB domain*) and a part that is used as input to the DHT's hash function (the *CLB suffix*). In SkipNet the special character '!' is used as a delimiter between the two parts of the name.

For example, suppose we stored a document using the name *msn.com/DataCenter!*
TopStories.html. The CLB domain indicates that load balancing should occur over all nodes whose names begin with the prefix *msn.com/DataCenter*. The CLB suffix, *TopStories.html*, is used as input to the DHT hash function, and this determines the specific node within *msn.com/DataCenter* on which the document will be placed.

To search for a data object that has been stored using CLB, we first search for any node within the CLB domain using search by name ID. To find the specific node within the domain that stores the data object, we perform a search by numeric ID within the CLB domain for the hash of the CLB suffix.

The search by name ID is unmodified from the description in Section 2.2, and takes $O(\log N)$ message hops. The search by numeric ID is constrained by a name ID prefix and thus at any level must effectively step through a doubly-linked list rather than a ring. Upon encountering the right boundary of the list (as determined by the name ID prefix boundary), the search must reverse direction in order to ensure that no node is overlooked. Reversing directions in this manner affects the performance of the search by numeric ID by at most a factor of two, and thus $O(\log N)$ message hops are required in total.

2.5   Enhancements

Links in the routing structure shown in Figure 2 are determined strictly by nodes' name IDs and numeric IDs, which means that the SkipNet overlay is constructed without consideration of the physical network topology. To improve routing performance, SkipNet maintains two additional *proximity* routing tables, one per address space, that provide pointers that reflect network proximity of nodes much the way that Pastry's proximity-aware routing tables do [2]. Further details can be found in both [4] and [3].

An important point to understand is that both proximity tables are used only to optimize routing efficiency. Message routing reverts to using an R-Table pointer whenever use of a proximity table pointer would violate path locality or the relevant proximity table pointer is invalid (e.g. due to organizational disconnect).

To maintain the root ring correctly, each SkipNet node also maintains a *leaf set* that points to additional nodes along the root ring, for redundancy. In our current implementation we use a leaf set size of 16, just as Pastry does. Whereas root ring pointers are monitored and repaired in an expedited manner, all other SkipNet state is updated and repaired in a background fashion.

3   Failure Recovery Algorithms

When an organization is disconnected from the Internet, its nodes will be able to communicate with each other over IP but will not be able to communicate with nodes outside the organization. If the organization's nodes' names employ only a few organizational prefixes then the nodes are mostly contiguous in Skip-Net, and hence the global SkipNet will partition itself into several disjoint, but internally well-connected, segments. This is illustrated in Figure 3.

Because of SkipNet's path locality property, message traffic within each segment will be unaffected by disconnection and will continue to be routed with $O(\log M)$ efficiency, where M is the number of nodes within the segment. Assuming that the disconnecting organization constitutes a small fraction of the global SkipNet, cross-segment traffic among the global portions of the SkipNet will also remain largely unaffected because most cross-segment pointers among global segments will remain valid. This will not be true for the segments of the disconnected organization.

Gracefully handling a partition in the underlying IP network has two aspects: continuing to provide internal connectivity for the duration of the partition, and efficiently repairing the overlay when the underlying IP network partition heals. Maintaining internal connectivity of the overlay requires that communications be possible both within each overlay segment and across segments that still have IP connectivity to each other. Repairing the overlay when the partition heals involves reestablishing communications between overlay segments that were formerly unreachable by IP. Thus, the primary repair task after both disconnection and reconnection is the merging of overlay segments.

The algorithms employed in both the disconnection and reconnection cases are very similar: SkipNet segments must discover each other and then be merged together. For the disconnect case, the organization segments are merged into a separate SkipNet and the global segments are merged to reform the global SkipNet. For the reconnect case, all segments from the two separate SkipNets are merged into a single SkipNet.

3.1   Discovery Techniques

When an organization disconnects from the Internet there is no guarantee that the resulting non-contiguous segments will have pointers into each other. Therefore its segments may not be able to find each other using only SkipNet pointers. To solve this discovery problem we assume that organizations will divide their

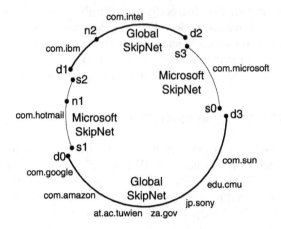

Fig. 3. Two partitioned SkipNets to be merged

nodes into a relatively small number of name segments and that they designate some number of nodes in each segment as "well-known". For instance,
Microsoft might maintain well-known members of segments with name prefixes
microsoft.com, *hotmail.com*, *xbox.jp*, etc. Each node in an organization maintains
a list of these well-known nodes and uses them as contact points between the
various overlay segments.

When an organization reconnects to the Internet, the organizational and
global SkipNets discover each other through their segment edge nodes. Since
each node maintains a leaf set, if a node discovers that one side of its leaf set,
but not the other, is completely unreachable then it concludes that a disconnect
event has occurred and that it is an edge node of a segment. These edge nodes
keep track of their unreachable leaf set pointers and periodically ping them for
reachability; should a pointer become reachable, the node initiates the merge
process. Note that merging two previously independent SkipNets together—for
example, when a new organization joins the system—is functionally equivalent
to reconnecting a previously connected one, except that an alternate means of
discovery is needed.

3.2 Connecting Root Ring Segments

The segment merge process is comprised of two steps: repair of the root ring
pointers and repair of the pointers for all higher-level rings. The first step can
be done quickly, as it only involves repair of the root ring pointers of the edge
nodes of each segment. Once the first step has been done it will be possible to
route messages correctly among nodes in different segments and to do so with
$O(S \log M)$ efficiency, where S is the total number of segments and M is the
maximum number of nodes within a segment. As a consequence, the second, more
expensive step can be done as a background task, as described in Section 3.3.

```
ConnectRootLevel(n1, n2) {
  edgeNodes = GatherEdgeNodeInfo(n1, n2, null)
  Connect edge node pairs.
}

GatherEdgeNodeInfo(n1, n2, msg) {
  n2 routes msg to n1 in its SkipNet.
  Msg will arrive at d1.
  d1 appends d1 and next neighbor, d0, to msg contents.
  d1 sends msg directly to n1 over IP.
  n1 routes msg to d0 in its SkipNet.
  Msg will arrive at s1.
  if (memberOf(s0, msg contents))  // => all segments
    return msg contents            //     traversed
  else  // => Message needs to discover more edge nodes
    s1 appends s1 and next neighbor, s0, to msg contents.
    return GatherEdgeNodeInfo(s0, d0, msg)
}
```

Fig. 4. SkipNet root ring connection algorithm

The key idea for connecting SkipNet root ring segments is to discover the relevant edge nodes by having a node in one segment route a message towards the name ID of a node in the other segment. This message will be routed to the edge node in the first segment that is lexicographically nearest to the other node's name ID. By repeating this process one can enumerate all edge nodes and hence all segments.

The actual inter-segment pointer updates are then done as a single atomic operation among the segment edge nodes, using distributed two-phase commit. This avoids routing inconsistencies where a message destined for a specific node on one segment inadvertently ends up at a different node in another overlay segment because the segments to be merged do not yet form a fully connected root ring.

To illustrate, Figure 3 shows two SkipNets to be merged, a Microsoft SkipNet and a global SkipNet, each containing two different name segments. Suppose that node $n1$ knows of node $n2$'s existence. Node $n1$ will send a message to node $n2$ (over IP) asking it to route a search message towards $n1$ in the global SkipNet. $n2$'s message will end up at node $d1$ and, furthermore, $d1$'s neighbor on the global SkipNet will be $d0$. $d1$ sends a reply to $n1$ (over IP) telling it about $d0$ and $d1$. $n1$ routes a search message towards $d0$ on the Microsoft SkipNet to discover $s1$ and $s0$ in the same manner. The procedure is iteratively invoked using $s0$ and $d0$ to gain information about $s2$, $s3$, $d2$, and $d3$. Figure 4 presents the algorithm in pseudo-code.

Immediately following root ring connection, messages sent to cross-segment destinations will be routed efficiently. Cross-segment messages will be routed to the edge of each segment they traverse and will then hop to the next segment using the root ring pointer connecting the segments. This leads to $O(S \log M)$ routing efficiency. When an organization reconnects its fully repaired SkipNet root ring to the global one, traffic destined for nodes external to the organization

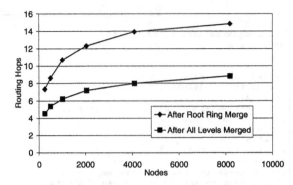

Fig. 5. Number of routing hops taken to route inter-organizational messages, as a function of network size, after an organization's internal SkipNet has been reconnected to the global SkipNet root ring and after the merge has been fully completed

will be routed in $O(\log M)$ hops to an edge node of the organization's SkipNet. The root ring pointer connecting the two SkipNets will be traversed and then $O(\log N)$ hops will be needed to route traffic within the global SkipNet. Note that traffic that does not have to cross between the two SkipNets will not incur this routing penalty.

To experimentally confirm the behavior of SkipNet's disconnection and merge algorithms we implemented them and then ran them in an extended version of the packet-level discrete event simulator available from [10]. The simulator was extended to support disconnection of AS subnetworks. The details of our experiments and experimental setup are described in [3]. Figure 5 shows the routing performance we observed between a previously disconnected organization and the rest of the system once the organization's SkipNet root ring has been connected to the global SkipNet root ring. We also show the routing performance observed when all higher level pointers have been repaired.

3.3   Repairing Routing Pointers Following Root Ring Connection

Once the root ring connection phase has completed we can update all remaining pointers that need repair using a background task. We present here an algorithm for doing this that avoids unnecessary duplication of work through appropriate ordering of repair activities.

The key idea is that we recursively repair pointers at one level by using correct pointers at the level below to find the desired nodes in each segment. All pointers at one level must be repaired across a segment boundary before repair of a higher level can be initiated. To illustrate, consider Figure 6, which depicts a single boundary between two SkipNet segments after pointers have been repaired. Figure 7 presents an algorithm in pseudo-code for repairing pointers above the root ring across a single boundary. We begin by discussing the sin-

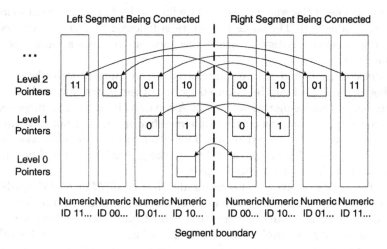

Level 2 Pointers: 11 00 01 10 | 00 10 01 11

Level 1 Pointers: 0 1 | 0 1

Level 0 Pointers

NumericNumeric Numeric Numeric | NumericNumeric Numeric Numeric
ID 11... ID 00... ID 01... ID 10... | ID 00... ID 10... ID 01... ID 11...

Segment boundary

Fig. 6. Nodes whose pointers have been repaired at the boundary of two SkipNet segments

```
// Called initially with level h=0 at node
// to the left of the merge point
PostMergeRepair(h) {
  Find closest node to left whose numeric ID matches
      mine in the first h bits and whose ID differs from
      mine in the next bit, by following level h
      pointers to the left.
  On my node:
    cont = FixMyRightPointer(h+1)
    if (cont) PostMergeRepair(h+1)
  In parallel, on the other node:
    cont2 = FixMyRightPointer(h+1)
    if (cont) PostMergeRepair(h+1)
}

FixMyRightPointer(h) {
  Search right using level h-1 pointers until a~node is
      found that matches my numeric id in h bits.
  Connect our level h pointers.
  if (pointers are already equal)
    return false
  else
    return true
}
```

Fig. 7. Level h ring repair algorithm for a single inter-segment boundary

gle boundary case, and later we extend our algorithm to handle the multiple boundary case.

Assume that the root ring pointers have already been correctly connected. There are two sets of two pointers to connect between the segments at level 1: the ones for the routing ring labeled 0 and the ones for the routing ring labeled 1 (see Figure 2). We can repair the level 1 ring labeled 0 by traversing the root (level

0) ring from one of the edge nodes until we find nodes in each segment belonging to the ring labeled 0. The same procedure is followed to correctly connect the level 1 ring labeled 1. After the level 1 rings, we use the same approach to repair the four level 2 rings.

Because rings at higher levels are nested within rings at lower levels, repair of a ring at level $h + 1$ can be initiated by one of the nodes that had its pointer repaired for the enclosing ring at level h. A repair at level $h + 1$ is unnecessary if the level h ring (a) contains only a single member or (b) does not have an inter-segment pointer that required repair. The latter termination condition implies that most rings—and hence most nodes—in the global SkipNet will not, in fact, need to be examined for potential repair.

The total work involved in this repair algorithm is $O(M \log(N/M))$, where M is the size of the disconnecting/reconnecting SkipNet segment and N is the size of the external SkipNet. Note that rings at level $h+1$ can be repaired in parallel once their enclosing rings at level h have been repaired across all segment boundaries. Thus, the repair process for a given segment boundary parallelizes to the extent supported by the underlying network infrastructure. The analysis behind these claims is omitted for space reasons and can be found in [3].

To repair multiple segment boundaries, we simply call the algorithm described above once for each segment boundary. In the current implementation, we perform this process iteratively, waiting for the repair operation to complete on one boundary before initiating the repair at the next boundary. In future work, we plan to investigate initiating the segment repair operations in parallel — the open question is how to avoid repair operations from different boundaries interfering with each other.

3.4   Repairing Proximity Table Entries

In normal operation, the routing table entries in both of a node's proximity routing tables are updated periodically using information gathered from the node's R-Table. Once the R-Table repair algorithms above have run then these periodic updates will likewise repair the node's proximity tables with no resulting increase in maintenance traffic.

4   Conclusion

Real-world data access patterns exhibit locality and hence we argue that peer-to-peer overlay networks should provide support for both content and path locality. One common form of locality that we expect is placement of globally accessible data within the organizations that own that data. We also expect that organizations will tend to access their own data more heavily than that of other organizations. Consequently there is value in enabling an organization's overlay network to continue functioning internally even when its member nodes have become partitioned from the rest of the overlay network.

SkipNet supports content and path locality by means of two separate, but related address spaces, one of which orders nodes lexicographically by their string names. The combination of the two spaces enables the definition of multiple globally accessible DHTs whose storage scopes span subsets of all overlay nodes. Assuming that organizations assign their nodes' names with a small number of unique organizational prefixes, they can thus store data locally while still making it globally available.

One of the more common forms of Internet failure is disconnection of an organization. The primary contribution of this paper is a description of how SkipNet enables efficient recovery from these failures. Because of the assumption that organizations' nodes will share one or a few name prefixes, a disconnect will result in a small number of internally well-connected overlay segments, each of which is able to route internal messages efficiently. Only a few routing pointers need to be repaired to connect segments into a functioning overlay network able to route with mildly degraded efficiency throughout the organization. Similarly, once a network partition has healed, the same approach can be used to reconnect the organization's SkipNet back into the global one.

Because efficient routing is quickly obtained, full repair of all nodes' routing tables can be done as a background task for both disconnection and reconnection. SkipNet's structure enables these repairs to be ordered in a manner that avoids unnecessary duplication of work.

Several important issues remain. Most notably, we have not yet explored how to initiate and perform multiple segment repair operations in parallel. Another problem is that segment edge nodes can become routing hot spots for both successful, as well as failed, cross-segment traffic. Finally, we also plan to find out how SkipNet behaves in practice by using it as the underpinning for the Herald global event notification service [1], which is currently being built to run on a large test bed cluster of machines.

References

[1] L. F. Cabrera, M. B. Jones, and M. Theimer. Herald: Achieving a global event notification service. In *Proceedings of the Eighth Workshop on Hot Topics in Operating Systems (HotOS-VIII)*, May 2001.

[2] M. Castro, P. Druschel, Y. C. Hu, and A. Rowstron. Topology-aware routing in structured peer-to-peer overlay networks. Technical Report MSR-TR-2002-82, Microsoft Research, 2002.

[3] N. J. A. Harvey, J. Dunagan, M. B. Jones, S. Saroiu, M. Theimer, and A. Wolman. SkipNet: A Scalable Overlay Network with Practical Locality Properties. Technical Report MSR-TR-2002-92, Microsoft Research, 2002.

[4] N. J. A. Harvey, M. B. Jones, S. Saroiu, M. Theimer, and A. Wolman. SkipNet: A Scalable Overlay Network with Practical Locality Properties. In *Proceedings of the Fourth USENIX Symposium on Internet Technologies and Systems (USITS '03)*, Mar. 2003.

[5] P. Keleher, S. Bhattacharjee, and B. Silaghi. Are virtualized overlay networks too much of a good thing? In *First International Workshop on Peer-to-Peer Systems (IPTPS '02)*, Mar. 2002.

[6] C. Labovitz and A. Ahuja. Experimental Study of Internet Stability and Wide-Area Backbone Failures. In *Fault-Tolerant Computing Symposium (FTCS)*, June 1999.

[7] D. Oppenheimer, A. Ganapathi, and D. A. Patterson. Why do Internet services fail, and what can be done about it? In *Proceedings of the Fourth USENIX Symposium on Internet Technologies and Systems (USITS '03)*, Mar. 2003.

[8] W. Pugh. Skip lists: A probabilistic alternative to balanced trees. In *Workshop on Algorithms and Data Structures*, pages 437–449, 1989.

[9] S. Ratnasamy, P. Francis, M. Handley, R. Karp, and S. Shenker. A Scalable Content-Addressable Network. In *Proceedings of the ACM SIGCOMM '01 Conference*, Aug. 2001.

[10] A. Rowstron and P. Druschel. Pastry: Scalable, distributed object location and routing for large-scale peer-to-peer systems. In *International Conference on Distributed Systems Platforms (Middleware)*, pages 329–350, Nov. 2001.

[11] I. Stoica, R. Morris, D. Karger, M. F. Kaashoek, and H. Balakrishnan. Chord: A scalable Peer-To-Peer lookup service for internet applications. In *Proceedings of the ACM SIGCOMM '01 Conference*, pages 149–160, Aug 2001.

[12] A. Vahdat, J. Chase, R. Braynard, D. Kostic, and A. Rodriguez. Self-organizing subsets: From each according to his abilities, to each according to his needs. In *First International Workshop on Peer-to-Peer Systems (IPTPS '02)*, Mar. 2002.

[13] B. Y. Zhao, J. D. Kubiatowicz, and A. D. Joseph. Tapestry: An infrastructure for fault-resilient wide-area location and routing. Technical Report UCB//CSD-01-1141, U. C. Berkeley, Apr. 2001.

Semantic-Free Referencing
in Linked Distributed Systems

Hari Balakrishnan[1], Scott Shenker[2], and Michael Walfish[1]

[1] Laboratory for Computer Science
Massachusetts Institute of Technology
Cambridge, MA. {hari,mwalfish}@lcs.mit.edu
[2] ICSI Center for Internet Research (ICIR), Berkeley, CA.
shenker@icsi.berkeley.edu

Abstract. Every distributed system that employs linking requires
a Reference Resolution Service (RRS) to convert link references to locations. We argue that the Web's use of DNS for this function is a bad
idea. This paper discusses the nature, design, and use of a scalable
and dynamic RRS. We make two principal arguments about the nature of reference resolution: first, that there should be a *general-purpose*
application-independent substrate for reference resolution, and second
that the references themselves should be *unstructured* and *semantic-free*.
We observe that distributed hash tables (DHTs) provide an elegant and
convenient platform for realizing these goals, and we present a general-
purpose DHT-based Semantic-Free Referencing (SFR) architecture.

1 Introduction

The Web, whose links can direct readers to a vast array of remote documents,
has revolutionized the nature of information dissemination by putting a global
set of resources into the hands of each individual author and reader. However,
the idea of using *links* to point to remote "objects" (of various types) is far
more general than the Web. Links are used in a variety of distributed systems
for identifying objects and invoking remote code [2, 4], for organizing data in
sensornets [7], for locating devices [1], and for many other purposes where one
wants to refer to objects by name, not IP address.

In general, we define a "link" as being composed of a *directive* and a *reference*.
The reference tells the client where to find the *target* (*i.e.*, the object being linked
to) while the directive tells the client how to process the target. For example, the
Web link <img src=http://www.mit.edu/ocw.jpg> has a directive telling the
client that the target of reference http://www.mit.edu/ocw.jpg is an image
that should be rendered.

In order to use a link, clients need a way of resolving the reference to a location
(*i.e.*, an IP address). Thus, every linked distributed system requires a *reference
resolution service* (RRS). To be useful for many distributed Internet applications,
an RRS should be *scalable*, performing well as the number of names and queries

F. Kaashoek and I. Stoica (Eds.): IPTPS 2003, LNCS 2735, pp. 197–206, 2003.

increases, and *dynamic*, able to accommodate fairly rapid changes in the binding between names and addresses.

This paper discusses the nature, design, and use of such a scalable and dynamic RRS. We make two principal arguments about the nature of reference resolution: first, that there should be a *general-purpose* application-independent substrate for reference resolution, and second that the references themselves should be *unstructured* and *semantic-free*.

After noting that distributed hash tables (DHTs) [5] provide an elegant and convenient platform for realizing these goals, we present a general-purpose DHT-based Semantic-Free Referencing (SFR) architecture and illustrate its use with some examples.

2   Shared and Semantic-Free

Every linked distributed application requires a scalable and dynamic method to translate references to locations. Since this is a complex problem requiring careful design and significant infrastructure, we should solve it exactly once with a shared substrate usable by all linked distributed systems.[1] Currently, no *general-purpose* RRS system exists. One might posit that Web URLs could fulfill this function. However, though the Web is wildly successful at providing its intended service, its DNS-based URLs are laden with application-specific semantics.

Today, because of these semantics, people often think of DNS names as branding mechanisms. As a result, there is tremendous legal contention for ownership of domain names [6]. Moreover, DNS's association between locations and well-known, delegated names makes it undesirable as a general-purpose RRS—while this association is merely inconvenient for Web publishers, who must acquire a DNS name before exposing content, it is clearly unnatural for linked systems in networks of sensors and devices in which administrative hierarchy and delegation are irrelevant, undesirable, or unavailable. Finally, because of their location-dependence, DNS-based Web URLs make it difficult to handle content replication, caching, and migration. Typically, new routing functionality for converting Web URLs to network locations requires baroque DNS hacks.

The argument for location-independent naming in linked systems is not new, and our position echoes the case made for Universal Resource Names (URNs) [8]. The various URN proposals advocated an architecture in which each linked system would have *its own* reference resolution service that would implement similar functionality in an application-specific manner. This contrasts with our contention that applications should use the *same* underlying method for reference resolution, and each linked system *share* the reference resolution infrastructure.

---

[1] There may be cases, such as in isolated sensornets, where the use of a common Internet-based RRS infrastructure is not possible. However, even in cases where a separate infrastructure is needed, we believe that the presence of a general-purpose RRS *design* would be of significant benefit.

The URN proposals also assumed that achieving scalability required both hierarchy and namespace delegation. One of our goals, however, is to eliminate these for the reasons mentioned above: using semantic-free references avoids human contention and an unstructured namespace is more natural and general-purpose, given the variety of applications requiring access to this shared infrastructure.

These aspects of the system imply that the RRS must support a "flat" namespace, making it difficult to design a hierarchical resolution method. Indeed, DNS scales very well in large part because of hierarchy based on administrative delegation, and until recently, there was no known RRS that could scale well without such hierarchy.

Fortunately, the recently developed DHT techniques offer a solution to the problem of designing a scalable, dynamic, and unstructured RRS, because they provide a general mapping between an unstructured key and a network location responsible for the key. The rest of this paper describes the design and use of a DHT-based RRS. We start by discussing the general concerns that any distributed linking infrastructure must address.

3   Link Infrastructure Components

We identify four basic, distinct concerns that must be addressed by any linking infrastructure and discuss how the Web implements them today.

Reference Routing: This is fundamental to a linking infrastructure: Given a reference, the system must locate the target. Currently, the Web uses DNS to convert a URL to an IP address and then point-to-point IP unicast routing for client-server communication.

Reference Integrity: The system must prevent the same reference from being used for two different intended targets,[2] a problem that becomes interesting when the set of link creators is distributed. Most previous systems have addressed this by embedding semantics in references, creating a reference namespace; the Web, for example, relies on DNS's administrative delegation for achieving reference integrity.

User-Level Names: Users need to be able to translate their goals (*e.g.*, "reach American Airlines") and context into an appropriate reference. In some cases, links are both generated and used by programs that require no outside context. But in many cases, the links will be exposed to human users, and for them the system must expose useful handles.

---

[2] It is of course possible and sometimes desirable for two different references to point to the same target.

On the Web, URLs themselves are an important user-level naming mechanism; URLs are usually human-readable and occasionally memorable. As a consequence, corporations sometimes fight for "choice" DNS names. However, an increasingly common and reliable way for discovering document locations on the Web is to use search engines.[3]

Confidence and Authentication: In most cases, users of a linking infrastructure would like some assurance that the reference they followed has taken them to the appropriate object. Formal methods can provide cryptographically-derived verification of server and content authenticity, but in many cases more informal *confidence-building* hints could satisfy users that they have reached their intended target.

Strict server (and content) authenticity on the Web is verified via certificates issued by trusted authorities. We note that the certificate infrastructure is largely independent of the Web architecture and can be used by any general link infrastructure. However, most information on the Web is not authenticated in the strict sense of the term. Instead, users often rely on informal assurances that they have found the correct reference (*e.g.*, seeing the DNS name of the content provider at the top of a browser page gives the user some confidence in the displayed data). While it is unclear to us precisely how important this notion of "confidence" is, it appears to provide something useful to Web users.

We note that the Web, instead of cleanly separating the four necessary features described above, uses DNS and the name registries to implement each of them: Reference routing occurs via DNS's name-to-IP address translation; DNS name registration helps achieve reference integrity; and some aspects of both the user-level naming and confidence features derive from the readability of DNS names.

As we described in Section 2, the human friendliness of DNS-based URLs, as well as its static associations between names and locations, results in consequences that are undesirable for a generic linking infrastructure. The next section details our proposal for a system free of those problems.

4   SFR Architecture

This section outlines our proposed SFR architecture in terms of the four link components. We emphasize that there are several open problems in each part. In designing the architecture to support semantic-free references, we seek to implement the four components as independently as possible (in contrast to the Web's overloading of DNS with responsibilities for which it was not intended and for which it is not well-suited). This gives us the benefits of modularity: tailoring components to their tasks, permitting different versions of components

---

[3] In fact, some say Google has supplanted URLs as the user-level naming method of choice [9].

for different applications, and freeing applications to use only those components necessary for them.[4]

Only one of the components—reference routing—is *essential*, and it forms the central piece of our proposed SFR architecture. Traversing links requires clients to locate remote targets, and so all distributed applications need this functionality. Because our solution is free of application-level semantics, we expect global sharing of this component by *all* SFR applications.

To implement scalable **reference routing**, the SFR architecture uses DHTs, which provide a mapping between a 160 bit reference, which we call an *SFRTag*, or simply—to emphasize its semantic-free nature—a *tag*, and an application-defined object-record (O-record). Our intent is for the O-record to provide a general-purpose scalable object location method that: (1) allows applications to embed semantics into objects while being oblivious to those semantics and (2) handles object replication, object mobility and object updates. The O-record has the following fields:

```
class O-record {
    UniqueID SFRTag;    // 160-bit id
    IP:Port Location;   // current locn.
    ObjectInfo O-info;  // app-specific
}
```

When the application creates an object, it also creates a new O-record and inserts it into the reference routing infrastructure (*i.e.*, the DHT) by calling SFR_Insert(SFRTag, O-record). (We address the issue of how SFRTag is generated later in this section.) In addition to the network location of the object, the O-record contains object information, defined and consumed only by the application. Examples of this information include the object's name in the application's namespace, the retrieval method for this object (*e.g.*, HTTP, SMTP), and a timestamp indicating last-modified-time. The O-info could even contain code that the searching client can use to retrieve the object. It is important to note that, although the O-info can be quite sophisticated, the reference routing machinery remains general-purpose because it operates below the application's namespace.

Once an O-record is in the SFR infrastructure, users who wish to retrieve the corresponding object first call SFR_Lookup(SFRTag). (The user-level naming component, which we discuss below, will allow the user or the user's application to obtain the SFRTag corresponding to her particular goals.) The infrastructure then returns the O-record of the object. The O-record's Location and O-info fields together have enough information for the searching client to retrieve the object. In some cases, the contents of the O-info field may signal to the client that object retrieval is unnecessary; a timestamp field, for example, would allow the client application to decide if a cached copy is current enough.

---

[4] For example, a system without human involvement does not need a user-level naming component.

While many of the DHT proposals were in the context of pure P2P systems on arbitrary hosts, we envision a decentralized but managed collection of machines in different administrative domains, somewhat akin to the DNS infrastructure, with reasonable stability and trustworthiness. Many groups are working to make such a DHT-based system a core component of the Internet's future infrastructure, and there are many open research questions (such as caching, replication, and security) that require further work. We don't address those research questions here and instead presume the presence of a working DHT infrastructure in our design.

We note that by using a DHT to resolve references, we are losing some of the *fate-sharing* that exists in current RRSs, such as DNS. Currently, with DNS, if an administrative domain is partitioned from the network, individuals in that administrative domain can often resolve references local to that domain (*e.g.*, they can successfully browse internal Web sites). Providing a form of fate-sharing within the SFR insfrastructure is an area of ongoing investigation for us.

Reference Integrity must be ensured by the application that creates a new object and inserts the corresponding SFRTag. Generation of unique tags is completely up to applications (which are free to employ a variety of techniques, including choosing random tags or hashing the contents of the O-record). The important points here are twofold: first, whatever method the application chooses, the SFR infrastructure will attempt to prevent the same tag from being inserted twice (updates and deletions are of course permitted). Second, the application can *check* whether the candidate tag has already been claimed (by calling SFR_Lookup() on the candidate) and then *reserve* its candidate. Because the namespace is massive, one need not worry that an adversarial application or user could preemptively reserve a significant chunk of potential identifiers. If an adversary reserved one new identifier each nanosecond for ten years, this would result in approximately 2^{58} identifiers being reserved, which, assuming the identifiers are 160 bits, represents a tiny fraction—only $1/2^{102}$—of the entire namespace.

We envision that various directory services will provide mappings between **user-level meanings** and the associated tags. Just as search engines now provide a mapping between keywords and URLs, in the future we envision that a plethora of directory services, each with its own intended audience and its own economic model, will provide a similar mapping service between keywords and other descriptions into tags. Far from being an unfortunate consequence of the semantic-free restriction, we believe that directory services are a more robust, extensible, reliable, and convenient method of advertising resources than non-permanent, forgettable URLs.

It is important to note that these directory services are not part of the core SFR architecture. Furthermore, their listings would not be decided at standards meetings or by official bodies. Some directory services could be funded by user contributions and would be designed to offer responses closest to the user's intent. Other directories could be funded by businesses seeking to have their name associated with certain keywords (payments would assure that a given airline would be one of the first items on the list of responses to a search for airlines, for example). Universities and other research non-profits could band together to offer directory services providing reliable listings in the research arena.

There are two aspects to **confidence and authentication**: first, only the "owner" or other authorized party should be allowed to modify a particular O-record. One way to implement this is to permit the entity inserting O-records to present a public key along with its SFR_Insert() request. If the entity presents a public key, then the SFR infrastructure ensures that the insert message and all modification messages have been signed with the corresponding private key. We note that the tag routing infrastructure should offer this level of authentication to applications, but it should not require them to take advantage of it.[5]

The second aspect to confidence and authentication is that clients (or their end-systems) should be able to verify the authenticity of references, and for this function, we envision different services using different mechanisms. Some services would use a trusted certificate authority and certificate chains much like the Web certificate infrastructure does today. However, the design of more informal confidence-building measures in an SFR infrastructure is an interesting problem, since references no longer convey semantic information to human users. For certain applications like the Web, a reasonable approach might be to rely on information provided by a search engine (such as a cryptographic hash) to validate content. We note that our proposal neither precludes any of these approaches nor mandates an authentication scheme.

5   Using Semantic-Free Links

The previous section's SFR architecture overview presented a preliminary design that, with many details to be fleshed out, will be the subject of future work. To give a more concrete idea of how the SFR architecture might be used in practice, we now describe two possible applications.

5.1   Web

One possible SFR-based redesign of the Web would be to use search engines as essentially the only way of reaching targets. This elevates search engines, already important, to a critical position in how documents are accessed.

Search engines will continue to index documents by their content but will associate documents with tags, instead of URLs. Since the reference in the link exposes no semantics, showing the corresponding bitstring when the user hovers over a link isn't particularly useful. We propose to handle this user-interface issue by instead displaying the meta-data corresponding to the target.[6]

---

[5] It is possible that for certain kinds of objects, the entity inserting an O-record would want any other user to be able to update the contents of the O-record without bothering with public and private keys.

[6] We emphasize that there are certainly many other interface questions to be worked through in this proposal for the Web; for example, we will have to develop a user-

In this SFR-based Web, two traditionally difficult issues—content replication and mobile Web servers—are handled without significant additional effort or specialized infrastructure because of the layer of indirection provided by the DHT. To handle replication, a tag (mapping to a DHT key) would have multiple values corresponding to the different nodes that contain some content. To handle server mobility, any change in the IP address/port of a target can be implemented using an O-record update mechanism.

Authentication is separate from link naming and would use a trusted certificate infrastructure as the Web does today. Search engines that produce the tags would give some degree of confidence, but exposing additional confidence-building hints is a trickier issue; one might envision a scheme in which each document has meta-data descriptions that are authenticated using signatures.

5.2 Directory Services

Directory services are an important primitive in many distributed systems, since they allow participants to rendezvous with each other (e.g., clients with servers). Invocations to a directory service often take the form of a remote procedure call (RPC) in a program—for instance, a program that has a link requiring email to be sent might invoke a DNS gethostbyname, or discovering a nearby color printer might require a suitable call to INS [1] or a SOAP call encoded in XML syntax [2]. The problem of finding suitable nodes that can answer an RPC is common to these applications, and can be implemented using SFR. Recent work has shown how this can be done in DNS [3] and in INS, using mappings between intentional names and SFRTags [1]. The same approach can be adapted to SOAP RPC, eliminating the need for HTTP encodings of SOAP.

6 Discussion

DNS is an excellent system for identifying static nodes in the Internet, and, at the time the Web was invented, it was also the best choice for reference routing. However, it has been over a decade since the Web was first deployed, and a system that statically maps well-known names to locations is not a good choice for the key component of a general linked infrastructure. We believe that DNS should continue to perform its original function but that there are now three reasons to reconsider the design of reference resolution systems: (1) the importance of links as a general concept in distributed systems is better understood, (2) we are more familiar with the weaknesses of embedding semantics in references, and (3) DHTs promise scalable, dynamic reference routing. Our thesis is that a general-purpose linking infrastructure will empower a variety of distributed services, and that *semantic-free* reference routing is the organizing principle for designing it.

---

interface to HTML composition that would allow content providers to embed tags in their document while protecting them from unwieldy bitstrings.

We conclude with an analogy between virtual memory in traditional operating systems and our proposal. Most programming languages today support typed objects that have references to other objects.

The compiler for the language converts all references to virtual (rather than physical) addresses, which are in turn translated to physical addresses by a language-independent OS and memory management unit.

Now consider a typical distributed linked application. It has objects, which have references to other objects, defined in an application-specific syntax. However, despite the ubiquity of remote linking, there is currently *no* notion of virtual addressing for linked applications.

Our SFR proposal aims to fill this void. For linked distributed applications it provides a general virtual-to-physical translation that allows application-specific links to be layered over the abstraction. We believe that an SFR infrastructure is timely, viable, and worthy of further research.

Acknowledgments

We thank Frank Dabek, Mark Handley, and Karen Sollins for useful discussions. We thank the anonymous reviewers for their comments.

This research was conducted as part of the IRIS project

http://project-iris.net/

supported by the National Science Foundation under Cooperative Agreement No. ANI-0225660.

References

[1] M. Balazinska, H. Balakrishnan, and D. Karger. INS/Twine: A Scalable Peer-to-Peer Architecture for Intentional Resource Discovery. In *Proc. International Conf. on Pervasive Computing*, Zurich, Switzerland, August 2002.

[2] D. Box et al. Simple Object Access Protocol (SOAP) 1.1. http://www.w3.org/TR/SOAP, May 2000. W3C Note.

[3] Russ Cox, Athicha Muthitacharoen, and Robert Morris. Serving DNS using a Peer-to-Peer Lookup Service. In *1st International Workshop on Peer-to-Peer Systems (IPTPS'02)*, Cambridge, MA, March 2002.

[4] Markus Horstmann and Mary Kirtland. DCOM Architecture. http://msdn.microsoft.com/library/default.asp?url=/library/en-us/ dndcom%/html/msdn_dcomarch.asp , July 1997.

[5] Infrastructure for Resilient Internet Systems. http://www.project-iris.net/, 2002.

[6] M. Mueller. *Ruling the Root: Internet Governance and the Taming of Cyberspace.* MIT Press, Cambridge, MA, May 2002.

[7] Scott Shenker, Sylvia Ratnasamy, Brad Karp, Ramesh Govindan, and Deborah Estrin. Data-Centric Storage in Sensornets. In *Proc. Hotnets-I*, October 2002.

[8] K. Sollins. Architectural Principles of Uniform Resource Name Resolution, Jan 1998. RFC 2276.

[9] R. Wiggins. The Effects of September 11 on the Leading Search Engine. *First Monday: Peer-Reviewed Journal on the Internet*, 7(10), October 2001. Available from `http://www.firstmonday.org/issues/issue6_10/wiggins/index.html`.

On the Feasibility
of Peer-to-Peer Web Indexing and Search

Jinyang Li[1], Boon Thau Loo[2], Joseph M. Hellerstein[2], M. Frans Kaashoek[1],
David R. Karger[1], and Robert Morris[1]

[1] MIT Lab for Computer Science
{jinyang,kaashoek,karger,rtm}@lcs.mit.edu
[2] UC Berkeley
{boonloo,jmh}@cs.berkeley.edu

Abstract. This paper discusses the feasibility of peer-to-peer full-text keyword search of the Web. Two classes of keyword search techniques are in use or have been proposed: flooding of queries over an overlay network (as in Gnutella), and intersection of index lists stored in a distributed hash table. We present a simple feasibility analysis based on the resource constraints and search workload. Our study suggests that the peer-to-peer network does not have enough capacity to make naive use of either of search techniques attractive for Web search. The paper presents a number of existing and novel optimizations for P2P search based on distributed hash tables, estimates their effects on performance, and concludes that in combination these optimizations would bring the problem to within an order of magnitude of feasibility. The paper suggests a number of compromises that might achieve the last order of magnitude.

1   Introduction

Full-text keyword search of the Web is arguably one of the most important Internet applications. It is also a hard problem; Google currently indexes more than 2 billion documents [1], a tiny fraction of the estimated 550 billion documents on the Web [2]. While centralized search engines such as Google work well, peer-to-peer (P2P) Web search is worth studying for the following reasons. First, Web search offers a good stress test for P2P architectures. Second, P2P search might be more resistant than centralized search engines to censoring or manipulated rankings. Third, P2P search might be more robust than centralized search as the demise of a single server or site is unlikely to paralyze the entire search system.

A number of P2P systems provide keyword search, including Gnutella [3] and KaZaA [4]. These systems use the simple and robust technique of flooding queries over some or all peers. The estimated number of documents in these systems is 500 million [5]; documents are typically music files, and searches examine only file meta-data such as title and artist. These systems have performance problems [6] even with workloads much smaller than the Web.

F. Kaashoek and I. Stoica (Eds.): IPTPS 2003, LNCS 2735, pp. 207–215, 2003.

Another class of P2P systems achieve scalability by structuring the data so that it can be found with far less expense than flooding; these are commonly called distributed hash tables (DHTs) [7, 8, 9, 10]. DHTs are well-suited for exact match lookups using unique identifiers, but do not directly support text search. There have been recent proposals for P2P text search [11, 12, 13][14] over DHTs. The most ambitious known evaluation of such a system [11] demonstrated good full-text keyword search performance with about 100,000 documents. Again, this is a tiny fraction of the size of the Web.

This paper addresses the question *Is P2P Web search likely to work?* The paper first estimates the size of the problem: the size of a Web index and the rate at which people submit Web searches. Then it estimates the magnitude of the two most fundamental resource constraints: the capacity of the Internet and the amount of disk space available on peer hosts. An analysis of the communication costs of naive P2P Web search shows that it would require orders of magnitude more resources than are likely to be available. The paper evaluates a number of existing and novel optimizations, and shows that in combination, they should reduce costs to within an order of magnitude of available resources. Finally, the paper outlines some design compromises that might eliminate the last order of magnitude difference.

The main contribution of this paper is an evaluation of the fundamental costs of, and constraints on, P2P Web search. The paper does not claim to have a definitive answer about whether P2P Web search is likely to work, but it does provide a framework for debating the question.

2   Background

A query consists of a set of *search terms* (words) provided by a user. The result is usually a list of documents that contain the terms, ranked by some scoring mechanism. Search engines typically precompute an *inverted index*: for each word, a *posting list* of the identifiers of documents that contain that word. These postings are intersected in a query involving more than one term. Since the intersection is often large, search engines usually present only the most highly ranked documents. Systems typically combine many ranking factors; these may include the importance of the documents themselves [15], the frequency of the search terms, or how close the terms occur to each other within the documents.

3   Fundamental Constraints

Whether a search algorithm is feasible depends on the workload, the available resources, and the algorithm itself. We estimate the workload first. Google indexes more than 2 billion Web documents [1], so to be conservative we assume 3 billion. Assuming 1000 words per document, an inverted index would contain $3 * 10^9 * 1000$ document identifiers (docIDs). In a DHT, a docID would likely be a key with which one could retrieve the document; typically this is a 20-byte hash of the document's content. The large docID space simplifies collision avoidance as different peers independently generate docIDs when inserting documents into the P2P network. The total inverted index size for the Web is about $6 * 10^{13}$ bytes. We assume the system would have to serve about 1000 queries per second (Google's current load [1]).

A P2P search system would have two main resource constraints: *storage* and *bandwidth*. To simplify subsequent discussion, we present concrete estimates based on informed guesses.

- **Storage Constraints:** Each peer host in a P2P system will have a limit on the disk space it can use to store a piece of the index; we assume one gigabyte, a small fraction of the size of a typical PC hard disk. It is not atypical today for some large desktop applications to have an installed size of around 1GB. An inverted index of size $6 * 10^{13}$ bytes would require 60,000 PCs, assuming no compression.
- **Communication Constraints:** A P2P query consumes bandwidth on the wide-area Internet; the total bandwidth consumed by all queries must fit comfortably within the Internet's capacity.

  Given the importance of finding information on the Web, we assume that it is reasonable for it to consume a noticeable fraction of Internet capacity. DNS uses a few percent of wide-area Internet capacity [16]; we optimistically assume that Web search could consume 10%. One way to estimate the Internet's capacity is to look at the backbone cross-section bandwidth. For example, the sum of the bisection bandwidths of Internet backbones in the U.S. was about 100 gigabits in 1999 [17]. Assuming 1,000 queries per second, the per-query communication budget is 10 megabits, or roughly one megabyte. This is a very optimistic assessment.

  Another way to derive a reasonable query communication cost is to assume that the query should send no more data than the size of the document ultimately retrieved. Assuming that the average Web page size is about 10 kilobytes, this leads to a pessimistic query communication budget of 10 kilobytes.

  The rest of this paper assumes the more optimistic budget of one megabyte of communication per query.

4 Basic Cost Analysis

This section outlines the costs of naive implementations of two common P2P text search strategies: *partition-by-document* and *partition-by-keyword*.

4.1 Partition by Document

In this scheme, the documents are divided up among the hosts, and each peer maintains a local inverted index of the documents it is responsible for. Each query must be broadcast or flooded to all peers; each peer returns its most highly ranked document(s). Gnutella and KaZaA use partition by document.

Flooding a query to the 60,000 peers required to hold an index would require about 60,000 packets, each of size 100 bytes. Thus a query's communication cost would be 6 megabytes, or 6 times higher than our budget. Of course, if peers were able to devote more disk space to storing the index, fewer would be required, and the communication cost would be proportionately less.

4.2 Partition by Keyword

In this scheme, responsibility for the words that appear in the document corpus is divided among the peers. Each peer stores the posting list for the word(s) it is responsible for. A DHT would be used to map a word to the peer responsible for it. A number of proposals work this way [11][14].

A query involving multiple terms requires that the postings for one or more of the terms be sent over the network. For simplicity, this discussion will assume a two-term query. It is cheaper to send the smaller of the two postings to the peer holding the larger posting list; the latter peer would perform the intersection and ranking, and return the few highest-ranking document identifiers.

Analysis of 81,000 queries made to a search engine for `mit.edu` shows that the average query would move 300,000 bytes of postings across the network. 40% of the queries involved just one term, 35% two, and 25% three or more. `mit.edu` has 1.7 million Web pages; scaling to the size of the Web (3 billion pages) suggests that the average query might require 530 megabytes, requiring a factor of **530×** improvement.

Some queries, however, are much more expensive than this average. Consider a search for "the who". Google reports that $3 * 10^9$ documents contain "the", and $2 * 10^8$ contain "who". This query would send 4 GB over the network, exceeding our budget by **4000×**.

Our analysis seems to imply that partition-by-document is the more promising scheme, requiring only a factor of 6× improvement. However, we focus instead on partition-by-keyword because it allows us to draw on decades of existing research on fast inverted index intersection. As we will see later, by applying a variety of techniques we can bring the partition-by-keyword scheme to the same order-of-magnitude bandwidth consumption as the partition-by-document approach.

5   Optimizations

In this section, we discuss optimization techniques for partition-by-keyword. We evaluate the optimizations using our data set of 81,000 `mit.edu` queries and 1.7 million web pages crawled from MIT.

5.1   Caching and Precomputation

Peers could cache the posting lists sent to them for each query, hoping to avoid receiving them again for future queries. This technique reduces the average query communication cost in the MIT query trace by 38%. The modest improvement can be attributed to the fact that many queries appear only once in the trace.

Precomputation involves computing and storing the intersection of different posting lists in advance. Precomputing for all term pairs is not feasible as it would increase the size of the inverted index significantly. Since the popularity of query terms follows a Zipf distribution [11], it is effective to precompute only the intersections of all pairs of popular query terms. If 7.5 million term pairs (3% of all possible term pairs) from the most popular terms are precomputed for the MIT data set, the average query communication cost is reduced by 50%.

5.2   Compression

Compression provides the greatest reduction in communication cost without sacrificing result quality.

Bloom Filters A Bloom filter can represent a set compactly, at the cost of a small probability of false positives. In a simple two-round Bloom intersection [11], one node sends the Bloom filter of its posting list. The receiving node intersects the Bloom filter and its posting list, and sends back the resulting list of docIDs. The original sender then filters out false positives. The result is a compression ratio of 13 [1].

When the result set is small, we propose multiple rounds of Bloom intersections. In this case, the compression ratio is increased to 40 with four rounds of Bloom filter exchange [2]. Compressed Bloom filters [18] give a further 30% improvement, resulting in a compression ratio of approximately 50.

Gap Compression *Gap compression* [19] is effective when the gaps between sorted docIDs in a posting list are small. To reduce the gap size, we propose to periodically remap docIDs from 160-bit hashes to dense numbers from 1 to the number of documents. In the MIT data set, gap compression with dense IDs achieves an average compression ratio of 30. Gap compression has the added advantage over Bloom filters as it incurs no extra round-trip time, and the compression ratio is independent of the size of the final intersection.

Adaptive Set Intersection Adaptive set intersection [20] exploits structure in the posting lists to avoid having to transfer entire lists. For example, the intersection $\{1, 3, 4, 7\} \cap \{8, 10, 20, 30\}$ requires only one element exchange, as $7 < 8$ implies an empty intersection. In contrast, computing the intersection $\{1, 4, 8, 20\} \cap \{3, 7, 10, 30\}$ requires an entire posting list to be transferred.

Adaptive set intersection can be used in conjunction with gap compression. Based on the MIT data set, an upper bound of 30% improvement could be achieved on top of gap compression, resulting in a compression ratio of 40.

---

[1] This is a best case compression ratio which assumes that the intersection is empty and that the two posting lists have similar sizes.

[2] More than 4 rounds yield little further improvement.

Table 1. Optimization Techniques and Improvements

Technique	Improvement
Caching	1.5×
Precomputation	2×
Bloom Filters	50×
Gap Compression (GC)	30×
Adaptive Set (AS) + GC	40×
Clustering + GC + AS	75×

Clustering Gap compression and adaptive set intersection are most effective when the docIDs in the posting lists are "bursty". We utilize statistical clustering techniques to group similar documents together based on their term occurrences. By assigning adjacent docIDs to similar documents, the posting lists are made burstier. We use Probabilistic Latent Semantic Analysis (PLSA) [21] to group all the MIT Web documents into 100 clusters. Documents within the same cluster are assigned contiguous docIDs. Clustering improves the compression ratio of adaptive set intersection with gap compression to 75.

6 Compromises

Table 1 summarizes the performance gains of different techniques proposed so far. The most promising set of techniques result in a 75× reduction in average communication costs. However, achieving this improvement would require distributed renumbering and clustering algorithms which are rather complex. Even a 75× reduction leaves the average query communication cost an order of magnitude higher than our budget. An extra 7× improvement is still needed. This leads us into the softer realm of accepting compromises to gain performance.

6.1 Compromising Result Quality

Reynolds and Vahdat suggest streaming results to users using *incremental intersection* [11]. Assuming users are usually satisfied with only a partial set of matching results, this will allow savings in communication as users are likely to terminate their queries early. Incremental intersection is most effective when the intersection is big relative to the postings so that a significant number of matching results can be generated without needing to transfer an entire posting list [3].

While incremental results are useful, the likelihood that users will terminate their queries early will be increased if the incremental results are prioritized based on a good ranking function. To achieve this effect, Fagin's algorithm (FA) [22]

---

[3] This suggests that it might be preferable to precompute term pairs with big posting lists and small intersections, which would also reduce the storage overhead of precomputation.

is used in conjunction with a ranking function to generate incremental ranked results. The posting lists are sorted based on the ranking function, and the top ranked docIDs are incrementally transferred from one node to another for intersection. Unfortunately, not all ranking functions are applicable. Examples of applicable ranking functions include those based on PageRank, term frequencies or font sizes. An example of a ranking function that can *not* be used with FA is one based on proximity of query terms. By limiting the choices of useful ranking functions, we are left with incremental results that are not as well-ranked compared to the results of commercial search engines. To alleviate this shortcoming, we propose the use of mid-query relevance feedback [23] that allows users to control and change the order in which the posting list intersections are performed. This leads to potential improvements in user experiences, and may result in earlier query termination. However, incorporating user feedback in the middle of a search query introduces a number of challenges in designing appropriate result browsing and feedback interfaces.

As we mentioned earlier, incremental intersection results are more effective when the final result set is big relative to the intersecting posting lists. To illustrate, consider two posting lists X and Y, and the corresponding intersection Z where $|X| > |Y| > |Z|$. Computing 10 matching results will require transferring an average of $\frac{10*|Y|}{|Z|}$ elements from the smaller posting list Y. We quantify the savings of incremental results based on the MIT data set. On average, computing 10 results using incremental intersection results in a $50\times$ reduction in communication cost [4]. We would expect even greater performance gains for the larger Web corpus. The savings of incremental intersection is especially significant for expensive queries such as "the who". Google reports that there are 10^7 results, hence roughly $\frac{2*10^8}{10^7} * 10 = 200$ docIDs need to be shipped to retrieve the top 10 ranked documents containing "the" and "who". This reduces the communication cost significantly to $200 * 20B \approx 4KB$ which is well within our budget of one megabyte per query.

6.2   Compromising P2P Structure

The one megabyte communication budget is derived from the bisection backbone bandwidth of the Internet. The *aggregate* bandwidth summed over all links is probably much larger than the bisection. We could compromise the P2P network structure to exploit Internet aggregate bandwidth for better performance. One proposal is to replicate the entire inverted index, with one copy per ISP. As a rough analysis, if the entire inverted index can be replicated at 10 ISPs, there is a $10\times$ increase in the communication budget per query.

---

[4] Incremental ranked intersection can be combined with compression, but unfortunately the compression ratio will be reduced as a result.

7   Conclusion

This paper highlights the challenges faced in building a P2P web search engine. Our main contribution lies in conducting a feasibility analysis for P2P Web search. We have shown that that naive implementations of P2P Web search are not feasible, and have mapped out some possible optimizations. The most effective optimizations bring the problem to within an order of magnitude of feasibility. We have also proposed two possible compromises, one in the quality of results, and the other in the P2P structure of our system. A combination of optimizations and compromises will bring us within feasibility range for P2P Web search.

Acknowledgments

This research was conducted as part of the IRIS project[5], supported by the National Science Foundation under Cooperative Agreement No. ANI-0225660.

References

[1] Google Press Center: Technical Highlights.
     http://www.google.com/press/highlights.html
[2] The Deep Web: Surfacing Hidden Value.
     http://www.press.umich.edu/jep/07-01/bergman.html
[3] Gnutella. http://gnutella.wego.com
[4] Kazaa. http://www.kazza.com
[5] Ingram: Record Industry Plays Hardball with Kazaa.
     http://www.globeandmail.com/
[6] Why Gnutella Can't Scale. No, Really.
     http://www.darkridge.com/ jpr5/doc/gnutella.html
[7] I. Stoica and R. Morris and D. Karger and F. Kaashoek and H. Balakrishnan: Chord: Scalable Peer-To-Peer Lookup Service for Internet Applications. Proceedings of the ACM SIGCOMM Conference (2001) 149–160
[8] S. Ratnasamy and P. Francis and M. Handley and R. Karp and S. Shenker: A Scalable Content Addressable Network. Proceedings of the ACM SIGCOM Conference (2001)
[9] A. Rowstron and P. Druschel: Pastry: Scalable, Decentralized Object Location, and Routing for Large-Scale Peer-to-Peer Systems Lecture Notes in Computer Science (2001) Vol 2218
[10] B. Y. Zhao and J. D. Kubiatowicz and A. D. Joseph: Tapestry: An Infrastructure for Fault-tolerant Wide-area Location and Routing. UC Berkeley Technical Report (2001) UCB/CSD-01-1141
[11] P. Reynolds and A. Vahdat: Efficient Peer-to-Peer Keyword Searching. Unpublished Manuscript (2002)
[12] C. Tang and Z. Xu and M. Mahalingam: pSearch: Information Retrieval in Structured Overlays. The First Workshop on Hot Topics in Networks (HotNets-I) (2002)

---

[5] http://project-iris.net/

[13] M. Harren and J. M. Hellerstein and R. Huebsch and B. T. Loo and S. Shenker and I. Stoica: Complex Queries in DHT-based Peer-to-Peer Networks. 1st International Workshop on Peer-to-Peer Systems (IPTPS) (2002)

[14] O. D. Gnawali: A Keyword Set Search System for Peer-to-Peer Networks. Master Thesis, Massachusetts Institute of Technology (2002)

[15] L. Page and S. Brin and R. Motwani and T. Winograd: The PageRank Citation Ranking: Bringing Order to the Web. Stanford Digital Library Technologies Project (1998)

[16] K. Thompson and G. Miller and R. Wilder: Wide-area Traffic Patterns and Characteristics. IEEE Network, (1997) Vol. 11, No. 6, 10-23

[17] Boardwatch Magazine's Directory of Internet Service Providers (1999)

[18] M. Mitzenmacher: Compressed Bloom Filters. Twentieth ACM Symposium on Principles of Distributed Computing (2001)

[19] I. H. Witten and A. Moffat and T. C. Bell: Managing Gigabytes: Compressing and Indexing Documents and Images. (1999)

[20] E. D. Demaine and A. López-Ortiz and J. Ian Munro: Adaptive Set Intersections, Unions, and Differences. Proceedings of the 11th Annual ACM-SIAM Symposium on Discrete Algorithms (SODA 2000)

[21] T. Hofmann: Probabilistic Latent Semantic Analysis. Proceedings of Uncertainty in Artificial Intelligence (1999)

[22] R. Fagin and A. Lotem and M. Naor: Optimal Aggregation Algorithms for Middleware. Symposium on Principles of Database Systems (2001)

[23] J. M. Hellerstein and R. Avnur and A. Chou and C. Olston and V. Raman and T. Roth and C. Hidber and P. Haas: Interactive Data Analysis with CONTROL. IEEE Computer (1999)

Studying Search Networks with SIL

Brian F. Cooper and Hector Garcia-Molina

Department of Computer Science
Stanford University
{cooperb,hector}@db.stanford.edu

Abstract. We present a general model, called the Search/Index Link (SIL) model, for studying peer-to-peer search networks. This model allows us to analyze and visualize existing network architectures. It also allows us to discover novel architectures that have desirable properties. Finally, it can be used as a starting point for developing new network construction techniques.

1 Introduction

The recent explosion in popularity of peer-to-peer search networks has sparked great interest in the problem of designing "good" networks. Although P2P systems hold the promise of harnessing large numbers of distributed resources, so far it has been difficult to achieve scalability. Similarly, the autonomy of peers and redundancy of links should enhance fault tolerance, and yet many networks are vulnerable if failures occur at the wrong place in the network.

Our approach to dealing with these issues is to construct a general model, called the Search/Index Link (SIL) model, for studying alternative architectures for peer-to-peer search networks. The SIL model is useful for visualizing as well as analyzing existing search networks in terms of scalability, fault tolerance and other metrics. However, the simplicity and generality of the model also makes it useful for discovering new types of networks that have desirable properties. Using the SIL model, we can examine the inherent properties of an existing or new network topology, and tune the basic architecture for a given goal, such as reduced load. We have also begun to use the insights gained from the SIL model to study "ad hoc, self-supervising networks," or networks where nodes simply make and break links at will, and the network evolves and becomes increasingly efficient over time.

The focus of the SIL model is on flooding-based networks (such as Gnutella or supernode networks), and not necessarily routing-based networks (such as distributed hash tables or DHTs [11, 10]). Although DHTs have significant advantages in many situations, we feel that the potential of flooding-based networks has not been fully realized, and that there are still many interesting research questions about flooding networks. SIL is an attempt to see what else is possible with flooding networks, beyond what has been developed so far. Moreover, flooding networks are especially adept at content-discovery, in contrast to DHTs, whose main strength is in file location once a name is known (as pointed out

F. Kaashoek and I. Stoica (Eds.): IPTPS 2003, LNCS 2735, pp. 216–224, 2003.
© Springer-Verlag Berlin Heidelberg 2003

in [10]). Finally, flooding networks continue to have huge popularity and wide deployment; on a typical day, Kazaa supports several million simultaneous users, and allows them to search for hundreds of millions of files and multiple petabytes of data. Optimizing such widely used systems continues to be an important research challenge. Although we could generalize SIL to model DHTs as well, the simplicity of the model as it is now gives us great power to describe and analyze P2P search networks.

In this position paper, we describe the SIL model, illustrate its usefulness for discovering novel topologies and developing network construction techniques, and discuss interesting research challenges.

2   The Search/Index Link Model

A primary goal of a peer-to-peer search network is to allow member peers to search for and retrieve content stored at other peers. Searching is usually accomplished by sending queries to peers, and these peers respond with search results if they have content matching the query. Often, indexing is employed to enhance scalability and efficiency. Indexing can be used to allow a single peer to answer queries for multiple other peers without the need for those other peers to process the queries themselves. Indexing can also improve availability, since a peer can be searched even if it is temporarily unreachable.

The Search/Index Link (SIL) model generalizes the basic techniques of querying and indexing in a search network. SIL models a peer-to-peer search network overlay as a set of nodes in a graph with specialized links connecting the nodes. There are four kinds of directed links in the model:

- A *forwarding search link* (FSL) carries search messages from peer X to peer Y. Peer Y processes the query and also forwards it on outgoing FSLs. FSLs can be graphically represented as $X \Longrightarrow Y$.

- A *non-forwarding search link* (NSL) carries search messages from peer X to peer Y. Peer Y processes the query but does not forward it. NSLs are represented as $X \longrightarrow Y$.

- A *forwarding index link* (FIL) carries index updates from peer X to peer Y. These index updates inform Y about new, modified or deleted content at peer X. Peer Y integrates the index updates into its own index, and also forwards the updates on outoing FILs. FILs are represented as $X = \Rightarrow Y$.

- A *non-forwarding index link* carries index updates from X to Y. Peer Y should add the updates to its own index but does not forward them. NILs are represented as $X - \Rightarrow Y$.

Under this model, there are two basic types of activity: indexing and searching. Peers construct indexes over their own content to assist in answering searches. These indexes may be inverted lists of words, sets of metadata or simply a list of filenames. When a peer receives a search, that peer searches its index for matching documents and returns any matches as search results. Whenever a peer A updates its own index, it should also send those index updates along outgoing index links. The peers that receive these updates will effectively have a copy of A's index, and can perform searches over A's content just as well as A can. Note that these peers do not store a replica of A's content, but only index entries that aid in searching that content. For example, imagine a peer B that has a copy of A's index. When B receives a search message, B processes that search over its own content as well as over A's index, and returns search results for matches at either A or B.

We say that a node X searches a node Y *directly* by sending searches to Y, or that X searches Y *indirectly*, by sending searches to a node Z that has a copy of Y's index. The total number of nodes that X can search directly or indirectly is X's *coverage*.

The SIL model can be used to describe a variety of existing peer-to-peer search networks. For example, a supernode network can be represented using FSLs and NILs, as shown in Figure 1a. Supernodes (the central nodes in the figure) are connected using FSLs ($\Longrightarrow$). Non-supernodes ("normal nodes") are connected to supernodes using one FSL and one NIL ($- \ni$). Then, supernodes have a copy of the indexes of normal nodes, and when a normal node generates a search, it is forwarded to all of the supernodes.

Another example is a network of peers that construct and forward index updates to other peers. Global indexing servers collect and store all of the updates, and peers can search for archived content at the indexing servers. Such a network is shown in Figure 1b. As the figure shows, updates flow along FILs ($= \ni$) between nodes and to the central index servers. Peers can search the index server, and these searches are carried by NSLs ($\longrightarrow$). The global indexing topology is similar to the Usenet structure, where updates flow around the network and centralized servers (such as DejaNews, now known as Google Groups) retain the updates and answer queries.

3   Discovering Topologies

The SIL model is useful for visualizing existing topologies and network organizations. However, the model's simplicity and generality also allows us to use it to suggest and study new and novel topologies. Using the same link types that form the basic building blocks of existing networks (such as supernodes), we can construct networks that have different and desirable properties.

One novel topology that we have found using SIL is called *parallel search clusters*. An example is shown in Figure 1c. In this architecture, peers are organized into search clusters of FSLs, similar to the Gnutella pure search network. Separate clusters are joined by index links, either FILs or NILs. Figure 1c shows three clusters, with NILs connecting cluster 1 to the other clusters. This graph would also have outgoing NILs from clusters 2 and 3, but we have omitted them for clarity. If the nodes in a cluster collectively have indexes for all the nodes outside the cluster, full coverage can be achieved even though nodes only directly search other nodes in their own cluster.

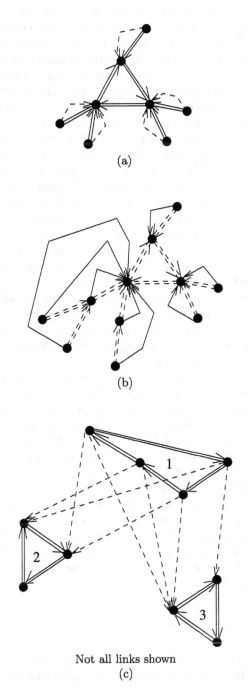

(a)

(b)

Not all links shown
(c)

Fig. 1. Networks represented using the SIL model: (a) supernodes, (b) Usenet and (c) parallel search clusters

A parallel search cluster network has several advantages when compared to other network topologies. For example, in a cluster network, the processing required to answer queries is shared among all the nodes in the network. In contrast, in a supernode network, each supernode must process all of the queries in the network, and may become overloaded. If there are few or no nodes with very high capacity, then a supernode network is simply not feasible. Even if some nodes have much higher capacity than others, a parallel cluster network offers more flexibility by allowing nodes to contribute whatever they can. In a supernode network, a node either handles all searches or no searches.

Another advantage of parallel cluster networks is that they can be tuned depending on the load in the network. For example, index updates might occur much more frequently than searches. Then, the network should be constructed with a few large clusters, so that there are relatively fewer index links and thus fewer indexes to be updated. Moreover, if clusters are larger, each node is responsible for fewer indexes, and the load on individual nodes is further reduced. On the other hand, if there are many more searches than updates, the network should be constructed as a large number of small clusters. In this case, each node only has to handle searches from a few nodes and the search load on each node is reduced. Thus, we can change the number of clusters to minimize total load on nodes. Supernode networks are less flexible. If searches comprise the bulk of the load, we cannot increase or decrease the number of supernodes to spread the search load, since every supernode handles all searches regardless of how many supernodes there are.

We have conducted simulation studies to quantify these advantages. In our simulations, we constructed networks that followed the parallel cluster model, and compared them to supernode networks and pure search networks (e.g. Gnutella). The full details of our experiments are outside the scope of this position paper; see [3]. As an example, we evaluated the load on nodes in parallel cluster networks versus supernode networks and pure search networks (such as Gnutella). The maximum load on a node in a cluster network was significantly lower (by up to a factor of 7) than the maximum load on a node in a supernode or pure search network. At the same time, the average load on a node in a cluster network was comparable to the average load on a node in a supernode network. In other words, the high load on supernodes was avoided without significantly overloading the average node in the network. These results illustrate that the SIL model is useful for identifying networks that are more effective in some cases than existing architectures.

4 Research Challenges

The SIL model also provides a framework for examining a variety of interesting research problems in the area of studying and optimizing search networks.

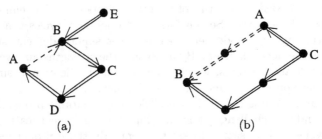

Fig. 2. Features that cause redundancy: a. one-index-cycle, b. search fork

4.1 Topological Properties

One research challenge is to identify "desirable" properties of search networks, so that we can discover topologies and build networks that exhibit these properties. We can use SIL as a method for expressing and studying these properties.

Consider, for example, the problem of minimizing the load on peers in the system. One cause of load is *redundancy*, which we define as peers performing work that is duplicated by other peers in the system. A peer A may try to shed load by replicating its index to peer B, so that B can answer queries over A's content without requiring processing on the part of A. However, if A still receives and processes queries that are also being answered by B, then A is doing unnecessary, redundant work. We can specify a general property of SIL graphs as follows:

- *Redundancy* exists in a SIL graph if a link can be removed without reducing query coverage.

In other words, if a link is carrying messages to A, and A need not process these messages in order to ensure that the query is answered, then there is redundancy.

We can make this property more concrete by identifying topological features of SIL graphs that lead to redundancy. One feature that causes redundancy is a specific type of cycle called a *one-index-cycle*: a node A has an index link to another node B, and B has a search path to A. An example is shown in Figure 2a. This construct leads to redundant processing, since B will answer queries over A's index, and yet these queries will be forwarded to A who will also answer them over A's index. More formally, a one-index-cycle fits our definition of *redundancy* because at least one link in the cycle can be removed without affecting coverage: the index link from A to B.

Another feature that causes search/index redundancy is a *search fork*: a node C has a search link to A and a search path to B that does not include A, and there is an index path from A to B. An example is shown in Figure 2b. Again, A will process any searches from C unnecessarily, since B can process the queries for A. The redundant link in this example is the link $C \Longrightarrow A$. We specify that there is a search path from C to B that does not include A because if the only path from C to B included A there would be no link that could be removed without reducing coverage.

Research is needed to identify other graph properties that enhance the efficiency of search networks. Search forks and one-index-cycles can be avoided when constructing supernode networks, and yet supernodes can still become overloaded as the network grows. By analyzing the strengths and weaknesses of various network architectures, we can elucidate desirable or undesirable graph properties, and apply them when constructing networks.

In summary, there is the challenge of defining desirable properties (like redundancy), and the challenge of identifying the topological features (e.g., no one-index cycles and no search forks) that embody those properties. Knowing the properties and features will make it easier to construct "good" SIL networks.

4.2 Dynamic Search Networks

In the discussion so far, we have assumed that graphs are static. In order to properly model real peer-to-peer networks, we must also represent the process of nodes joining and leaving. Such dynamic networks can easily be modeled by SIL: adding a new node and links to the graph represents a peer joining, while removing a node and all of its incoming and outgoing links represents a node leaving.

However, a dynamic network presents an interesting research question: when a node joins, what connections should it make? The traditional approach is to pick a particular architecture (such as supernodes or parallel search clusters) and force nodes to join in such a way as to preserve that architecture. A different and novel approach is to allow a node to join in any way it likes, creating links as appropriate, as long as it does not introduce undesirable topological features. For example, we might specify that a node could join a network as long as it does not introduce a one-index-cycle or a search fork. If a node could verify that adding a link did not create one of those features, then it could join the network in an ad hoc way while preserving desirable properties such as efficiency or fault tolerance. Nodes could form whatever connections they needed without damaging the efficiency of the network, and the network would evolve and adapt to best meet the needs of member nodes and changing load conditions.

If a dynamic network is not tied to a specific topology, then the topology can more easily change over time depending on the needs of the network. For example, we have begun to study ways for overloaded nodes to shed load by simply disconnecting from some of their neighbors. These neighbors would then reconnect to other, less loaded nodes, spreading the work around the network more evenly. Moreover, a node may find that it is overloaded with search messages, and drop only search links. Then, neighbors would be encouraged to replace those search links with index links. In this way, the nature of the network would change from search-centric to index-centric as a reflection of the current load conditions.

SIL provides a framework for trying out different ad hoc graph-construction methods and examining their effects. We have examined several techniques, and our results are described in more detail in [2]. Our experiments indicate that ad hoc methods can be effective in many situations in significantly improving the efficiency of the network.

5 Related Work

Optimization of peer-to-peer search networks is a hot topic among distributed systems researchers. Some investigators are examining techniques for more effective searching of existing networks, for example using random walk searches [7]. Others have examined how to build better versions of existing networks [12, 9], how to "fix-up" an inefficient network [8], or how to better index an existing network [4]. The SIL model is an attempt to provide a framework for generalizing these approaches. Complementary to the SIL model is work that explicitly models the location of content, such as systems that attempt to replicate content to reduce search latency [1]. It may be useful to extend our model to describe content as well as nodes and links.

Another current research trend is to focus on networks that allow users to locate objects by name instead instead of by content. Such networks are typically designed as distributed hash tables (DHT) and several DHT architectures have been proposed [11, 10]. There are still interesting research questions in the space of flooding-based networks, and as discussed in Section 1, the advantages of DHTs do not mean that we should not study SIL. Yet another focus of many investigators is designing networks for privacy, security or anonymity (such as SOS [6] or FreeHaven [5]). Our focus on content discovery is complementary to these approaches.

6 Conclusion

The SIL model is a general mechanism for describing the topology and properties of peer-to-peer search networks. It is useful as:

- A framework for evaluating networks in terms of metrics such as efficiency or fault tolerance.
- A tool for discovering new and interesting network architectures.
- A mechanism for defining and studying desirable topological properties of networks.
- A platform for studying new ways of constructing and maintaining dynamic networks.

References

[1] E. Cohen and S. Shenker. Replication strategies in unstructured peer-to-peer networks. In *Proc. SIGCOMM*, August 2002.
[2] B. F. Cooper and H. Garcia-Molina. Ad hoc, self-supervising peer-to-peer search networks, 2003. Technical Report.

[3] B. F. Cooper and H. Garcia-Molina. SIL: Modeling and measuring scalable peer-to-peer search networks, 2003. Technical Report.

[4] A. Crespo and H. Garcia-Molina. Routing indices for peer-to-peer systems. In *Proc. Int'l Conf. on Distributed Computing Systems (ICDCS)*, July 2002.

[5] R. Dingledine, M. J. Freedman, and D. Molnar. The FreeHaven Project: Distributed anonymous storage service. In *Proc. of the Workshop on Design Issues in Anonymity and Unobservability*, July 2000.

[6] A. Keromytis, V. Misra, and D. Rubenstein. SOS: Secure overlay services. In *Proc. SIGCOMM*, Aug. 2002.

[7] Q. Lv, P. Cao, E. Cohen, K. Li, and S. Shenker. Search and replication in unstructured peer-to-peer networks. In *Proc. of ACM International Conference on Supercomputing (ICS'02)*, June 2002.

[8] Q. Lv, S. Ratnasamy, and S. Shenker. Can heterogeneity make gnutella scalable? In *Proc. of the 1st Int'l Workshop on Peer to Peer Systems (IPTPS)*, March 2002.

[9] G. Pandurangan, P. Raghavan, and E. Upfal. Building low-diameter P2P networks. In *Proc. IEEE Symposium on Foundations of Computer Science*, 2001.

[10] S. Ratnasamy, P. Francis, M. Handley, R. Karp, and S. Shenker. A scalable content-addressable network. In *Proc. SIGCOMM*, Aug. 2001.

[11] I. Stoica, R. Morris, D. Karger, M. F. Kaashoek, and H. Balakrishnan. Chord: A scalable peer-to-peer lookup service for internet applications. In *Proc. SIGCOMM*, Aug. 2001.

[12] B. Yang and H. Garcia-Molina. Designing a super-peer network. In *Proc. ICDE*, March 2003.

Efficient Peer-To-Peer Searches
Using Result-Caching

Bobby Bhattacharjee, Sudarshan Chawathe, Vijay Gopalakrishnan,
Pete Keleher, and Bujor Silaghi

Department of Computer Science
University of Maryland
College Park, Maryland, USA
{bobby,chaw,gvijay,keleher,bujor}@cs.umd.edu

1 Introduction

Existing peer-to-peer systems implement a single function well: data lookup. There is now a wealth of research describing how to reliably disseminate, and to later retrieve, data in a scalable and load-balanced manner.

However, searching has received less attention. The current state of the art is to distribute inverted indexes in the name space. Intersection of distributed sets can be made more efficient by exchanging bloom filters prior to moving objects [2].

This paper proposes an orthogonal and complementary technique: using result-caching to avoid duplicating work and data movement. For example, assume that indexes a_i, a_j, and a_k are located on distinct nodes in the network. Computing $a_i \wedge a_j \wedge a_k$ directly from these indexes is much more expensive than intersecting the result of a prior $a_i \wedge a_j$ operation together with a_k.

The main contribution of the paper is a new data structure, the *view tree*, that can be used to efficiently store and retrieve such prior results. These results, which can also be thought of as materialized views, can then be used to efficiently answer future queries. Note that object attributes could either be derived from application semantics (e.g. meta-data from files in a filesystem) or computed via techniques such as latent semantic indexing.

1.1 Data and Query Model

We assume that each data item in the namespace has a unique name, and has some searchable meta-data associated with it. We assume the meta-data is represented as an ordered set of attribute-value pairs. The attributes may be boolean or may be real valued. It is possible to extend our search scheme to handle more complex meta-data schemes, including hierarchically arranged attribute trees, but we do not consider this extension in this paper.

Our queries have the form $(a_i \wedge a_j \wedge \ldots \wedge a_k) \vee (b_i \wedge b_j \wedge \ldots \wedge b_k) \vee \ldots \vee (n_i \wedge n_j \wedge \ldots \wedge n_k)$. The solution to such a query is the union of the solutions of each conjunctive clause. For example, if the query is $(a \wedge b) \vee (b \wedge c)$, where

F. Kaashoek and I. Stoica (Eds.): IPTPS 2003, LNCS 2735, pp. 225–236, 2003.
© Springer-Verlag Berlin Heidelberg 2003

a, b, c are boolean predicates, then the result is the union of the items that have either attribute $(a \wedge b)$ or attribute $(b \wedge c)$. We use the term "view query", or just "query", to refer to such boolean queries, and the term "view" to refer to a set of namespace elements that satisfy a particular view query.

The rest of the paper is organized as follows. Section 2 presents the details of our search algorithm, together with the creation and maintenance of the view tree. Section 3 describes preliminary results, Section 4 discusses prior work, and we conclude in Section 5.

2   The View Tree

The core of our method works with conjunctive queries. Queries with disjunction are first converted to disjunctive normal form (disjunction of conjunctions), and each conjunction is evaluated as a separate conjunctive query. The results of the conjunctions are cached separately. For example, the evaluation of the query $(a \wedge b) \vee (b \wedge c)$ results in two views being cached: $(a \wedge b)$ and $(b \wedge c)$. These views can subsequently be used to answer the original query, and also other queries that contain these views. Henceforth, we shall discuss only conjunctive queries.

The views corresponding to conjunctive queries can be located by searching for the view using a canonical representation. In a distributed hash tree (DHT), the views are stored at nodes where the hash of the canonical name maps to. For example, in Chord, the view $a \wedge b$ is stored at the successor of $H(\text{"}a \wedge b\text{"})$. Note that the same technique is used to find the nodes where each attribute index should be stored. In a hierarchical system, the views can be stored in a hidden part of the name tree with each view stored at the server that initially creates the view. Obviously, more sophisticated techniques that balance the storage load can also be used in a hierarchical system. In both cases, views are located by searching the namespace using the canonical representation.

Unfortunately, merely storing each view in the namespace with a canonical name is not sufficient to efficiently answer view queries, even if the underlying namespace can very efficiently locate each materialized view. For a single conjunctive query $a_1 \wedge a_2 \wedge \ldots \wedge a_k$ with k attributes, the number of views that are useful for evaluating the query is exponential in k. Clearly, for moderately large k, it is not feasible to search the namespace to for each of these views to determine which ones exist. One solution is to maintain a central, consistent list of currently materialized views. Useful views that are materialized can then be obtained by locating this list in the namespace. The problems with a naive central list are many and obvious. For example, it has to be updated whenever any new view is created or destroyed in the system, which can happen whenever a new query is satisfied or when a node storing a view fails. Further, the storage required at the node holding the list is of the order of the number of views in the system.

Therefore, we propose the *view tree* for maintaining a distributed snapshot of the set of currently materialized views. The view tree can be traversed to find all relevant views for a particular query. The view tree can easily be implemented as a trie and, as we discuss later, does not have the state and update scalability problems of a central list solution. An example of a view tree is depicted in Figure 2. Nodes in the view tree are labeled with attributes. To locate the node at which a view $a_1a_2\ldots a_k$ is stored, we descend from the root of the view tree, in standard trie manner, first to the child labeled a_1, then to its child labeled a_2, and so on. If this process stops before we reach the end of the string representing the view, the view is stored as a child of the last node reached. Thus, the view tree is a trie in which each node that has no siblings is merged with its parent.

Since we wish to always provide efficient attribute-based access to objects, we require that all single-attribute views be materialized. There are therefore as many nodes at depth one in the view tree as there are attributes in our domain, and each node stores the view for the corresponding attribute. Thus, the method for adding a node to the underlying namespace is augmented to also update the index for each attribute that is part of the new node's meta-data. Similarly, these attribute indexes are also updated as nodes are deleted from the namespace.

We define a canonical order on the attributes and use this order to uniquely identify equivalent conjunctive queries (and views). For example, assuming an alphabetic ordering of attributes, $a \wedge b$ and $b \wedge a$ map to the canonical form $a \wedge b$ (or simply ab in our abbreviated notation). Henceforth, we will assume that all queries and views are in canonical form. Since the canonicalization is performed by the system, this assumption is without loss of generality and is transparent to the user of our system.

2.1   Answering Queries Using the View Tree

Given a view tree and a conjunctive query over the attributes, finding the smallest set of views to evaluate the query (using only the views) is NP-hard even in the centralized case (by reduction from Exact Set Cover [10]). Thus, an exact solution is not practical, especially in a distributed setting. Instead, we use the following guidelines for a method for locating views for answering a query: (1) *exact match* - If a view that matches the query exactly exists, that view must be located. (2) *forward progress* - If there is no exact match, then each view tree node that is visited must result in locating a view that contains at least one attribute from the query that does not occur in the views located so far.

Our search algorithm is outlined in Figure 1. We use $p(n)$ to denote the parent of a node n, $l(n)$ to denote the string formed by the concatenation of attributes indexed at n, and $r(n)$ to denote the suffix of $l(n)$ such that $l(n) = l(p(n)) \| r(n)$. We use the notation $s \ominus X$ to denote the string obtained by deleting from s the characters that occur in set X. Given a query q, the algorithm is invoked as $S(r, q)$, where r is the root of the view tree. The computation at a node n (i.e., $S(n, q)$) is based on selecting a set of suitable children to which the computation is propagated (recursively). Results from the children indicate the attributes of q that have been covered. As noted earlier, an exhaustive search is impracticable. It is easy to verify that the test on line 12 ensures that both the conditions in our guidelines (exact match and forward progress) are satisfied. The rest of the

```
 1: Let {n' : p(n') = n} = {c₁, ..., cₙ}
 2: q_w ← q
 3: r_w ← ∅
 4: loop
 5:    if q_w = ε then
 6:       return r_w
 7:    else
 8:       Let q_w = a₁ ... a_m
 9:       if ∄i, j, s₁, s₂ : s₁‖aᵢ‖s₂ = r(cⱼ) then
10:          return r_w
11:       else
12:          (i*, j*) ← min{(i, j) : ∃s₁, s₂ : s₁‖aᵢ‖s₂ = r(cⱼ)}
13:          r_w ← r_w ∪ {r(c_{j*})}
14:          r' ← S(c_{j*}, a_{i*+1} ... a_m)
15:          q_w ← q_w ⊖ r'
16:          r_w ← r_w ∪ r'
17:       end if
18:    end if
19: end loop
```

Fig. 1. Search for query q at node n: $S(n, q)$

pseudo-code is concerned with bookkeeping of the attributes of the query that have been covered by the views encountered so far.

For example, Figure 2 shows a search for "cbagekhilo", which proceeds as follows. The algorithm first locates the best prefix match, which is "cbag" in this case. Even though the next clause in the prefix, "cbage" has not been materialized, the "cbagh" child of "cbag" is useful for this query, and thus this node is visited next. The algorithm is now in the "forward progress" component of the search and proceeds in depth-first manner visiting nodes that add more unresolved literals.

2.2 Creating a Balanced View Tree

In our description, we have implicitly assumed that a view of the form $(a \wedge b \wedge \ldots \wedge x)$ can only be part of the subtree starting at a, since a occurs first in the canonical representation of $(a \wedge b \wedge \ldots \wedge x)$. This will result in well-defined trees, but they will be heavily imbalanced with most of the views stored under the attributes which occur first in the canonical representation. For example, all views of the form $a \wedge \ldots \wedge x$ will be stored under the a subtree. Obviously, a view of the form $(a \wedge b \wedge \ldots \wedge x)$ can equally well be stored under a clause of the form $(b \wedge \ldots \wedge x)$ under the b subtree and so on. However, doing so will not allow us to efficiently locate this materialized view, since again, there are an exponential number of sub-views that are potential parents of this clause.

We solve this tree-imbalance problem as follows: Let $\mathcal{E}$ represent the clause $(a \wedge b \wedge c \wedge \ldots \wedge x)$ which we want to add to the view tree. First, we deterministically pick a permutation $\mathcal{P}$ of $\mathcal{E}$ uniformly at random among all the possible

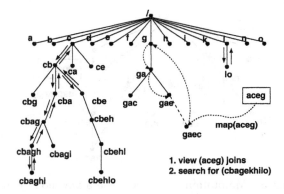

Fig. 2. Example of a node joining the View Tree

permutations of $\mathcal{E}$. For example, the clause $(a \wedge b \wedge c)$ will be mapped with same $1/6$ probability to the $(a \wedge b \wedge c)$, $(a \wedge c \wedge b)$, etc. There are well known methods for generating random permutations, e.g. by exchanging array elements initialized with the array index, which can be used to generate random permutations deterministically. We then place the view $\mathcal{P}$ in the view tree such that the parent of $\mathcal{P}$ is the longest existing prefix of $\mathcal{P}$.

We illustrate this scheme in Figure 2. Suppose $a \wedge c \wedge e \wedge g$ deterministically maps to $g \wedge a \wedge e \wedge c$. This clause is now added to the view tree under its best current prefix in the tree, which is $g \wedge a \wedge e$. We discuss how the tree is maintained as new clauses are added below.

2.3 Maintaining the View Tree

The view tree must be updated to reflect new materialized views. This is done when a view is materialized using the procedure described in Section 2.2. The tree must also be updated when nodes holding already materialized views depart, or when views are simply discarded.

Tree integrity requires that the owner of a new node updates all attribute indexes corresponding to attributes of the new node. If the application requires this new node must be part of each resolved query immediately, then the node owner must also traverse each attribute subtree and update all existing materialized views before the node is added to the system. The view tree provides exactly the pointers that must be traversed for these updates. Further, the tree has the property that in order for a node to be updated, the entire path to the root must also be updated. Thus, if the update ever reaches a view that it does not need to update, it can discard the entire subtree under this view. For most applications, it is probably sufficient to only update the attribute indexes, and *not* update any of the materialized views. In this case, the materialized views should be periodically refreshed using its parent node and other appropriate view searches. For these applications, new nodes will not appear in a few queries immediately after they are added to the system.

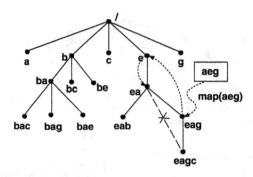

Fig. 3. Maintaining the tree when a new node joins

We use a soft state refresh to maintain the integrity of the view tree. Child views periodically send heartbeat messages to their parent node in the view tree. If these messages are not received for a timeout period, the parent node simply discards state for the child view (and correspondingly its entire subtree). If a parent node is not alive, then the child re-inserts itself in the view tree.

Lastly, as views are added to the system, the child pointers need to be reassigned. Figure 3 shows a new clause, "aeg", being added to the tree. The deterministic permutation maps "aeg" to "eag", and the exact prefix "ea" is found in the tree. The old child of "ea", "eagc", now becomes a child of the newly inserted node "eag".

3   Preliminary Results

This section presents preliminary results from simulations of the algorithms described above. We begin with a description of the data and query sources we used in the simulations along with the methodology we employed in deriving the input to drive our simulations.

3.1   Data Source and Methodology

We chose a random sets of documents from the TREC-Web data set as the source data for our experiments. We used HTML pages that exported the `keyword` meta-tag, and nominally used 64K different pages for each experiment.

We ran each experiment with 500,000 queries; this number was sufficient in all experiments for the caching behavior to stabilize. The queries were generated as follows: we first chose a representative sample of WWW queries from the publicly available `search.com` query database[1]. Unfortunately, the `search.com`

---

[1] We were also given access to 32K WWW queries by the IRCache project, and the query characteristics of the IRCache and `search.com` queries were comparable. We ran simulations with both data sets with similar results; we only present results from the (larger) `search.com` query set here.

query set does not provide an associated document set over which these queries would be valid: instead, we generated queries with the same statistical characteristics as the search.com queries using keywords from the TREC-Web data set. Specifically, we used the search.com queries to generate the distribution of number of attributes per query.

Next, we use the distribution of keywords in the set of source documents to map keywords to each attribute. For multi-attribute queries, we generated the set of 10,000 most popular keyword digrams, trigrams, etc. and used these, uniformly at random, as the input query set for multi-attribute queries. Note that the popular 10,000 covered all possible multi-attribute queries with non-null results for our source data.

For each experiment, we use a "working set", which is a set of unique queries to which some fraction of overall queries are directed. Nominally, we used a working set of size 50,000 to which 90% of the queries were directed. All queries (including the queries in the working set) were generated using the scheme described above; however, 90% of the queries were always directed to the queries in the working set, while 10% were unconstrained.

We also model updates to the data. Specifically, we consider the cases when attributes are added from, deleted from, and changed in existing documents. New attributes, for both addition and updates, are chosen using the original keyword distribution generated from the complete source data set. For deletion, attributes are selected uniformly at random. It is not clear exactly what the rate for such updates should be.

Our primary metric is the number of tuples intersected when answering multi-attribute queries. If an exact result is required, then the number of tuples intersected is also an upper bound on the number of tuples that must be transferred between hosts.

Both single- and multi-attribute indexes have to be updated as data items are added, updated, or removed from the namespace. We present results for the number of messages that are required to update the attribute indexes; we specifically account for the number of messages that are sent directly as a result of maintaining the view tree. Once again, we assume the worst case scenario in which each index is hosted by a different host. Thus, the overheads we present represent an upper bound on the number of messages and tuples that would have to be transferred in a deployed system.

3.2 View Tree Results

In our first result, we investigate the benefit of maintaining the view tree by simulating keyword searches over this data set. These experiments were run using our base parameter set: there were 500,000 total queries, 90% of which go to a working 50,000 queries, and the rest are chosen uniformly at random. In Figure 4, we show how the number of tuples intersected decreases as multi-attribute query results are cached. The x-axis shows the maximum depth of the view tree (e.g. depth 3 implies results of only two and two-attribute queries

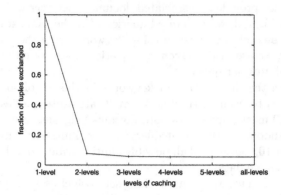

Fig. 4. Caching benefit by level

are cached). The y-axis is a measure of the benefit from maintaining the view-tree, and shows the normalized number of tuples transferred for each level of caching. For the normalization, we use the number of tuples transferred for the single attribute indexes only case as unity. From the plot, it is clear that there is potentially an immense benefit to maintaining a view tree: keeping only the second-level indexes reduces the number of tuples transferred by 92%. Extra levels of caching further reduces the intersection overhead by a further 30% compared to the two-level only caches (to less than 95% of the original). In terms of the actual number of tuples, the single-attribute indexes required 486M tuples to be intersected in total (972 tuples intersected/query). The two-level and all caches required 37M and 26M tuples intersected respectively. Recall that for exact queries, these numbers represent an upper bound on the number of tuples that have to be transferred over the network; for approximate methods, the number of tuples intersected is a lower bound on the amount of processing per query.

Obviously, the number of tuples that must be stored at each host increases as more indexes are maintained. For these experiments, the amount space required increased by a factor of 3.06 (0.6M tuples stored for the single attribute indexes vs. 1.84M tuples stored in 55K different multi-attribute caches for caching all levels) in the worst case. The two-attribute queries themselves require 1.5M tuples in 30K caches, which, in terms of tuple storage, is about 70% of all the multi-attribute queries.

The two attribute indexes consume most space since the indexes with more attributes tend to be smaller as it is less likely that documents will export the same three or more keywords.

An interesting footnote from our experiments was that the number of cache hits monotonically *decreases* (by about 25% as the caching level is increased from 2 to all) as the level of caches is increased. This is because with more caches, queries have a higher probability of a direct cache hit in a cache with

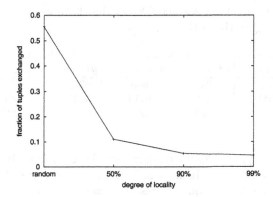

Fig. 5. Effect of locality on caching efficiency

many attributes; however, with only a subset of caches, the popular subqueries get used over and over again.

3.3 Query Locality

It is important to understand exactly how sensitive our results are to the degree of locality in the query stream. In our base experiments, we choose a working set of 50,000 queries, and direct 90% of all queries this working set. In this experiment (Figure 5), we quantify the benefits from result caching as the degree of locality is varied. The x axis represents the degree of locality: specifically, it shows what fraction of the queries were chosen from the working set of 50,000 queries[2]. The rest of the queries are chosen uniformly at random. For the leftmost set of points, all queries are chosen uniformly at random, i.e. there is no locality in the query stream. The y-axis shows the normalized benefit from maintaining a full view tree (i.e. it is the ratio of the number of tuples intersected with and without a view tree).

We should note that the *number* of caches created for different localities vary by an order of magnitude (288K caches for no locality vs. only 29K caches when 99% of the queries are directed to the working set). There are only 64K cache hits in case of the random queries, thus, the view tree is of limited use when the query stream is random. However, even the random set of queries do get some benefit from the view tree (50% reduction in the number of intersected tuples). This is somewhat counterintuitive, since there is no locality in the queries. The benefit derives from the observation that even though the queries themselves are uncorrelated, there is correlation in the individual *attributes* that make up the queries. The attributes are chosen using their distribution in the exported keywords, and thus, the view tree becomes useful. We did conduct experiments

---

[2] We have experimented with other working set sizes, and these results are representative.

Table 1. Update overhead for 100,000 queries. 90% locality refers to 90% of the queries directed to the 50K working set

Update:Query ratio	90% locality		Random Queries	
	#Caches	#Update Hops	#Caches	#Update Hops
1:10	28244	106683	62607	33758
1:100	28253	10774	62619	3430
1:1000	28255	923	62608	296

in which both the queries and attributes are chosen uniformly at random. As expected, in this case, there is no benefit from the view tree; further, the vast majority of multi-attribute queries result in zero or a very small number of tuples.

3.4   View Maintenance: Updates

In the previous two results, we have shown that result caching reduces query resolution overhead, and is relatively robust as long as there is reasonable locality in the input. In this section, we show that the update overhead of the view tree is essentially negligible for almost all deployment scenarios. In Table 1 we report the number of caches updated, and the number of distinct nodes visited, over two 100,000 query simulations with different input distributions, and query vs. update ratios. "Update hops" includes the cost of finding caches via the view tree. In these simulations, attributes (keywords) are added or deleted from documents, and these updates are reflected in *every* cache that holds a pointer to this document. In the worst case scenario, there are only ten queries in the entire system before an attribute is changed in some document. Note that in the first row (1:10), there are 10,000 updates during the course of the simulation. The effect of locality in the query stream is apparent: query locality reduces the number of caches, but *increases* the overall update overhead to a popular document now has to update multiple caches. Specifically, the updates with a random query stream results in, on average, 3 different caches being updated, while the query stream with locality has to update approximately 10 different caches, again on average. Thus, in the worst case, each update would cause a single tuple to be transferred to ten different hosts. In practice, overheads will be lower since updates will be batched, and the update to query ratio is likely to be very low for most data.

4   Previous Work

Most closely related to this work are other efforts to provide a search infrastructure over peer-to-peer systems. Harren et al. [1] propose traditional relational database operators on top of DHT-based systems to resolve queries. Reynolds and Vahdat [2] discuss a search infrastructure using distributed inverted indexing. Each entry corresponds to a keyword and the set of documents that contain the keyword. Each node in the system is responsible for all keywords that map the node. Tang et al. [4] argue for context-based and semantic-based text searches on top of DHTs. They extend vector space model (VSM) and latent semantic indexing (LSI), and support keyword-based queries. Annexstein et al. [5] argue for combining text data to speedup search queries, at the expense of more work done attaching/ detaching a node to a super-node. The indexes are kept as suffix trees. Kubiatowicz [3] proposes to use transactional query support. The set cover problem and a greedy approximation algorithm is discussed by Cormen et al. [10].

5 Summary and Discussion

This paper presents the design of a scalable and efficient search infrastructure using a new structure called the view tree. Our preliminary results show that 1) use of result caches can eliminate the vast majority of tuples retrieved across the network for queries with multiple terms, 2) result caches are effective even with no locality in the query stream (but with locality in the distribution of attributes across documents), and 3) update cost should be relatively insignificant.

In addition to testing with a wider variety of input data, we need to address a number of significant issues before a real system can be designed. These issues include result cache placement policies, result cache replacement policies, fault tolerance, availability, and interactions with the underlying DHT system. Finally, both application consistency requirements and available system resources should ideally be taken into account by view maintenance policies. Cached results, and even the basic distributed index scheme, also open up a wealth of new security problems.

References

[1] M. Harren, J. M. Hellerstein, R. Huebsch, B. T. Loo, S. Shenker, and I. Stoica, "Complex queries in dht-based peer-to-peer networks," in *The 1st International Workshop on Peer-to-Peer Systems (IPTPS)*, Cambridge, MA, March 2002.

[2] P. Reynolds and A. Vahdat, "Efficient Peer-to-Peer Keyword Searching," *unpublished*.

[3] J. Kubiatowicz, D. Bindel, Y. Chen, S. Czerwinski, P. Eaton, D. Geels, R. Gummadi, S. Rhea, H. Weatherspoon, W. Weimer, C. Wells, and B. Zhao., "Oceanstore: An architecture for global-scale persistent storage," in *Proc. of the 9th International Conference on Architectural Support for Programming Languages and Operating Systems*, Cambridge, MA, November 2000, pp. 190–201.

[4] C. Tang, Z. Xu, and M. Mahalingam, "pSearch: Information retrieval in structured overlays," *SIGCOMM Computer Communication Review*, vol. 33, no. 1, January 2003.

[5] F. S. Annexstein, K. A. Berman, M. Jovanovic, and K. Ponnavaikko, "Indexing techniques for file sharing in scalable peer-to-peer networks," in *Proc. the 11th IEEE International Conference on Computer Communications and Networks*, Miami, FL, October 2002.

[6] B. H. Bloom, "Space/time trade-offs in hash coding with allowable errors," *Communications of the ACM*, 13(7):422-426, 1970.

[7] M. Stonebraker, "Concurrency control and consistency of multiple copies of data in distributed INGRES," *IEEE Transactions on Software Engineering*, vol. 5, no. 3, pp. 188–194, May 1979.

[8] P. Slavik, "A tight analysis of the greedy algorithm for set cover," in *ACM Symposium on Theory of Computing*, Philadelphia, PA, May 1996, pp. 435–441.

[9] Y. Minsky, A. Trachtenberg, and R. Zippel, "Set reconciliation with nearly optimal communications complexity," in *IEEE International Symposium on Information Theory*, Washington DC, June 2001.

[10] T. H. Cormen, C. E. Leiserson, and R. L. Rivest, *Introduction to Algorithms*, MIT Press, Cambridge, Massachusetts, 1997.

[11] I. Wegener, *The Complexity of Boolean Functions*, John Wiley & Sons Ltd., and B. G. Teubner, Stuttgart, July 1987, ISBN: 0-471-91555-6.

Adaptive Peer Selection

Daniel S. Bernstein, Zhengzhu Feng, Brian Neil Levine, and Shlomo Zilberstein

Department of Computer Science
University of Massachusetts
Amherst, Massachusetts 01003
{bern,fengzz,brian,shlomo}@cs.umass.edu

Abstract. In a peer-to-peer file-sharing system, a client desiring a particular file must choose a source from which to download. The problem of selecting a good data source is difficult because some peers may not be encountered more than once, and many peers are on low-bandwidth connections. Despite these facts, information obtained about peers just prior to the download can help guide peer selection. A client can gain additional time savings by aborting bad download attempts until an acceptable peer is discovered. We denote as peer selection the entire process of switching among peers and finally settling on one. Our main contribution is to use the methodology of machine learning for the construction of good peer selection strategies from past experience. Decision tree learning is used for rating peers based on low-cost information, and Markov decision processes are used for deriving a policy for switching among peers. Preliminary results with the Gnutella network demonstrate the promise of this approach.

1 Introduction

In a peer-to-peer file-sharing system, data is replicated among the peers participating in the system. Replicated data, while providing scalability and fault-tolerance, introduces the problem of source selection. After determining the locations of a desired file, a client must decide where to download from in order to receive the file quickly. We assume that only one peer can send data at a time, but our work can be extended to multi-source downloading (see the discussion section).

This problem has been studied mainly in the context of mirrored Web data, where it is called the *server selection* problem. Various solutions have been proposed and validated with experiments on the Internet [1, 2, 3, 4, 5, 6, 7, 8, 9]. However, many of the existing techniques rely on assumptions that render them inapplicable in the dynamic setting of peers. For instance, selection strategies based on experience with specific hosts do not apply when hosts are not likely to be encountered more than once. In addition, selection strategies that rely on network-layer assistance are not feasible.

In this paper, we introduce techniques for efficiently obtaining replicated content in peer-to-peer networks. We assume that the client has obtained a list

F. Kaashoek and I. Stoica (Eds.): IPTPS 2003, LNCS 2735, pp. 237–246, 2003.

of peers, each possessing a desired file. No assumptions are made about whether the client has previously encountered any of the peers on the list. The client has access to limited information about its bandwidth to each of the peers. In addition, the client can perform partial downloads from peers before finally settling on one. We define as *peer selection* the problem of switching among peers and finally settling on one, while keeping the total time to a minimum.

The novel aspect of our approach to this problem is that it is based on the machine learning methodology from artificial intelligence. Our approach is *not* to introduce a new strategy for peer selection, but rather to introduce techniques by which a client can automatically derive a selection strategy based on its own experience. The strategies that are eventually produced are actually *adapted* to the client (hence the title).

The two phases of selection strategy execution proceed as follows. First, passively collected information is used to rate each peer on the list in terms of expected transfer time. In the Gnutella network, this information includes attributes from the search response messages regarding each peer's current load, current bandwidth, and past uploading experience. A *decision tree*, learned using data from previous downloads, rates never-before-seen peers based on attribute values. One benefit of using decision trees as a basis for the rating system is that they allow us to rate peers based on combinations of attributes. When individual attributes are unreliable, as is the case in peer-to-peer networks, this becomes important.

In the second phase of peer selection, the client uses the rating system to sort its list of peers, and then executes a policy for performing partial file downloads from the most promising ones and finally settling on a peer. An appropriate framework for deriving such a policy is the *Markov decision process (MDP)* framework. The peer selection process can be modeled as an MDP, the parameters of which are obtained from previous experience. The MDP can be solved for a selection policy that is optimal with respect to the model.

We implemented our ideas using the Gnutella network as our experimental platform. Downloading data was collected from four different client sites. Using this data, a different decision tree was learned for each of the clients. The resulting rating systems turned out to be fairly accurate in their predictions. In addition, we constructed an MDP for each client and solved each MDP for a complete peer selection strategy. Although mostly the same, the resulting policies did show some interesting differences across clients. We are in the process of evaluating the complete selection strategies with respect to other possible strategies.

As we mentioned, by focusing on peer selection, we address issues not dealt with in the classical server selection work. In addition, there been little research on combining attributes to yield better predictions. Two exceptions are [6], in which prior bandwidth and round-trip latency were combined, and [5], in which linear regression was used to combine round-trip latency and current available bandwidth. Finally, our focus on techniques for automatically learning a peer selection strategy from experience is novel.

2   Data Collection

Our machine learning approach requires that we have a set of training data from which to learn. To this end, a period of approximately two weeks was set aside to perform several downloads and record statistics about them. We note that, in practice, this training data could be produced as a byproduct of actual system use. This is left for future work and is discussed briefly in the final section of the paper.

For data collection, we modified a version of Gtk-Gnutella 0.85. The program was run at four client sites: University of Massachusetts in Amherst, University of Maryland in College Park, University of California in San Diego, and on an AT&T Broadband cable modem connection in Boston, Massachusetts. During this time the clients repeatedly attempted to download the first megabyte of randomly selected mp3 files from randomly selected peers. For each peer contacted, the following attributes were recorded from its search response message: an indication of whether all of the peer's upload slots were currently full (busy flag), an indication of whether the peer had successfully uploaded at least one file (uploaded flag), an indication of whether the peer was firewalled (firewall flag), a number representing the connection speed (speed field), and an indication of whether the speed field was measured or set by the user (measured flag). Note that the accuracy of this information is dubious, as different client programs have different policies for providing it. If the client was able to connect to the peer, the connection time was recorded, and if the client was able to download from the peer, the number of bytes received was recorded every 0.5 seconds.

Data was collected separately at each of the four clients. The derivation of each client's selection strategy, as described in the following sections, relied only on that client's data.

3   Rating Peers

In this section, we describe how to use training data to learn a decision tree for rating peers. We begin with a brief introduction to decision trees. A more thorough treatment can be found in [10].

3.1   Decision Trees

The decision trees we consider are used to approximate noisy binary-valued functions. The input to a decision tree consists of a set of attributes. In order to compute the output of a decision tree, one traverses down from the root, following the branches dictated by the attribute values, until a leaf is reached. Each leaf contains an output value. A decision tree can also be viewed as a list of if-then rules, one for each leaf. A decision tree is learned using a dataset of input-output pairs from the function. In our case, the inputs were search message attributes, and the output was an indication of whether the download from the corresponding source was fast (above the median speed) or slow (below

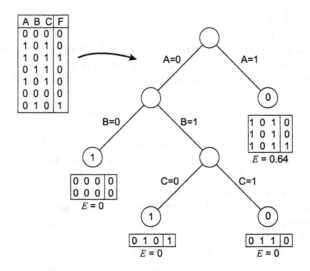

Fig. 1. A dataset along with a decision tree that could have been learned from the dataset

the median speed). Figure 1 shows an artificial dataset along with a decision tree that could have been learned from the dataset.

Given a dataset, one desires a reasonably-sized decision tree that returns outputs with a high degree of certainty. In other words, for a given leaf, one would like most of the training instances associated with that leaf to agree on the output. Notice that in the decision tree in the figure, only one of the leaves contains a disagreement. One quantitative measure of the confidence of a leaf is the *entropy* of the leaf. The entropy of a leaf is defined as

$$E = -p_0 \log p_0 - p_1 \log p_1,$$

where p_0 is the fraction of instances with output 0, and p_1 is the fraction of instances with output 1.

3.2   Application to Rating Peers

Preliminary experiments revealed that the busy flag is strongly correlated with connection success. Thus we did not use the busy flag in the decision tree and decided to assign all instances with the busy flag set the lowest rating, B. Furthermore, we used only training downloads that completed successfully for learning a decision tree with the remaining four attributes.

We used the ITI decision tree algorithm [11] to learn a decision tree for each client site. The leaves of the decision trees are rated in the following way. First the leaves are sorted according to how many instances each contains. The bottom 50% are assigned the rank U (uncertain). These leaves contain too few instances to provide reliable information. Any of the remaining leaves with $E > 0.918$ are

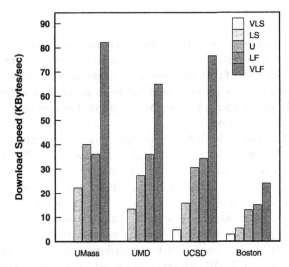

Fig. 2. The average download speed corresponding to the ratings for each client, measured on the test data. Note that the UMass and UMD decision trees had no VLS leaves

assigned rank U because of the high uncertainty inherent in them. For each of the remaining leaves, if the majority of the leaf's instances are above the median speed, and $E > 0.65$, then the leaf is assigned LF (likely fast). A similar rule holds for categorizing leaves as LS (likely slow). For the leaves still remaining, if the majority of the leaf's instances are above the median speed, then the leaf was assigned VLF (very likely fast). A similar rule holds for categorizing leaves as VLS (very likely slow). This completes the rating system (from least to most desirable): B, VLS, LS, U, LF, VLF.

Examining the resulting rating systems, we were able to extract some general rules. For the campus connections, a measured high speed along with a positive firewall flag were indicative of a fast download. The measured high speed makes sense, but there is not a clear explanation of why firewalled hosts would be faster; we speculate that "always on," high-speed hosts tend to employ firewalls more often, but we have no data to back this claim. Our cable modem was behind a firewall, which prevented it from downloading from firewalled peers (the Gnutella protocol does not allow this), and consequently rendered the firewall flag irrelevant. The best indicators of a fast download in this case seem to be previous upload success and a high measured speed. The indicators of a slow download seem to be that the peer has not successfully uploaded before and has a low value in its speed field.

Figure 2 provides evidence of the rating system's utility. It illustrates how rating correlates with download speed on test data (a small part of the dataset not used for training). We see that peers rated as VLF give significantly faster downloads than those with other ratings.

4   Peer Selection

In the preceding section, we showed how to construct a rating system for peers based on low-cost attributes. After sorting its list according to rating, the client can perform a sequence of partial downloads, eventually settling on a peer. Since partial downloads consume time, the client must proceed in an intelligent manner. It basically needs to make a sequence of good decisions, ending with the decision to commit to a peer.

An elegant framework for addressing this kind of sequential decision-making problem is the *Markov decision process (MDP)* framework [12]. An MDP models an agent acting in a stochastic environment with the aim of minimizing expected long-term cost. Our agent is the Gnutella client, and its long-term cost is the total time to obtain the first megabyte of a file, including the time for connection establishment and aborted downloads. To achieve this goal, it has a policy that indicates the situations in which it should abort its current download and start over with the next peer on the list. After describing the MDP framework in more detail, we show how an MDP can be constructed from training data and solved to yield a selection strategy.

4.1   Markov Decision Processes

We consider a type of MDP in which the agent tries to minimize the expected total time to reach a goal. The process proceeds through a sequence of stages $t = 0, 1, 2, 3, \ldots$ At each stage, the agent perceives the state of the process, $s_t \in S$, and chooses an action, $a_t \in A$. One stage later, the process produces a numerical cost, c_t, and a next state, s_{t+1}. This continues until a zero-cost absorbing state is reached, which indicates the attainment of the goal and the end of an *episode*.

Formally, an MDP is a tuple $\langle S, A, T, C \rangle$, where S is a finite set of states; A is a finite set of actions; $T(s, a, s')$ is a transition function representing the probability of transitioning from state s to state s' under action a; and $C(s, a, s')$ is a cost function giving the cost for executing action a in state s and transitioning to state s'. Actions are chosen according to a *policy*, $\delta : S \rightarrow A$. The *cost-to-go function*, $J_\delta(s)$, for a policy δ gives the expected (discounted) sum of future costs upon executing δ from state s. The aim is to find a policy δ that minimizes $J_\delta(s)$ for all states s. MDPs can be solved efficiently using dynamic programming [13].

4.2   Peer Selection as an MDP

We first provide a high-level description of the MDP model that is constructed from the training data. This MDP is an idealized model of the peer selection process, in which the client desires a 1 MB file and has access to an unlimited list of peers possessing the file. At any given time, it interacts with only one peer, denoted the *active peer*. The interaction consists of two phases. First is the *connecting* phase, which lasts a maximum of 3 seconds. If no connection is made during that time, a new peer is randomly drawn from the list. If a connection *is* established, the *downloading* phase begins. After 3 seconds of downloading have passed, the client automatically commits to downloading the rest of the file from the currently active peer, and the episode is over. Failures can only occur during the connecting phase. For the first 3 seconds after a connection is made, the download speed may fluctuate, but it remains constant from the 3 second point on. Some aspects of our model may seem unrealistic; however, our objective is not realism but a model that can be solved quickly to yield an effective policy.

We now describe the model in more detail. The action set contains two elements. At each stage, the agent may either continue its download attempt with the active peer or start over with a new peer. In the connecting phase, an action is chosen every 0.5 seconds, and in the downloading phase, an action is chosen every 1.0 seconds. The states of the problem are as follows. The pre-connecting states,

$$P = \{\text{B}, \text{VLS}, \text{LS}, \text{U}, \text{LF}, \text{VLF}\},$$

indicate the rating of the active peer. The connecting states,

$$N = \{\text{B}, \text{VLS}, \text{LS}, \text{U}, \text{LF}, \text{VLF}\} \times$$
$$\{0.5, 1.0, 1.5, 2.0, 2.5, 3.0\},$$

indicate the rating of the active peer and how much time has passed since the active peer was first contacted. The downloading states,

$$D = \{\text{B}, \text{VLS}, \text{LS}, \text{U}, \text{LF}, \text{VLF}\} \times \{1.0, 2.0, 3.0\} \times$$
$$\{(0\text{-}1), (1\text{-}2), (2\text{-}4), (4\text{-}8), (8\text{-}16),$$
$$(16\text{-}32), (32\text{-}64), (64\text{-}128), (128\text{-}\infty)\},$$

indicate the rating of the active peer, the time spent downloading so far, and the (discretized) average speed so far (KB/sec). Finally we have an absorbing state, a, which is entered at the end of the downloading phase. Thus $S = P \cup N \cup D \cup \{a\}$, and $|S| = 205$.

Since the only cost in our problem is time, our cost function is relatively straightforward. A transition into a pre-connecting state incurs no cost. For transitions into connection and download states, the immediate costs are 0.5 and 1.0, respectively. Upon entry into the absorbing state, a final cost is incurred. This cost is the time that it would take to download the rest of a 1 MB file, assuming the speed from the first 3 seconds persists. Given this cost function, the total cost for an episode is equal to the time taken to download a complete 1 MB file, including the overhead for connection establishment and aborted downloads.

The parameters for the transition dynamics are derived using the training data. The initial pre-connecting state is drawn from a distribution that matches the distribution over ratings observed in the data. The rating component of the state remains fixed until the episode ends or an abort action has been performed. At any stage, an abort action causes a transition to a new pre-connecting state, drawn from the distribution mentioned above. For transitions into connecting states, the probabilities are determined from the distribution over connect times in the training data. If the 3 second point of the connecting phase is reached, an automatic transition to a new pre-connecting state occurs on the next step. The probabilities for transitions into downloading states are determined from the training data. At the end of the downloading phase, there is a deterministic transition into the absorbing state.

4.3   The Resulting Policies

We solved each of the clients' MDPs using a dynamic programming algorithm. Not surprisingly, the policies are similar. In most cases, the policy aborts if no connection has been made in 0.5 seconds, or if a connection has been made but the speed at 1 second is below a threshold. The threshold is usually 32 KB/sec. For the cable modem connection, there are a few ratings for which the threshold is lower. This makes intuitive sense. As connection speed decreases, the client's connection becomes more of a bottleneck, and it makes less sense for the client to be choosy about which peer it downloads from. We conjecture that a modem would have a very low threshold.

There are some exceptions to the aforementioned policy rules. Some are difficult to explain and could be due to modeling assumptions and noise in the data. There is however, one apparently meaningful exception. If a peer is highly rated, policies are sometimes willing to wait longer to establish a connection. This makes sense, as it is worth investing extra time when the potential payoff is high.

We performed some preliminary experiments integrating the complete selection strategies into a client and using the client to obtain popular files. Our strategies are competitive with random strategies and strategies based on round-trip latency because they often quickly find peers with high bandwidth connections. A careful assessment of our strategies under a variety of conditions remains to be done.

5   Discussion

We have presented an approach to peer selection based on the machine learning methodology. Decision trees were used for learning peer rating systems, and our experiments showed the resulting rating systems to be accurate. The MDP framework was used for deriving policies for aborting downloads. These policies decide whether to continue or abort based on the state of the current download, so as to minimize the total time to receive the file.

By adding more information to the client's state, more sophisticated and better-performing policies should be possible. Information about peers other than the active peer should be useful—whether or not it is advantageous to abort sometimes depends on whether other promising peers are available. In situations where a client will be downloading files of varying sizes, it may also be useful to base decisions on the size of the desired file. As files get larger, it is probably worth investing more time in trying to find a well-performing one. Finally, it may be a good idea to incorporate performance estimators such as hop count and round-trip latency into the MDP.

One natural question that arises from this work is whether the rating system and MDP can be updated online, based on data from actual system use. This is often referred to as *reinforcement learning* [14] in the artificial intelligence community. We see no major obstacles to doing this, and it has advantages over offline training. One advantage is that the time and congestion incurred by gathering large batches of training data are eliminated. In addition, an online approach allows for adaptation to changes in the Gnutella network and in local traffic conditions, which could in turn lead to better overall performance. Also interesting are *model-free* online learning techniques, which learn a policy without first constructing an MDP (see, e.g., [15]). These more direct approaches can alleviate some the burdensome assumptions implicit in an MDP model, but usually require more data.

In our study, we restricted the number of concurrent download attempts to be one. It has been shown, however, that parallel access to multiple sources can lead to lower transfer times [16, 17]. Indeed, many of today's peer-to-peer clients employ multi-source downloads. We believe that our methods can be extended to provide intelligent management of parallel transfers. A set of promising peers can be identified before the start of the download, and peers can be switched into and out of the set during the download. Intelligent parallel transfers should achieve maximal performance with fewer connections than naive parallel transfers, thus reducing congestion in the network. Some evidence of this is provided in [18], in which round-trip latency is used to select a set of servers for a parallel download.

Acknowledgments

We are grateful to Geoff Volker and Stephen Savage at UCSD and Samrat Bhattacharjee at UMD for providing the remote accounts used in our experiments. We also thank Zihui Ge for helping with our data collection. This work was supported in part by the National Science Foundation under grants IIS-9907331, ANI-0133055, and EIA-0080119. Daniel Bernstein was supported by a NASA GSRP Fellowship. Any opinions, findings, and conclusions or recommendations expressed in this material are those of the authors and do not reflect the views of the NSF or NASA.

References

[1] Gwertzman, J., Seltzer, M.: The case for geographical push-caching. In: Proceedings of the 1995 Workshop on Hot Operating Systems. (1995) 51–55

[2] Guyton, J.D., Schwartz, M.F.: Locating nearby copies of replicated Internet servers. In: Proceedings of SIGCOMM '95, Boston, MA (1995) 288–298

[3] Yoshikawa, C., Chun, B., Eastham, P., Vahdat, A., Anderson, T., Culler, D.: Using smart clients to build scalable services. In: Proceedings of the First USENIX Symposium on Internet Technologies and Systems. (1997)

[4] Sayal, M., Breitbart, Y., Scheuermann, P., Vigralek, P.: Selection algorithms for replicated web servers. Performance Evaluation Review **26** (1998) 44–50

[5] Carter, R.L., Crovella, M.E.: On the network impact of dynamic server selection. Computer Networks **31** (1999) 2529–2558

[6] Dykes, S.G., Robbins, K.A., Jeffery, C.L.: An empirical evaluation of client-side server selection algorithms. In: Proceedings of INFOCOM '00. (2000) 1361–1370

[7] Stemm, M., Katz, R., Seshan, S.: A network measurement architecture for adaptive applications. In: Proceedings of INFOCOM '00. (2000)

[8] Zegura, E.W., Ammar, M.H., Fei, Z., Bhattacharjee, S.: Application-layer anycasting: A server selection architecture and use in a replicated web service. IEEE/ACM Transactions on Networking **8** (2000) 455–466

[9] Hanna, K.M., Natarajan, N., Levine, B.N.: Evaluation of a novel two-step server selection metric. In: Proceedings of IEEE International Conference on Network Protocols, Paris, France (2001)

[10] Quinlan, J.R.: C4.5: Programs for Machine Learning. Morgan Kaufmann, San Mateo, CA (1993)

[11] Utgoff, P.E., Berkman, N.C., Clouse, J.A.: Decision tree induction based on efficient tree restructuring. Machine Learning **29** (1997) 5–44

[12] Puterman, M.L.: Markov Decision Processes. J Wiley & Sons, New York (1994)

[13] Bellman, R.E.: Dynamic Programming. Princeton University Press, Princeton, NJ (1957)

[14] Sutton, R.S., Barto, A.G.: Reinforcement Learning: An Introduction. MIT Press, Cambridge, MA (1998)

[15] Williams, R.J.: Simple statistical gradient-following algorithms for connectionist reinforcement learning. Machine Learning **8** (1992) 229–256

[16] Byers, J., Luby, M., Mitzenmacher, M.: Accessing multiple mirror sites in parallel: Using tornado codes to speed up downloads. In: Proceedings of INFOCOM '99. (1999)

[17] Rodriguez, P., Biersack, E.W.: Dynamic parallel-access to replicated content in the Internet. IEEE/ACM Transactions on Networking **10** (2002) 455–464

[18] Zeitoun, A., Jomjoom, H., El-Gendy, M.: Scalable parallel-access for mirrored servers. In: Proceedings of IASTED International Conference on Applied Informatics, Innsbruck, Austria (2002)

Rateless Codes and Big Downloads

Petar Maymounkov and David Mazières

New York University
New York NY 10003, USA
{petar,dm}@cs.nyu.edu
http://www.scs.cs.nyu.edu/~petar
http://www.scs.cs.nyu.edu/~dm

Abstract. This paper presents a novel algorithm for downloading big files from multiple sources in peer-to-peer networks. The algorithm is simple, but offers several compelling properties. It ensures low hand-shaking overhead between peers that download files (or parts of files) from each other. It is computationally efficient, with cost linear in the amount of data transfered. Most importantly, when nodes leave the net-work in the middle of uploads, the algorithm minimizes the duplicate information shared by nodes with truncated downloads. Thus, any two peers with partial knowledge of a given file can almost always fully ben-efit from each other's knowledge. Our algorithm is made possible by the recent introduction of linear-time, rateless erasure codes.

1 Introduction

One of the most prominent uses of peer-to-peer systems is to download files—often very large files, such as movies [9]. More often than not, these files are available at least in part at more than one node on the network. This observation has inspired a number of different algorithms for multi-source file download [2], including some that have already been deployed [6].

The basic multi-source download problem is simple. A set of nodes, called *source nodes*, have complete knowledge of a certain file. A set of nodes we call *requesting nodes* wish to obtain a copies of that file. The goal is to transfer the file to the requesting nodes in a fast and bandwidth-efficient manner. In practice, the task is complicated by the fact that nodes can join or leave the system, aborting downloads and initiating new requests at any time. Thus, a download algorithm can make very few assumptions about the uptime or bandwidth capacity of participating nodes.

Most multi-source download algorithms take the same general approach. When a requesting node needs a file, it first locates a set nodes with full or partial knowledge of that file. It then contacts as many of them as necessary to download the file efficiently. For each source node the requesting node contacts, the two must reconcile the differences in their knowledge of the file. Then either the requesting node downloads any non-overlapping information, or often both nodes exchange any non-overlapping information they have about the file.

F. Kaashoek and I. Stoica (Eds.): IPTPS 2003, LNCS 2735, pp. 247–255, 2003.

An effective multi-source download algorithm should meet two main challenges. First, it should maximize the utility of nodes with partial knowledge of a file to each other. This, in turn, means minimizing the amount of overlapping information nodes are likely to have. We call this property the *availability* aspect of the algorithm, because it allows nodes with truncated downloads to reconstruct a file even in the event that every source node with the complete file has left the network.

The second challenge of a multi-source download algorithm is to make the reconciliation phase as bandwidth-efficient as possible. This phase is an instance of the more general set reconciliation problem [10, 3, 11, 1]. Unfortunately, existing set reconciliation algorithms are not practical for multi-source download algorithms. They are either too computationally costly, suboptimal in terms of message complexity, or simply too complicated to implement.

In this paper, we propose an algorithm that combines near-optimal availability with a simple yet practical reconciliation phase not based on the general set reconciliation problem. Our approach is made possible by the recent introduction of locally-encodable, linear-time decodable, rateless erasure codes. It exploits particular properties of the way file contents tend to disperse over nodes in a peer-to-peer system. The paper is presented in terms of a new erasure code called on-line codes [8]. The recently published LT-codes [7] are similar to on-line codes, but have $O(n \log n)$ running time, compared to linear time for on-line codes.

The next section gives an overview of erasure codes and their use in multi-source downloads and introduces on-line codes. Section 3 details on-line codes and their implementation. Section 4 describes our multi-source download algorithm. Section 5 discusses aspects of the algorithm and open questions.

2   Loss-Resilient Codes

Erasure codes transform a message of n blocks into an encoding of more than n blocks such that one can recover the message from only a fraction of the encoded blocks. A block is just a fixed-length bit string, with block size a parameter of the algorithm. Many erasure codes, including the on-line codes in this paper, support blocks of arbitrary size, from a single bit to tens of kilobytes or more. Choice of block size is driven by the fact that a fragment of an encoded block conveys no useful information about the original message. Thus, blocks should be small enough that aborted block transfers do not waste appreciable bandwidth.

Conventional erasure codes also have a *rate* parameter, specifying the fraction of the encoded output blocks required to reconstruct the original message. An *optimal* erasure code with rate R transforms a message of n blocks into n/R blocks such that any n suffice to decode the original message. Because of the cost of optimal codes, people often employ *near-optimal* codes, which require $(1 + \epsilon)n$ output blocks to reconstruct the message for any fixed $\epsilon > 0$. The cost of a smaller ϵ is increased computation. Currently there is only one instance of linear-time, near-optimal, conventional erasure codes, called Tornado codes [4].

Linear-time, near-optimal erasure codes have already been used for multi-source downloads [2]. The basic approach is for source nodes to encode files with rate $R < 1/2$ to achieve a large expansion factor. When a node downloads files, the source node sends a pseudo-random permutation of the encoded blocks to the requesting node, deriving the permutation from the requesting node's ID. Using this technique, two nodes that each have downloaded $0.6n$ encoded blocks of an n-block file will likely have enough information between them to reconstruct the file. Thus, the file will remain available even if all source nodes leave the network. To generalize the technique to more requesters, however, the expansion factor $1/R$ would need to grow proportionally to the number of truncated downloads. Unfortunately, even Tornado codes become impractically expensive and memory-intensive for rates $R < 1/4$.

A new class of erasure codes, *rateless, locally-encodable codes*, addresses the problem. The two novel properties of these codes—ratelessness and local encodability, go hand-in-hand. Ratelessness means that each message of size n has practically infinite encoding. Local encodability means that any one encoding block can be computed quickly and independently of the others. Replacing conventional fixed-rate codes with rateless, locally-encodable ones in the above scenario and making some additional use of the unique properties of rateless codes leads to the multi-source download algorithm presented in section 4 of this paper.

There are two instances of practical rateless codes, LT codes [7] and on-line codes [8], both recently proposed. We present our algorithm in terms of on-line codes because they are more efficient, requiring $O(1)$ time to generate each encoding block and $O(n)$ time to decode a message of length n. LT codes, in contrast, take $O(\log n)$ and $O(n \log n)$ time respectively (though they are asymptotically optimal and require no preprocessing, which may make them more convenient for other settings). The next section describes the implementation of on-line codes in greater detail.

3   On-Line Codes

This section explains how to implement on-line codes. A more detailed description and analysis of the algorithm is available in [8]. On-line codes are characterized by two parameters, ϵ and q (in addition to the block size). ϵ determines the degree of suboptimality—a message of n blocks can, with high probability, be decoded from $(1 + 3\epsilon)n$ output blocks. q, discussed subsequently, affects the success probability of the algorithm—it may fail to reconstruct the message with negligible probability $(\epsilon/2)^{q+1}$.

The overall structure of on-line codes has two layers, depicted in Figure 1. To encode a message, in an outer encoding, we first generate a small number of *auxiliary blocks* and append them to the original message to produce a *composite message*. The composite message has the property that knowledge of any $1 - \epsilon/2$ fraction of its blocks is sufficient to recover the entire original message. Next, in a second, inner layer, we continuously generate blocks to form an infinite, rateless encoding of the composite message. We call these blocks *check blocks*, because they serve as a kind of parity check during message reconstruction.

The decoding process is the inverse of the encoding. We first recover a $1 - \epsilon/2$ fraction of the composite message from (received) check blocks, then recover the entire original message from the this fraction of the composite message. In practice, auxiliary blocks and check blocks are similar in nature, allowing implementations to combine both layers of the decoding process.

3.1 Outer Encoding

The first step of the encoding process is to produce a composite message by generating $0.55q\epsilon n$ auxiliary blocks and appending them to the original message. Each auxiliary block is computed as the XOR of a number of message blocks, chosen as follows. We first seed a pseudo-random generator in a deterministic way. Then, using the pseudo-random generator, for each block of the original message, we chose q auxiliary blocks, uniformly. Each auxiliary block is computed as the XOR of all message blocks we have assigned to it. We append these auxiliary blocks to the original message blocks, and the resulting $n' = (0.55q\epsilon + 1)n$ blocks form the composite message.

With this construction, knowledge of any $1 - \epsilon/2$ fraction of the composite message is sufficient to recover the entire original message with probability $1 - (\epsilon/2)^{q+1}$. The decoding process is described at the end of this section, though the analysis is beyond the scope of this paper and described in [8].

3.2 Inner Encoding

We now describe how to generate check blocks from the composite message. The inner encoding depends on global values F and $\rho_1, \ldots, \rho_F$ computed as follows:

$$F = \left\lceil \frac{\ln(\epsilon^2/4)}{\ln(1 - \epsilon/2)} \right\rceil$$

$$\rho_1 = 1 - \frac{1 + 1/F}{1 + \epsilon}$$

$$\rho_i = \frac{(1 - \rho_1)F}{(F - 1)i(i - 1)} \quad \text{for } 2 \leq i \leq F$$

Each check block is named by a unique identifier, taken from a large ID space, such as 160-bit strings. The check block is computed by XORing several blocks of the underlying composite message. These blocks of the composite message are chosen as follows, based on the check block ID.

We begin by seeding a pseudo-random generator with the check block ID. Using the pseudo-random generator, we chose a *degree* d from 1 to F for the check block, biased such that that $d = i$ with probability ρ_i. We then pseudo-randomly and uniformly select d blocks of the composite message and set the check block to the XOR of their contents.

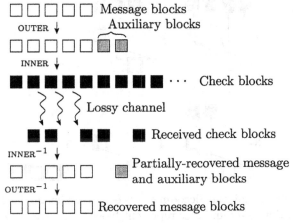

Fig. 1. Overall design of online codes

Any set of $(1+\epsilon)n'$ check blocks generated according to this procedure will be sufficient to recover a $1 - \epsilon/2$ fraction of the underlying composite message. The price to pay for a smaller ϵ is an increase by a constant factor in the decoding time. Specifically, the decoding time is proportional to $n\ln(1/\epsilon)$.

3.3 Decoding

We call the message blocks that were XORed to produce a check or auxiliary block its *adjacent* message blocks. Decoding consists of one basic step: Find a check or auxiliary block with exactly one unknown adjacent message block and recover the unknown block (by XORing the check block and all other adjacent message blocks). Repeat this step until the entire original message has been recovered.

The decoding process is depicted in Figure 2. Initially, the only useful check blocks will be those of degree 1, which are just copies of composite message blocks. Once the degree-1 check blocks have been processed, more check blocks become usable. As the number of decoded message blocks continues to increase, more and more higher-degree check and auxiliary blocks will become usable. Note that one can execute this decoding procedure on-the-fly, as check blocks arrive.

To see that the decoding process takes linear time, following the approach of [4, 5], we think of the composite message blocks and the check blocks as the left and right vertices, respectively, of a bipartite graph G. A check block has edges to and only to the message blocks that comprise it in terms of the XOR. We say that an edge has *left* (respectively *right*) degree d if the left-end node (respectively right-end node) of this edge is of degree d. Using the graph language, the decoding step is: find an edge of right degree 1 and remove all edges incident to its left-end node. In the graph context, decoding completes

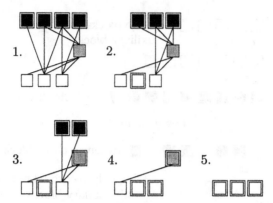

Fig. 2. Evolution of the decoding process of an example 3-block message. Squares with double-boundaries represent blocks that are known (recovered)

when all edges have been removed. Since the total number of edges is bounded by $(1 + \epsilon)Fn'$ (specifically it is roughly equal to $n' \ln F$), the decoding process runs in linear-time. A similar argument applies to the auxiliary blocks as well.

3.4 Practical Considerations

On-line codes are proven to be good asymptotically in n. Thus, as messages get too small, the suboptimality of the erasure code increases. However, with $\epsilon = 0.01$ and $q = 3$, one can decode messages of as few as 1,000 blocks after receiving only 3% more check blocks than the size of the message, and with probability of failure 10^{-8}.

To estimate the performance on large files, we used a non-optimized, 150-line Java implementation to encoded and decoded a message of size 1 million blocks. The decoding took roughly 10 seconds for blocks of size zero, and would have required approximately 11 million block XORs for a non-zero block size.

We recommend the parameters $\epsilon = 0.01$ and $q = 3$ to implementors, resulting in $F = 2114$ and an average check block degree of 8.23.

4 Multi-source Download

We now address the question of how to implement multi-source download with on-line codes. One approach might be for source nodes simply to send check blocks with random IDs to requesting nodes. This solution yields nearly optimal availability. However, if source nodes disappear and requesting nodes begin exchanging check blocks, two communicating nodes may still have significant overlap in their knowledge of check blocks. (This can only happen, if the overlapping check blocks came from the same third node earlier in time. Avoiding this effect is within the scope of another topic—deciding how nodes choose whom to exchange information with in the first place.) Exchanging only useful blocks would essentially boil down to the set reconciliation problem.

To improve on the above solution, a multi-source download algorithm should allow nodes to produce concise descriptions of large numbers of check blocks. Fortunately, requesting nodes tend to download large numbers of blocks from the same source before being interrupted. Thus, we can divide a node's check blocks into a small number of *streams*—one for each aborted download from a source node to a particular requesting node.

We define a *stream with ID* $s^* \in \{0,1\}^{160}$ to be the sequence of 160-bit numbers $a_0, a_1, a_2, \ldots$, where $a_i = \text{SHA-1}(s^*, i)$. For a given file f, we refer to a sequence of check blocks with IDs $a_1, a_2, \ldots$ as the *encoding stream with ID s^**.

Each requesting node downloading a file f can keep a small state table of pairs *(stream ID, last position)*. A pair (s^*, p) is in the table if and only if the node has the first p check blocks of the encoding stream with ID s^*. The pair (q^*, r), where q^* is the node's ID in the peer-to-peer system, is always in this table, even if $r = 0$.

To download a file, a requesting node, v, first uses a peer-to-peer lookup system to locate and select a node with information about the file. Preference is always given to a source with complete knowledge of the file, if one is available and has spare capacity. When downloading from a source node, a requesting node always downloads the encoding stream with ID equal to its own node ID in the peer-to-peer system. When resuming an aborted download, the requesting node simply informs the source of which stream position to start at.

When a requesting node v downloads a file from another node w that has only incomplete information, v begins by sending its entire state information table to w. In this way, w can send v only streams or stream suffixes that v does not already have. Furthermore, v can optionally request that w simultaneously upload any of its streams or stream suffixes. Blocks can be transfered one stream at a time, or else multiple streams can be interleaved, so long as each encoding stream is sent in order and starting from the correct position. There is a lot of freedom in the ordering of streams transfered, allowing for some optimizations we discuss later.

5 Discussion

Rateless codes are a promising new tool for the peer-to-peer community, offering the prospect of improved file availability and simplified reconciliation of truncated downloads. We expect even the simple multi-source download algorithm in the previous section to outperform most other schemes, either proposed or implemented. Rateless codes guarantee that almost every data block transmitted by a source node contains unique information about a file, thus minimizing the amount of duplicate information amongst nodes with partial file information. Moreover, the freedom to chose encoded block IDs from a large identifier space allows files to be encoded in concisely specifiable streams so that nodes can inexpensively inform each other of what blocks they know.

5.1   Open Questions

We speculate that the reconciliation costs upon initiation of interaction between two nodes are minimal. The message cost of reconciliation between two nodes is no bigger than the cost of sending the state information table, whose size is directly proportional to the number of different streams from which a node has check blocks. This number is generously upper-bounded by the total number of nodes that had partial knowledge of the file within the life-span of the download. In our experience, this number has actually never exceeded 20. As a result, the reconciliation data sent upon initiation of interaction between two nodes will in practice always fit in one IP packet. This is likely more efficient than algorithms based on compact summary data structures [1] for set reconciliation.

To make the algorithm truly scalable, however, one needs to consider scenarios with dramatically larger numbers of nodes with partial file knowledge. In this case, we believe we can limit the growth of state tables by clustering peers into smaller groups within which nodes exchange partial file information. How big these clusters need to be, and how to design the algorithms for forming these clusters poses an open question.

Another open question is whether availability guarantees can be further improved. The specification of the algorithm in Section 4 leaves some freedom of interpretation. When a node v requests help from a node w with partial knowledge, w can choose the order in which it sends streams to v. For example, w could send blocks from one stream until the stream is exhausted, or it could interleave blocks from different streams. The choice becomes important if the connection between the two nodes is unexpectedly interrupted. By choosing what specific approach to use, and which stream(s) to send first, one can pick a favorable trade-off between higher reconciliation costs and higher file availability in the presence of unexpected disconnects. It is an open problem to find good strategies and understand the nature of this trade-off.

Finally, our multi-source download algorithm uses TCP. One could alternatively imagine UDP-based downloads. In particular, people often want peer-to-peer traffic to have lower priority than that of other network applications. A user-level UDP download protocol less aggressive than TCP could achieve this. With erasure codes, such a protocol might also avoid the need to retransmit lost packets, but at the cost of complicating state tables with gaps in streams.

6   Conclusion

We hope that this paper will motivate further studies of applications of rateless codes to peer-to-peer problems. Our experiments show that due to their simplicity of implementation and speed, on-line codes are a good candidate for practical solutions.

The download algorithm that we propose shows that rateless codes offer increased file availability and decreased reconciliation costs. Interestingly, the decrease of reconciliation costs is due to the limit on how many streams a cluster of nodes may need. This shows that one can avoid difficult information-theoretical problems, like set reconciliation, by making use of a wider range of properties of the underlying peer-to-peer system. Moreover, since the limit on the number of streams is, in some sense, a global property of the multi-source setting, further research should be done to better use other such global properties.

Acknowledgments

We thank Yevgeniy Dodis, Srinivasa Varadhan and Maxwell Krohn for helpful feedback on this work.

This research was supported by the National Science Foundation under Cooperative Agreement #ANI–0225660 (http://project-iris.net), and by DARPA and the Space and Naval Warfare Systems Center under contract #N66001–01–1–8927.

References

[1] J. Byers, J. Considine, and M. Mitzenmacher. Fast Approximate Reconciliation of Set Differences. In *Draft paper, available as BU Computer Science TR 2002-019*, 2002.

[2] J. Byers, J. Considine, M. Mitzenmacher, and S. Rost. Informed Content Delivery Across Adaptive Overlay Networks. In *SIGCOMM*, 2002.

[3] M. Karpovsky, L. Levitin, and A. Trachtenberg. Data verification and reconciliation with generalized error-control codes. In *39th Annual Allerton Conference on Communication, Control, and Computing*, 2001.

[4] M. Luby, M. Mitzenmacher, A. Shokrollahi, D. Spielman, and V. Stemann. Practical Loss-Resilient Codes. In *STOC*, 1997.

[5] M. Luby, M. Mitzenmacher, and A. Shokrollahi. Analysis of Random Processes via And-Or Tree Evaluation. In *SODA*, 1998.

[6] Jed McCaleb. EDonkey2000. http://www.edonkey2000.com/.

[7] Michael Luby. LT codes. In *The 43rd Annual IEEE Symposium on Foundations of Computer Science*, 2002.

[8] Petar Maymounkov. Online Codes. Technical Report TR2002-833, New York University, October 2002.

[9] Stefan Saroiu, Krishna P. Gummadi, Richard J. Dunn, Steven D. Gribble, and Henry M. Levy. An analysis of internet content delivery systems. In *Proceedings of the 5th Symposium on Operating Systems Design and Implementation*, pages 315–327, December 2002.

[10] Y. Minsky, A. Trachtenberg, and R. Zippel. Set Reconciliation with Nearly Optimal Communication Complexity. In *International Symposium on Information Theory*, 2001.

[11] Y. Minsky and A. Trachtenberg. Practical Set Reconciliation. In *40th Annual Allerton Conference on Communication, Control, and Computing*, 2002.

Understanding Availability

Ranjita Bhagwan[1]*, Stefan Savage[2], and Geoffrey M. Voelker[2]

[1] Department of Electrical and Computer Engineering
University of California, San Diego
[2] Department of Computer Science and Engineering
University of California, San Diego

Abstract. This paper addresses a simple, yet fundamental question in the design of peer-to-peer systems: What does it mean when we say "availability" and how does this understanding impact the engineering of practical systems? We argue that existing measurements and models do not capture the complex time-varying nature of availability in today's peer-to-peer environments. Further, we show that unforeseen methodological shortcomings have dramatically biased previous analyses of this phenomenon. As the basis of our study, we empirically characterize the availability of a large peer-to-peer system over a period of 7 days, analyze the dependence of the underlying availability distributions, measure host turnover in the system, and discuss how these results may affect the design of high-availability peer-to-peer services.

1 Introduction

Inevitably, real systems stop working. At some point, disks fail, hosts crash, networks partition, software miscalculates, administrators misconfigure or users misuse. Consequently, the principal challenge in designing highly available systems is to tolerate each failure as it occurs and recover from its effects. However, engineering such systems efficiently requires the designer to make informed decisions about the availability of individual system components.

Webster's dictionary defines *availability* as "the quality of being present or ready for immediate use". However, this seemingly simple definition can conceal tremendous complexity. In traditional data storage systems, the components of interest are devices like disks, SCSI interfaces, and NVRAM buffers, each of which have well-understood statistical failure properties that are usually assumed fail-stop and independent (e.g., redundant disk arrays [4]). In peer-to-peer storage systems, however, the component of interest is the host, whose availability is poorly understood by comparison.

While the failure of individual hardware components can still compromise the availability of a host, a peer-to-peer system designer must also anticipate transient software failures, partial or total communication interruption, and users who join and leave the system independently of their own volition. Moreover, these components can be time varying. For example, a peer-to-peer system may

---

* Department of Electrical and Computer Engineering, UCSD.

F. Kaashoek and I. Stoica (Eds.): IPTPS 2003, LNCS 2735, pp. 256–267, 2003.

replicate some file F on n machines at time t. However, by time $t + k$ some m machines may be turned off as their owners go to work, returning at some later time. The availability of the hosts is therefore dependent on time of day, and hence, the availability of the file F is a function of time. Another issue is whether the availability of a host is dependent on the availability of another host, or, whether two host availabilities are interdependent. This issue is important since many peer-to-peer systems [3,11] are designed on the assumption that a random selection of hosts in a P2P network do not all fail together at the same time.

Consequently, host availability is not well modeled as a single stationary distribution, but instead is a combination of a number of time-varying functions, ranging from the most transient (e.g., packet loss) to the most permanent (e.g., disk crash). Traditionally, distributed systems have assumed that transient failures are short enough to be transparently masked and only the long-term components of availability require explicit system engineering. In peer-to-peer systems, though, this abstraction is grossly insufficient. A new "intermittent" component of availability is introduced by users periodically leaving and joining the system again at a later time. Moreover, the set of hosts that comprise the system is continuously changing, as new hosts arrive the system and existing hosts depart it permanently on a daily basis. A peer-to-peer system designed on this substrate will need to incorporate arriving hosts into it without much overhead, while being able to provide all the functionality it promises to provide in the face of regular departures.

We were motivated to study peer-to-peer host availability in part to shape the design and evaluation of a highly available, wide-area peer-to-peer storage system [14]. A primary goal of the system is to provide efficient, highly available file storage even when the system is comprised of hosts with relatively poor and highly variable availability. Even so, our results can apply to any peer-to-peer system constructed from a similar collection of hosts.

The remainder of this paper examines these issues empirically by characterizing host availability in a large deployed peer-to-peer file sharing system over a 7 day period. We make four principal contributions in this work: First, we show that a minor methodological limitation of previous availability measurements has lead to underestimated P2P host availability [12, 2, 13]. Second, we show that host availability in peer-to-peer systems is a complex enough metric to warrant specification by more than just a fractional value between 0 and 1. Thirdly, we show that, for the purposes of storage placement, the availability of hosts is dependent on time-of-day, but is roughly independent of the availability of other hosts. Finally, we measure the system-wide dynamics of the P2P network by calculating the rate at which new hosts arrive the system for the first time, and existing ones depart. We conclude with a summary of our findings.

2   Related Work

Saroiu et al. [12] and Chu et al. [2] have characterized host availability in the Gnutella [5] peer-to-peer network by actively probing TCP/IP addresses gathered using a Gnutella crawler. Sen and Wang [13] described a similar study using passive measurement of flow-level data from multiple routers across a large tier-1 ISP backbone. Finally, Long et al. [7] measured workstation availability in the Internet using an active probing methodology. Unfortunately, all of these approaches rely on IP addresses to uniquely identify individual hosts over time. This assumption was likely accurate for Long's 1995 study, but modern dynamic address assignment protocols such as DHCP can easily cause the same host to be counted multiple times and thereby underestimate host availability. Moreover, the growth in the use of NAT boxes can affect the correctness of a TCP/IP address-probing technique.

Weatherspoon et al. [15] analyzed the impact of failure on peer-to-peer block storage systems using a model based on disk mean time-to-failure. In a separate paper, the authors also address the issue of independence between host failures. They mention the need to quantify dependence between failures at a coarse-grained level, i.e., failures due to network disconnectivity, OS version, etc. [16] However, these efforts do not capture the complexity of the peer-to-peer environment – particularly the user-controlled transient outages that dominate host availability in most real systems. The dependence of host availabilities on time and whether there is any interdependence between host availabilities stemming from user behavior have yet to be studied in detail.

3 Experimental Methodology

To study host availability in peer-to-peer systems, we actively measure the availability of hosts in the Overnet file-sharing network [10]. In this section, we describe Overnet and our reasons for choosing it over other popular systems. We then describe our experimental methodology for periodically identifying hosts and subsequently probing them.

3.1 Overnet

The Overnet peer-to-peer file-sharing system is based on Kademlia [8] and is structured on a distributed hash table (DHT). Overnet has no hierarchy, i.e., all hosts have identical functionality. When a new client joins Overnet, it randomly generates an ID for itself. This is the client's ID, and it remains unchanged on subsequent joins and leaves of the client until the user deletes the file containing the client's preferences. For lookup and routing purposes, each host maintains a list of neighbors and their IP addresses. The details of this list can be found in [8].

We measure the Overnet system to model host availability for two reasons:

- Overnet users are identified by immutable IDs, enabling us to track hosts by ID rather than by IP address. Using IDs eliminates the problem of host aliasing via DHCP and NATs.

– Host availability studies need to use a sufficiently widely-deployed peer-to-peer network for measurements to be valid and acceptable. To our knowledge, Overnet is the only widely deployed DHT-based peer-to-peer network.

Note that Overnet is not an open-source system or protocol. As a result, to perform our availability measurements we had to reverse engineer various aspects of the Overnet protocol. Other popular open-source systems would have been more convenient to measure, but they do not meet the requirements of our study (in particular, identifying hosts by unique ID).

3.2 Methodology

Our measurement infrastructure consists of two components; the *crawler* and the *prober*. The crawler provides us with a global view of host membership in the system. The prober allows us to get detailed and fine-grained information on individual host behavior.

Crawler: The purpose of the crawler is to collect a snapshot of the IDs of the active hosts in the network at a particular point in time. It does so by repeatedly requesting 50 randomly generated IDs. These requests lead to the discovery of some number of hosts. The crawler repeats the process by sending requests for the same 50 IDs to all the newly discovered hosts. Thus the crawler uses a recursive algorithm to discover the IDs of hosts in the network by performing lookups to as many hosts as it can find. The crawler runs once every 4 hours to minimize impact on the system as it locates these hosts.

Prober: The purpose of the prober is to periodically probe a set of hosts to determine whether they are available in the system or not at that particular time. It uses a random subset of host IDs discovered by the crawler and probes them every 20 minutes. We chose only a subset of hosts to probe because the overhead of probing hosts limits the frequency at which we can cycle through them. The prober determines the availability of a host with ID I by performing a lookup for I. The lookup succeeds only if the host with ID I responds to the probes. So a successful lookup implies an available host running an Overnet peer.

All our probes look exactly like normal Overnet protocol traffic. This is in contrast to previous measurement studies of peer-to-peer networks [12,2] that use TCP SYN packets. This strategy has two main advantages. First, it eliminates the problem of IP address aliasing due to the use of DHCP, NAT, and multiple users using the same machine. Second, due to Overnet's lookup procedure, we do not repeatedly send probes to hosts that have been unavailable for long periods of time, thus keeping our experiments non-intrusive.

4 Results

In this section, we present the results of our measurements and the inferences that we can draw from them. First, we summarize the data obtained from the crawler and the prober. Then, we show the effects of aliasing on measured availability. Next, we show how the distribution of host availability varies depending on the time over which it is calculated. We then characterize time-of-day effects on host availability and characterize host availability interdependence. Finally, we measure global host membership turnover in terms of host arrivals and departures in Overnet.

4.1   Experiment Summary

The crawler ran every four hours for a period of 15 days, from January 14 through January 28, 2003[1]. Each pass of the crawler yielded approximately 40,000 host IDs, while in a single day, or six passes of the crawler, between 70,000 and 90,000 host IDs were seen

Out of the roughly 84,000 IDs that the crawler gathered on the first day, We chose 2,400 at random for the prober to trace at fine-grained time intervals. . It probed these hosts every 20 minutes for 7 days, from January 15 to January 21, 2003. Out of the 2,400 hosts, 1,468 responded at least once to the probes.

4.2   Aliasing Effects

Although only 1,468 unique hosts responded to the prober, a total of 5,867 unique IP addresses responded to the prober. This results in a unique host ID to IP address ratio of approximately 1:4. Clearly, host IP address aliasing is a significant issue in deployed peer-to-peer systems such as Overnet. The aliasing effects could be due to various reasons. Most likely, the main cause is the use of DHCP. It is common that, when a host leaves the system and joins it at a later time, it does so with a different IP address. NATs also introduce aliasing into the network by making use of private IP addresses for hosts behind them. Another possible cause of aliasing is multiple users using the same machine; they will have different unique IDs, but the same IP address.

Figure 1 provides more insight into the nature of aliasing. It shows the percentage of hosts that have more than one IP address over varying periods of time. For example, even over just one day, almost 40% of all probed hosts use more than one IP address. This number increases to 50% after 4 days. These results show that measuring host availability by probing hosts using IP addresses can be very misleading. In fact, 32% of all probed hosts used five or more IP addresses, and 12% used 10 or more! These numbers will only get larger with longer periods of probing. So, probing by IP address does not accurately capture the availability characteristics of the hosts. IP address probing would consider each IP address a new host, thus greatly overestimating the number of hosts in the system and underestimating their availability.

To evaluate the implications of IP address aliasing on modeling host availability, we derive the host availability distributions for both probing techniques.

---

[1] There was a disruption on of January 21 for roughly 24 hours due to storage problems.

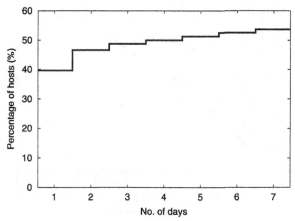

Fig. 1. Percentage of hosts that have more than one IP address across different periods of time

Figure 2 shows the cumulative distribution of host availability calculated over seven days. We calculate host availability for each host by dividing the number of probes that a host responds to by the total number of probes. The darker line shows the accurate distribution obtained by using host IDs to identify individual hosts, while the lighter line shows the distribution calculated by using the first IP address that was seen for each host ID; the lighter curve is reminiscent of the availability curve in the popular Gnutella study [12]. There is a significant difference between the two curves, with the IP address-based calculation greatly underestimating host availability.

The difference in these distributions demonstrates the extent to which using IP addresses to identify hosts is inaccurate. For example, the darker curve shows that 50% of hosts have availability 0.3 or less, but, if we had used the IP address-based probing denoted by the lighter curve, we would conclude that 50% of all hosts have availability 0.07 or less. Using IP addresses would thus understimate availability by a factor of four. If we had used the IP address methodology to parameterize the design of a highly available storage system, we would make more replicas of files than required to compensate for the apparently low availability and waste storage space. For example, in one model of peer-to-peer file availability [1], the number of file replicas required to maintain a 99% file availability given a mean host availability of 0.07 is five times the storage overhead compared to the number of replicas required given a mean host availability of 0.3.

4.3   Host Availability

We calculated host availability in Figure 2 over seven days, the entire period of our active probe measurements. However, the period of time over which host availability is calculated can change the distribution. To determine the extent of

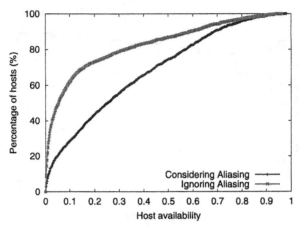

Fig. 2. Host availability derived using unique host ID probes vs. IP address probes

this effect, we varied the time period over which we calculate host availability. Figure 3 shows the results of this experiment. Over a period of 10 hours, the distribution curve is slightly concave, while for a period of 4 days, the distribution curve becomes convex. Over 7 days, the convexity of the curve increases. And we suspect that with longer periods of measurement this will only increase. Put differently, the distribution curve moves more and more to the left as the period over which availability is calculated increases. This stems from the fact that we are probing the same hosts over the entire period, and the longer the period of time, the greater the chances of a host being unavailable. We are continuing our probing measurements for longer periods of time to validate this hypothesis.

The implication is that, when using an availability distribution to characterize hosts in the system or simply using a fractional value to reflect mean host availability in models of system behavior (e.g., [3]), one needs to also specify the period of time over which the availability measurement holds. Also, the fact that host availability decreases over longer periods of time motivates the need for periodic file refreshes (redistributions, or re-insertions) in the system.

4.4   Time-of-Day Effects

Next, we characterize the effect of time-of-day on host availability. To do this we need to see how the host availability pattern varies with local time, where local time is based on the geographic location of each host. To calculate local time for each host, we use CAIDA's Netgeo tool [9] to determine the longitude of the host using its current IP address at the time at which it was probed. We then map host longitude to a local time zone.

Figure 4 shows the number of available hosts as a function of local time at the hosts' geographic location. The ticks on the x-axis correspond to midnight on

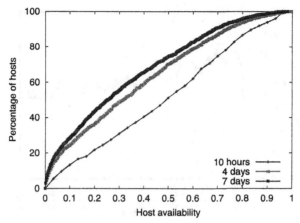

Fig. 3. The dynamic nature of the availability distribution. It varies with the time period over which availability is calculated

the days that are labeled, and this applies to all following time-series graphs. As with other studies of peer-to-peer systems, the graph shows a diurnal pattern [2]. The difference between the maximum and minimum number of available hosts in a single day is roughly 100.

We also found that on average, there were 9413 host joins and leaves per day, or 6.4 joins and leaves per host per day. This figure is considerable, given that the number of hosts that were probed and responded to probes were only 1468. In a system such as CFS, which actively replicates objects immediately when it learns of a host join or leave, this could cause a large amount of overhead in terms of the amount of data transferred between hosts.

The other feature to notice in this graph is the steady decrease in the total number of hosts that are available over subsequent days, which was reflected in our availability distribution measurement. Although limited by a short trace duration, the trend indicates a decay of about 32 hosts per day. The fact that there is a steady decay in the number of hosts with time indicates that in a system such as Oceanstore [6], frequent and periodic file refreshes are required to maintain high file availability.

4.5   Host Availability Interdependence

The diurnal pattern indicates that availability varies with time-of-day. At non-peak hours a number of hosts become unavailable. Most structured peer-to-peer storage systems, e.g., [3, 8], assume that this happens with very low probability, failing which, objects stored in the system could be lost forever. To our knowledge, this is the first study to investigate the extent that this assumption holds.

We characterize the dependence between every host pair using conditional probabilities. Consider two hosts X and Y. We need to determine the conditional

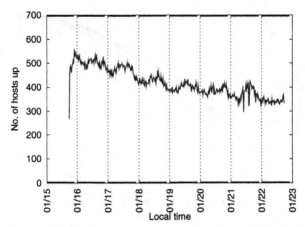

Fig. 4. Diurnal patterns in number of available hosts

probability of Y being available given that X is available for a given time-of-day t. Call this value $P(Y=1/X=1)$. If this is equal to the probability that Y is available whether or not X is available, or $P(Y=1)$, then X and Y are independent. If independent, then the availability of X at time t does not imply anything about the availability of Y at that time.

We calculated $P(Y=1/X=1)$ and $P(Y=1)$ for every host pair from our empirical data for each hour in the trace. Figure 5 shows the probability density function of the difference between these two values. The graph shows that more than 30% of all pairs have 0 difference. Further, 80% of all host pairs lie between +0.2 and -0.2, indicating that there is significant independence between host pairs. So if we were to pick a small subset of hosts randomly, it is highly unlikely that the availabilities of all of them are strongly dependent on each other, even though each may show a strong correlation with time of day. For example, in CFS, the size of this subset is 6, while in Kademlia, it is 20. The probability of all these hosts failing together would be very low.

4.6 Arrivals and Departures

Host turnover is important for peer-to-peer systems that rely upon long-term host membership. For example, archival peer-to-peer storage systems like Oceanstore use a high degree of redundancy to mask host failures and departures over time. The rate of host turnover fundamentally determines the rate at which the system must refresh and restore the redundancy in the system to maintain file availability [1, 15], and the overhead that this process entails.

To characterize host membership turnover in Overnet, we would like to determine the rate at which new hosts enter the system for the first time (*arrive*) and the rate at which existing hosts leave the system permanently (*depart*). Note the distinction with host joins and leaves, which refer to intermittent disconnections

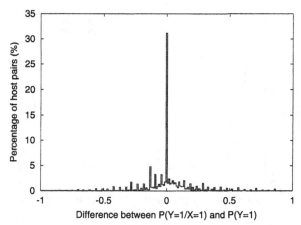

Fig. 5. Probability density function of the difference between P(Y=1/X=1) and P(Y=1)

of hosts from the system. We estimate arrival and departure rates in Overnet using the 15-day crawler trace of active hosts. We consider the first occurrence of a host ID in the trace as an arriving host, and the last occurrence of a host ID as a departing host.

Figure 6 shows host arrivals and departures as a fraction of the number of active hosts in the system for each day in the trace. For perspective, during this period the crawler found that roughly 85,000 hosts in Overnet were active each day. From the graph, we see that Overnet has a significant degree of turnover. Each day, new hosts never seen before in the trace comprise over 20% of the system (or roughly 17,000 hosts/day). At the same time, existing hosts are departing at roughly the same rate. As a result, the overall size of Overnet stayed constant over our trace period. Since our trace is only 15 days, though, these results only capture short-term turnover. We are continuing our trace to capture long-term turnover as well.

5 Summary

In this paper we studied several characteristics of host availability in the Overnet peer-to-peer file sharing system, and discussed the implications of our findings on the design and operation of peer-to-peer systems. We found that IP address aliasing is a significant problem in these systems, and that measurements according to host IP address significantly underestimate peer-to-peer host availability. We also argue that availability is not well-modeled by a single-parameter distribution, but instead is a combination of two time-varying distributions: (1) short-term daily joins and leaves of individual hosts, and (2) long-term host arrivals and departures. In our Overnet trace, both behaviors significantly impact host availability. For a given set of hosts probed at a fine time granularity, each

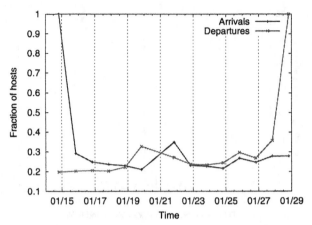

Fig. 6. New host arrivals and existing host departures in Overnet as a fraction of all hosts in the system (approximately 85,000 during this period). The high values at the beginning and end of the period are artifacts of starting and ending the trace

host joined and left the system 6.4 times a day on average. For a global crawl of all active hosts in the system at a coarser granularity, we also found that host turnover in the system is considerable: over 20% of the hosts in system arrive and depart every day. Peer-to-peer systems must take into account both sources of host unavailability to gracefully and efficiently provide highly available service.

References

[1] R. Bhagwan, S. Savage, and G. M. Voelker. Replication strategies for highly available peer-to-peer systems. Technical Report CS2002-0726, University of California, San Diego, Nov 2002.

[2] J. Chu, K. Labonte, and B. Levine. Availability and locality measurements of peer-to-peer file systems. In *Proceedings of ITCom: Scalability and Traffic Control in IP Networks*, July 2002.

[3] F. Dabek, M. Kaashoek, D. Karger, R. Morris, and I. Stoica. Wide-area cooperative storage with cfs. In *proceedings of the 18th ACM Symposium on Operating System Principles (SOSP)* , 2001.

[4] G. Gibson. *Redundant Disk Arrays: Reliable, Parallel Secondary Storage.* PhD thesis, University of California at Berkeley, 1990. Report UCB/CSD 91/613.

[5] Gnutella homepage, http://www.gnutella.com.

[6] J. Kubiatowicz, D. Bindel, Y. Chen, P. Eaton, D. Geels, R. Gummadi, S. Rhea, H. Weatherspoon, W. Weimer, C. Wells, and B. Zhao. Oceanstore: An architecture for global-scale persistent storage. In *Proceedings of ACM ASPLOS*, 2000.

[7] D. Long, A. Muir, and R. Golding. A longitudinal study of internet host reliability. In *Proceedings of the Fourteenth Symposium on Reliable Distributed Systems*, September 1995.

[8] P. Maymounkov and D. Mazieres. Kademlia: A peer-to-peer information system based on the xor metric. In *Proceedings of the 1st International Workshop on Peer-to -Peer Systems (IPTPS'02)*, March 2002.

[9] Netgeo - the internet geographic database, http://www.caida.org/tools/utilities/netgeo/.

[10] Overnet website, http://www.overnet.com.

[11] A. Rowstron and P. Druschel. Storage management and caching in past, a large-scale, persistent peer-to-peer storage utility. In *Proceedings of the 18th ACM Symposium on Operating Systems Principles(SOSP '01)*, 2001.

[12] S. Saroiu, P. K. Gummadi, and S. D. Gribble. A measurement study of peer-to-peer file sharing systems. In *Proceedings of MMCN*, 2002.

[13] S. Sen and J. Wang. Analyzing peer-to-peer traffic over large networks. In *Proceedings of ACM SIGCOMM Internet Measurement Workshop*, November 2002.

[14] Total recall website, http://ramp.ucsd.edu/projects/recall/.

[15] H. Weatherspoon and J. Kubiatowicz. Erasure coding v/s replication: a quantitative approach. In *Proceedings of the First International Workshop on Peer-to-peer Systems*, 2002.

[16] H. Weatherspoon, T. Moscovitz, and J. Kubiatowicz. Introspective failure analysis: Avoiding correlated failures in peer-to-peer systems. In *Proceedings of the International Workshop on Reliable Peer-to-peer Distributed Systems*, October 2002.

PeerNet: Pushing Peer-to-Peer Down the Stack

Jakob Eriksson, Michalis Faloutsos, and Srikanth Krishnamurthy*

University of California, Riverside

Abstract. An unwritten principle of the Internet Protocol is that the
IP address of a node also serves as its identifier. We observe that many
scalability problems result from this principle, especially when we consider mobile networks. In this work, we examine how we would design
a network with a separation between address and identity. We develop
PeerNet, a peer-to-peer-based network layer for large networks. *PeerNet
is not an overlay on top of IP*, it is an alternative to the IP layer. In
PeerNet, the address reflects the node's current location in the network.
This simplifies routing significantly but creates two new challenges: the
need for consistent address allocation and an efficient node lookup service. We develop fully distributed solutions to address these and other
issues using a per-node state of $O(\log N)$, where N is the number of nodes
in the network.
PeerNet is a radically different alternative to current network layers, and
our initial design suggests that the PeerNet approach is promising and
worth further examination.

1   Introduction

How would we design a network layer with mobile nodes and peer-to-peer interactions in mind? This question would have seemed like a theoretical exercise
a few years back, but it has become legitimate, if not necessary, with the current
technological trends and commercial initiatives. In fact, we observe an over-
whelming popular and commercial interest in mobile wireless connectivity [1, 7],
consumer owned networks [3, 2, 4] and mesh networking [5, 6]. A vision that we
share with [12] involves pockets of peer-to-peer wireless connectivity interconnected with traditional wired lines. Implementing such a vision introduces new
networking requirements, and we may need a novel network architecture. Here,
we focus on the network layer of such a future architecture.

Although the Internet Protocol (IP) has been a spectacular success, this
should not prevent us from assessing its suitability for the networks of the future. Most of the above initiatives seem to rely on the Internet Protocol. An
implicit principle of this protocol is that the IP address of a node is tightly coupled with its identity. This has worked well so far, since the Internet supports
mostly stationary nodes with wireline links and well defined consumer-provider

* This material is based upon work supported by the National Science Foundation
under CAREER Grant No. 9985195, DARPA award FTN F30602-01-2-0535.

F. Kaashoek and I. Stoica (Eds.): IPTPS 2003, LNCS 2735, pp. 268–277, 2003.

relationships. However, the *address as identifier* paradigm may encounter problems in highly mobile networks. We have already seen mobility and scalability push IP to its limits. While it is possible to satisfy most new requirements with patches such as NAT, DHCP, Mobile IP, the end result is seldom elegant and often plagued by new problems. One striking example of the above paradigm failing is the fact that a TCP session will break if one of the end points changes its address. This is an important issue as networks are becoming increasingly mobile.

The overarching question is how we would design the network layer for future networks if we were to start from scratch. Our target environment is very large potentially wireless and mobile networks. Therefore, we want an agile, plug and play, fault-tolerant, and scalable networking layer. A source of inspiration is application layer peer-to-peer networking, an area that has seen tremendous advancements recently. Therefore, we pose the question: what can we gain by bringing the peer-to-peer concept from the application layer down to the networking layer? We develop a set of guidelines that seems to satisfy our networking vision. We want the new network layer to: *a) minimize the need for manual configuration, b) avoid centralized solutions and node specialization in favor of distributed and peer-to-peer solutions, and c) localize control overhead.*

In this paper, we present PeerNet, a network layer with integrated support for routing between peers. PeerNet makes an explicit distinction between node identity and address. The address of a node reflects its current location in the network at all times. This simplifies routing but introduces two new challenges. First, we need a node lookup service that will provide the address for a given a node identifier. Second, PeerNet needs to maintain addresses dynamically: as a node moves, its address changes to reflect the new location. Our initial design suggests that PeerNet is feasible and potentially fundamental component of our vision for future networks.

Our Work in Perspective. PeerNet is a radically new architecture that brings peer-to-peer concepts to the network layer. Although the design presented here is not complete, it provides the backbone and several non-trivial algorithmic solutions. In our upcoming implementation, we expect to complete and finetune our design. Furthermore, we expect this work to provoke a constructive reevaluation of current networking architectures.

Related Work. Area Routing [11] and Landmark routing [16] are classical papers on hierarchical routing. LANMAR [13] and L+ [9] are modern extensions of Landmark routing, whereas PeerNet to our knowledge is the first protocol for dynamic networks with similarity to Area Routing. For a survey of ad hoc routing, see [10], and for a survey of distributed hash tables, see [14]. Recently, several efforts such as [15, 8] address some of the same issues as PeerNet but do so by adding functionality to the existing IP infrastructure.

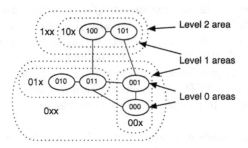

Fig. 1. A 3-level area network. Level-0 areas are single nodes and Level-n areas consist of up to two Level-$(n-1)$ areas

2   Operations Overview

The key idea in PeerNet is the separation of the *identity* and the *address* of a node. For now, we can assume that each PeerNet node has one unique identifier and one unique address. The address is dynamic and changes with node movement to reflect the node's location in the network. The ID of the node remains the same throughout, reliably identifying the node despite address changes. An integrated distributed node lookup service maps identifiers to addresses.

Joining the Network. To join a PeerNet network, a node establishes a physical connection to at least one node already in the network and requests an address. The receiving node(s) answer(s) with an available address. The joining node then "registers" its identifier together with the address in the distributed node lookup service. As a node moves, it requests and receives new addresses from its new neighbors. On each address change, the node updates its entry in the lookup service.

Packet Routing. The sender node only needs to know the *identifier* of the receiver. Before sending its first packet to some destination, the sender looks up the current address of the destination node using the lookup service. PeerNet packets contain both the identifier of the destination and the last known address and routing is done in a Distance Vector fashion[1], one hop at a time. If the destination cannot be reached, the lookup table is consulted along the way to find the new address of the destination.

3   The PeerNet Network Layer

PeerNet targets networks consisting of a large number of mobile and stationary nodes, connected by bidirectional links using any current MAC technology.

---

[1] Note this is not regular Distance Vector routing. Routing entries point to predetermined positions in a virtual hierarchy of nodes, thereby reducing the size of the routing table to $O(logN)$.

Node addresses are dynamically assigned depending on the node's current position in the network. More specifically, the addresses are organized as leaves of a binary tree. We call this the *address tree*. By selecting node addresses carefully, we guarantee that nodes within a subtree are able to communicate using only nodes inside that subtree. We will also use the term *area*, which we define as follows:

Area: An area is a set of network nodes such that for every pair of nodes in the area, there exists a path between them that consists only of nodes in the area.

A subtree of the address tree is an area, and we will use these terms interchangeably.[2]

As shown in figure 1, a Level-0 area is a single network node. A Level-n area is recursively defined as consisting of two connected Level-$(n-1)$ areas. The following is crucial to all PeerNet operations:

PeerNet Area Invariant: All nodes belong to a nested sequence of areas, one area of each level. All nodes within an area share a unique address prefix.

In figure 1, each node belongs to a Level-0, 1 and 2 area respectively, with the Level-0 area being the node itself. In a PeerNet with addresses consisting of l bits, there would be l corresponding area levels. To maintain the area invariant, a node that violates the invariant resigns from the network and request a new address from a neighboring node.

The PeerNet network layer consists of three major parts. First, *address allocation* maintains one address per node, in compliance with the area invariant. Second, *routing* disseminates enough information about the global state of the network and uses this information to efficiently deliver packets to their destination. Third, *node lookup* is a distributed network service mapping a node identifier to its current network address. We describe these areas in more detail below.

Finally, there are several issues that the current paper has not attempted to address. Security is one such issue which we are currently examining, other issues include the performance effects of network partitioning and merging.

3.1   Address Allocation

PeerNet assigns addresses to nodes dynamically, so that the PeerNet area invariant is preserved. For increased efficiency and stability, address allocation must result in a well balanced address tree and nodes within an area should be well connected.

A PeerNet address consists of l bits. These bits describe a position in a corresponding l level binary address tree. Figure 2 illustrates the idea for $l = 3$. All physical nodes reside at the leaf level, and hold complete l-bit addresses.

---

[2] Not all areas correspond to an address subtree, but we are not interested in such areas, and will not refer to them in this paper.

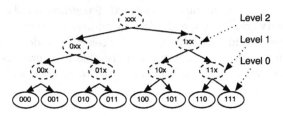

Fig. 2. 3-bit address space as a binary tree. Physical nodes exist only at the leaf level

To join a network, a new node requests an available address from an existing PeerNet node. Finding an available address can be implemented in different ways, attempting to balance two somewhat conflicting factors. On the one hand, we want the address allocation to be based on local information. This way, we can improve the scalability of the network and minimize the necessary control overhead. On the other hand, we would like to utilize the address space efficiently. We present our framework to strike the balance in this trade-off. Our solution hides several subtleties; we only provide a high level overview here.

Obtaining an Address. We develop a protocol hat enables nodes to allocate addresses in a local and conflict free fashion. At any given time, each node "manages" a range of addresses including its own address. Every time a new node requests an address, the responding node splits its *address range* in half, and delegates control of the upper half to the new node. The address of the new node is set to be the lowest address within the delegated range. In this manner, nodes are evenly distributed throughout the address space.

Figure 3 illustrates this procedure for 3-bit addresses. Node A starts out alone and has address 000. Furthermore, it controls the entire 3-bit address space. When node B joins the network, it is assigned the address 100. At this time Node A can no longer assign addresses that begin with '1'. Similarly when C joins the network by connecting to B, it gets assigned address 110 and Node B is then precluded from assigning the address 111. Finally, when D joins via A, it gets assigned address 010.

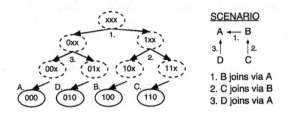

Fig. 3. Address tree for a small network topology. The numbers 1-3 show the order in which nodes were added to the network

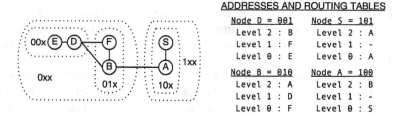

ADDRESSES AND ROUTING TABLES	
Node D = 001	Node S = 101
Level 2 : B	Level 2 : A
Level 1 : F	Level 1 : -
Level 0 : E	Level 0 : A
Node B = 010	Node A = 100
Level 2 : A	Level 2 : B
Level 1 : D	Level 1 : -
Level 0 : F	Level 0 : S

Fig. 4. In a 3-level network, each node keeps 3 routing entries. Those of S, A, B and D are shown on the right

The characteristics of the address allocation can have a major impact on the performance of the network. For example, if an available address can not be found, the request is refused. However, with a large enough address space and with efficient address tree maintanance, this is unlikely to happen. Two issues are critical for the address tree: a) we want to keep the address tree balanced, and b) we want to maximize the connectivity within an area. These two objectives may at times be conflicting, and we are currently evaluating techniques to find a good balance between tree balancing and inter-area connectivity.

Address Tree Balancing. We need a way to balance the tree while maintaining the PeerNet area invariant. If a particular area becomes congested, using up all locally available address space, new nodes that try to obtain an address may be unable to do so. Thus, in order to alleviate cases of local congestion in the tree, we would like nodes to proactively migrate in the tree in order to balance it. Migrating in this case, means simply to select a new address; without affecting connectivity and within the constraints of the area invariant.

Maximizing the Intra-area Connectivity. We want to select addresses in such a way that nodes within an area are well connected by physical links. This improves the routing performance and tolerance to link failures, and is especially desirable in mobile networks.

3.2 Routing

Intuitively, PeerNet routing can be seen as recursive procedure descending through the address tree. At each level, we decide through which of the two available subtrees to descend[3], starting from the top (the most significant bit). At the physical level, a packet is routed one level at a time. When the packet has reached any node in the correct subtree on one level, the packet is routed

---

[3] Although this is an intuitively appealing statement, we have to keep in mind that the address tree is not an actual network. In fact, only the leafs of the tree correspond to actual nodes. The internal nodes of the tree do not correspond to actual nodes.

to the nested lower level subtree, that contains the destination node. Given the PeerNet area invariant, every step takes us closer to the destination in both the network topology and along the address tree. Using a distance vector approach, the PeerNet routing table of each node requires only $l = \log N$ entries, that is, one entry per level in the address tree.

Let us revisit the address tree (figure 2) in order to understand some subtleties of PeerNet routing. For addresses of $l = 3$ bits, the entire address space can be represented by xxx, where $x \in \{0, 1\}$. The most significant bit divides the address space in two subtrees, $0xx$ and $1xx$. We refer to these as Level-2 subtrees. Similarly, the second bit divides the left Level-2 subtree, into the two Level-1 subtrees 00x and 01x. We refer to such pairs of trees as *siblings*. Furthermore, we define a *k*-**sibling** of a node to mean the sibling subtree of the Level-*k* subtree to which the node belongs. In figure 2, 1xx is the Level-2 sibling of 010, whereas 00x is the Level-1 sibling of 010.

To route a packet, a PeerNet node will compare the destination address with its own address. If the most significant bit differs in the two addresses, then the destination is in the "other half" of the address space, the $(l - 1)$-level sibling subtree. In general, a node compares its own address and that of the destination one bit at a time, starting with the most significant bit. If it finds a bit that differs, say the ith bit, it will forward the packet towards the *i*-sibling. Eventually, all the bits will be identical, at which point the destination is reached.

The Routing Table. Every node maintains a routing table that has l entries. The kth entry in this table contains the next hop to the *k*-sibling subtree.

As an example, let us assume that node S[101], where 101 is the address of the node S, wants to route a message to D[001] in figure 4. Given the difference in the most significant (Level-2) bit , S[101] forwards the packet to A[100], as indicated by S[101]'s Level-2 routing table entry. Similarly, A[100] looks at the most significant (Level-2) bit and forwards the message to node B[010], which is inside the Level-2 area 0xx. B[010] and the packet destination D[001] have the same Level-2 bit which means that the message is in the correct Level-2 area. Node B[010] looks at the next (Level-1) bit of the address, and forwards the message according to the Level-1 routing entry, which points to D[001]. Once there, D[001] looks at the third (Level-0) bit and realizes that it is the recipient.

PeerNet uses a distance vector approach in updating its routing tables. Although link state routing is also an option, we choose distance vector for its low overhead, low computational cost per router, and ease of implementation. PeerNet can be made cycle free with little overhead, thanks to the area invariant. It can be shown that cycle-free PeerNet routing requires $O(l) = O(logN)$ per-node state, but we will omit the details due to space constraints.

3.3   Node Lookup

Since the ID of a node is not its address, PeerNet provides a distributed node lookup service for looking up an address given an identifier. Intuitively, each identifier is mapped though some function to a single address and the node that currently controls that address is required to store the mapping. Let us initially assume that an identifier is an m-bit number $m \geq l$ that uniquely identifies a node. In contrast, an address is an l-bit number that determines a position in the network topology. We call the pair $(identifier, address)$ a *lookup entry*.

Mapping Entries to Nodes. In the basic case, each lookup entry is globally mapped onto a single node. This node is responsible for storing the entry and responding to requests for that entry. In our current design, the node is chosen so that its address minimizes the integer value of the expression $nodeAddress\ XOR\ identifier$.[4] We call this the **xor-distance criterion**. Finding the minimum *xor-distance* node for an identifier is a process similar to packet routing, where an update is routed towards the identifier rather than a particular address. We observe that the cost of performing this mapping is the same as that of regular packet routing, but omit further details due to space constraints.

Challenges due to Node Movement. Moving nodes present two challenges to the lookup service. First, node movement leads to address change which means lookup entries have to be updated. Second, when the address of a node changes, it is likely that some of its lookup entries need to be moved to a new node according to the *xor-distance criterion*. The area invariant guarantees that the new node will be in the vicinity of the moving node, so the second issue is a minor one.

If we were to simply use *xor-distance* mapping without modification, any locality in the communication patterns would be lost. An example of this is node X looking up the address of node Y, which happens to be just a few hops away. Y's lookup entry could potentially be mapped to a very distant node, forcing X to perform a long-distance lookup to set up short-distance communication with Y. Similarly, nodes that change address would occasionally have to send their updates long distances, which may be too expensive in very mobile scenarios. We will now briefly describe how to address these problems.

Solution A: Preserving Locality of Lookups. Instead of storing the entry in a single location in the network, we store it in multiple locations. These locations are chosen so that a lookup initiated in the vicinity of the desired node will find a locally stored entry instead of sending a query across the whole network. More specifically, the extra entries are stored in nodes that satisfy *minimum xor-distance* with 1 or more of the most significant bits removed from both address and identifier. Our improved locality preserving lookup starts with a very local scope and iteratively tries larger and larger subtrees until the entry is located.

Solution B: Creating Locality of Updates. We observe that a moving node is likely to change its lower order bits more frequently than the higher

---

[4] Since $m \geq l$ the expression is applied only to the l most significant bits of m.

order bits. We can use this to reduce the cost of updating the entries of moving nodes. Instead of storing the whole address in the abovementioned locations, local nodes keep the less significant bits of the address, while more remote nodes store the more significant bits of the target address. This way, non-local nodes will need less frequent updates.

The lookup process is further modified so that once the more significant bits of the address have been located, the query is forwarded to that area. Once in the local area, additional less significant parts of the address can be located. We are currently studying the tradeoff between additional lookup steps and increased locality of communication.

Identifiers as Communication Abstractions. By allowing identifiers to map to more than one address, we can efficiently implement **multicast** and **anycast** in PeerNet. In doing that, we extend the role of the identifier from that of uniquely identifying a node, to that of uniquely identifying a node *or a group of nodes*. A node would subscribe to a multicast group by adding a mapping between the multicast group identifier and its current address. Similarly, anycast can be implemented by mapping a single service identifier to a set of service providing nodes. A local lookup of the anycast identifier would then return the closest node providing the requested service.

3.4   Implementation and Deployment

In our ongoing implementation, we have decided to use addresses of size $l = 128$, which is the size of the IPv6 address. As a result, the corresponding routing table size is 128 entries. For maximum portability, we are developing the kernel code in C, and expect to release kernel modules for Darwin/MacOS X and Linux initially.

Leveraging the Existing Infrastructure. PeerNet does not need the support of a wireline infrastructure, but we want to be able to leverage any available infrastructure. We envision tunneling through the Internet to interconnect disconnected PeerNet networks initially and when available. In addition, we want to develop protocols and tools to facilitate the communication between Peer-Net and Internet nodes. We also want to enable TCP/IP emulation for IP-only software, which we may want to run on PeerNet nodes.

4   Conclusion

We present PeerNet, a radically different network layer. Recent trends in wireless technology, popular demand, and commercial interest impose new requirements on networks. This has prompted us to re-evaluate the role of IP in future networks. We envision dynamic networks with pockets of peer-to-peer wireless connectivity interconnected with traditional wired lines.

There are two fundamental and complementary novelties in PeerNet. First, there is a distinction between the identity and address of a node. This distinction enables us to handle mobility in a novel way, improving the scalability of the system. Specifically, the effect of node mobility is confined to the neighborhood of a moving node in most cases. Second, PeerNet supports peer-to-peer routing at the network layer. Critical functions like address allocation and routing are addressed in a distributed and cooperative fashion using a per node state of $O(\log N)$. In addition, PeerNet requires no manual configuration, and is fully distributed.

To summarize, PeerNet is a promising new network layer with the potential to scale to very large dynamic networks. In our ongoing implementation, we will validate and refine the ideas presented here.

References

[1] Boingo inc. `www.boingo.com`
[2] Community wireless. `www.communitywireless.org`
[3] Consume.net project: Trip the loop, make your switch, consume the net! `www.consume.net`
[4] Freenetworks. `www.freenet.org`
[5] Mesh networks inc. `www.meshnetworks.com`
[6] Mitre mobile mesh. `www.mitre.org/tech_transfer/mobilemesh/`
[7] Starbucks inc. `www.starbucks.com`
[8] M. Beck, T. Moore, and J. S. Plank An end-toend approach to globally scalable network storage. In *SIGCOMM*, August 2002
[9] B. Chen and R. Morris. L+: Scalable landmark routing and address lookup for multi-hop wireless networks, 2002
[10] X. Hong, K. Xu, and M. Gerla. Scalable routing protocols for mobile ad hoc networks. *IEEE NETWORK*, 16(4), 2002
[11] L. Kleinrock and F. Kamoun. Hierarchical routing for large networks: Performance evaluation and optimization,. *Computer Networks*, 1, 1977
[12] N. Negroponte. Being wireless, 2002.   `www.wired.com/wired/archive/10.10/wireless.html`
[13] G. Pei, M. Gerla, and X. Hong. Lanmar: Landmark routing for large scale wireless ad hoc networks with group mobility. In *ACM MobiHOC'00*, 2000
[14] S. Ratnasamy, S. Shenker, and I. Stoica. Routing algorithms for DHTs: Some open questions. IPTPS, 2002
[15] I. Stoica, D. Adkins, S. Zhuang, S. Shenker, and S. Surana. Internet indirection infrastructure. In *ACM SIGCOMM 2002*, August 2002
[16] P. F. Tsuchiya. The landmark hierarchy : A new hierarchy for routing in very large networks. In *SIGCOMM*. ACM, 1988

Lighthouses for Scalable Distributed Location

Marcelo Pias[1], Jon Crowcroft[2], Steve Wilbur[1], Tim Harris[2], and
Saleem Bhatti[1]

[1] University College London (UCL)
Computer Science Dept.
Gower Street, WC1E 6BT, London, UK
{m.pias,s.wilbur,s.bhatti}@cs.ucl.ac.uk
[2] University of Cambridge
Computer Laboratory
15 JJ Thomson Avenue, CB3 0FD, Cambridge, UK
{jon.crowcroft,tim.harris}@cl.cam.ac.uk

Abstract. This paper introduces *Lighthouse*, a scalable location mechanism for wide-area networks. Unlike existing vector-based systems such as GNP, we show how network-location can be established without using a fixed set of reference points. This lets us avoid the communication bottlenecks and single-points-of-failure that otherwise limit the practicality of such systems.

1 Introduction

Recent years have seen prolific research into large-scale distributed Internet applications drawing on the foundations laid by file-sharing systems, such as Napster, and other *unstructured* peer-to-peer systems such as Gnutella and Freenet (see [11]). This research has developed self-organising content addressable storage based on distributed hash tables (DHT) [15, 12, 7, 2] and distributed trees (DT) [1, 10].

However, the efficiency metrics considered in original versions of these protocols have simply been the number of overlay hops taken while routing a message [13]. This might be appropriate for some very constrained scenarios, but is rarely suitable for realistic deployments. This inflexibility leads to perverse routing policies; a message might be routed in the overlay network via the Europe-US transatlantic link when the two nodes willing to communicate are nearby with a fast local connection, for example, one in London and other in Cambridge.

Distributed network games are another large-scale example which has recently engaged the research community. Among the multiuser games, First person shooters (FPS) are one of the most popular types [17]. In FPS games, network proximity information about the players and servers is an important system requirement. With suitable information, the game discovery mechanism can return a list of servers that are close to a prospective player (e.g. a 'k-Nearest Neighbours' query).

Motivated by the current lack of network proximity information in these systems, we started from the following questions: could we characterise network

F. Kaashoek and I. Stoica (Eds.): IPTPS 2003, LNCS 2735, pp. 278–291, 2003.

proximity in a scalable model? Could this model help the systems in selecting appropriate close peers?

Network proximity, in the context of this paper, refers to how close node A is to node B in respect to the underlying IP topology. We characterise it with measures of IP network performance. The propagation delay, for instance, can indicate whether or not two nodes are close neighbours.

To capture the proximity between nodes, we can compute their location in the Internet using a set of coordinates. How we calculate such locations is the main idea of this paper.

We shall now make two definitions before we introduce the the problem of interest. First, a **general space** M is defined by the pair $(\mathbf{X}, \mathbf{d})$ where $\mathbf{X}$ represents the set of valid objects and $\mathbf{d}$ is a function, either metric or non-metric, that represents the distance between these objects such that $\mathbf{d} : \mathbf{X} \times \mathbf{X} \rightarrow \mathbb{R}$. In contrast, a **vector space** is a set $\mathbf{V}$ that is closed under appropriate vector addition and scalar multiplication operations.

These definitions have a broad scope. A general space represents objects and their mutual distances; whereas a vector space represents objects, their distances and locations. In the Internet case, the space M may be a set of network nodes (objects) spaced according to a particular network performance metric (distance). For instance, properties such as propagation delay and bandwidth can define two types of distance measures; consequently under certain assumptions, they create two metric spaces.

The problem then is defined as follows. We refer to it as the *mapping* problem and it consists of:

- finding a scalable mapping method to transform *objects* $\{x_1, ..., x_n\}$, in our case, network nodes, of the original space M onto *points* $\{v_1, ..., v_n\}$ in a target vector space $\mathbf{V^k}$ (k is the dimensionality) in such a way that the distance measures (i.e. delay) are preserved, i.e. $d(\mathbf{x_i}, \mathbf{x_j}) \sim D(\mathbf{v_i}, \mathbf{v_j})$ for $i, j > 0$; where D is another distance function.
- *constraint*: we only know a few distance measures between these objects. This is because we want the system to scale and having a full distance matrix $|X| \times |X|$ is impractical.

The constraint above leads us to use *pivoting* techniques to map the location of an object in a general space onto a vector-space location. These techniques consider the distance from a given object to a number of pre-selected *pivots* $\{p_1, ..., p_n\} \in X$. Pivoting is the common framework for a large class of nearest neighbour algorithms [4, 16].

In this paper we study two distinct techniques that employ pivoting to solve the 'mapping' problem. First, we introduce *absolute* or *global* coordinates-based approaches that always use the same set of well-known pivots. Because of this, such techniques create potential bottlenecks. This is not to mention the consequences when a pivot node becomes unavailable (e.g. pivot failure). The GNP framework [18] is included in this category.

To overcome the issue of well known pivots, we then introduce *Lighthouse*, an alternative technique that uses *relative* or *multiple local* coordinates-systems.

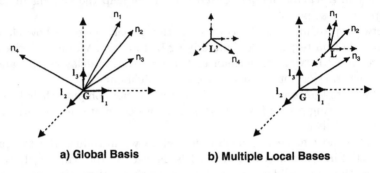

a) Global Basis   **b) Multiple Local Bases**

Fig. 1. Global x Multiple Local Bases

Lighthouse is (a) scalable: by relying on any arbitrary set of pivots, it avoids a single set of reference points (pivots) forming bottlenecks; (b) accurate: by solving the *mapping* problem, it devises accurate coordinates for a node.

In what follows, we give an overview of the GNP framework in Section 2, describe the Lighthouse design in more detail in Section 3. We then discuss our initial results and raise a list of questions in Section 4.

2   GNP

The GNP (Global Network Positioning) framework [18] for predicting Internet network distances is based on *absolute* coordinates computed by modelling the Internet as a real vector space. In outline, the GNP architecture is formed from two parts. First, a small set of well known hosts (pivots) called landmarks locate themselves into a real vector space by measuring their mutual distances (delay). These coordinates are taken by hosts that wish to join the system as a global, and therefore unique, basis of the vector space. The landmarks' coordinates are calculated through the solution of a relative error minimization problem:
$\sum_{i,j} Error(d_{ij}, \hat{d}_{ij})$ where d_{ij} and $\hat{d}_{ij}$ are the measured and estimated distances between the landmarks i, j.

The second part of the architecture relates to how an arbitrary host calculates its own absolute coordinates based on the landmarks' own coordinates. The joining host measures its round-trip delay to the landmarks and then casts the computation as an overall error minimization problem: $\sum_{i,j} Error(d_{ij}, \hat{d}_{ij})$ where now d_{ij} and $\hat{d}_{ij}$ are the measured and estimated distances respectively from host i to the landmark j; $Error()$ is an error measurement function.

3   Lighthouse

We start by introducing Figure 1a. The basis **G** of this 3-D vector space comprises vectors $\{l_1, l_2, l_3\}$. The second observation is that **G** must be formed by

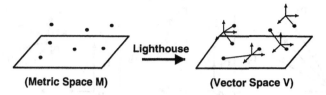

Fig. 2. Lighthouse Overview

well-known pivot nodes, i.e., the same nodes must be contacted by every joining node. In fact, this is a characteristic of GNP, 'binning' [14] and 'beaconing' [9] frameworks in terms of how they manage reference points. It turns out that this characteristic has the disadvantage that it makes the system not fully self-organised. What happens if the pivot nodes (e.g. landmarks/beacons) are not available at a given instant of time? Who should a joining node contact instead to locate itself in the system?

To overcome the above issue of *well-known pivots*, we present Lighthouse[1], a technique that explores two concepts: multiple local bases together with a transition matrix in vector spaces. Lighthouse allows the flexibility for any host to determine its coordinates relative to any set of pivot nodes provided it maintains a transition matrix. Such a matrix does what the maritime chart does for navigation. It gives a basic instrument for gauging a global position when this is deemed necessary. With the idea of local positioning, better scalability of the system can be achieved. Figure 1b shows a follow-up configuration of the global basis scenario achieved with the Lighthouse framework. Now nodes n_1, n_2, n_3, n_4 are located in different local basis, $\mathbf{L}$ and $\mathbf{L'}$, in a decentralised manner.

Figure 2 presents an example of our technique applied to a 3-D real vector space. Points at the left side plot network nodes as they might be observed in the IP network (metric space $\mathbf{M}$). The right side shows the same points mapped onto a vector space $\mathbf{V}$. With pivoting, we choose arbitrary $k + 1$ local reference points, which we call *lighthouses*. Unlike GNP, our framework relies on a set of nodes from which different joining hosts may select differently. However, each of these hosts has to preserve the invariant: a transition matrix $\mathbf{P}$, which is only applicable to calculating a global position, has to be correctly maintained.

We shall now introduce details of the four step procedure followed by a joining host.

---

[1] Historically, lighthouses played a vital role to navigation. The first and most notorious lighthouse, Pharos of Alexandria (Egypt), was built about 270 B.C. When looking at this unique tower with a bright light at the top, a ship's crew can compute their local position relative to it (local reference). Eventually, the position can be transformed into a global one by using maritime charts and the like. Nowadays, GPS (Global Positioning System) with its replicated service has made this method redundant.

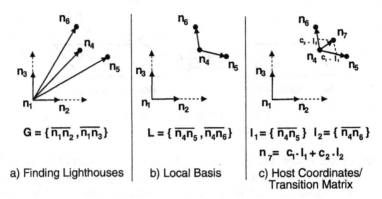

Fig. 3. 2-D Example

3.1 Finding Lighthouses

The bootstrap of the system occurs as follows:

- **Joining Node:** a new node n_i finds an entry point node n_j, i.e. any node that is already in the system. Node n_j provides to n_i a list of nodes that can potentially act as n_i lighthouses. The joining node selects $k + 1$ nodes among those in this list. It then constructs a local basis $L = \{l_1, l_2, ..., l_k\}$, where each vector l is a pair of lighthouses. This basis spans the V^k.
- **First Nodes:** when n_i is the m-th node such that $m \le k+1$, n_i is considered as one of the first nodes. As n_i cannot have other $k + 1$ lighthouses, it constructs a local basis with the lighthouses that already joined. The idea is to build the first basis after $k + 1$ nodes have joined in the system.

Once the joining node n_i has been given a list of nodes that can act as its lighthouses, it then measures a set of network performance metrics between itself and the lighthouses. The technique by which these measurements are undertaken will vary according to the context. The IDMAPS project [5] found that the propagation delay can be triangulated, so the delay between points (a,c) can be estimated based on the delay between (a,b) and (b,c). As a result, the round-trip time (RTT) measured through ICMP ECHO packets may be a practical tool to incorporate delay as a metric. Additionally, techniques that measure the available bandwidth look promising. However, we have only explored the network delay metric in this paper.

With a $k \times k$ matrix of network performance metric values, the joining node computes the coordinates of a local basis L.

Figure 3 introduces a 2-D example. We assume that there are six nodes already in the system: $\{n_1, n_2, n_3, n_4, n_5, n_6\}$ (Figure 3a). Suppose a new node, n_7, wants to join in. As the first step, it contacts a node in the system, say n_4, in order to get a list of lighthouses. In this example, n_4 sends a list of three nodes to act as n_7 lighthouses: $\{n_4, n_5, n_6\}$. At this time, n_7 start measuring the distance, propagation delay, between itself and the three lighthouses.

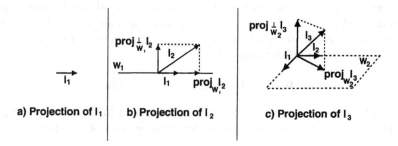

a) Projection of l_1 | b) Projection of l_2 | c) Projection of l_3

Fig. 4. Gram-Schmidt Process

The following sections describe the method that calculates a local basis **L** using the lighthouses.

3.2   Local Basis Coordinates

Any node that wants to take part in the system has to compute its own coordinates relative to a local basis. However, it must first determine the coordinates of the basis that it will be using. To do this, node n_i calculates $L = \{l_1, ..., l_k\}$ where l_i is a pair of lighthouse nodes $\overline{n_r n_s}$. It applies the Gram-Schmidt process [3] described as follows.

$$
\begin{cases}
l_1 = proj_{w_0}l_1 + proj^{\perp}_{w_0}l_1; \\
l_2 = proj_{w_1}l_2 + proj^{\perp}_{w_1}l_2; \\
\quad\vdots \\
l_k = proj_{w_{k-1}}l_k + proj^{\perp}_{w_{k-1}}l_{k-1}.
\end{cases}
\tag{1}
$$

Where $proj_{w_{i-1}}l_i$ is the projection of l_i along the finite-dimensional subspace $\mathbf{W}_{i-1}$ of $\mathbf{V}^k$; whereas the vector $proj^{\perp}_{w_0}l_1$ is called the the component of l_i orthogonal to $\mathbf{W}_{i-1}$.

We shall explain the Gram-Schmidt process, with a 3-D basis construction example. In the first step (Figure 4a), l_1 is projected into subspace $\mathbf{W}_0$. Vector l_1 now spans the one dimensional subspace $\mathbf{W}_1$. In the second step (Figure 4b), vector l_2 is projected along and orthogonal to $\mathbf{W}_1$. Over the last step (Figure 4c), vector l_3 is calculated as the sum of its component along the subspace $\mathbf{W}_2$, spanned by l_1 and l_2, and by its component orthogonal to $\mathbf{W}_2$.

The joining node, n_7, uses the Gram-Schmidt process to compute a local basis $L = \{\overline{n_4 n_5}, \overline{n_4 n_6}\}$ (Figure 3b).

3.3   Host Coordinates

At this stage, node n_i has fresh coordinates of its local basis. It may now calculate its own set of coordinates. However, as a side-effect of choosing arbitrary $k + 1$ lighthouse nodes to span the vector space $\mathbf{V}^k$, it is probable that these vectors will form an alternate basis, not necessarily an orthogonal one. Chances are that the computed basis will be oblique. In that case, we have to be able to use any type of basis (oblique/orthogonal), so that node n_i coordinate vectors will be a linear combination of the local basis $\mathbf{L}$:

$$n_i = c_1 l_1 + c_2 l_2 + \cdots + c_k l_k \tag{2}$$

By taking the inner product $<, >$ of both sides of Eq.2 with every vector in $\mathbf{L} = \{l_1, l_2, ..., l_k\}$, we are left with the following system of equations:

$$\begin{cases} < n_i, l_1 > = < c_1 l_1, l_1 > + \cdots + < c_k l_k, l_1 > \\ < n_i, l_2 > = < c_1 l_1, l_2 > + \cdots + < c_k l_k, l_2 > \\ \quad \vdots \\ < n_i, l_k > = < c_1 l_1, l_k > + \cdots + < c_k l_k, l_k > \end{cases} \tag{3}$$

Solving the system 3, we obtain the scalars c_i. As the only given input to our technique is the distance measures (e.g. delay) from the joining node to a set of lighthouses, an expansion of the system above is essential. Thus, two formulae of the Algebra are required.

$$< \mathbf{u}, \mathbf{v} > = \|\mathbf{u}\| \|\mathbf{v}\| \cos(\widehat{\mathbf{u}, \mathbf{v}}) \tag{4}$$

$$< \mathbf{u}, \mathbf{u} > = \|\mathbf{u}\|^2 \tag{5}$$

Formula 4 gives the cosine of the angle between two vectors $\mathbf{u}$ and $\mathbf{v}$; whereas formula 5 is a derivation of the first since the angle θ between identical vectors is 0. Substituting these two formulae in the system 3 yields:

$$\begin{cases} c_1 \|l_1\| + \cdots + c_k \|l_k\| \cos(\widehat{l_1, l_k}) = \|n_i\| \cos(\widehat{n_i, l_1}) \\ \quad \vdots \\ c_1 \|l_1\| \cos(\widehat{l_1, l_k}) + \cdots + c_k \|l_k\| = \|n_i\| \cos(\widehat{n_i, l_k}) \end{cases} \tag{6}$$

In synthesis, the node's coordinates are calculated by solving the system of linear equations (6). Geometrically, this represents the projections of the node distance measures along the vectors of the local basis L.

In our 2-D example (Figure 3c), node n_7 solves a simple linear system in two variables: c_1 and c_2. As a result, the coordinates of n_7 become $c_1.l_1 + c_2.l_2$, where $l_1 = \overline{n_4 n_5}$ and $l_2 = \overline{n_4 n_6}$.

3.4   Transition Matrix

We allow nodes to arbitrarily choose their lighthouse nodes (local basis) provided they preserve the invariant of rightly maintaining a transition matrix $\mathbf{P}$. The question is how a joining node knows about the global basis $\mathbf{G}$ without measuring any property between itself and the nodes that form such a basis. To answer this question, we bring the idea of *basis changing* into our technique.

If we change the basis for a vector space $\mathbf{V}^k$ from some old basis $\mathbf{B} = \{\mathbf{u_1}, ..., \mathbf{u_k}\}$ to some new basis $\mathbf{B'} = \{\mathbf{u'_1}, ..., \mathbf{u'_k}\}$, then the old coordinate matrix $[\mathbf{v}]_B$ of a vector $\mathbf{v}$ is related to the new coordinate matrix $[\mathbf{v}]_{B'}$ of the same vector by the equation:

$$[\mathbf{v}]_{B'} = P^{-1}[\mathbf{v}]_B \tag{7}$$

where the columns of $\mathbf{P}$ are the coordinate matrices of the new basis vectors relative to the old basis, that is, the column vectors of $\mathbf{P}$ are:

$$P = \begin{bmatrix} [\mathbf{u'_1}]_B \\ \cdots \\ [\mathbf{u'_k}]_B \end{bmatrix} \tag{8}$$

As a result, node $\mathbf{n_i}$ computes a transition matrix $\mathbf{P}$ between its local basis $\mathbf{L}$ and the global basis $\mathbf{G}$. This does not require any additional distance measurements. The only requirement is that the entry point node $\mathbf{n_j}$ supplies either the coordinates of $\mathbf{G}$ or its own $\mathbf{P}$ transition matrix.

The transition matrix P calculated by n_7 (Figure 3c) contains the coordinates of the local basis $\mathbf{L} = \{\mathbf{l_1}, \mathbf{l_2}\}$ relative to the global basis G. This in fact the coordinates of the lighthouses that compose L, i.e., $\{n_4, n_5, n_6\}$. Therefore, n_7 devises $\mathbf{P}$ with nothing more than the information it already has.

We expect nodes to re-calculate their coordinates from time to time due to frequent network topology changes (i.e. an optical link was shut down). Such changes are captured by the network performance metrics used such as the propagation delay. In this case, a participating node re-computes its coordinates following the four steps above. If for some reason, a lighthouse node becomes unavailable during this re-calculation process, the participating node then chooses an alternate lighthouse to devise the transition matrix.

4   Experimental Evaluation

In this section, we present an initial analysis of our technique. We compared the accuracy of Lighthouse delay estimates against the GNP estimates. Accuracy, in this context, is how close the distance predicted by our technique is to the real distance measured. If we achieve high level of accuracy that means we can compute accurate node locations.

The data used in this experiment was the *global* data set collected by the GNP project[2]. It consists of two matrices with delay measures. The *probe matrix* holds the mutual distance measures between 19 probes. The second matrix, called *target matrix*, contains the delay measures between 869 target hosts and the 19 probes. The delay was measured by ICMP ECHO packets.

---

[2] Measurement data available at
http://www-2.cs.cmu.edu/~eugeneng/research/gnp

Table 1. Key Parameters

Dimensions	Distance	Probes	Tolerance
3	L_2 (Euclidean)	4	10^{-6} (GNP only)

Table 1 shows the key parameters used in both implementation of these two techniques. The tolerance parameter was the convergence error of the minimization method used by the GNP code.

The strength of Lighthouse, as explored in the previous sections, is its capability of working with multiple local bases through oblique projections. To fairly compare our technique to GNP, we limited the experiment to a single and global basis.

We chose four arbitrary probes among the nineteen to serve as the lighthouses and landmarks nodes. With distance between four probes, Lighthouse code computed a local basis for a 3-D vector space; whereas the GNP code calculated a global solution for the distance error minimization problem.

Moreover, a common framework was required to compare both techniques. Hence, we divided the evaluation in two sub-processes. The first one, called *calibration*, relates to how accurate a technique is when computing the local basis (Lighthouse) or the global basis (GNP). Distances measures between the four chosen probes were required for this sub-process. The *extrapolation*, the second sub-process, tells how accurate a technique is to predicting/extrapolating distance measures between arbitrary nodes. In order to help the comparison two accuracy metrics were used.

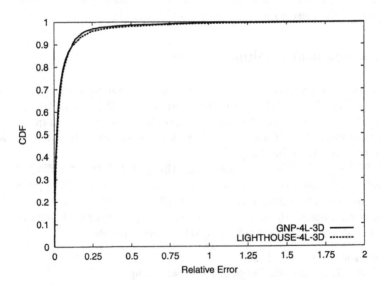

Fig. 5. Accuracy of Lighthouse: Calibration

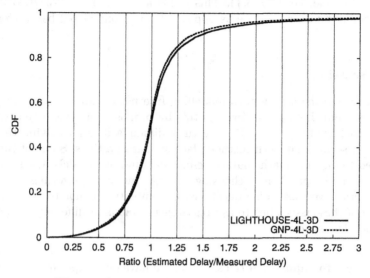

Fig. 6. Accuracy of Lighthouse: Extrapolation

$$\text{RelativeError} = \frac{|\text{Measured} - \text{Estimated}|}{\text{Measured}} \qquad (9)$$

$$\text{Ratio} = \frac{\text{Estimated}}{\text{Measured}} \qquad (10)$$

Formula 10 gives the ratio of an estimated to a measured distance. Ideally, a curve resulting from this metric is a vertical line at x=1. On the other hand, the relative error metric (formula 9) results in zero when the estimated matches the measured distance by 100%.

In Figure 5, we plot the CDFs of the relative error of Lighthouse and GNP for the calibration sub-process.

As we expected, both techniques achieved high levels of accuracy measured by their relative errors. We should point out that the measured distances between the four probes should match the distances computed by each technique. This property determines how well the technique can extrapolate distance measures. Lighthouse presented almost the same average accuracy of GNP. Both techniques could estimate 99% of the distances within a relative error of 0.5 or less.

Figure 6 compares the CDFs of the ratios of Lighthouse and GNP delay estimates to those measured. Despite the fact that the two techniques presented equivalent results, Lighthouse was slightly better than GNP for ratios less than 1. On the other hand, 70.34% of GNP estimates were within a 25% error margin as opposed to 69.61% of Lighthouse estimates. As much as 41% of Lighthouse and GNP estimates were within an error of 10%.

Finally, we offer some back-of-the-envelope numerical support for why Lighthouse should scale better than GNP. We used in our experiments 869+19 hosts. Lighthouse could have used any local basis from a combination of 888 hosts taken 4 at a time, i.e. $C(888,4)$. This yields a selection of 25733706090 bases that a joining node can choose as opposed to only one global basis offered by GNP.

4.1   Discussion

GNP represents the first step to modelling Internet distances with a single co-ordinate system. Lighthouse furthers this by proposing a system that can use multiple coordinate systems. Despite their dissimilarities for solving the same problem, it seems that both methods face similar questions. Some of them are connected to ongoing mathematical refinements in both models. Others are associated with the problem of choosing the right network performance metrics. In this section we raise some questions. Our intention is not to cover the full spectrum of these issues but to ask researchers to look at different perspectives at this problem space.

Network Performance Metrics. So far we have only experimented with Internet delay as it can be triangulated [5]. What are the additional metrics that could be used? How could these metrics be *practically* measured? Is 'available bandwidth' a feasible metric? If so, could we characterise it as we did with network delay?

Distance Function. In our experiments we tested the L_p family of functions with $L_p = \left(\sum_{i=1}^{k} |x_i - y_i|^p \right)^{1/p}$. When $p = 2$ we have the L_2, which is the Euclidean distance. In contrast, for $p = 1$, we have the 'Manhattan' or block distance. Additionally, $p < 1$ results in a non-metric distance function used where the distances do not obey the triangle inequality [8]. We varied p from 0.0 to 6.0 in our experiments and found that the L_2 function has given better delay estimates than any other derivation of L_p. However, the question is: could the L_2 distance function be applied to other network performance metrics such as the available bandwidth?

The Curse of Dimensionality. Network performance metrics may suffer from large differences between their *representational* dimensions k in a vector space and their *intrinsic* dimensionality. This is related to the real number of dimensions that have to be used while maintaining the original distance and it is called *the curse of dimensionality*. To match the *intrinsic* dimensionality of Internet delay distances about 5 to 7 dimensions were required [18] . This prompts the question: do we need to experimentally find out the intrinsic dimensionality of other network performance metrics such as the available bandwidth? Or, could we assume that a vector space with 5 to 7 dimensions can model any network performance metric?

Complex versus Real Scalars. We are investigating the benefits of using complex numbers rather than real scalars. Therefore, a $\mathbb{C}^3$ complex vector space may suit the intrinsic dimensionality of Internet delay. But why should we use complex vector spaces? As Lighthouse relies on projections, usually oblique, it uses the cosine of angles between the projected segments. With a non-metric distance function, we may also be able to model distances that do not obey the triangle inequality. In doing so we turn the metric space into a non-metric space.

On-Line versus Off-Line Measurements. On-demand measures of network distances might be too costly to be carried out. This has motivated our work. In contrast, King [6], a latency measurement tool based on the DNS infrastructure, measures on-line latency. What are the trade-offs of using an off-line or on-line measurement tool? A comparison of King to Lighthouse may give some clues of which type of technique we can apply in different contexts.

Choosing Lighthouse Nodes. Lighthouse nodes form a local basis **L** which spans a vector space **V**. To be sure that **L** is a proper basis, we need to show that the vectors of **L** are linear independent, i.e. every vector in **V** is expressible as a linear combination of the vectors in **L**. There might be cases where the chosen Lighthouse nodes do not form a linear independent basis, therefore, yielding multiple solutions to the system (6). For example, suppose we want to span a 2-D vector space but the three chosen points lie on the same line. They are linear dependent vectors that can only span a 1-D space. To address this issue, the joining node can check locally, during the second step of our algorithm, whether or not the selected Lighthouse nodes form a vector space basis. Such a test consists of making sure that the following matrix **L** has a nonzero determinant:

$$det(L) = \begin{vmatrix} [\mathbf{l_1}] \\ \cdots \\ [\mathbf{l_k}] \end{vmatrix} \neq 0 \tag{11}$$

where the columns of **L** are the coordinate matrices of the basis vectors.

In contrast, GNP requires a similar test as it encounters the same problem. Unlike Lighthouse, this checking cannot be done locally by the joining node but it should be implemented while selecting the GNP global landmarks.

5 Conclusions

In this paper we have presented a technique, called Lighthouse, that maps objects, i.e. nodes and their distance measures such as delay, onto points in a k-dimensional vector space. Our framework avoids the scalability problem of systems that employ 'well-known' pivots as their reference points. Hence, it gives enough flexibility to a joining host in choosing its set of lighthouses. We believe that Lighthouse is accurate as shown by our initial results. With the same information, a 4x4 matrix of distance delay measures, we were able to achieve similar

levels of accuracy as GNP with a 3-D vector space. As for future work, we will
be investigating the issues raised in the previous section.

Acknowledgments

We thank Sugih Jamin for discussions on distance metrics and triangulation on
the Internet. We thank Adam Greenhalgh, Socrates Varakliotis, Tolga Uzuner,
Andrew Twigg, Igor Sobrado, Arnaud Jacquet, Jose Suruagy, Kennedy Cheng,
Senthil Ayyasamy and the anonymous reviewers for their valuable feedback.

References

[1] B. Silaghi, S. Bhattacharjee, and P. Keleher. Query Routing in the TerraDir
Distributed Directory. In *Submitted for Publication*, 2001.

[2] B. Zhao, J. Kubiatowicz, and A. Joseph. Tapestry: An Infrastructure for Fault-
Tolerant Wide-Area Location and Routing. In *Technical Report UCB CSD-01-
1141, University of California at Berkeley*, November 2001.

[3] L. Corwin and R. Szczarba. *Calculus in Vector Spaces: 2nd edition*. Marcel Dekker
Inc., 1994.

[4] A. Farago, T. Linder, and G. Lugosi. Fast nearest-neighbor search in dissimilarity
spaces. *IEEE Trans. on Pattern Analysis and Machine Intelligence*, 15(9):957–
962, 1993.

[5] P. Francis, S. Jamin, C. Jin, D. Raz, Y. Shavitt, and L. Zhang. Idmaps: A global
internet host distance estimation service. *IEEE/ACM Trans. on Networking*,
9(5):525–540, 2001.

[6] K. P. Gummadi, S. Saroiu, and S. Gribble. King: Estimating latency between arbitrary internet end hosts. In *ACM SIGCOMM Internet Measurement Workshop
(IMW'02)*, Marseille, France, November 2002.

[7] I. Stoica, R. Morris, D. Karger, F. Kaashoek, and H. Balakrishnan. Chord:
A Scalable Peer-to-Peer Lookup Service for Internet Applications. In *ACM SIG-
COMM'01 Conference*, San Diego, USA, August 2001.

[8] D. Jacobs, D. Weinshall, and Y. Gdalyahu. Classification with non-metric distances: Image retrieval and class representation. *IEEE Trans. on Pattern Analysis
and Machine Intelligence*, 22(6):583–600, 2000.

[9] C. Kommareddy, N. Shankar, and B. Bhattacharjee. Finding close friends on the
internet. In *ICNP'01*, Riverside (CA), USA, November 2001.

[10] M. Freedman and R. Vingralek. Efficient Peer-To-Peer Lookup Based on
a Distributed Trie. In *1st International Workshop on Peer-to-Peer Systems
(IPTPS'02)*, MIT, Cambridge, USA, March 2002.

[11] Andy Oram. Peer-to-peer: Harnessing the power of disruptive technologies.
O'Reilly, March 2001.

[12] P. Druschel and A. Rowstron. Pastry: Scalable Distributed Object Location and
Routing for Large-scale Peer to Peer Systems. In *18th IFIP/ACM Middleware
2001*, November 2001.

[13] S. Ratnasamy, , S. Shenker, and I. Stoica. Routing Algorithms for DHTs:
Some Open Questions. In *1st International Workshop on Peer-to-Peer Systems
(IPTPS'02)*, MIT, Cambridge, USA, March 2002.

[14] S. Ratnasamy, M. Handley, R. Karp, and S. Shenker. Topologically-aware Overlay Construction and Server Selection. In *IEEE INFOCOM' 02*, New York, USA, June 2002.

[15] S. Ratnasamy, P. Francis, M. Handley, R. Karp, and S. Shenker. A Scalable Content-Addressable Network. In *ACM SIGCOMM'01 Conference*, San Diego, USA, August 2001.

[16] M. Shapiro. The choice of reference points in best-match file searching. *Communication of the ACM*, 20(5), 1977.

[17] T. Henderson. Observations on Game Server Discovery Mechanisms. In *ACM SIG MULTIMEDIA NetGames 2002: First Workshop on Network and System Support for Games*, Braunschweig, Germany, April 2002.

[18] T. S. Eugene Ng and Hui Zhang. Predicting Internet Network Distance with Coordinates-Based Approaches. In *IEEE INFOCOM' 02*, New York, USA, June 2002.

SplitStream:
High-Bandwidth Content Distribution
in Cooperative Environments*

Miguel Castro[1], Peter Druschel[2], Anne-Marie Kermarrec[1], Animesh Nandi[2],
Antony Rowstron[1], and Atul Singh[2]

[1] Microsoft Research
7 J J Thomson Avenue, Cambridge
CB3 0FB, UK.
[2] Rice University
6100 Main Street, MS-132, Houston, TX 77005, USA

Abstract. In tree-based multicast systems, a relatively small number
of interior nodes carry the load of forwarding multicast messages. This
works well when the interior nodes are dedicated infrastructure routers.
But it poses a problem in cooperative application-level multicast, where
participants expect to contribute resources proportional to the benefit
they derive from using the system. Moreover, many participants may not
have the network capacity and availability required of an interior node in
high-bandwidth multicast applications. SplitStream is a high-bandwidth
content distribution system based on application-level multicast. It distributes the forwarding load among all the participants, and is able to
accommodate participating nodes with different bandwidth capacities.
We sketch the design of SplitStream and present some preliminary performance results.

1   Introduction

End-system or application-level multicast [4, 13, 23, 8, 20, 16, 3] has become an
attractive alternative to IP multicast. Instead of relying on a multicast infrastructure in the network, which is not widely available, the participating hosts pool
their resources to route and distribute multicast messages using only unicast network services. In this paper we are particularly concerned with application-level
multicast in *cooperative* environments. In such environments the participants
contribute resources in exchange for using the service and they expect that the
forwarding load be shared among all participants.

Unfortunately, conventional tree-based multicast is inherently not well
matched to a cooperative environment. The reason is that in any efficient (i.e.
low-depth) multicast tree a small number of interior nodes carry the burden of
splitting and forwarding multicast traffic, whilst a large number of leaf nodes

---

* This research was supported in part by Texas ATP (003604-0079-2001) and by NSF
(ANI-0225660), http://project-iris.net.

F. Kaashoek and I. Stoica (Eds.): IPTPS 2003, LNCS 2735, pp. 292–303, 2003.

contribute no resources. This conflicts with the expectation that all members should share the forwarding load. The problem is further aggravated in high-bandwidth applications like video or bulk file distribution, where many nodes may not have the capacity and availability required of an interior node in a conventional multicast tree. SplitStream is designed to address these problems.

SplitStream enables efficient cooperative distribution of high-bandwidth content, whilst distributing the forwarding load among the participating nodes. SplitStream can also accommodate nodes with different network capacities and asymmetric bandwidth on the inbound and outbound network paths. Subject to these constraints, it balances the forwarding load across all the nodes.

The key idea is to *split* the multicast content into k stripes, and multicast each stripe in a separate multicast tree. Participants join as many trees as there are stripes they wish to receive. The aim is to construct this *forest* of multicast trees such that an interior node in one tree is a leaf node in all the remaining trees. In this way, the forwarding load can be spread across all participating nodes. We show that it is possible, for instance, to efficiently construct a forest in which the inbound and outbound bandwidth requirements of each node are the same, while maintaining low delay and link stress across the system.

The SplitStream approach also offers improved robustness to node failure and sudden node departures. Since ideally, any given node is an interior node in only one tree, its failure can cause the temporary loss of at most one of the stripes. With appropriate data encodings such as erasure coding [5] of bulk data or multiple description coding (MDC) [15, 17] of streaming media, applications can thus mask or mitigate the effects of node failures even while the affected tree is being repaired.

SplitStream assumes that the available network bandwidth among nodes is typically limited by the hop connecting the nodes to the wide-area network (WAN), rather than the WAN backbone. This scenario is increasingly common as private and business subscribers move to dedicated Internet connections with DSL-level or better bandwidth, and the capacity of the Internet and corporate Intranet backbones is rapidly increasing.

The key challenge in the design of SplitStream is to efficiently construct a forest of multicast trees that distributes the forwarding load, subject to the bandwidth constraints of the participating nodes in a decentralized, scalable, and self-organizing manner. SplitStream relies on a structured peer-to-peer overlay network called Pastry [21], and on Scribe [8], an application-level multicast system built upon this overlay to construct and maintain these trees.

The rest of this paper is organized as follows. Section 2 outlines the SplitStream approach in more detail. A brief description of Pastry and Scribe is given in Section 3. We sketch the design of SplitStream in Section 4. Section 5 describes related work and Section 6 concludes.

2   The SplitStream Approach

In this section, we give a more detailed overview of SplitStream's approach to cooperative, high-bandwidth content distribution.

Tree-Based Multicast In all multicast systems based on a single tree, participating nodes are either interior nodes or leaf nodes. The interior nodes carry all the burden of forwarding multicast messages. In a k-level balanced tree with arity f, the number of interior nodes is $\frac{f^{k+1}-1}{f-1}$ and the number of leaf nodes is f^k. Thus, the fraction of leaf nodes increases with f. For example, more than half of the nodes are leaves in a binary tree, and over 90% of nodes are leaves in a tree with arity 16. In the latter case, the forwarding load is carried by less than 10% of the nodes; whilst all nodes have equal inbound bandwidth, the internal nodes have an outbound bandwidth requirement of 16 times the inbound bandwidth. Even in a binary tree, which would be impractically deep in most circumstances, the outbound bandwidth required by the interior nodes is twice that of their inbound bandwidth.

SplitStream SplitStream is designed to overcome the inherently unbalanced forwarding load in conventional tree-based multicast systems. SplitStream strives to distribute the forwarding load over all participating nodes, and respects different capacity limits of individual participating nodes. SplitStream achieves this by splitting the multicast content into multiple stripes, and using separate multicast trees to distribute each stripe.

Figure 1 illustrates how SplitStream balances the forwarding load among the participating nodes. In this simple example, the original content is split into two stripes and multicast in separate trees. For simplicity, let us assume that the original content has a bandwidth requirement of B, and that each stripe has half the bandwidth requirement of the original content. Each node other than the source subscribes to both stripes, inducing an inbound bandwidth requirement of B. As shown in Figure 1, each node is an internal node in only one tree and forwards the stripe to two children, yielding an outbound bandwidth requirement of no more than B.

In general, the content is split into k stripes. Participating nodes may subscribe to a subset of the stripes, thus controlling their inbound bandwidth requirement in increments of B/k. Similarly, participating nodes may control their outbound bandwidth requirement in increments of B/k by limiting the number of children they adopt. Thus, SplitStream can accommodate nodes with different bandwidths, and nodes with unequal inbound and outbound network capacities.

Applications SplitStream provides a generic infrastructure for high-bandwidth content distribution. Any application that uses SplitStream controls how the content it distributes is encoded and divided into stripes. SplitStream constructs the multicast trees for the stripes while adhering to the inbound and outbound

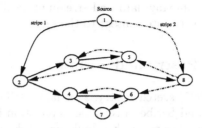

Fig. 1. A simple example illustrating the basic approach of SplitStream. Original content is split into two stripes. An independent multicast tree is constructed for each stripe such that a node is an interior node in one multicast tree and a leaf in the other

bandwidth constraints of the nodes. Applications need to *(i)* encode the content such that each stripe requires approximately the same bandwidth; *(ii)* ensure that each stripe contains approximately the same amount of information and there is no hierarchy among stripes; and *(iii)* provide mechanisms to tolerate the intermittent loss of a subset of the stripes.

In order to tolerate the intermittent loss of a subset of stripes, some applications may provide explicit mechanisms to fetch content from other peers in the system, or applications may choose to use redundancy in encoding content, requiring more than B/k per stripe in return for the ability to reconstitute the content from less than k stripes. For example, a media stream could be encoded using MDC so that the video can be reconstituted from any subset of the k stripes, with video quality proportional to the number of stripes received. If an interior node in the multicast tree for the stripe should fail, then clients deprived of the stripe are able to continue displaying the media stream at reduced quality until the multicast tree is repaired. Such an encoding also allows low-bandwidth clients to receive the video at lower quality by explicitly requesting fewer stripes.

Another example is the multicasting of file data, where each data block can be encoded using erasure codes to generate k blocks, such that only a subset of the k blocks are required to reconstitute the original block. Each stripe is then used to multicast a different one of the k blocks. Participants subscribe to all stripes and once a sufficient subset of the blocks is received, the clients are able to reconstitute the original data block. If a client misses a number of blocks from a particular stripe for a period of time (while the stripe multicast tree is being repaired after an internal node has failed), the client can still reconstitute the original data blocks due to the redundancy. An example where multicasting of file data could be useful is the distribution of software patches and upgrades to institutions or end-users.

In general, while the contributed nodes could be the computers belonging to individual Internet subscribers or the desktop machines in a corporation, they could also be dedicated servers. For example, in Enterprise Content Delivery Networks (eCDNs), dedicated servers are placed through out a corporate network to facilitate access to company data and streaming media. Such eCDNs could utilize SplitStream to distribute content to the servers.

3   Background: Pastry and Scribe

In this section, we briefly sketch Pastry, a scalable, self-organizing, structured p2p overlay network, and Scribe, a scalable application-level multicast system based on Pastry. Both systems are key building blocks in the design of Split-Stream.

Pastry In Pastry, nodes and objects are assigned random identifiers (called *nodeIds* and *keys*, respectively) from a large sparse id space. Keys and nodeIds are 128 bits in length and can be thought of as a sequence of digits in base 2^b (b is a configuration parameter with a typical value of 3 or 4). Given a message and a key, Pastry routes the message to the node with the nodeId that is numerically closest to the key, which is called the key's *root*.

In order to route messages, each node maintains a routing table and a leaf set. A node's routing table has about $log_{2^b} N$ rows and 2^b columns. The entries in row n of the routing table refer to nodes whose nodeIds share the first n digits with the local node's nodeId; the $(n + 1)$th nodeId digit of a node in column m of row n equals m. The column in row n corresponding to the value of the $(n + 1)$th digits of the local node's nodeId remains empty. Routing in Pastry requires that at each routing step, a node normally forwards the message to a node whose nodeId shares with the key a prefix that is at least one digit longer than the prefix that the key shares with the present node's id. If no such node is known, the message is forwarded to a node whose nodeId shares a prefix with the key as long as the current node, but is numerically closer to the key than the present node's id.

Each Pastry node maintains a leaf set of neighboring nodes in the nodeId space, both to ensure reliable message delivery, and to store replicas of objects for fault tolerance.

The expected number of routing hops is less than $log_{2^b} N$. The Pastry overlay construction observes proximity in the underlying Internet. Each routing table entry is chosen to refer to a node with low network delay, among all nodes with an appropriate nodeId prefix. As a result, one can show that Pastry routes have a *low delay penalty*: the average delay of Pastry messages is usually less than twice the IP delay between source and destination [7]. Similarly, one can show the *local route convergence* of Pastry routes: the routes of messages route to the same key from nearby nodes tend to converge at a nearby intermediate node. Both of these properties are important for the construction of efficient multicast trees, described below. A full description of Pastry can be found in [21].

Scribe Scribe is an application-level multicast system built upon Pastry. A pseudo-random Pastry key, known as the *groupId*, is chosen for each multicast group. A multicast tree associated with the group is formed by the union of the Pastry routes from each group member to the groupId's root (which is also the root of the multicast tree). Messages are multicast from the root to the members using reverse path forwarding [11].

The properties of the Pastry overlay ensure that the multicast trees are efficient. The delay to forward a message from the root to each group member is low due to the low delay penalty of Pastry routes. Pastry's local route convergence ensures that the load imposed on the physical network is small because most message replication occurs at intermediate nodes that are close in the network to the leaf nodes in the tree.

Group membership management in Scribe is decentralized and highly efficient, because it leverages the existing, proximity-aware Pastry overlay. Adding a member to a group merely involves routing towards the groupId until the message reaches a member of the tree, followed by adding the route traversed by the message to the group multicast tree. As a result, Scribe can efficiently support large numbers of groups, arbitrary numbers of group members, and groups with highly dynamic membership.

The latter property, combined with an anycast [9] primitive recently added to Scribe, can be used to perform distributed resource discovery. As we will show in the next section, SplitStream uses this mechanism to discover nodes with spare forwarding capacity. A full description and evaluation of Scribe multicast can be found in [8]. Scribe anycast is described in [9].

4   SplitStream Design

In this section, we sketch the design of SplitStream.

Building Interior-Node-Disjoint Trees SplitStream uses a separate Scribe multicast tree for each of the k stripes. SplitStream exploits the properties of Pastry routing to construct trees with disjoint sets of interior nodes (called *interior-node-disjoint* trees). Recall that Pastry normally forwards a message towards nodes whose nodeIds share progressively longer prefixes with the message's key. Since a Scribe tree is formed by the routes from all members to the groupId, the nodeIds of *all* interior nodes have a common prefix of at least one digit with the tree's groupId. Therefore, we can ensure that k Scribe trees have a disjoint set of interior nodes simply by choosing groupIds for the trees that all differ in the most significant digit.

Setting $k = 2^b$ ensures that each participating node has an equal chance of becoming an interior node in some tree. If k is chosen such that $k = 2^i$ and $i \leq b$, then it is still possible to ensure this fairness by exploiting certain properties of the Pastry routing table, but we omit the details to conserve space. Without loss of generality, we assume that $k = 2^b$ in the rest of this paper.

Limiting Node Degree The resulting forest of Scribe trees is interior-node-disjoint and satisfies the nodes' constraints on the inbound bandwidth, but it does not necessarily satisfy the individual nodes' outgoing bandwidth constraints. Let us first consider the inbound bandwidth. A node's inbound bandwidth is proportional to the number of stripes to which the node subscribes. Note that every node has to subscribe to at least one stripe, the stripe whose stripeId shares a prefix with its nodeId, because the node may have to serve as an interior node for that stripe.

The number of children that may attempt to attach to a node is bounded by its indegree in the Pastry overlay, which is influenced by the physical network topology. In general, this number may exceed the number of children a node is able to support. For a SplitStream node to limit its outbound network bandwidth, it must limit its outdegree in the SplitStream forest, i.e., the total number of children it takes on.

Scribe has a built-in mechanism to limit a node's outdegree. When a node that has reached its maximal outdegree receives a request from a prospective child, it provides the prospective child with a list of its current children. The prospective child then seeks to be adopted by the child with lowest delay. This procedure continues recursively down the tree until a node is found that can take another child. In Scribe, this procedure is guaranteed to terminate because a leaf node is required to take on at least one child.

However, this procedure is not guaranteed to work in SplitStream. The reason is that a leaf node in one tree may be an interior node in another stripe tree, and may have already reached its outdegree limit with respect to that stripe tree. Next, we describe how SplitStream resolves this problem.

Locating Parents The following algorithm is used to resolve the case where a node that has reached its outdegree limit receives a join request from a prospective child. First, the node adopts the prospective child regardless of the outdegree limit. Then, it evaluates its new set of children to select a child to reject. This selection is made in an attempt to maximize path independence and to minimize delay and link stress in the SplitStream forest.

First, the node looks for children that are subscribed to stripes whose stripeIds do not share a prefix with the local node's nodeId. (How the node could have acquired such a child in the first place will become clear in a moment). If the prospective child is among them, it is selected; else, one is chosen randomly from the set. If no such child exists, then the current node is an interior node for only one stripe tree, and it selects the child whose nodeId has the shortest prefix match with that stripeId. If multiple such nodes exist and the prospective child is among them, it is selected; else, one is chosen randomly from the set. The chosen child is then notified that it has been orphaned for a particular stripeId.

The orphaned child then seeks to locate a new parent in up to three steps. In the first step, the orphaned child attempts to attach to a former sibling that shares a prefix match with the stripeId for which it seeks a parent. The former sibling either adopts or rejects the orphan, using the same criteria as described above. This process continues recursively down the tree until the orphan either finds a new parent or no children share a prefix match with the stripeId.

Spare Capacity Group If the orphan has not found a parent, it sends an anycast message to a special Scribe group called the *spare capacity group*. All SplitStream nodes whose total number of stripe children is below their forwarding capacity limit are members of this group. Scribe delivers this anycast message to a node in the spare capacity group tree that is near the orphan in the physical network. This node forwards the message to a child, starting a depth-first search (DFS) of the spare capacity group tree. If the node has no children or they have all been checked, the node checks whether it receives the stripe to which the orphaned child seeks to subscribe. If so, it verifies that the orphan is not an ancestor in the corresponding stripe tree, which would create a cycle. To enable this test, each node maintains its path to the root of each stripe tree of which it is a member.

If both tests succeed, then the node takes on the orphan as a child; if as a result, the node has now reached its outdegree limit, it leaves the spare capacity group. If one of the tests fails, the node forwards the message to its parent, continuing the DFS of the spare capacity group tree until an appropriate member is found.

Anycasting to the spare capacity group may fail to locate an appropriate parent for the orphan, even after an appropriate number of retries with sufficient timeouts. There are two circumstances in which this can happen. If the spare capacity group is empty, then the SplitStream forest construction is infeasible, since an orphan remains after all forwarding capacity has been exhausted. In this case, the application on the orphaned node is notified that there is no forwarding capacity left in the system.

Deadlocks Otherwise, each member of the spare capacity group either does not provide the desired stripe, or it is a successor of the orphan in the stripe tree. If follows that none of the nodes in the desired stripe tree has unused forwarding capacity, although forwarding capacity exists in other stripes. This is a type of deadlock and can be resolved as follows. The orphan sends an anycast message to the desired stripe tree, which performs a randomized search of the stripe tree until it reaches a leaf node. The forwarding capacity of this leaf node must either be zero, or it must be consumed by children in different stripes (else, it would have been a member in the spare capacity group). In the former case, we ask the leaf's parent to drop the leaf and attach the orphan instead. Otherwise, the leaf node adopts the orphan and drops one of its current children randomly.

One can show that the above procedure is guaranteed to locate an appropriate parent for the orphan if one exists. Moreover, the properties of Scribe trees and the DFS of the spare capacity tree ensure that the parent is near the orphan in the physical network, among all prospective parents. This provides low delay and low link stress in the physical network. However, the algorithm as described may sacrifice interior-node-disjointedness, because the new parent may be already an interior node in another stripe tree. Thus, should the node fail, it may cause the temporary loss of more than one stripe for some nodes. Simulation results show that only a small number of nodes and stripes are typically affected.

Maintaining Path Independence It is possible to minimize this partial loss of path independence at the expense of higher delay, link stress, and cost of the forest construction. Note that completely path independent forest construction may be impractically expensive if the problem is highly constrained. However, one can bias the construction towards path independence at moderate cost.

One approach to preserving path independence is to add a third test during the DFS in the spare capacity group tree, which verifies that the prospective parent is not a predecessor to the orphan in any of the stripes to which the orphan subscribes. This ensures path independence, but may require a more extensive exploration of the spare capacity group tree, may yield a parent that is more distant in the physical network, and may not always locate a parent in the absence of sufficient excess forwarding capacity. One may balance these concerns by limiting the scope of the DFS, and relax the third test if no parent was found within that scope.

SplitStream can allow applications to control this tradeoff between independence, delay, link stress, total required forwarding capacity and overhead of forest construction according to its needs. A full evaluation of heuristics to maximize path independence is the subject of ongoing work.

Preliminary Results We have performed a preliminary performance evaluation of SplitStream, by running 40,000 SplitStream nodes over an emulated network with 5050 core routers based on the Georgia Tech network topology generator. We constructed a SplitStream forest with 16 stripes, and assigned per-node inbound and outbound bandwidth limits that follow a distribution measured among Gnutella clients in May 2001 [22].

The result are very encouraging. During the SplitStream forest construction, the mean and median number of control messages handled by each node were 56 and 47, respectively. When multicasting a message in each stripe, the medians of the relative average delay penalty (RAD) and the relative maximum delay penalty (RMD), compared to IP multicast, where 2.17 and 2.88, respectively. These value are about 1.35 and 1.8 times higher, respectively, than the values measured in a single Scribe tree on the same topology. This increase reflects the principal cost of balancing the forwarding load across all participants in SplitStream.

We also considered the degree of independence in the SplitStream forest. Without any of the independence-preserving techniques described above, and with a highly constrained bandwidth allocation (outbound bandwidth not to exceed inbound bandwidth at any node), we found that over 95% of the nodes had independent (i.e., node disjoint) paths to the source in 12 or more of the 16 stripes to which they subscribed. Thus, even in pessimal cases, the loss of independence is modest. A more comprehensive evaluation of SplitStream will be presented in a forthcoming full paper.

5   Related Work

Many application-level multicast systems have been proposed recently, e.g. [10, 16, 20, 23, 8, 3]. All are based on a single multicast tree.

Several systems use application-level multicast for streaming media [16, 12, 19]. SpreadIt [12] utilizes the participants, as SplitStream does, but creates a single multicast tree. However, unlike SpreadIt, SplitStream distributes the forwarding load over all participants using multiple multicast trees, thereby reducing the bandwidth demands on individual peers and increasing robustness.

Overcast [16] organizes dedicated servers into a source-rooted multicast tree using bandwidth estimation measurements to optimize bandwidth usage across the tree. The main differences between Overcast and SplitStream are *(i)* that Overcast uses dedicated servers whilst SplitStream utilizes the participants; *(ii)* Overcast creates a single bandwidth optimized multicast tree whereas SplitStream creates a forest of multicast trees assuming that the available network bandwidth among peers is typically limited by bandwidth of the links connecting nodes to the network rather than the network backbone. This scenario is increasingly common as the capacity of the Internet and corporate Internet backbones rapidly increase.

CoopNet [19] implements a hybrid system for streaming media, which utilizes multiple application-level trees with striping and Multiple Description Encoding (MDC) [15, 17]. The idea of using MDCs and exploiting path diversity for robustness was originally proposed by Apostolopoulos [1, 2] to increase robustness to packet loss when streaming media. In CoopNet a centralized server is used to stream media. Clients contact the server requesting the media stream. If the server is not overloaded, it supplies the client with the stream. If the server becomes overloaded, then it redirects clients to already participating nodes. The stream is striped and several application-level multicast trees rooted at the server are created. There are two fundamental differences between CoopNet and SplitStream: *(i)* CoopNet uses a centralized algorithm (running on the server) to build the trees whilst SplitStream is completely decentralized and more scalable; and *(ii)* CoopNet does not explicitly attempt to manage the bandwidth contribution of individual nodes; however, it is possible to add this capability to CoopNet.

Nguyen and Zakhor [18] propose streaming video from multiple sources concurrently, thereby exploiting path diversity and increasing tolerance to packet loss. They subsequently extend the work in [18] to use Forward Error Correction [5] encodings. The work assumes that the client is aware of the set of servers from which to receive the video. SplitStream constructs multiple end-system based multicast trees in a decentralized fashion and is therefore more scalable.

In [6], algorithms and content encodings are described that enable parallel downloads and increase packet loss resilience in richly connected, collaborative overlay networks by exploiting downloads from multiple peers. SplitStream provides a complete system for content distribution in collaborative overlay networks. It explicitly stripes content and creates a multicast tree for each stripe. Also, SplitStream's primary goal is to spread the forwarding load across all participants.

FCast [14] is a reliable file transfer protocol based on IP multicast. It combines a Forward Error Correction [5] encoding and a data carousel mechanism. Instead of relying on IP multicast, FCast could be easily built upon SplitStream, for example, to provide software updates cooperatively.

6   Conclusions

We have sketched the design of SplitStream, a high-bandwidth content distribution system based on end-system multicast in cooperative environments. Preliminary performance results are very encouraging. The system is able to distribute the forwarding load among the participating nodes, subject to individual node bandwidth limits. When combined with redundant content encoding, SplitStream yields resilience to node failures and unannounced departures, even while the affected multicast tree is repaired. The overhead of the forest construction is modest and well balanced, and the resulting increase in delay penalty and link stress is modest, when compared to a conventional tree-based application-level multicast system. A forthcoming paper will present comprehensive results, including results of experiments using the PlanetLab Internet testbed.

References

[1] J. G. Apostolopoulos. Reliable video communication over lossy packet networks using multiple state encoding and path diversity. In *Visual Communications and Image Processing*, Jan. 2001.

[2] J. G. Apostolopoulos and S. J. Wee. Unbalanced multiple description video communication using path diversity. In *IEEE International Conference on Image Processing*, Oct. 2001.

[3] S. Banerjee, B. Bhattacharjee, and C. Kommareddy. Scalable application layer multicast. In *ACM SIGCOMM*, Aug. 2002.

[4] K. Birman, M. Hayden, O. Ozkasap, Z. Xiao, M. Budiu, and Y. Minsky. Bimodal multicast. *ACM TOCS*, 17(2):41–88, May 1999.

[5] R. Blahut. *Theory and Practice of Error Control Codes*. Addison Wesley, MA, 1994.

[6] J. Byers, J. Considine, M. Mitzenmacher, and S. Rost. Informed content delivery across adaptive overlay networks. In *SIGCOMM'2002*, Pittsburgh, PA, USA, Aug. 2002.

[7] M. Castro, P. Druschel, Y. C. Hu, and A. Rowstron. Exploiting network proximity in peer-to-peer overlay networks, 2002. Technical report MSR-TR-2002-82.

[8] M. Castro, P. Druschel, A.-M. Kermarrec, and A. Rowstron. SCRIBE: A large-scale and decentralized application-level multicast infrastructure. *IEEE JSAC*, 20(8), Oct. 2002.

[9] M. Castro, P. Druschel, A.-M. Kermarrec, and A. Rowstron. Scalable peer-to-peer anycast for distributed resource management, 2003. Submitted.

[10] Y. Chu, S. Rao, and H. Zhang. A case for end system multicast. In *ACM Sigmetrics*, pages 1–12, June 2000.

[11] Y. K. Dalal and R. Metcalfe. Reverse path forwarding of broadcast packets. *CACM*, 21(12):1040–1048, 1978.

[12] H. Deshpande, M. Bawa, and H. Garcia-Molina. Streaming live media over a peer-to-peer network, Apr. 2001. Stanford University, CA, USA.

[13] P. Eugster, S. Handurukande, R. Guerraoui, A.-M. Kermarrec, and P. Kouznetsov. Lightweight probabilistic broadcast. In *DSN*, July 2001.

[14] J. Gemmell, E. Schooler, and J. Gray. Fcast multicast file distribution. *IEEE Network*, 14(1):58–68, Jan 2000.

[15] V. K. Goyal. Multiple description coding: Compression meet the network. *IEEE Signal Processing Magazine*, 18(5):74–93, Sept. 2001.

[16] J. Jannotti, D. Gifford, K. Johnson, M. Kaashoek, and J. O'Toole. Overcast: Reliable multicasting with an overlay network. In *OSDI 2000*, San Diego, CA, 2000.

[17] A. Mohr, E. Riskin, and R. Ladner. Unequal loss protection: Graceful degredation of image quality over packet erasure channels through forward error correction. *IEEE JSAC*, 18(6):819–828, June 2000.

[18] T. Nguyen and A. Zakhor. Distributed video streaming with forward error correction. In *Packet Video Workshop*, Pittsburgh, USA., 2002.

[19] V. Padmanabhan, H. Wang, P. Chou, and K. Sripanidkulchai. Distributing streaming media content using cooperative networking. In *NOSSDAV*, Miami Beach, FL, USA, May 2002.

[20] S. Ratnasamy, M. Handley, R. Karp, and S. Shenker. Application-level multicast using content-addressable networks. In *NGC*, Nov. 2001.

[21] A. Rowstron and P. Druschel. Pastry: Scalable, distributed object location and routing for large-scale peer-to-peer systems. In *IFIP/ACM Middleware 2001*, Heidelberg, Germany, Nov. 2001.

[22] S. Saroiu, P. K. Gummadi, and S. D. Gribble. A measurement study of peer-to-peer file sharing systems. In *MMCN*, San Jose, CA, Jan. 2002.

[23] S. Zhuang, B. Zhao, A. Joseph, R. Katz, and J. Kubiatowicz. Bayeux: An architecture for scalable and fault-tolerant wide-area data dissemination. In *NOSSDAV*, June 2001.

Efficient Broadcast in Structured P2P Networks

Sameh El-Ansary[1], Luc Onana Alima[2], Per Brand[1], and Seif Haridi[2*]

[1] Swedish Institute of Computer Science
Kista, Sweden
{sameh,perbrand}@sics.se
[2] IMIT-Royal Institute of Technology
Kista, Sweden
{onana,seif}@imit.kth.se

Abstract. In this position paper, we present an efficient algorithm for performing a broadcast operation with minimal cost in structured DHT-based P2P networks. In a system of N nodes, a broadcast message originating at an arbitrary node reaches all other nodes after exactly $N - 1$ messages. We emphasize the perception of a class of DHT systems as a form of distributed k-ary search and we take advantage of that perception in constructing a spanning tree that is utilized for efficient broadcasting. We consider broadcasting as a basic service that adds to existing DHTs the ability to search using arbitrary queries as well as dissiminate/collect global information.

1 Introduction

Research in P2P systems resulted in the creation of many Data/Resource- location systems. Two approaches were used to tackle this problem; the flooding approach and the Distributed Hash Table approach. The common characteristic of both approaches is the construction of an application-level overlay network. Table 1 includes some of the major differences between the two approaches.

The DHT approach with a structured overlay network, determinism, relatively low traffic and high guarantees is currently perceived in the P2P research community as the "reasonable" approach. Many systems were constructed based on that approach such as Tapestry [17], Pastry [13], CAN [10], Chord [14], Kademlia [8]. In contrast, the flooding-based approach represented by [5] [4] is mainly considered as unscalable based on a number of traffic analyses such as [7, 12].

A missing feature in most DHTs is the ability to perform search based on an arbitrary query rather than key lookups. Extensions to existing DHTs are needed to supply this feature. Arbitrary querying is realized in flooding-based systems via broadcasting. However, the random nature of the overlay network renders the solution costly and with low guarantees.

In this position paper, we show the status of our work on extending DHTs with an efficient broadcast layer. We are primarily investigating how to take

___

* This work is funded by the Swedish funding agency VINNOVA, PPC project, the European IST-FET PEPITO project and by the PIRATES project at UCL, Belgium.

F. Kaashoek and I. Stoica (Eds.): IPTPS 2003, LNCS 2735, pp. 304–314, 2003.
© Springer-Verlag Berlin Heidelberg 2003

Table 1. Flooding Approach vs. DHT Approach

	Flooding	DHT
Queries	Arbitrary	Key Lookup
Query-Induced Traffic	$O(N)$	$O(log(N))$
Hit Guarantees	Low	High
Connectivity Graph	Random	Structured

advantage of the structured nature of the DHT overlay network in performing efficient broadcasts. We provide broadcasting as a basic service in DHTs that should be deployed for any kind of global dissemination/collection of data.

In the next section, we describe related work. In section 3, we explain our approach based on the perception of a class of DHTs as systems performing *distributed k-ary search*. In section 4, we present a broadcast algorithm for one of the DHTs, namely Chord. Some preliminary simulation results are presented in section 6. Finally, we conclude and show intended future work in section 7.

2   Related Work

Our work can be classified as an arbitrary-search-supporting extension to DHTs. From that perspective, the following research shares the same goal:

Complex Queries in DHTs. In [6], an extension to existing DHT systems was suggested to add the ability of performing complex queries. The approach constructs search indices that enable the performance of database-like queries. This approach differs from ours in that we do not add extra indexing to the DHT. The analysis of the cost of construction, maintenance, and performing database-like join operations is not available at the time of writing of this paper.

Multicast. Since broadcast is a special case of multicast, a multicast solution developed for a DHT such as [15, 11, 2] can provide broadcast. Nevertheless, a multicast solution would require the additional maintenance of a multicast group which is, in the case of broadcast, a large group containing all the nodes of the network. In our approach, we do not require such an additional cost, we depend on the routing information of the already-maintained overlay network.

3   Our Approach

3.1   DHTs as Distributed *k*-ary Search

By looking at the class of DHT systems that have logarithmic performance bounds such as Chord, Tapestry, Pastry, and Kademlia, one can observe that

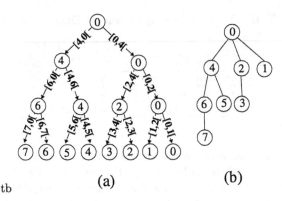

tb   (a)   (b)

Fig. 1. (a) Decision tree for a query originating at node 0 in a fully-populated 8-node Chord network. (b) The spanning tree derived from the decision tree by removing the virtual hops

the basic principle behind their operation is performing a form of distributed k-ary search. In the case of Chord, a binary search is performed. For other systems like, e.g., Tapestry and Pastry, the search arity is higher.

In this paper, we explain the perception of the Chord system as a special case of distributed k-ary search. The arguments apply to higher search arities as well.

The familiarity of the reader to the Chord system and its terminology is assumed. However, we restate the structure of the routing tables. Every Chord node has an identifier that represents its position in a circular identifier space of size N. Each Chord node maintains a table of $M = \log_2(N)$ routing entries, called the fingers. We denote the table of fingers at a node by *Finger*. At a node n, *Finger*[i] contains the address of the successor of $n + 2^{i-1}$, $1 \leq i \leq M$.

To illustrate the idea of the distributed k-ary search, without loss of generality, we assume a Chord system with identifier space of size $N = 8$. The system is fully populated, i.e. a node is present for every identifier in the space. In Figure 1 (a), we show the decision tree of a lookup query originating at node 0. Given a query for a key whose identifier is x, node 0, starts to lookup for the node responsible for x by considering the whole identifier space as the search space. Based on the interval to which x belongs (arc labels in figure 1 (a), the query is forwarded and the process is repeated with the search space reduced to a half of the previous search space. Hence, all nodes are reachable by a query-guided path of at most $H = \log_2(N)$ hops.

Notice that some of the hops are made from one node to itself. We call such hops, virtual hops. An important observation to be made from the decision tree shown in Figure 1 (a) is that a spanning tree can easily be derived by removing virtual hops. Figure 1 (b) shows a spanning tree derived from the decision tree by removing virtual hops. A more elaborate explanation on the idea of distributed k-ary search is presented in [1, 3].

3.2   Problem Definition

Having highlighted the idea of distributed k-ary search, we can now state the problem we solve in this paper.

Problem. *Given an overlay network constructed by a P2P DHT system, find an efficient algorithm for broadcasting messages. The algorithm should not depend on global knowledge of membership and should be of equal cost for any member in the system.*

Note that in the problem definition, we emphasize the P2P assumptions, i.e. the absence of central coordination and where every peer pays the same cost for running the algorithm.

3.3   Solutions

Efficient Broadcast. We base our solution on the fact that from the decision tree of the distributed k-ary search, a spanning tree can be derived by removing virtual hops. Figure 1 (b) shows a spanning tree derived from the binary decision tree for the 8-node Chord system. In section 4, we show how to construct this tree in a distributed fashion.

Gnutella-like Broadcast. A simple solution for the above-mentioned problem is to apply a Gnutella-like algorithm, where every node forwards a received query to its neighbors. This approach has an extra advantage when applied in a structured overlay network compared to a random network, namely, the ability to determine the diameter of the network. Speaking of the class of DHTs with logarithmic performance, one can set the Time-To-Live (TTL) parameter of the queries to the logarithm of the total number of nodes and be sure that the flooding process covers the whole network instead of using a heuristic TTL that results in unknown guarantees. However, this solution retains the main property of non-scalability. In section 6, we compare Gnutella-like broadcasting to efficient broadcasting.

Ring Traversal. As the overlay network of a system like Chord is organized in a ring, traversing that ring by following the successor pointers is also a possible solution. The solution differs from our solution in execution time. That solution requires the sequential traversal of the ring while our algorithm reaches different parts of the network in parallel.

4   The Broadcast Algorithm

4.1   System Model & Notation

We assume a distributed system modeled by a set of nodes communicating by message passing through a communication network that is: (i) Connected, (ii) Asynchronous, (iii) Reliable, and (iv) providing FIFO communication.

A distributed algorithm running on a node of the system is described using rules of the form:

$$\frac{\textbf{receive}(Sender : Receiver : \text{MESSAGE}(arg_1, .., arg_n))}{\text{Action(s)} ....}$$

The rule describes the event of receiving a message MESSAGE at the *Receiver* node and the action(s) taken to handle that event. A *Sender* of a message executes the statement **send**(*Sender* : *Receiver* : MESSAGE($arg_1, .., arg_n$)) to send a message to *Receiver*.

4.2   Rules

Initiating a Broadcast. A broadcast is initiated at any node as a result of a user-level request. That is, a user-level layer entity P can send to a node Q a message INITBROADCAST(*Info*) where *Info* is a piece of information that must be broadcast e.g. an arbitrary search query, a statistics gathering query, a notification, etc.

The role of the node Q is to act as a root for a spanning tree. As shown in the rule in Figure 2, Q does that by sending a BROADCAST message to all its neighbors. Note that, unless the identifier space is fully populated, the table *Finger* of a node contains many redundant fingers. For a sequence of redundant fingers, the last one is used for forwarding while the others are skipped.

A BROADCAST message contains the *Info* to be broadcast and a *Limit* argument. A *Limit* is used to restrict the forwarding space of a receiving node. The *Limit* of a *Finger*[i] is *Finger*[$i + 1$], $(1 \leq i \leq M - 1)$ where M is the number of entries of the routing table. The Mth finger's limit is a special case where the *Limit* is set to the sender's identifier. As an example, we use the sample Chord network given in section 3.1. When node 0 initiates a broadcast, it sends to nodes 1, 2, and 4. Giving them the limits of 2, 4, and 0 respectively. By doing that it is actually telling node 4 to cover the interval $[4, 0[$, i.e. half of the space. It is telling node 2 to cover the interval $[2, 4[$, i.e. quarter of space and finally, telling node 1 to cover the interval $[1, 2[$, i.e. an eighth of the space.

receive($P : Q$: INITBROADCAST(*Info*))

```
for i in 1 to M − 1 do
    //Skip a redundant finger
    if Finger[i] ≠ Finger[i + 1] then
        R := Finger[i]
        Limit := Finger[i + 1]
        send(Q:R:BROADCAST(Info, Limit))
    fi
od
//Process the Mth finger
send(Q:Finger[M]:BROADCAST(Info, Q))
```

Fig. 2. Initiating a Broadcast Message

receive($P : Q :$ BROADCAST($Info, Limit$))

//Take some action to deliver to application layer ...
for i **in** 1 **to** $M - 1$ **do**
   //Skip a redundant finger
   if $Finger[i] \neq Finger[i + 1]$ **then**
   //Forward while within "Limit"
    if $Finger[i] \in]Q, Limit[$ **then**
     $R := Finger[i]$
     //NewLimit must not exceed Limit
     if $Finger[i + 1] \in]Q, Limit[$ **then**
      $NewLimit := Finger[i + 1]$
     else
      $NewLimit := Limit$
     fi
     send($Q:R:$BROADCAST($Info, NewLimit$))
    else
     exit for
    fi
   fi
od

Fig. 3. Processing a Broadcast Message

Processing a Broadcast. A node Q receiving a BROADCAST($Info, Limit$) message delivers it to its application layer and continues the broadcast in a subtree confined in the interval $]Q, Limit[$. In addition to skipping the redundant fingers, Q forwards to every finger whose identifier is before the $Limit$. Moreover, when forwarding to any finger, it supplies it with a $NewLimit$, defining a smaller subtree. Note that, this will only happen if $NewLimit \in]Q, Limit[$, i.e. the $NewLimit$ is not exceeding the $Limit$ given by the parent. Figure 3 contains the rule for processing a broadcast message.

Note that for any node other than the initiating node, the Mth finger will never be used, so we do not try to forward to it. In general, after h hops, the $(M-h)^{th}$ finger at most is used in forwarding. An additional invariant of the two rules that is not shown in the figures, for the simplicity of presentation, is that a node never sends a BROADCAST message to itself. A finger of a node n can point to n only in the rare case that half or more of the identifier space does not contain any nodes which is most unlikely given the assumption of a uniform distribution of node identifiers.

Replies. We are considering the issue of replying to the broadcast source to be an orthogonal issue that depends on the $Info$ argument of the BROADCAST message. Several strategies could be considered for replying, for example : (i) Sending the broadcast source with every broadcast message and it is contacted directly by a node willing to reply (*ii*) The reply is propagated to the root over the same spanning tree.

4.3 Correctness Argument

Coverage of All Nodes. As a DHT system constructs a *connected* graph of nodes and as every node that receives a broadcast message forwards it to all of its neighbors (except those it knows by DHT construction properties that they are going to be contacted by other nodes), therefore, *eventually* every node in the system receives the broadcast message.

No Redundancy. The algorithm ensures that disjoint (non-overlapping) intervals are considered for forwarding. Consequently every node receives the broadcast message exactly once.

5   Cost versus Guarantees

While presenting an efficient algorithm for broadcast in DHT-based P2P networks, we are aware that the cost of N-1 messages, especially in large P2P systems can be prohibitive for many applications. The point is that we offer broadcasting as a basic service available for a system that is willing to pay its cost. Our algorithm offers strong guarantees and utilization of traffic for that endured cost. In order to offer the same guarantees on a network, of the same size, in a Gnutella-like broadcast, a substantially higher cost is paid. The next section elaborates more on this comparison.

Predictable Guarantees. The broadcast as presented in section 4, offers strong guarantees as it explores every node in the network. Minor modifications to the algorithm could be applied to, deterministically, reduce the scope of the broadcast and thus offer weaker, yet predictable guarantees. For example, by sending only to the Mth (or all but the Mth) finger while initiating a broadcast, only 50% of the network is covered in the broadcast. Similar pruning policies could be applied to achieve different coverage percentages.

Different Traversal Policies. The algorithm could also be modified to support an iterative deepening policy. This policy was suggested in [16] for use in unstructured overlay networks. We believe that combining this policy with our algorithm can decrease the messaging cost, especially, when one query hit suffices as a result.

6   Simulation Results

In this section, we show preliminary simulation results for the presented broadcast algorithm. We are primarily interested to see that all nodes are covered in

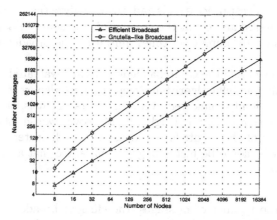

Fig. 4. Comparison of number of messages needed to cover all nodes using efficient broadcast and Gnutella-like flooding in a structured network

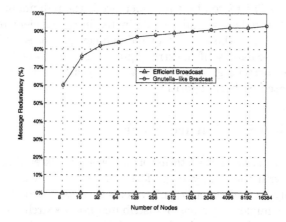

Fig. 5. Comparison of percentage of redundant messages generated by efficient broadcast and Gnutella-like flooding in a structured network

the broadcast process and that no redundant messages are sent. Additionally, we want to compare the messaging cost of the efficient broadcast algorithm with that of the Gnutella broadcast algorithm over the same size of the network and with the same guarantees offered. The experiments were conducted on a distributed algorithms simulator developed by our team and using the Mozart [9] programming platform.

Experiments Setting. To study the messaging cost, we create an identifier space of size 2^{16} and we vary the number of nodes in the space, from 2^3 up to 2^{14} with increasing powers of 2. For each network size, after all the nodes join the system, we initiate a broadcast process starting at a randomly-chosen node. We wait until the broadcast process ends and, then, analyze the messages to see if all the nodes are covered and count the amount of redundant messages. We repeat the same experiment a number of times, initiating the broadcast from different sources.

Both the efficient and the Gnutella algorithms are evaluated in the same way. We use the basic Gnutella algorithm except that we deploy it on a structured rather than a randomly-connected overlay network. That is, the unique fingers of the Chord nodes are used as neighbors. Moreover, we set the Time-To-Live (TTL) parameter of the Gnutella broadcast to the diameter of the network , i.e. $\log_2(N)$ which should be just enough to guarantee that all the nodes of the network are covered.

Results. For the number of messages, the efficient broadcast algorithm constantly produces N-1 messages for the different network sizes. The Gnutella algorithm succeeds to cover all the nodes, thanks, to the TTL parameter, but does that with a substantially larger amount of messages. The comparison is shown in figure 4. The reason for that difference is the redundant messages that are sent in the Gnutella case and are eliminated in the efficient broadcast case. It is worth noting that the amount of redundancy increases with system size, strongly affecting scalability if the strong guarantees are to be maintained. Figure 5 shows the percentage of redundant messages from the total number of messages generated by both algorithms.

7   Conclusion and Future Work

In this paper, we showed the status of our work in extending the functionality of DHTs with the ability to perform efficient broadcasts. Our approach depended mainly on the perception of systems such as Chord, Tapestry, Pastry, and Kademlia as implementations of distributed k-ary search. We gave an algorithm for traversing the k-ary search tree and thus, constructing a spanning tree of an overlay network formed by a DHT.

We based all our explanation on Chord as a simple system implementing binary search. In future papers, we intend to elaborate more on how to construct a spanning tree in systems with higher arities.

We suggested a number of strategies by which a peer deploying the efficient broadcast algorithm can reduce its scope by pruning a spanning tree in order to generate less traffic, yet with the ability to deterministically decide the percentage of network members that are covered in the broadcast and thus offering predictable guarantees. More experiments need to be done for the evaluation of those strategies.

For the issue of dynamic network (joins/leaves), more experimental results are needed to: (i) Quantify the effect of outdated routing tables on the properties offered by the efficient broadcast algorithm. (ii) Guide the design of a more fault-tolerant version of the algorithm. In its current state, our algorithm, depends heavily on the ability of the underlying DHT system to cope quickly with the dynamic nature of the network.

References

[1] Luc Onana Alima, Sameh El-Ansary, Per Brand, and Seif Haridi. Dks(n; k; f): A family of low communication, scalable and fault-tolerant infrastructures for p2p applications. In *To appear in the 3rd International workshop on Global and Peer-To-Peer Computing on large scale distributed systems*, Tokyo, Japan, May 2003.

[2] M. Castro, P. Druschel, A-M. Kermarrec, and A. Rowstron. Scribe: A large-scale and decentralised application-level multicast infrastructure. In *IEEE Journal on Selected Areas in Communications (JSAC) (Special issue on Network Support for Multicast Communications*, 2002.

[3] Sameh El-Ansary, Luc Onana Alima, Per Brand, and Seif Haridi. A framework for peer-to-peer lookup services based on k-ary search. Technical Report TR-2002-06, SICS, May 2002.

[4] FreeNet. http://freenet.sourceforge.net, 2003.

[5] Gnutella. http://www.gnutella.com, 2003.

[6] Matthew Harren, Joseph M. Hellerstein, Ryan Huebsch, Boon Thau Loo, Scott Shenker, and Ion Stoica. Complex queries in dht-based peer-to-peer networks. In *The 1st Interational Workshop on Peer-to-Peer Systems (IPTPS'02)*, 2002.

[7] E. P. Markatos. Tracing a large-scale peer to peer system: An hour in the life of gnutella. In *Second International Symposium on Cluster Computing and the Grid*, 2002.

[8] Petar Maymounkov and David Mazires. Kademlia: A peer-to-peer information system based on the xor metric. In *The 1st Interational Workshop on Peer-to-Peer Systems (IPTPS'02)*, 2002.

[9] Mozart Consortium. http://www.mozart-oz.org, 2003.

[10] Sylvia Ratnasamy, Paul Francis, Mark Handley, Richard Karp, and Scott Shenker. A scalable content addressable network. Technical Report TR-00-010, Berkeley, CA, 2000.

[11] Sylvia Ratnasamy, Mark Handley, Richard Karp, and Scott Shenker. Application-level multicast using content-addressable networks. In *Third International Workshop on Networked Group Communication (NGC '01)*, 2001.

[12] M. Ripeanu, I. Foster, and A. Iamnitchi. Mapping the gnutella network: Properties of large-scale peer-to-peer systems and implications for system design, 2002.

[13] Antony Rowstron and Peter Druschel. Pastry: Scalable, decentralized object location, and routing for large-scale peer-to-peer systems. *Lecture Notes in Computer Science*, 2218, 2001.

[14] I. Stoica, R. Morris, D. Karger, M. Kaashoek, and H. Balakrishnan. Chord: A scalable peer-to-peer lookup service for internet applications. Technical Report TR-819, MIT, January 2002.

[15] Ion Stoica, Dan Adkins, Sylvia Ratnasamy, Scott Shenker, Sonesh Surana, and Shelley Zhuang. Internet indirection infrastructure. In *The 1st Interational Workshop on Peer-to-Peer Systems (IPTPS'02)*, 2002.

[16] Beverly Yang and Hector Garcia-Molina. Efficient search in peer-to-peer networks. In *The 22nd International Conference on Distributed Computing Systems (ICDCS 2002)*, 2001.

[17] Ben Y. Zhao, John D. Kubiatowicz, and Anthony D. Joseph. Tapestry: An infrastructure for fault-tolerant wide-area location and routing. U. C. Berkeley Technical Report UCB//CSD-01-1141, April 2000.

Author Index

Lecture Notes in Computer Science

For information about Vols. 1–2680
please contact your bookseller or Springer-Verlag